The History of Civilisation
Edited by C. K. OGDEN, M.A.

Roman
Political Institutions

Roman
Political Institutions
from City to State

By
LEON HOMO

LONDON
ROUTLEDGE & KEGAN PAUL LTD
BROADWAY HOUSE: 68-74 CARTER LANE, E.C.4

First published 1929
by Kegan, Paul, Trench, Trubner & Co. Ltd
This edition with an additional bibliography first published 1962
by Routledge & Kegan Paul Ltd
Broadway House, 68-74 Carter Lane
London, E.C.4

Translated by
M. R. DOBIE

Printed in Great Britain by
Lowe & Brydone (Printers) Ltd
London, N.W.10

CONTENTS

v

CONTENTS

BOOK TWO

FROM OLIGARCHY TO MILITARY RULE

BOOK THREE

CÆSARISM : PRINCIPATE AND "DOMINATE"

CONTENTS

BOOK FOUR

IMPERIAL BUREAUCRACY. ADMINISTRATION AND GREAT PUBLIC SERVICES

FOREWORD

ROME THE ORGANIZER

THE PERFECTING OF THE STATE

THE first volumes of this series have enabled us to observe that prehistory and the earliest history, little as they tell us for certain about the wanderings of racial groups, the part played by individuals, the order of chiefs, and contingent things of all kinds, reveal a development of institutions—as of material and intellectual civilization—which, although doubtless not regular nor continuous, is at least certain. In laying stress upon these aspects of the past, and in particular upon public and private law, we do not misrepresent history, nor enlarge its scope unduly. It cannot be repeated too often that history has no limits but the activity of men gathered in societies, in its various forms. As a synthesis, therefore, it comprises all those special studies the progress of which involves its own progress, and which have a higher end in it. In respect of sociology, we say once again that, if it has been legitimate to constitute a comparative study of societies, taking the facts of history and the data of ethnology as a basis, the result of these labours must be claimed and assimilated by the science of history as a whole.[1]

It is useful to define society, to determine the institutions which answer to its essential needs and enable it to work, and to distinguish the stages of its evolution ; but in reality there are only societies. In order both to check sociology and to make history intelligible, we must weave our sociological generalizations back into the historical synthesis with the other elements which analysis has disentangled and which it is the task of historical theory to enumerate. Sociology, it may be said, emerges from history only to return into it.

Two previous volumes of our synthesis have been devoted to following, in history, the development of that primary function

---

[1] See General Introduction to *The Earth before History*, and Foreword to *From Tribe to Empire*, both in this series.

*of a society, its politico-juridical function, which is differentiated
by its very progress and allows law to detach itself as a distinct
institution—conspicuously so in the case of Rome.*

In From Tribe to Empire *we saw the beginnings of social
organization, the political evolution from primitive clan to
rudimentary state, and from that state to empire. It should
be noted, moreover, that the difference between the original cell,
the clan, and the early state, and that between the state and the
empire, consist chiefly in the extension of the human group and
therefore of the territory which are covered by the power of the
chief, in the systematization of that power. From the beginning
the chief has a religious character, which becomes more definite
as time goes on [1] ; he is a god or the representative of a god.
" Centralized monarchy by right divine " constitutes a remarkable attempt to unite men and, by uniting them, to increase the
resources, the possibilities of enjoyment, of the King, the great
men, and, to a certain extent, sometimes, of the whole people,
rathc· than to rule the whole united mass as well as possible.[2]*

*In contrast to the vast unifications of men, the " cosmo-
cracies ", as they have been called, of the boundless plains and
tablelands of the East, we find the small political organisms of
Greece. There the country, by the mountainous formation
which divides it into compartments, and man, by his spirit of
independence, combine to create something new—the city. In*
The Greek City *and its Institutions,* Professor Glotz *has set
himself to show how the city, emancipating the individual from
family collectivism, grew in power and prosperity by that very
individualism which it encouraged ; and how, after triumphing
over the conservative elements, democracy followed its natural
course, broke down the balance of rights and duties, and permitted
the individual to make selfish encroachments—which would,
little by little, destroy the city.[3]*

*So we have on the one hand territorial empire and hypertrophy
of the person of the sovereign, and on the other a tiny state and
development of the personality of the citizen. On the one hand,
unlimited extension : it has been observed that empires always
go beyond their fertile and densely-populated districts, being*

---

[1] See *From Tribe to Empire*, p. 356.

[2] Egypt and Persia, however, differ from the Semitic Empires. See below,
pp. xv–xvi.

[3] See also Jardé, *The Formation of the Greek People*, and Jouguet, *Macedonian Imperialism*, Foreword, pp. xi–xiii, both in this series.

*obliged to defend themselves against the hungry nomads who
besiege their marches, and let themselves be drawn further and
further forwards into almost empty spaces. On the other hand,
narrow limits and expansion instead of extension : through
the initiative and daring of the individual, the city sends out
swarms, founding " colonies " to exploit the world and pump
it of its riches. In the Empire of Alexander and the kingdoms
into which that Empire broke up, cities would still come into
being, Greek in origin and tradition, but they would be markets
or garrisons, and the city would remain, in the empire or kingdom,
a sort of foreign body.*

*It is quite otherwise with Rome. Here the starting-point
is the city, but here the city grows in size. Rome extends the
civitas to Italy, to the provinces, to the world, and ends by
assimilating cities and kingdoms. Rome becames " Romania ".[1]
And her institutions, becoming codified, assume a character
of universality, an absolute value.*

*That is the evolution which Professor Homo presents so
luminously in this work. In a previous volume of this series,
he has explained the formation of the empire ; here he gives us
the development, the perfecting of the State.*

In the Foreword to his Primitive Italy, *we have drawn attention
to his ingenious attempt to recover, beneath the arrangement
of the Annals, the truth of Roman origins. Here he continues
the attempt, extracting the complex, evolutionary truth from a
tradition which simplifies facts and obscures stages of development. He starts from the Gens, the social germ-cell, and goes
through the horde, a group of Gentes, the City, Greek and
Etruscan in origin, and the various forms of empire down to the
partition, giving a cautious but definite account of fifteen centuries*

[1] " At its origin (the Roman City) had contained only Patricians and
Clients ; then the Plebeian class had gained admission, then the Latins,
then the Italians, and last of all came the provincials. . . . All the cities
vanished little by little, and the City of Rome, the last left standing, was itself
so much changed that it became a union of a dozen great peoples under a
single master. So fell the municipal system " (Fustel de Coulanges, *La Cité
antique,* 14th ed., p. 456).

The Edict of Caracalla of 212, which conferred the citizenship on all free
inhabitants of the Empire who did not already possess it (*dediticii* excepted),
marks " a turning-point in the history of Italy and of the world " (below,
p. 339). In the course of the third century the word *Romani* acquired a
universal acceptation ; see the remarks of G. Bloch, *L'Empire romain*, p. 209,
and J. Declareuil, *Rome the Law-giver*, in this series, pp. 52 ff.

*of constitutional development. Of the institutions which
followed one another—the mixed system of the village, the
Etruscan Kingship, the Republic, Patrician, Plebeio-Patrician,
and oligarchic, the Principate, and the " Dominate "—he has
himself given in his Conclusion such a vigorous summary
that to resume it here would be almost to repeat it. It
will be more useful to dwell on certain points of especial
importance.*

*Nothing is more interesting, in our eyes, than the study to
which Professor Homo devotes himself of the causes which
determined the long, slow development of Roman political
institutions. He shows forcibly that in that constitutional work
theory played a small part and only came in late. Among the
Greeks, political speculation throve, and created a literature.
Well into the Hellenistic period, in the cities which Hellas
sowed all over the East, the debates of the Agora were a passion
and a sport. In Rome, the theory of public law does not appear
before the second century. Then men went in for speculation,
but about what is rather than about what ought to be. Polybios
declared that the Roman constitution was a realization of the
best type of constitution possible, by the combination of the
three principles of monarchy, aristocracy, and democracy [1];
but at the time when he was thus defining it and lauding its
composite originality, it was already developing under the
action of causes which had nothing to do with theory.*

*We know that the Roman was essentially conservative,[2] and
that was why speculation did not attract him. We know, too,
that he was fundamentally practical, and that was why, although
he had little bent for the play of the creative imagination, he
had no positive objection to change. Although his character was,
naturally, a factor in the creation of institutions, these are
chiefly explained—in virtue of that same character which was
ready to learn from experience—by the succession of circumstances. In Primitive Italy we have seen the empire being
created under the pressure of facts much more than by any
preconceived plan ; here we see the constitution evolving under
the same pressure as gave rise to the empire.*

*It is interesting to compare Professor Homo's book with
La Cité antique. In that very systematic masterpiece, Fustel
de Coulanges shows, no doubt, the series of revolutions which*

---

[1] See below, pp. 113 ff.   [2] See especially pp. 31, 238.

" *weakened and exhausted* " *the City* [1] *and was to lead, in the case of Rome, to empire ; but he believes that everything can be explained, at bottom, and for all ancient cities, by* " *that part of our being which changes from age to age* ", *our intelligence.* " *It is,*" *he says,* " *always moving, almost always progressing, and because of it our institutions and our laws are subject to change. Man does not think to-day as he thought twenty-five centuries ago, and that is why he does not govern himself now as he used to govern himself.*" *All ancient politics are bound up with* " *the history of a belief* " ; " *such was the law of ancient times.*" [2] *In Professor Homo's view, a thesis stated in too absolute terms* " *is always in danger of distorting and more or less contradicting the complex reality of things* ",[3] *and he lays weight, with much reason, on what, in spite of these analogies, makes Rome profoundly different from the Greek cities.*

The great difference was that Rome never knew true democracy. " *Our constitution,*" *Thucydides said through the lips of Pericles,* " *is called a democracy because it is made not for the advantage of a few, but for the good of the majority* " ; *and* " *liberty, not for the Athenian only, but for the Greek in general . . . consisted essentially in participation in the government and in equality before the law* ".[4] *Now, in Rome, at the time when the Republican constitution was moving towards its full development, from the fifth to the third century, the swelling mass of citizens (there were 350,000 in the fifth century) remained* " *traditionally and temperamentally* " *respectful of the social scale and readily accepted the ascendancy first of a Patrician and then of a Patricio-Plebeian nobility.*[5] *The Plebs entered into political life, and* " *democratic disturbances* " *were frequent, but democracy never fully developed. We know how quickly the agrarian element was absorbed by the town, and how the middle class of true Roman stock was submerged among newly created, low-class citizens and then superseded by a servile proletariate,* " *sold body and soul to the army and money.*" [6] *No doubt, Rome has handed down to modern times, especially in Livy's speeches, the sentiments of democracy ; but it is chiefly the legacy of the Greek city that posterity has taken up through Roman literature. Rome left something else to the world as her*

---

[1] *La Cité antique*, p. 441. [2] Ibid., pp. 2, 464. [3] Below, p. 122.
[4] M. Croiset, *La Civilisation hellénique*, vol. ii, p. 83.
[5] Below, p. 82. [6] Below, p. 365.

own legacy—the perfect model of a military empire and a strong administrative organization.

Professor Homo is so much interested in the characteristics which differentiate the Roman constitution and in their connection with particular circumstances, that it is doubtful whether the development of a body of institutions has ever been studied and explained in such careful detail. He is, and means to be, a historian, *to bring out all the contingent circumstances which have acted on social organization and coloured with their changing shades the institutions necessary to collective life. But, while avoiding an over-rigid system, he has too penetrating a mind, he is too much of a psychologist, to fail to show the internal logic which to a great extent determined the development of those institutions, just as he previously recognized the share of deep-lying instincts and human tendencies in the genesis of imperialism.*

In the initial period, the development of institutions is commanded by two logical tendencies—that which makes for the strengthening of the State with a view to the extension of the City and later to the unification of Italy, and that which makes for the establishment of a balance between the various elements of the City. In respect of the Plebs, whose military activity increases, " the spirit of the ancient city and, one must add, logic *demanded that the process of assimilation should, soon or late, extend from duties to rights." [1] The creation and co-ordination of magistracies sharing the* imperium *of the King (the religious character of the primitive kingship being, as it were, detached from it) answered both to the interests of the conflicting classes and to the needs of a society which desired to live and to grow.*

But at an early date constitutional history becomes the " faithful reflection " of external history, that is, of growing imperialism. " Circumstances," military, economic, and moral, may explain the details, the moment, and certain methods of the transformations of institutions, but the direction of those changes is determined by an imperative social logic. The development of imperialism had, in respect of the power, its unity, its permanence, not only " inexorable necessities " but also " inevitable " consequences. When the size of a society and the distribution of its elements change, institutions are adapted

---

[1] Below, p. 40.

accordingly.[1] *Professor Homo is well aware of this ; so far
as it is possible, he uses statistics to show the exact relation
which existed between the results of the conquest on population
and wealth on the one hand and the continual readjustment
of the Roman constitution on the other—a readjustment which
consisted in an increasing concentration of the power : oligarchy,
principate, monarchy.*[2]

*For a long time the logic to which this movement towards
monarchy answered was, like imperialism itself, only half-
conscious. It arose from an agreement between the needs of the
group, dimly felt by all members of it, and the initiative of
individuals, who had an intuition of those needs, were* social
agents, *and at the same time acted out of personal ambition,
having the temperament of* leaders, regius mos.[3] *Loyalty to a
chief tended to take the place of devotion to one's country.
Although the ruling idea of the Imperial system was born of
realities, it was " slow to emerge ".*[4] *That " inevitable end " of
an evolution which had been going on for three hundred years
first became really conscious in the " lucid genius " of Cæsar.*[5]
*From then onwards, individuals played the part of social
inventors, fully aware of what they were doing ; after Cæsar
came Octavian, Diocletian, Constantine. We follow the stages
which, in the course of five centuries, led to the final formula
of " the two great parallel creations of the Imperial system,
Cæsarism and bureaucracy ".*[6]

*Professor Homo does not, of course, omit to show what the
organization of the Empire owed to the examples of the past* [7]—
*to Alexander, whose absolute world-monarchy Cæsar had taken
for his political ideal,*[8] *to Egypt, from which Rome, in the course
of the first three centuries of our era, learned much, both in
politics and in administration,*[9] *and from the Sassanian
monarchy, whose " influence on the transformation of the Imperial*

---

[1] On social morphology, see my *Synthèse en histoire,* pp. 135–8.
[2] See below, pp. 109–10, 145–6, 202, 277.
[3] See below, pp. 104–5. Cf. von Stern, *Staatsform und Einzelpersön-
lichkeit im klassischen Altertum,* analysed in *Anhée sociologique,* N.S., vol. i,
p. 659.
[4] Below, pp. 202, 368–9.
[5] Below, pp. 193, 197, 202.   [6] Below, p. 242.
[7] Below, pp. 239, 371.   [8] Below, p. 196.
[9] Below, pp. 239–40.

government of Rome began with the Illyrian Emperors and went on until the last days of the Western Empire ".[1] *In the transfiguration of the* Princeps, *whose tradition was Roman, into a* Dominus *of the Oriental kind, and then into a* Deus,[2] *and also in the organization of the civil service, imitation and suggestion evidently counted for much. But that does not detract from the achievement of Rome. Her practical, socially creative genius brought into being a pattern state, which in some respects remains the final model.*

From Rome the modern world has got the conception of " really absolute monarchy ". The Emperor was the " master of the whole Roman State "[3]; *he could say, "L'État, c'est moi." All the legislative and judicial powers of the State which belonged to the* Comitia *and* Senate *were gradually absorbed by the Emperor, who at the very most preserved appearances.[4] The* magistracies cum imperio *in the end were nothing but " an empty show* ".[5]

That State, which was so vast that the Emperor presently had to double himself, as it were, preparatory to doubling the Empire, was united in the person of the sovereign, but it could not be governed by him direct. The magistrates, elected and furnished with power, were superseded by officials, whom he appointed and delegated. A central administration was formed, and true ministries, and great specialized public services, and a whole civil bureaucracy, quite distinct from the military element. Administrative unification took away the privileges of Italy, assimilated the provinces one to another, and even split them up, when the time came, to make them politically weaker and materially more prosperous.[6]

---

[1] Below, pp. 268, 275–7.

[2] Below, pp. 269, 278.

[3] Below, pp. 265,306. The power of the Cæsar, the Imperator, which religion came to consecrate by a kind of return to the origins of kingship, was based on the army. Now, that instrument of conquest which had become an instrument of power became in the end a power itself, and a dangerous one, a factor of anarchy (pp. 240–6. In Professor Homo's two volumes there is also much matter for reflection on the part played by the army and military power ; cf. Foreword to *Primitive Italy*, pp. ix–x). Therefore later absolute monarchies endeavoured to eliminate that element of instability, chiefly by basing themselves on the hereditary principle. That principle was never known to Roman law, although there were attempts to establish hereditary succession in practice.

[4] His authority extended even over the " Senatorial " provinces.

[5] Below, p. 306.

[6] Below, pp. 336–7, 341.

This organization of bureaucracy and great public services whose progress he describes, as "they gradually took on their complete and permanent form under the Empire", Professor Homo rightly calls a "supremely original creation of the Romans ".[1] That is what, together with law, Rome has " brought into the common possession of mankind ", and especially in societies of the Western type.[2]

We do not believe that the needs which drew the Roman State "along the road to unification and centralization " [3] can be called national. *There was a* res publica Romana,[4] *but no* natio Romana, *if by nation one means something whose elements are united not only by a common organization but by a common heritage, are animated by a collective will-to-live, and assert their unity by opposing it to foreign collectivities.[5] The Roman world was made up of elements which, after all, were too disparate to constitute a nation.[6] It was from a combination of a patriotism like that of the city with an organization like that of the Roman State that modern nations were born.*

Centralization, civil service, and bureaucracy, the creations of Cæsarism, have their value even without Cæsarism. If democracy failed here, monarchy perfected the organization which would afterwards be of service even to democratic nations.

One of the strongest impressions left by this book is that of the internal drive and the necessities which govern political evolution. "Inexorable " necessities, "relentless " evolution, "inevitable " results—these are some of the striking expressions which we have noted on the way. In these pages we find the sociology of a historian, rising from the very nature of the

[1] Below, p. 320.

[2] Below, p. 370. For the deficiencies of the Roman State, see p. 372, and H. G. Wells, *The Outline of History*, London, 1919–22 (fortnightly parts ed.), pp. 285, 302–4, 332–9, 380–1, which are explained by his personal dislike of Rome.

[3] Below, p. 337.

[4] See M. Gelzer, " Altertumswissenschaft und Spätantike," in *Historische Zeitschrift*, cxxxv, p. 175.

[5] For the word *nation*, see the 3rd *Bulletin* of the *Centre international de Synthèse* (sec. of Historical Synthesis).

[6] See Chapot, *The Roman World*, in this series. The heterogeneous nature of the Empire seems to have been one great cause of the difficulty of establishing Imperial hereditary succession. See G. Bloch, *L'Empire romain*, p. 71, and R. Hubert, *Manuel de sociologie*, p. 211.

subjects treated (as in Professor Moret's contribution to From Tribe to Empire), *which happily confirms the sociology of comparative sociologists. With the sureness of critical sense, wealth of knowledge, liveliness of portraiture, and vigour of phrase, it is one of the merits of this valuable book, and in our eyes it is its chief interest.*

HENRI BERR.

BOOK ONE

THE INSTITUTIONS OF THE EARLY CITY

CHAPTER I

THE BIRTH OF THE ROMAN STATE.   THE ETRUSCAN KINGSHIP

BIBLIOGRAPHY.—*Ancient Authors* : Livy, i (cf. Florus, i, 1–3 ; Eutropius, i, 1–8 ; Orosius, ii, 4) ; Dionysios Hal., i–iv ; *H.R.F.*, *passim* ; Cicero, *Rep.*, ii, 1–30 ; Dion. C., i–iii (fragments ; cf. Zonaras, vii, 1–12) ; Diodoros, iv, 21 ; v, 40 ; vii, 22–3 ; Plutarch, *Romulus*, *Numa, Publicola* ; Appian, *Basil.* (fragments) ; Velleius, i, 8 ; *De Viris illustr.*, 1–9.

Inscriptions : *C.I.L.*, i, 2nd ed., 1, p. 189, 1–4 (*Elogia* of Æneas, Lavinia, Æneas Silvius, Romulus).

Modern Works : **XXIII,** i, 381–810 ; **XXII,** i, 241–70, 423–65 ; **XXIV,** i, 193 ff. ; **XXIX,** i, 171–255, 344–400 ; **XXI,** 30–9 ; **II,** 1–50 ; **X,** iii, 164–5 (K. J. Beloch), 436–9 (K. J. Neumann) ; **XXVI,** 360–4 (K. J. Neumann) ; **IX,** i, 1–26 ; **XXXI,** 19–52 ; **XXVII,** 7–8 ; **XVI,** i, 1–108 ; **XIX,** iii, 2–18 ; **XXX,** i, 78–132, and add. iii–x ; **XIII,** Eng., pp. 67–128 ; **CXX,** 244–67 ; **CXXIV** ; **LIX,** 105–13, 255–75 ; **XVIII,** i, 3–49 ; E. Kornemann, " Zur italischen Verfassungsgeschichte," in **XXXVIII,** 1914, 190–206 ; *id.*, " Urbs et Polis," *ibid.*, 1905, 78–88 ; W. Schulze, in **XXXII,** Neue Folge, v (1904), *passim*.

I

THE CONSTITUTION OF THE AUTONOMOUS ROMAN VILLAGES

THAT the political life of Rome began with kingship, that the first of her Kings, Romulus, was the father of the Roman constitution which was to have such a long and glorious future—these are two fundamental assertions on which the whole of annalistic tradition, mainly represented for us to-day by Livy, Dionysios of Halicarnassos, Cicero, and Plutarch, shows itself unanimous. Romulus, the hero founder, gave Rome both the framework of her political life and the organs of her government.

For the framework of her political life, he gave her the three primitive tribes—Ramnes, Tities, and Luceres—each divided into ten Curiæ, which were in turn divided into a number of Gentes, so that the whole city consisted of three Tribes, thirty Curiæ, and about three hundred Gentes.

---

*See also Supplementary Bibliography with Prefatory Note (p. 405)

Next, there were the organs of government. The King was the head of the State, invested with civil, military, judicial, and religious powers, the administrator, commander-in-chief, supreme judge, and high-priest, elected by the Assembly of the thirty Curiæ and confirmed by the Senate in the form of the *auctoritas Patrum*, for life. The Curiate Assembly was a gathering of the members of the Gentes, which elected the King, decided on peace and war, voted laws, and had a sovereign voice in matters of justice. The Senate, a body permanently representing the Gentes, was a Council of State which assisted the King in the exercise of his power. Except for a few constitutional changes in detail, which, according to tradition, were introduced under the successors of Romulus, the Roman constitution, with the Tribes and their subdivisions, Curiæ and Gentes, with the King, Curiate Assembly, and Senate, was provided, at the very dawn of the city's history, with its characteristic and fundamental organs.

But the whole of this conception of the constitution, in the form in which the Roman Annals have preserved it for us, presupposes one thing—that a united Rome existed before the Etruscan conquest—and this point of view modern criticism, based largely on archæological discovery and the progress of philology, no longer allows us to accept. In the early centuries the soil of Rome bore only a number of humble villages—Germal, Palatual, Velia, Oppius, Cispius, Fagutal, Querquetu(a)l—which were independent until about the end of the eighth century B.C., and were later collected in a fairly loose political and religious federation, the League of the Seven Hills, which was rudely brought to an end in the middle of the seventh century by the Etruscan conquest.[1]

This state of things had one logical consequence of capital importance from the constitutional point of view. In the period before the League of the Seven Hills was formed, while the Roman villages were still self-governing, and even later, at the time of the League, there was no Roman State, and therefore no one constitution. So in this respect the tradition of the Annals is entirely fictitious, and, disagreeable

[1] On the formation and development of primitive Rome, see **XIII**, Eng. pp. 75–98.

as such a drastic operation may be for the historian of early Rome, there is nothing for him but to draw his pen through it. At the very most, one might suppose that at the end of the time of the League a further step towards unification was taken, and Rome gave herself organs of centralization— Tribes and Curiæ, King, Curiate Assembly, and Senate— which she did not possess before. But against this theoretical possibility, besides a number of various difficulties, there is one decisive argument : the names of the three primitive Tribes are Etruscan, and the institution cannot be disassociated from the Etruscan conquest itself.

To sum up, before the Etruscan conquest, which occurred at the middle of the seventh century B.C., just as there was no town of Rome, properly speaking, so there was no Roman State, nor, consequently, any single Roman constitution. Having thus cleared the ground of the artificial structures of the Annals, can we, at least, make out a few historical features of this primitive and mainly legendary period ?

In the absence of a coherent and authoritative history of these early times, which the Romans of the classical period did not possess any more than ourselves, let us try at least to stake out a few points which may guide us. The constitutional history of Rome, like all her history, begins for us in an age prior to the city-system, the age of the horde, and just at the moment when these hordes, still in the rudimentary form of refuge-villages or *oppida*, take a first step towards permanent settlement.[1] Archæology, a fragmentary source, but the most certain for this early period, gives us, at the outset, a first-class starting-point— the nature and conditions of existence of the various villages scattered over the soil of Rome. The finds show that they were little agglomerations, with a small population— most of them, such as Germal, Palatual, Velia, Cispius, and Fagutal, having a few hundred inhabitants, while there may have been a thousand in the largest, such as Oppius, or the Sabine colony on the Quirinal, which was not one of the primitive Latin villages and only entered the Roman community during the Etruscan domination. Unfortunately, the excavations which inform us about the topography and material life of these various settlements tell us nothing—

[1] **XIII,** Eng. pp. 70 ff. ; E. Kornemann, " Urbs et Polis," in **XXXVIII,** 1905, pp. 8–88.

and it is not surprising—about their political organization. It is in distant memories of the past and the mists of legend that we must seek the necessary evidence.

One thing appears quite certain—the existence of local kingships in Italy, and particularly in Latium, at the beginning of their history. The various Etruscan cities had their kings, or Lucumos ; in the heart of Latium itself, memories survived afterwards of the Kings of Alba, Lavinium, and Cænina and the King of the Grove, to mention no others. We also know that, beside the kingship, the two other fundamental organs of the ancient city, the Assembly of the people and the Council of Elders, or Senate, were customary in the Italian world—and especially in Latium— as elsewhere. We must therefore imagine these different villages dotted about the site of Rome as having a King, who was the civil, military, judicial, and religious head, a popular Assembly, and a Senate. So, when the annalistic tradition endowed Rome, before the Etruscan conquest, with a single constitution which she had not possessed and could not have possessed, it merely transferred to an imaginary state genuine elements taken from the constitutional life of the Roman villages during the earliest centuries of their history. Here again, it did not so much invent as distort and transpose. This method is so familiar to it that, in this point as in so many others, it need not surprise the historian or baffle the critic.

Another *point d'appui*, no less valuable, is furnished by the constitution of the Gens. The existence of the Gens, the primitive family in the wide sense of the word, still in its undivided state, which left lasting traces, not only in historical tradition, but also in later Roman law, remains beyond all possible doubt. The Gens was a collection of families whose members claimed, rightly or wrongly, that they were descended from a common ancestor ; it had its family worship, its common burying-place, its head, and, by the side of the family group based on natural kinship, it contained an artificial, adventitious element, constituted by a body of men dependent on it and protected by it, the " Clients ". Here we are in the presence of historical, indisputable facts ; but two observations, both essential, must be made.

We may suppose, as the most likely solution, that the Gens existed in time before the first political groupings, and that there was, therefore, a time when the Gens lived on the soil of Rome as an autonomous, isolated unit ; but we cannot reconstruct that social state except as a pure hypothesis, for neither historical tradition nor the archæological finds take us beyond a period when the grouping of the Gentes in larger organizations, the villages, appears as an accomplished fact.

Secondly, it is important, when considering the Gens, as in all historical problems, to distinguish carefully between periods. Directly after Porsenna's retreat, Livy [1] shows us the Sabine Attus Clausus coming to Rome and settling with his Gens, the future Gens Claudia.

" Attus Clausus, whose name afterwards became Appius Claudius in Rome, finding himself, as head of the peace-party, hard-driven by the fomenters of war, and unable to stand up against their faction, fled from Regillum with a great company of Clients to Rome " (Plutarch and Dionysios of Halicarnassos give a total of 5,000 men, plus women and children).

Some years later, in the year 479 B.C., according to the traditional dating, another Roman Gens, the Gens Fabia, took the war against the Veians upon itself.

" Then the Gens Fabia," Livy tells us,[2] " went to the Senate. The Consul (Kaesio Fabius) spoke in the name of the Gens . . . Leaving the Senate, he went home, accompanied by the whole body of the Fabii, who had stayed in the vestibule of the Curia awaiting the decree of the Senate. Having been ordered to be at the Consul's door with their arms the next day, they went to their homes . . . Next day, the Fabii took their arms, and met where they had been bidden. The Consul came out, wearing the *paludamentum*, and found his whole Gens drawn up in marching-order in the vestibule. He took his place in their midst, and ordered the standards to advance. Never did an army smaller in numbers or more glorious in renown and the admiration of men march through the city. Three hundred and six fighting-men, all Patricians, all of one Gens . . . went out, threatening destruction to the whole people of Veii with the strength of one family. Behind them went the body of their kinsmen and *sodales* " (4,000 men in all, according to Dionysios of Halicarnassos)[3] " in whose minds there was no half measure, neither in their hopes nor in their fears, but everything was boundless."

It is a fine picture, full of swing, and we have not, for the period in which tradition places it, any serious reason for doubting it, but it was not until the time of the Etruscan

[1] ii, 16, 4-5.   [2] ii, 48, 7, to 49, 5.   [3] ix, 15.

domination, as a result of the general prosperity and the increase of the number of Clients, that the Gens-system reached its height and, therefore, Gentes with large numbers made their appearance. In the earliest centuries of Roman history we should imagine the Gens on a much smaller scale, as a group of a few families, perhaps four or five at the most, making a total of about fifty members, true *gentiles* and Clients all told. Therefore, the primitive Roman villages might, according to their size, comprise from fifteen to thirty of these Gentes, the heads of which, the Patres, formed, by right of birth, the Council of Elders, or Senate.

A King, appointed for life or hereditary (we do not know which), an Assembly of the People, from one to two hundred in number, and a Senate of from fifteen to thirty members— such is the idea which we can form, if not with certainty, at least with very great likelihood, of these early constitutions, into which the subsequent formation of the League of the Seven Hills, a mere federation of villages which were still autonomous, introduced no fundamental change.[1] Anything else is a fiction of the annalists or an arbitrary construction of modern scholars.

II

The Etruscan Conquest and the Organization of the State

The conquest of the Roman villages by the Etruscans, which had the twofold consequence of the foundation of the town of Rome and the creation of the Roman State, marks the beginning of a period of military kingship, which goes on for nearly a century and a half and ends in the catastrophe which history describes as the Revolution of 509.[2]

From the constitutional point of view, the Etruscan domination represents a tremendous revolution. The Roman villages, at first isolated, and afterwards brought together, still only loosely, by the introduction of the federal system, are replaced by the City, a system unknown in Italy except to the most highly developed peoples of the peninsula,

[1] **XIII**, Eng. pp. 86–98.   [2] **XIII**, Eng. pp. 111–28.

the Etruscans and the Greeks. The Etruscans gave this system to the new Rome, with its two fundamental, correlative characteristics—the predominance of the town, the residence of the conquerors and centre of government, and the effacement of the countryside, which was methodically deprived of all autonomous organization and reduced to a politically subordinate position.

The first of the Etruscan Kings, Tarquin the Elder, the conqueror who effected the unification of the League of the Seven Hills by force of arms, and, by the drainage of the low-lying ground, gave the new town the physical unity without which it could not exist, was also the man who, by a correlative and parallel innovation, gave the Roman State the administrative framework—Tribes and Curiæ—and political organs—King, Curiate Assembly, and Senate—which were henceforward indispensable to it.

The question of the Tribes and their subdivisions, the Curiæ, has given rise to many and varied controversies. Even in ancient times, the historians who wrote of primitive Rome disagreed about them. While they were unanimous in dating the very beginnings of the Roman kingship before the Etruscan period, they were not agreed over the nature of the institution. According to some, the Roman people was formed by the juxtaposition of three different neighbouring tribes, the Ramnes, Latins of the Palatine, the Tities, Sabines of the Quirinal, and the Luceres, who were a source of doubt, but were generally regarded as Etruscans, of the Cælian. Others said that the Tribes were created purely by an administrative division, after the foundation of the town. One fact is sufficient to dispose of these diverse theories. The names of the primitive Tribes—Ramnes, Tities, and Luceres—are of Etruscan origin, and, far from being earlier than the conquest of the Roman villages by the Tarquins, the creation of this administrative framework was a consequence of it.

A second question is the nature of the Tribes. The etymology of the word, whether we see in it the mere idea of apportionment (*trib* ; cf. *tribuere*) or more especially that of division into three (*ter*), tells us nothing precise about it ; but it is possible to discern the truth by indirect means. Each of the three Tribes contained ten Curiæ—probably an

Etruscan importation, like the Tribes themselves—that is, there were thirty Curiæ in all, each of which, like the Tribes, had its own name, " being called," says Cicero,[1] " after the Sabine maidens, whose prayers led to peace and alliance."

This gallant explanation might well leave us sceptical ; what is more, we have definite proof that it is wrong. Out of the thirty Curiæ, the number of which remained unaltered throughout the classical period, the names of six have come down to us—Titia, Faucia, Velitia, Rapta, Foriensis, and Veliensis. Of two of these, Rapta, whose name may have been handed down incorrectly, and Velitia, we can say nothing. Two of the others, Titia and Faucia, take their names from Gens-names, and therefore tell us nothing definitely about their character. In the case of the two last, Foriensis and Veliensis, there can be no doubt ; they are topographical names, taken from two quarters of the new Rome, the Forum and the Velia. Therefore, by all our evidence, the Curiæ were territorial divisions, and the same is necessarily true of the Tribes themselves.

Moreover, the three Tribes of Rome, being aggregates of Curiæ and territorial divisions, cannot have constituted racial groups. When the Etruscans conquered the Roman League of the Seven Hills, it included only Latin villages, for the annexation of the Sabine settlement of the Quirinal and Viminal must have taken place later, during the second phase of the Etruscan domination. The Tribes were, therefore, purely and simply quarters of early Rome, similar to the municipal districts of modern cities. Their number was due to the nature of the ground. The villages whose fusion constituted the Etruscan Rome in the first form given to it by Tarquin the Elder were divided into three natural regions, the Palatine, Esquiline, and Cælian, which were logically made into three distinct districts. The three Tribes were given Etruscan names—Ramne, Titie, Luχre,[2] transcribed in Latin as Ramnes, Tities, Luceres—which were the names of three especially important families which had settled there at the time of the conquest. The site of their districts hardly seems certain except for the Palatine, the abode of the Ramnes ; this leaves the two other regions, the Esquiline and Cælian, for the Tities and Luceres, but we cannot place

[1] *Rep.*, ii, 8, 14. [2] **CXXX**, p. 218.

these two with certainty. As for the Curiæ, the fact that there were thirty of them, ten to a Tribe, is enough to prove that both territorially and numerically they were very small—about nine acres, three or four Gentes, and an average of a hundred souls to each.

So much for the framework of united Rome. The government, of which annalistic tradition, represented for us by Livy, Dionysios of Halicarnassos, Cicero, and Plutarch, has left a picture which claims to be faithful, comprised three essential organs—King, Curiate Assembly, and Senate.

The kingship was an elective appointment for life. The King was elected by the Curiate Assembly, which, in virtue of a distinct and complementary act, the *Lex Curiata de Imperio*, invested him with the *imperium*, the whole of the executive power, which was confirmed by the Senate, in virtue of the *auctoritas Patrum*. On his death, his authority reverted to the State, to the community permanently represented by the Senate. The Senate drew a provisional King, the Interrex, by lot among its own members, and he held office for a period limited to five days. When that time had expired, the Interrex nominated a successor to himself, and so it went on, the possible number of Interreges being unlimited, until one of them convoked the Curiate Assembly, which proceeded to elect a new King. As head of the State, in virtue of his *imperium*, the King held in his hands the whole executive power, civil, military, judicial, and religious.

In addition to the election of the King, the Assembly of the People had legislative powers (voting laws, declaring war, concluding peace) and judicial powers in criminal cases (hearing appeals against judgments given by the King or his delegates) and in civil cases (grants of citizenship, adoptions, wills). It voted by Curiæ, a majority of sixteen out of the thirty Curiæ being required.

Lastly, the Senate, comprising all the heads of Gentes, was a permanent council assisting the King in the exercise of his authority. It had no initiative, except only in the case of an interregnum, when, in the absence of a king, it assumed the executive power in the interim and governed the election of the new King in the manner described above.

Of all this constitutional picture, how much should be retained ? Not much, it seems. First of all, and on two essential points, its truthfulness is vitiated by a double error. The united constitution of the Roman State dates only from the Etruscan conquest, and not, as the annalists declare, from the very beginnings of Rome. Also, beyond mentioning the existence of the Etruscan Kings, whom it always presents in the innocent form of peaceful immigrants, it takes no account whatever of the conquering element in the new organization, although it must have kept a big place for itself, whether in the Assembly of the People or in the Senate.

Being wrong on these two points, the Roman annalists are suspect on others. Lacking authentic documents and true to their habit of anticipation, they transfer into the early constitution features taken, *mutatis mutandis*, from institutions of the later period. For example, the electoral machinery which tradition shows us governing the election of Kings was inspired directly by the procedure followed later in the election of the chief Republican magistrates, particularly the Consuls. In reality, the Etruscan tyrants owed their power solely to the force of arms, and were not in the least concerned with legal election by the Comitia. Whether we are dealing with constitutional or with foreign history, scepticism should be our prevailing attitude in respect of the earliest centuries of Rome. A strong military kingship of Etruscan type, concentrating all the executive power in its own hands (general administration, military command, justice, religion), a popular Assembly in Curiæ, having an essentially consultative function, and a Council of Elders, the Senate, composed of the heads of Roman or Etruscan Gentes, as a permanent representation of the conquerors and conquered at Court—such are the essential features, and the only ones which we can discern with any certainty, of the single constitution which the Etruscans imposed upon the subjugated Roman villages, henceforward fused in a synœcism on an equal footing. But this state of things was presently, through the duration and very character of the Etruscan rule, to undergo profound modifications. A new element, whose rôle was to be decisive in the constitutional development of Rome, the Plebs, very soon comes upon the scene.

III

THE ORIGINS OF THE PLEBS AND THE CONSTITUTIONAL REFORM OF SERVIUS TULLIUS

As the town of Rome grew under the powerful impulse of the Etruscan sovereigns, a new element had developed, which had a great future in store for it—the Plebs. What was this Plebs ? What was its origin ? What was its legal status ? [1] It can be defined in two ways, one negative and one positive.

First, the Plebs was not the Patriciate. The latter contained two elements, one natural, the Patricians born, and the other artificial, the Clients. The Plebeians were neither one nor the other. So, since the City was an aggregate of Gentes, and the Gentes contained only Patricians and Clients, the Plebeians did not form part of the City. They might live on its soil, but politically and legally they were foreigners to it.

From the positive point of view, the first question which arises is that of origins. The origins of the Plebs were very complex. It comprised three main elements—conquered populations, taken on the spot (Quirinal, Viminal, Capitol) or forcibly transplanted on to Roman soil (Aventine), Clients of the Patricians, emancipated by the natural extinction of their Gens or by a relaxation of the Client-system accompanying the gradual dissolution of the Gens-system, and, last but not least, domiciled aliens, the traders, manufacturers, and workmen who had settled in Rome, particularly on the Aventine or in the low quarters, such as the Velabrum, to carry on their profession or for some other personal advantage. Therefore, apart from the emancipated Clients, who were doubtless few at first, although they multiplied later, the Plebs, in its two main sections, conquered peoples and domiciled aliens, represented an element foreign to the early City. Its formation and its establishment on Roman soil were directly connected with the Etruscan conquest which created the Roman State and, for the first time,

---

[1] For the whole of the many theories regarding the Plebs, and particularly for the latest, see especially G. Bloch, " La Plèbe romaine : étude sur quelques théories récentes," in **XLVII**, 1911 (cvi), 241–75 ; (cvii), 1–42 ; A. Rosenberg, " Studien zur Entstehung der Plebs," in **XXXVI**, xlviii (1913), pp. 359–77 ; and A. Piganiol, **CXX**, pp. 247–51.

made Rome a big town; they were its immediate and direct result.

So, true to its origins, the Plebs presents the characteristics of an essentially urban population and, within the city itself, it is divided in definite localities. As a whole, the Plebs was the quarters of the new Rome—Quirinal, Viminal, Aventine, Capitol, Velabrum—as against the old Patrician Seven Hills and, outside the actual town, the Patriciate of the country. This distinction of place, no less than the legal differentiation, was to play a chief part in the later history of the struggle of the two orders.

The legal position of the Plebs, lastly, was a direct consequence of the principle of its composition. Being excluded from the city, the Plebs had nothing in common with it, not from the political point of view, nor from the civil, nor from the religious, a fact which was translated into practice by the lack of political and civil rights, in respect both of persons (*connubium*, right of marriage) and of things (*commercium*, right of property). This total absence of civic rights had as a strict corollary a parallel absence of duties; the Plebeians were not subject to either of the great burdens to which citizens were liable—military service and taxation.

Now, this very definite position of the Plebs ended by being completely transformed. The Plebs which was wholly foreign to the city entered it. This event, of capital importance in the history of Rome, is ascribed by tradition to Servius Tullius, who was the last King of Rome but one and must therefore be of the Etruscan dynasty. Livy may tell the story.[1]

" At that time, when there was peace, Servius Tullius undertook a very great work, so that, if Numa was the founder of legal institutions, posterity gives Servius the glory of having introduced difference of station and the orders into the State. For he established the census, a most salutary institution for an empire which was to be so great, by which the burdens of war and peace were not laid upon every man without distinction, as before, but depended on the wealth of each. On the basis of the census he then formed the Classes and the Centuries, and this present order, which has been as distinguished in peace as in war.

" Of those possessing 100,000 *asses* and more, he made eighty Centuries, forty of young men (*juniores*) and forty of older men (*seniores*). These were all called the First Class. The older men had

---

[1] i, 42, 4, to 44, 2 ; for this so-called Servian Centuriate organization, cf. Dion. Hal., iv, 16 ff. ; Cic., *Rep.*, ii, 22, 39–40.

to be prepared to defend the city, the younger to serve abroad. . . . To this Class two Centuries of smiths were added, who served without arms and had to look after the war-engines. The Second Class comprised all possessing between 75,000 and 100,000 *asses*, and contained twenty Centuries of citizens, Seniors and Juniors. . . . The minimum for the Third Class was 50,000 *asses* ; it had the same number of Centuries, divided into ages in the same way, as the Second Class. . . . The minimum for the Fourth Class was 25,000 *asses*, and the number of Centuries was the same. . . . The Fifth Class was larger, containing thirty Centuries . . . including the *accensi*, horn-blowers and trumpeters, divided into three Centuries. This class was assessed at 11,000 *asses*.[1] The rest of the multitude, whose fortune was less than that, was collected in a single Century exempt from military service.

" Having thus formed and divided his infantry, he raised twelve Centuries of cavalry from the first men of the city. He also created six other Centuries (three of which had been instituted by Romulus), under the names which they had had when instituted. The public treasury furnished 10,000 *asses* for the purchase of horses, the cost of whose upkeep was met by a tax on widows, who had to pay 2,000 *asses* a year. All these burdens fell on the rich, while the poor escaped.

" Then he dealt with honours. Instead of giving a vote of equal value to every man without distinction, as Romulus had done and the Kings after him, maintaining the tradition, he established grades, so that no one seemed to be excluded from the vote, yet all the real power was in the hands of the first men of the city. First the Knights (cavalry) were called ; then the eighty Centuries of the First Class of infantry. If these did not agree (which seldom happened), the votes of the Second Class were taken, but it was hardly ever necessary to go down to the bottom class. . . . When the census was completed, the work being expedited by the fear of the law, which threatened those who failed to enter their names with imprisonment and death, Servius issued an edict ordering all citizens, cavalry and infantry, to appear on the Campus Martius at day-break, each man in his Century. There he drew up his whole army in battle-order, and purified it with *suovetaurilia*. This sacrifice was called the closing of the *lustrum*, because it marked the end of the taking of the census."

So Roman tradition categorically stated two things : (i) that the Republican organization in Centuries, as we find it established before third century B.C., with its parallel scales of rights and duties and its political embodiment in the Comitia Centuriata, was created systematically by one single operation ; (ii) that that systematic and complete organization was the work of the sixth of the seven Kings of Rome, Servius Tullius. In this absolute form the tradition cannot be accepted, and, indeed, we have two proofs, one of a military and one of a political kind.

---

[1] 12,500, according to Dion. Hal.

The army of the Centuriate type originally contained only one category of men, the *classis* or levy, composed of all, Patricians and Plebeians alike, who owed military service. The various echelons, the five Classes of Livy and Dionysios of Halicarnassos, into which the *classis* itself was divided, are of a later time. All who were outside the *classis*, through not having the necessary wealth, were put together under the description of *infra classem*. Secondly, the Comitia Centuriata, the concrete expression of the political importance assumed by the army, did not really begin to work until the beginning of the Republic ; we must, therefore, deny the alleged reform of Servius Tullius any electoral or legislative character. From a number of definite indications, we know that military and financial organization developed gradually in the course of the fifth century B.C.; consequently, the complete reform ascribed by annalistic tradition to Servius Tullius was really the end of a slow development.

That being so, what was the Servian reform ? Here again our guiding clue will be supplied by foreign politics, by the position of Rome in Italy during the last phase of the Etruscan kingship. That period was for Central Italy an age of intense and continuous fighting, which ended with the capture by Rome of the Latin League and the establishment of Roman hegemony over Latium. A policy of conquest of this kind exposed the Roman State to new necessities ; it needed more men and more money. The last Etruscan Kings of Rome found that they had not always the material means to carry out their policy. What could they do ? There could be no question of asking the Patricians to make further sacrifices. Even in Royal times, the Patriciate was dwindling fast, and it would soon be necessary to fill its depleted ranks artificially, to keep it at a reasonable strength. Tradition tells us of many Gentes of the conquered cities—Claudii, Furii, Julii, Marcii, Papirii, Sergii, Sulpicii, Volumnii, etc.— being naturalized by the Etruscan Kings or immediately after their time and poured into the Roman Patriciate. It was therefore necessary to look outside the Patrician body for the increased means of action which had become a crying necessity for the foreign policy of Rome, and outside the Patriciate there was only the Plebs, that foreign element, domiciled on Roman soil but hitherto legally excluded from the city.

Moreover, as the Etruscan kingship more and more took on the character of a military tyranny, there was continuous and increasing tension between the two elements, and the Kings, making for centralization, and the Patricians, standing for particularism, confronted each other in an antagonism which daily became more acute. In this conflict the support of the Plebs, numerous and already very wealthy, might be decisive. Foreign policy, home policy, everything drove the Etruscan Kings to turn to it for support ; it is this two-fold necessity which explains the admission of the Plebs to the citizenship, that first constitutional widening of the Roman State which tradition unanimously fathers on Servius Tullius.

If it was to the King's advantage, and doubly so, to admit the Plebs to the citizenship, the Plebeians, on their side, asked nothing better than to fall in with his policy. They were foreign to the Roman State, and therefore had no protection whatever against arbitrary treatment ; in a reform of this kind, even limited, they would find serious guarantees for their persons and goods which could not leave them indifferent. For these guarantees, which the Etruscan dynasty had no intention of giving them for nothing, they were ready to pay by the military and financial sacrifices required. The advantage which King and Plebs alike had from the innovation was the great reason which justified the principle and explains its success.

There remains the question of application. To what extent was the principle applied and how far was it carried out in practice ? The traditional account, which credits Servius Tullius with the organization of the Comitia Centuriata in the form in which we find them working in the earliest centuries of the Republic, cannot be accepted. The reform developed gradually, after the expulsion of the Etruscan Kings, during the sixth and fifth centuries B.C. What share can the Kings claim in the organization which we find complete at the end of the fifth century or the beginning of the fourth ? First of all, one fact is certain. At the beginning of the Republican period the army contains a Plebeian element, and that element, in an army which has

long been exclusively Patrician, must date from the last
Kings. But the presence of Plebeians in the army at that
time does not prove that *all* Plebeians were then admitted.
Even in the Golden Age of the Republic, not all Plebeians
belonged to the Classes, that is, to the regular army. They
were only admitted bit by bit, by the gradual lowering of the
property-minimum of the lowest Class, which was 11,000 or
12,500 *asses* in the so-called Servian constitution and 4,000
asses (i.e. a reduction of two-thirds) in the middle of the
second century B.C. So the evolution of recruiting took the
form of an increasing incorporation of the Plebeian element.
The facts referred by annalistic tradition to the work of
Servius Tullius really date from the fifth century at the
earliest ; they represent, not a starting-point, but the logical
end of a movement which had begun in the Royal period
and had gone on relentlessly ever since. That the Plebeians
were admitted to the army in the time of the Etruscan Kings
appears undeniable, but they were only admitted by selection
and in limited numbers.

There is no doubt about the principle on which they were
incorporated ; it was, as tradition says, the principle of the
census. No doubt, there was no question of the complicated,
scientific system which Livy and Dionysios of Halicarnassos,
faithfully echoing the Annals, describe under the name of the
Servian organization ; it was a rudimentary form of census,
which did no more than distinguish between the Plebeians
to be incorporated (that is, the richest) and those to be
excluded (until further orders, at least, all the rest). For
this census, the State took into account only landed property,
the only kind, or almost, which mattered in those days.
The assessment in coin, of which tradition speaks, in a time
when coin did not yet exist, only represents an anticipation,
one anachronism the more. Even in this embryonic form,
the census implied an exact enumeration of the population,
both of persons and of goods. Now, the Plebeians—*rudis
indigestaque moles*—were not yet arranged in concrete
organisms like the Patrician Gentes. Therefore artificial
divisions had to be created for them. These could only be
imagined in topographical, territorial form, and, since the
Plebs at that time was essentially, if not entirely, urban,
the new divisions were confined to the town itself. These

were the four Urban Tribes—Suburane, Palatine, Esquiline, and Colline, the first three corresponding to the domain of the three early Tribes, the fourth to the Sabine villages of the Quirinal and Viminal, recently annexed—the origin of which was ascribed by tradition to Servius Tullius, and may with more safety be placed somewhere at the end of the Royal period. This creation of the Urban Tribes was an innovation which is interesting in two ways. (i) It applied to Patricians and Plebeians alike, thus giving, for the first time, divisions common to the two great classes of the population established on the soil of Rome ; (ii) it introduced into the organization of the City a new principle, that of domicile, which was to figure very largely in the constitutional history of Rome.

Such were the general principles on which, in the last period of the Etruscan domination, the Plebeians were admitted, still only partially, to Roman citizenship. How was this incorporation of the Plebeian element carried out in detail ? We do not know for certain, but at least the later development of the institution gives some valuable indications. When, directly after the Revolution which drove out the Etruscan Kings, the army, in the form of Comitia Centuriata, constituted itself an electoral and legislative assembly, we do not find it by any means an exclusively, or even mainly, Plebeian body. It was not, and it would not be, all through the struggle of the two orders down to the Licinian Laws, the centre of the activity and propaganda of the Plebeians. There were Plebeians in it, without a doubt, from the reform of Servius Tullius onwards, but they did not predominate in it, and do not even seem to have been very powerful. We lack accurate information about the early organization of the Centuries, but we at least know that of the following period, which affords an instructive element of comparison. In the governmental system of the fourth and third centuries B.C., the Patricio-Plebeian nobility, based on wealth, had not abolished but appropriated to itself (whether by right or in fact), the traditional political privileges of the Patriciate, such as the monopoly of magistracies and the Senatorial sanction (*auctoritas Patrum*). A process of the same kind is to be seen in the organization of the Centuries ; the less rich, who are also, as usual, the more numerous, are relegated to Centuries which are both fewer and less influential. At the end of the Royal period, when the Plebeians were first admitted to the citizenship, resort was had to a similar process. The wealthier Plebeians, on being admitted to an army which had hitherto been exclusively Patrician, probably formed fewer and less influential Centuries than the Patrician Centuries, and, from the technical point of view, constituted special corps which were held in less esteem, analogous to the Velites of Republican times. This would quite naturally explain the two characteristics of the Centuriate Assembly at the beginning of the Republic—the presence of the Plebeians and their limited influence.

Lastly, a final anachronism on the part of tradition, the reform ascribed to Servius Tullius must be reduced to its true value from the political point of view. In Royal times it most certainly did not take the form of the creation of a new assembly, the Centuriate Assembly, possessing electoral, legislative, and judicial powers and intended to duplicate or even to supplant the traditional Comitia Curiata. These powers were taken by the army after the fall of the Etruscan Kings, and the innovation was the direct consequence of the Revolution of 509, but it is certain that the Kings never meant to give the army these powers and never let it take them.

The reform of Servius Tullius was, in reality, purely military and financial. Its object was to give the State the new means which the requirements of its policy of conquest and those of national defence made an absolute necessity, in short, to supply it with the soldiers and taxpayers whom the Patriciate, already dwindling in numbers, could no longer guarantee by itself.

It is quite clear, so far, what advantage the Etruscan Kings expected when they decided to admit the Plebs to the city, at least in part ; but why should the Plebeians have welcomed a reform whose most obvious feature was a considerable increase of their own burdens, military and financial ? The reason was that these burdens were counterbalanced by the advantages which they obtained for certain at the present and those, still more considerable, on which they might reasonably count in the future. For the present, the Servian organization meant access, at least partial, to a citizenship from which they had legally been wholly excluded. Among the exact rights entailed by possession of the citizenship, one at least, the right of ownership (*commercium*) was given to them in full, and doubtless to all of them, as early as the Royal period. The future was still more promising. The old principle of birth, if it was not yet driven out, at least had to make room for two new principles, that of wealth, on which the census was based, and that of domicile, which was the foundation of the Urban Tribes. Neither of these new principles made any difference between the two great elements of the Roman population, the inhabitants of the two Romes, Patricians and Plebeians. As in all great political and social innovations, these two principles entered upon the scene in a doubtful and rudimentary form, but the mere appearance was, from the constitutional point of view, a real revolution, containing the seeds of all the future history, all the political development, of Republican Rome.

The warlike policy of the last Etruscan King of Rome, whom tradition calls Tarquin the Proud, Tarquinius Superbus, was the cause of an important transformation in the character of the Etruscan kingship. From a military kingship it became a tyranny in the full sense of the word. " With Servius Tullius," Livy writes, " both just and lawful kingship disappeared—*simul justa ac legitima regna occiderunt.*" [1] Tarquin the Proud seized the power by force, killing his father-in-law Servius Tullius, a first characteristic of tyranny, and, equally characteristically, he relied on a bodyguard and ruled as a tyrant. Let us hear Livy,[2] who gives a clear and precise account of the Etruscan political regime in its last phase :—

" Then Tarquin began to reign, who was given the surname of the Proud, because he refused burial to his father-in-law, saying that Romulus too had died and not been buried. He slew the chief men of the Senators, whom he believed to have supported the cause of Servius. Then, aware that his example of getting the kingship by ill means might be turned against himself, he surrounded himself with armed men ; for he had no right to the power save that of force, and reigned neither by the will of the people nor with the sanction of the Senate. Moreover, placing no hope in the affection of the citizens, he had to protect his kingship by fear. In order to inspire this as widely as possible, he judged capital cases by himself, without

[1] i, 48, 7.   [2] i, 49, 1–7.

advisers ; so he was able to visit death, banishment, and confiscation of goods, not only on men whom he viewed with suspicion or disfavour, but on those from whom he could merely expect plunder. When, as a result of this, the number of the Senators particularly decreased, he decreed that no new nominations should be made, that the order might be less influential, on account of its numerical weakness, and that it might complain less at being excluded from all business. For he was the first of the Kings to abandon the custom observed by his predecessors of consulting the Senate about everything. He governed with the advice of his own household alone, making and breaking off war, peace, treaties, and alliances by himself, with whom he pleased, without the orders of the people and the Senate."

The reign of Tarquin the Proud was one of brilliant success abroad and of prosperity and greatness at home. On the Capitol he built the Temple of Capitoline Jupiter which Tarquin the Elder is said by tradition to have decided to erect, and he carried out many great public works in addition to those undertaken by his predecessors. Seizure of the power by violence, development of the policy of national expansion abroad, permanent conflict with the aristocracy, but, at the same time, economic prosperity and intense artistic life at home—all these component elements and characteristic features of tyrannical government are found in full in the reign of Tarquin the Proud. The Etruscan monarchy ended as a tyranny ; as such we see it in its last days, as such it is depicted in the story of its fall.

The traditional account of the expulsion of the Etruscan Kings, in the form in which the historians of the classical period give it, is a mere tissue of legends.[1] The story of the death of Lucretia has nothing to do with history. Just as it had cast a decent veil over the Etruscan conquest, so Roman history-writing, logically inconsistent, was careful to distort the national character of the Latin reaction which made an end of it. But at least, through the accounts of Livy and Dionysios, in spite of distortions and gaps, we clearly see two features which are undeniably historical. The Etruscan kingship fell beneath the blows of the local aristocracy, and the Revolution of 509 was a revenge of the old Roman Patriciate after a century and a half of foreign domination. Secondly, the Plebs, if it did not directly bring about the fall of the Kings, at least allowed the movement to

<hr />

Livy, i, 59–60 ; Dion. Hal., iv, 64–85.

take place, and finally joined it. This passive attitude of the Plebeian element is surprising at first sight, but can be quite well explained. Constant wars abroad and the ever-lasting contributions required by great public works at home were in the long run too much for the Plebeians, who bore a very large part of the burden. Brutus, in the speech which Livy puts in his mouth,[1] dwells on the point with some complacency :—

> " He then spoke of . . . the miseries and toil of the Plebeians, thrown into ditches and sewers which they had to drain. Men of Rome, he said, who had conquered all the peoples round them, were turned into workmen and stone-cutters instead of soldiers."

Peoples readily forget the blessings of the past, to remember only the evils of the present. All the material hardships which the Etruscan tyranny brought with it caused the Plebeians to forget, for the time at least, what they owed to the monarchy, and what dangers an aristocratic reaction might have in store for them. In the end, when it was too late, they saw that with the kingship they had lost their natural support and their supreme protector. The advent of a jealous and oppressive aristocratic system, a century and a half of conflict between the two orders—that would be the price which they must pay for a political mistake and a day's blindness.

[1] i, 59, 9–10.

CHAPTER II

THE PATRICIAN REPUBLIC AND THE CONFLICT OF THE TWO ORDERS

BIBLIOGRAPHY.—*Ancient Authors* : Livy, ii–vi (cf. Florus, i, 4–8 ; Eutropius, i, 9 to ii, 4 ; Orosius, ii, 5, 12–13, 19 ; iii, 3) ; Dionysios Hal., v–x (to 443 B.C.) ; xi–xiii (fragments) ; *H.R.F.*, *passim* ; Cicero, *Rep.*, ii, 31–7 (to the end of the Decemvirate) ; Dion Cass., iv–vii, 29 (frags., cf. Zonaras, vii, 13–24, 9) ; Diodoros, xi–xv (*passim*) ; Plutarch, *Publicola, Coriolanus, Camillus* ; *De Viris ill.*, 10–25.

Inscriptions : Consular *Fasti* in *C.I.L.*, i, 2nd ed., pp. 98–126 ; *C.I.L.*, i, 2nd ed., 2, No. 1 (cippus from Forum) ; p. 189, 5 (*Elogium* of M. Valerius Maximus) ; p. 191, 6 (do. of L. Albinius (?)), 7 (do. of M. Furius Camillus).

Modern Works : **XXIII**, ii, 3–358, 454–563 ; iii, 94–116 ; **XXII**, i, 3–214, 271–335, 399–421 ; iv, 49–74 ; **XXIX**, i, 400–28 ; ii, 1–89, 192–217 ; **XXI**, 42–6, 58–64 ; **II**, 51–85 ; **X**, iii, 165–6 (K. J. Beloch), 439–42 (K. J. Neumann); **XXVI**, 364–87 ; **IX**, i, 31–43, 54–9 ; **XXVII**, 9–10, 13, 24–7; **XVI**, i, 109–219; **XX**, bk. ii, ch. i–iii, viii ; **XIX**, i–iv (magistracies) ; vi, 1–2, pp. 1–81 (people) ; vii (Senate) ; **XXXI**, 53–72 ; **XVIII**, i, 51 ff.; **XIII**, bk. ii, ch. v; **CXXIV**; **LVIII**; E. Meyer, " Der Ursprung des Tribunats und die Gemeinde der vier Tribus," in **XXXVI**, xxx (1895), 1–24; A. Rosenberg, " Studien zur Entstehung der Plebs," *ibid.*, xlviii (1913), 359–77 ; G. Bloch, " La Plèbe romaine : étude sur quelques théories récentes," in **XLVII**, 1911 (cvi), 241–75; (cvii), 1–42 ; **CXXXV**; E. Kornemann, " Zur altitalischen Verfassungsgeschichte," in **XXXVIII**, 1914, 190–206; **CXIV** ; W. Schur, " Zwei Fragen der älteren römischen Verfassungsgeschichte : i, Die militärische Grundlage der Centurienordnung," in **XXXIX**, li (1923), 193–201 ; " ii, Diktatur, Konsulartribunat, und Konsulat," *ibid.*, 202–9.

I

THE ORGANIZATION OF REPUBLICAN GOVERNMENT

THE period of a century and a half (from the end of the sixth century to middle of the fourth), known under the name of the conflict of the two orders, represents a decisive phase in the building-up of the Republican constitution. But we must first of all determine its true character and correct once again, and not for the last time, one of the many errors of perspective for which tradition is

*See also Supplementary Bibliography with Prefatory Note (p. 405)

responsible. The Republican constitution underwent a profound change during this time, but annalistic tradition, transmitted in the first place by Livy and Dionysios of Halicarnassos, is wrong and deceptive when it ascribes the important and lasting innovations then introduced into the nature and working of institutions entirely to the conflict of the two orders, Patricians and Plebeians, that is, to strictly internal causes. The internal question was, without a doubt, one of the great factors in the constitutional development, but it was not the only one, nor always the chief one. Here again, in accordance with the general rule which governs the whole of Roman history, the question of foreign policy has a right to claim its share, and a very large share. The great events of the foreign history of Rome during this long period of crisis—the expulsion of the Etruscan Kings in 509, the siege of Veii in the first years of the fourth century, the capture of Rome by the Gauls in 390, the unification of Latium under Roman hegemony, and the Italian wars of independence—were just the events which directly and logically gave rise to the most decisive changes in the constitution. The growing extension of the Roman State as a result of conquest, on the one hand, and, on the other, the constant increase of the population, economic development, and the appearance of new needs, led to the creation, both in the political constitution and in the administrative organism, of new and more complex machinery.

The appearance of the Roman magistracies, one after another, gives a definite example of this increasing constitutional complexity. The Quæstorship is the first to appear alongside of the Consulship. Originally the Quæstor was a mere assistant of the Consul, who doubtless appointed him, and he had quite a subordinate post. Later, as business at home and abroad increased and, in particular, the influx of booty and the creation of new revenues made it necessary to establish a specialized State chest, the number of Quæstors was increased to two, and then to four, two of whom resided permanently in Rome to administer the treasury, while the other two were attached to the Consuls and followed them to the field. At the same time the post was made a magistracy and, as such, was subject to election by the people, an innovation important in itself and still more so in its consequences. For the notion of a single magistracy, the Consulship was thus superseded by a new idea, that of the *cursus honorum*, or official career, which was to be one of the fundamental elements and corner-stones of the classical Republican constitution. The subsequent creation of the Censorship, the Prætorship, and the Curule Ædileship, that is, of special administrative offices, represented successive stages on the same road, and corresponded, at least to a great extent, to organic necessities of the same kind. So the external factor and the internal factor contributed simultaneously, in proportions which varied according to the needs of the moment, to the construction of a new fabric and constitutional life. A rapid survey of the facts will bring out this truth fully.

By pressing the principle of military monarchy to its logical conclusion, the Etruscan Kings had gradually weakened the Patriciate and, by increasing application of the principle of centralization, they had made a breach in the particularistic element which the old Roman Patriciate embodied in the State. In destroying the royal authority by driving out the Etruscan dynasty, the Patricians revenged themselves signally. But, if they were the chief victors, they were not the only victors. Powerless by themselves, they had needed the army in order to carry out the Revolution. In tradition the army plays a very important part in the affair. Revolution had just broken out in Rome, instigated by Brutus.

" The news had come to the camp, and as the King, agitated at the turn which things were taking, was making for Rome to put down the movement, Brutus, hearing of his coming, changed his route, so as not to meet him. They arrived almost at the same time, by different ways, Brutus at Ardea and Tarquin in Rome. Tarquin was met with closed gates and the order of banishment ; the deliverer of the city was hailed with joy by the army, and the King's sons were driven from its ranks." [1]

The so-called Revolution of 509 was, as we have seen, a Latin national reaction, led by the Patricians and supported by the army. The new constitution would take these two elements into account, exactly so far as they had contributed to the victory. The Patriciate, the chief victor, laid hands on the government and established, for nearly

[1] Livy, i, 60.

a hundred years, a purely aristocratic republic; but, to pay the army for its help, and also because, in the terrible ordeal to which the State was subjected, it needed its support against foreign enemies, it was to find itself, whether it liked or not, obliged to give it its place and allow it an effective share in the new system of government.

With the national defence to be ensured abroad and the political consequences of the Revolution of 509 to be drawn at home, the men who had to organize the new, or rather revised, constitution, found themselves faced with a peculiarly complicated situation and a very hard task. One fact must first be considered. What elements were at their disposal for solving the problem ? Around them, two types of republican constitution must necessarily have attracted their eyes and demanded their attention—constitutions of the Etruscan type and those of the Italian type.

In Etruria,[1] as early as the sixth century, the kingships had started to break down under the pressure of local aristocracies. The King was replaced by an annual magistrate, the Zilaχ, who took over from the fallen regime considerable power, with the pomp (purple dress, lictors) with which the Lucumos, the Etruscan sovereigns, traditionally loved to surround themselves. By his side we find two other magistrates, also annual, the Marunuχ or Marniu and the Πυρθne, who were doubtless a sort of Ædile and Quæstor respectively. Among the Italian peoples,[2] on the other hand, there were boards or colleges of magistrates —two Marones (a doubling of the Etruscan Marunuχ) among the Umbrians, eight Octovirs among the Sabines, and two Meddices, the Meddix Tuticus and the Lesser Meddix, among the Oscans—and in each case this was the only magistracy. So there were two different conceptions of the executive. Among the Etruscans there were many magistracies with a regularly organized *cursus honorum*, each magistracy being held by one man with very extensive powers. Among the Italians there was only one magistracy, held by more than one man at a time. Everywhere alike, office was annual, according to the general rule of republican

---

[1] A. Rosenberg, **CXXIV**, 51–71.
[2] *Ibid.*, 1–50, 71–117 ; E. Kornemann, " Zur altitalischen Verfassungs-geschichte," in **XXXVIII**, 1914, 190–206.

governments in Italy and elsewhere.   Such were the different elements which the Patricians, when they had driven out the Etruscan Kings, might use to construct the new constitution.   Now let us see how they did it.

In the Royal period the Patriciate had had its own organs as against the King—the Curiate Assembly and the Senate. Having rid itself of the royal power, it simply kept them both. There remained the very delicate task of organizing the executive and replacing the fallen Kingship, at least in its political attributions.   This the Patricians did by creating and organizing the Consulship.

National defence abroad and the safeguarding of the privileges of the Patriciate against the menacing Plebs at home required a particularly strong executive, but, on the other hand, the danger of kingship or tyranny made it absolutely necessary to take serious precautions in respect of it.   The Patricians, with that practical spirit of which the Romans are the standing embodiment, found the compromise required by the complicated position of the State in a wise combination of the Etruscan and Italian conceptions of government.   From the Etruscans they took the idea of the powerful magistrate, like the Zilaχ, and from the Italians that of many holders of one magistracy, like the Oscan Meddices, the Umbrian Marones, or the Sabine Octovirs.   The supreme power was given to two magistrates, whose titles—first Prætors (*prætores*, chiefs) and later Consuls (*consules*, colleagues), the latter appellation being destined later to supplant the former—reflected their fundamental characteristics.[1]

There is a last question, of capital importance for the history of the Roman magistracies at their origins.   With the principle of many holders of an office, did the Patricians find among the Italian peoples, Oscans, Umbrians, or Sabines, that of the college on a basis of *par potestas*, which was to be one of the chief features of the Republican constitution ? Of the mutual relationship of the two Marones of Umbria we know nothing precise.   About the Oscan Meddices, the Meddix Tuticus and the Lesser Meddix, there is no doubt ; their powers were not equal, and therefore they

---

[1] On the origin of the Roman magistracies, see especially W. Schur, art. cit., 202–9.

did not constitute an absolute college.   Among the Sabines, lastly, the college of the Octovirs was divided into four pairs of magistracies with special powers—two Octoviri Fanorum, two Ærarii, two Ædiles, and two Quæstors—but the principle of the college seems (although we cannot be quite certain) to have been maintained within each of these double magistracies.   So the question remains open.   It is possible, even probable, if one admits the precedent of the Sabine Octovirs, that the reformers of 509 found the principle of the college already in force among the Italic peoples and did no more than transplant it to Rome in the form of the Consulship ; it is also possible that the idea of two collegiate magistrates, armed with an equal *imperium*, as a precaution against possible attempts at absolute power, was a purely Roman invention, a constitutional discovery doing the greatest honour to the statesmen of the early Republic. Lacking sufficient evidence, we must be content to observe the fact, without being able to establish its genesis with certainty.

Livy [1] describes the Consulship in the following terms :—

" One should date the origin of liberty from this time because the period of a Consul's power was made one year rather than because the royal power was at all reduced, for the first Consuls kept all its rights and distinctions."

Cicero, too, in his essay *On the Laws*,[2] defined the new magistracy as a royal power, *regium imperium*. For no serious damage was done to the executive in its principle. The Consulship, as Livy says, inherited all the essential prerogatives of the kingship, civil, military, and judicial, and also its emblems of dignity, the curule chair and the lictors, but it did so—and here the novelty comes in— with a double limitation : it was a college and it was annual. Henceforward the executive power was divided between two magistrates having equal powers and, in virtue of their *par potestas*, the right of mutual control (*intercessio*) ; more- over (a provision likely to be acceptable to the governing aristocracy), in case of conflict they had to refer to the arbitration of the Senate. Secondly, the office was no longer held for life, but for one year, a double guarantee

---

[1] ii, 1, 7–8.   [2] iii, 8.

for the victorious Patriciate against any return to the offensive on the part of personal government.

The collegiate conception, which was so valuable and efficacious in the domain of home politics, had from the point of view of national defence grave disadvantages which the increasing danger abroad presently made plain.

> " In the anxiety of awaiting these great events," Livy writes of the year 501,[1] " there was talk for the first time of making a Dictator. But we do not know in what year, nor in whose Consulship . . . nor who was first made a Dictator."

At all events, the office was created in the first years of the Republic, and on account of the foreign danger resulting from the expulsion of the Etruscan dynasty. In the face of the enemy, unity of command was necessary. This the college of the Consuls was unable to give in complete form, so the old kingship of the Etruscan type, which in Etruria had become the annual magistracy of the Zilaχ, was revived, and was placed in the hands of one official, who was first called Magister Populi, and afterwards Dictator, which name, as in the case of the Consulship, eventually replaced the older title. But the royal power thus revived was subject to two limitations, one in time, the period of office being fixed at a maximum of six months, without possible prolongation, and one in power, since the Dictator had to be accompanied by a subordinate called the Master of Horse, who seems to have been suggested by the already existing Magister Juvenum, who is found in the Etruscan cities and Italian peoples of the time.

With a regular magistracy in the Consulship and an extraordinary magistracy, held in reserve, as it were, in the Dictatorship, the problem of the executive was completely solved by a double organization which seemed to meet every possible contingency. This elaboration of the Republican constitution was hardly original (except, perhaps, for the idea of the college), but, as always, when the statesmen of Rome found themselves faced by pressing, though partly contradictory, needs, they managed to find close to their hand the means to cope with them and, by the perfect adaptation of means to end, to create an institution which the future would show to be as original as it was effective.

[1] ii, 18.

Both as a national rising against Etruscan dominion and as a patrician reaction against military tyranny, the Revolution of 509 was, in all the force of the term, a violent breach with the past. Yet, at the time of the constitutional change which followed upon the expulsion of the Etruscan Kings, the victorious Patriciate did its best to save appearances. The kingship, a traditional and indispensable link between the Roman State and the powers above, between men and gods, was by no means abolished, and in this respect there was evolution much rather than revolution. Rome continued to have a king, and one who held his office for life, but he was reduced to purely religious functions. Later, in the early part of the fifth century, a second assault robbed him of still more of his importance; he lost all his religious attributions to the Pontifex Maximus except some show ceremonies, and was henceforth only the King of Sacrifices, Rex Sacrorum or Sacrificulus, of the Republican period. Conservative habits, sense of practical needs— the constitutional transformation of 509 reveals, in its essential features and its most profound tendencies, the whole spirit of Rome.

So far, all the organs of the Republican constitution— Curiate Assembly, Senate, executive power in the double form of Consulship and Dictatorship, and even the semblance of kingship—are exclusively patrician, and the government appears as a complete patrician monopoly. The Patriciate, master of the situation and provided with ample powers, would gladly have stopped there, but beside it there was the army, which had supported the Revolution, and was needed more and more every day against enemies outside. The army, too, must be paid for its services, past and future. This the Patriciate did by creating the Centuriate Assembly, that is, by allowing the army very wide legislative, electoral, and judicial powers.

The organization in Centuries effected by the last Etruscan Kings was, as we have seen, essentially of a military and financial nature; the army, which was its embodiment, had never exercised nor even possessed rights of a political kind. Immediately after the Revolution, and for the first time, it received the powers which were to make it, under the name of Comitia Centuriata, the great political assembly of the Roman State. We do not know the exact nature of the composition of that assembly at that early time, and the Centuriate organization described by annalistic tradition is a pure anachronism. All that we know is the very important fact that the assembly was simply the army, meeting in its divisions of Classes and Centuries under the command of its highest leaders, the Consuls, outside the city, on the Campus Martius. The Plebeians, newly admitted to the constitutional organism, still held only a very small place in it, and the Patricians, politically, and without a doubt numerically too, were definitely preponderant.

About the powers of the Comitia Centuriata we have more information. They were given three kinds of attribution, electoral, legislative, and judicial. They elected the chief magistrates of the State, the Consuls ; they voted on laws and had the supreme decision over peace and war ; they heard the appeal of men condemned to death (*provocatio*, as it was called) and pronounced on their case in the last resort.

However great the triumph of the Patricians appeared—and it was great—the new power of the army cast a cloud, and a dark one, on the picture of its victory. The serious thing was the presence of the Plebeian element in that army, and its position, now subordinate, but dangerous for the future. No doubt, they might have thought, as they can hardly have failed to do, of expelling the Plebeians from the military organization. But the introduction of the Plebeians into the cadres of the army was one of those necessary reforms which cannot be repealed ; the deep-seated reasons which had led to their incorporation (at least partial) in the city and in the army were as strong as ever, and when the Roman power was driven back and the fall of the kingship brought new dangers upon the State these reasons became yet more imperative.

But there is no situation to which one cannot adapt oneself. If the Plebeian element could not be expelled, at least an attempt could be made to nullify its influence, and the Patricians did not fail to do so. With this object, they took a double series of precautions, inside the Centuriate organization and outside it.

(*a*) The Patricians tried, in one way or another, to weaken

the influence of the Plebeians within the Centuriate organization as much as possible. Perhaps they were skilfully
distributed among the Centuries so as to be in a minority ;
perhaps smaller and less influential Centuries were created
for the Plebeians, like the Century of *capite censi*, in the later
organization of the end of the fifth century or the beginning
of the fourth. We do not know exactly what was done.
These beginnings of the Centuriate system have been missed
by our sources, which only tell us of the final term of the
development, that is, the Centuriate organization finally
established.

(*b*) The Patricians strove to limit the influence of the
Centuriate Assembly. By the side and on the edge of that
assembly they had at their disposal three exclusively Patrician
organs—the Comitia Curiata, the magistrates, and the
Senate. These three organs they used as a triple brake
against any possible powers and activity of the Centuriate
Assembly.

I. *The Comitia Curiata.*—The Comitia Curiata had been
the only legislative organ of the Royal period. When they
were compelled to make room for the new organ born of
the Revolution of 509, the Comitia Centuriata, they still
retained a great importance. The Consuls were elected
by the Comitia Centuriata, but they did not receive all their
authority from them. It was conferred in two stages,
corresponding to the two elements constituting the Consular
power, the *potestas*, or right to deal with the people and
Senate, and the *imperium*, or total civil, military, and judicial
power. The former was conferred by the Comitia Centuriata,
the latter by the Comitia Curiata, which invested the newly
elected candidate with his *imperium* by a special law, the
Lex Curiata de Imperio. So the election of a Consul was
not complete until the Comitia Curiata had stepped in
and ratified it.

II. *The Magistrates.*—The Consuls, who held all the
executive power in their hands, were chosen exclusively among
the Patricians. Now, the constitution gave them considerable means of acting on the Centuriate Assembly.
In an election, the Consul, as president of the Comitia,
played a very important active part. He held the auspices
which had been handed on to him by his predecessors, and

it was he who must transmit them to his successor ; without a definite statement and personal action on his part, the auspices, or, in modern language, the power, was not and could not be legally passed on. In practice, this privilege took the form of direct intervention in the election. As president of the Assembly, who had to read the list of candidates to the electors, he could refuse to announce (*nominare*) a candidate of whom he did not approve, and even to proclaim him (*creare*) if he was elected. In legislation the Consul exercised a similar control. The Comitia Centuriata could not initiate laws, and could only discuss such bills as the presiding Consul chose to put forward for deliberation and voting.

III. *The Senate.*—Lastly, the Senate, the stronghold of the Patriciate, which it permanently represented, enjoyed a still more complete right of control. In elections and in voting òf laws alike, the decision of the Centuriate Assembly must, to be fully valid and to produce its legal effects, be ratified afterwards by the Senate (*auctoritas Patrum*). Refusal of the Senate to ratify was an absolute veto ; it made every decision of the Comitia Centuriata null and void, and they had no legal recourse against it.

II

THE ATTACK ON THE PATRICIATE

So, being compelled to allow the Plebeians some place in the Comitia Centuriata, the Patricians had taken good care to nullify their influence as much as possible, and might hope that, at least for a long time, they would have nothing to fear from that quarter. The reasoning might be sound, but on one condition—that, being determined not to increase the rights of the Plebs, they were also wise enough not to multiply its duties. Unluckily for the Patricians, they were here faced with necessities of a national and military nature against which they were helpless. The fifth century and the first half of the fourth century were for the Roman State a time of prolonged and acute crisis abroad. Porsenna led the Etruscan reaction and took Rome. Latium rose against her hegemony. There were constant struggles with the highlanders of the east, Sabines, Æqui, Hernici, and in the south against the tribes of the Volsci. There was a long war with Veii, the powerful Etruscan neighbour on the north, which only ended with the destruction of that city at the beginning of the fourth century. Lastly, in 390, the Gauls took Rome, and there were forty years of Gallic invasions in consequence. Threatened, not only in her power, but in her very existence, Rome had to meet needs in men and money which were always renewed and always increasing.

Now, just at the moment when those necessities with which there is no arguing were increasing, the means for meeting them were dwindling, a phenomenon of first importance for the constitutional history of Republican Rome. The Patriciate, which had been an open class during the Etruscan domination and even in the first years of the Republic, had ceased to reinforce and rejuvenate itself by incorporating outside elements. Henceforward it was a closed caste, which, for lack of the necessary renewal, soon began to fall off in numbers, like all social categories of the kind.

The Patrician Gentes comprised two elements—Patricians and Clients. Both diminished simultaneously. The Gentes disappeared one after another, and consequently the Patricians became fewer and fewer. Even at the beginning of the Republic there was a serious shortage in the Patriciate. This shortage, thanks to losses in war and also to consanguine marriages within an ever narrowing caste, steadily increased. Out of sixty-one Patrician Gentes, whose existence is historically confirmed, thirty-seven disappeared in the fifth century and in the first half of the fourth; in 367 there were only twenty-four left. Moreover, as the Gentes gradually disappeared, their Clients were emancipated and went to swell the Plebs. So, as a result of these two connected phenomena, the Patriciate grew less and less numerous, just at the time when the safety of the city required more and more men and money. Therefore, since there were no longer enough Patricians, the State had, willy-nilly, to turn to the other element of the population, the element which was truly alive and constantly increasing, the Plebs. In accordance with these unavoidable necessities, the burdens laid on the Plebs, both military and financial, from the end of the sixth century to the middle of the fourth, gradually became very heavy.

Our sources, representing annalistic tradition, describe the Centuriate organization, we have seen, as if it had been created by Servius Tullius, lock, stock, and barrel. This is artificial simplification and flagrant anachronism. A scientific and complicated institution of this kind was only started in a very rudimentary form in the Royal period, and was brought to final completion by a series of modifications. In default of complete data, a certain number of indications allow us, at least, to determine the main features of its development.

First, there was the creation of the Censorship, which tradition places in 443. Livy [1] explains the innovation as follows :—

> " The same year saw the institution of the Censorship, which started from small beginnings. . . . No census had been taken for many years ; it could not be put off any longer, and the Consuls, with so many wars threatening, had no time to do it. A report was made to the Senate that this arduous task, which was not at all the business for Consuls, needed a magistracy of its own, with scribes to guard and keep up the books, which should decide for itself in what manner the census would be taken. Although these duties were unimportant, the Patricians were glad to have more Patrician magistracies in the Republic, being convinced, I think, that, as indeed happened, the wealth of those who received this office would lend it authority and dignity."

The real reason, lying much deeper than the historian will admit, was that the Censorship appeared on the day when the census became an operation of first importance, and the real explanation of that increasing importance lay in the development of the Centuriate organization.

We get a second indication from the increasing number of Military Tribunes with Consular Power, as is attested by the *Fasti*. The Military Tribunes took the place of the Consuls in 444 as the highest magistrates of the State. These senior officers, invested on this occasion with the Consular prerogative, were the traditional leaders of the contingents of a thousand men which together formed the Roman army. Originally they had been three, and this was their number in 444 when the Military Tribuneship with Consular Power was created. Twelve years later, in 432, the number was

[1] iv, 8, 2–5.

the same. In 428 we find four Consular Tribunes, in 405 there are six, and this number remains unchanged until the re-establishment of the Consulship in 367 by the Licinian Laws. This gradual increase of the number of corps-commanders reflects a gradual increase of the contingent; the three corps of a thousand men were increased to four, and then six, that is, they were doubled. The date of this doubling, which is particularly important, is 405 B.C., the very year in which the siege of Veii began and the Roman State, in order to carry out this great military operation, had to increase its effectives considerably. Now, this could only be done in two ways, either by laying a heavier burden on the Patricians, which was impossible, given the steady diminution of that order, or by calling upon the Plebs to take a larger part and introducing more and more Plebeians into the Centuriate organization, which was the only solution possible.

Lastly, a third fact was decisive for the development of the Centuriate institution and the increasing admission of the Plebs to the institutions of the city, and that was the siege of Veii. That siege was a military operation on a large scale, the first big operation undertaken by Rome outside Latium, and it represents the end of the crisis of the fifth century, which had nearly overwhelmed Rome, and the beginning of the counter-offensive. To face it, great changes had to be made in the army. As we have seen, the infantry contingent was increased, with two consequences, the division of the old *classis* into five differentiated echelons, Classes I–V, and the increase of the number of senior officers, the Military Tribunes. At the same time the strength of the cavalry was increased; hitherto it had been formed solely by the eighteen Equestrian Centuries (*Equites equo publico*), and now the duty of serving in the cavalry was extended to the whole of the First Class. This was an innova-tion of great importance, which would give rise to the Equestrian order of the classical period and would thereby profoundly affect the constitutional history of Rome. Lastly, to compensate troops who had been kept away from their homes for several years in succession, pay was instituted. It was at this time, under the pressure, I repeat, of necessities from outside, that the Centuriate organization was first given the complete form in which it is described (and incorrectly attributed to Servius Tullius) by our main sources, Livy,[1] Dionysios of Halicarnassos,[2] and Cicero.[3] The financial burdens of the Plebeians must have increased together with their military obligations, but our sources do not allow us to say this with certainty. The only fact of which we can be sure is the end of the evolution, as we find it in the complete and systematic organization of the end of the fifth century and the beginning of the fourth.

The Centuriate system, at the time of its full development, has two essential characteristics. First, under the conditions laid down for the census it comprises all Roman citizens without distinction, Patricians and Plebeians alike. Secondly, citizens are classified in the political and social organization in proportion to their wealth. So the principle of wealth definitely and absolutely supplants the old principle of birth.

In accordance with this double principle, the citizens are distributed into Classes, and the Classes are divided into Centuries. In addition there are, outside the Classes, the cavalry, or rather mounted infantry, of the eighteen Equestrian Centuries at the top of the scale and the Century of proletarians or *capite censi* at the bottom. So the people, according to our sources, was divided as follows :—

OUTSIDE THE CLASSES. Cavalry *equo publico*, 18 Centuries. 100,000 *asses* [4] (like the First Class).

FIRST CLASS. 80 Centuries, 40 of Seniors and 40 of Juniors. 100,000 *asses*.

SECOND CLASS. 20 Centuries, 10 of Seniors and 10 of Juniors. 75,000 *asses*.

THIRD CLASS. 20 Centuries, 10 of Seniors and 10 of Juniors. 50,000 *asses*.

FOURTH CLASS. 20 Centuries, 10 of Seniors and 10 of Juniors. 25,000 *asses*.

FIFTH CLASS. 30 Centuries, 15 of Seniors and 15 of Juniors. 11,000 *asses* (Livy) or 12,500 (Dionysios).

Add : 2 Centuries of workmen (carpenters and smiths— *Fabri tignarii, ærarii*), attached to the Second Class, and 2 Centuries of bandsmen (*cornicines* and *tubicines*) attached

---

[1] i, 42, 4, to 44, 2.   [2] iv, 16 ff.   [3] *Rep.*, ii, 22, 39–40.
[4] The figure in *asses* represents the minimum property required for the Class.

to the Fourth. Lastly, below and outside the Classes, the Century of proletarians and *capite censi*.

General total of Centuries, 193.

The duties of the citizen, military and financial, correspond to the place which his property gives him in the civic scale. The eighteen Equestrian Centuries, *Equites equo publico*, owe service in the cavalry. From the end of the fifth century onwards, the First Class may also be called to this service, as *Equites equo privato*. The First (so far as it is not serving in the cavalry), Second, Third, and Fourth Classes constitute the heavy or legionary infantry, the Fifth, the light infantry. The Century outside the Classes is exempt from service in normal conditions and only called up in case of very great danger, when the inexorable law of the public safety alone has authority.

The financial obligations to which citizens are liable number two.

(*a*) *Costs of Equipment.* Except the *Equites equo publico*, who have the right to an advance in coin for the purchase of a horse (1,000 *asses*) and an annual indemnity of 200 *asses* for its upkeep, all the costs of equipment fall on the citizen, and the higher his Class is, the heavier this burden is. First Class : helmet, cuirass, leg-pieces, round shield, spear, sword. Second Class : the same, less cuirass ; round shield covered with leather. Third Class : the same as the Second, less leg-pieces. Fourth and Fifth Classes : spear, javelin, shield.

(*b*) *Tax.* This is the tribute (*tributum*), a tax on capital imposed on all citizens in proportion to their wealth and, at least from the second half of the fifth century, paid in money.

In sum—and this is the capital fact from the constitutional point of view—in respect of military and financial burdens there was no longer any difference between Patricians and Plebeians at the end of the fifth century. All were soldiers and tax-payers, on the same terms, and the State recognized only citizens, on whom it laid burdens proportionate to their fortune.

The Patricians, being driven by the inexorable necessities of foreign policy to extend the military and fiscal duty of the Plebeians more and more, would have resigned themselves

to the situation, but it was impossible for the gradual participation of the Plebs in the city to take the form of burdens
only. The spirit of the ancient city and, one must add,
logic demanded that the process of assimilation should,
soon or late, extend from duties to rights.

The monopoly held by the Patriciate was political, judicial,
social and religious. The Plebeians naturally replied with
an equally complex programme of positive demands :

(i) In the social domain, they demanded the mitigation
of the regulations regarding debt and the solution of the
agrarian question ;

(ii) In the judicial domain, the establishment of a written
code, common to all, and the authorization of mixed
marriages ;

(iii) In the political domain, admission to the Consulship
and to the other magistracies as they were created, admission
to the Senate, and the legal validity of plebiscites ;

(iv) In the religious domain, admission to the priesthoods
on the same terms as Patricians.

Tradition, which has left a confused and often distorted
account of the conflict, has given us the names of the men
who, as Tribunes of the Plebs, guided the movement and led
the Plebs to victory—Icilius, the author of the plebiscite
of 492 which guaranteed the privileges of Tribunes, Publilius
Volero, whose plebiscite of 471 governed the organization
of the Concilia Plebis, the first Plebeian assemblies, Terentilius
Harsa, who proposed the Decemvirate in 461, Canuleius,
who by sheer energy forced the Patricians to authorize mixed
marriages in 445, and Licinius Stolo and L. Sextius who
fought for the Licinian Laws and the sharing of the Consulship until they carried them in 367. These men, so far as the
distortions of tradition allow us a glimpse of them, appear to
us as very intelligent party-leaders, knowing what they want
and where they are going, wary opportunists, who, the better
to obtain their object, excel in bringing out their questions
according to the conditions of the moment, and first-rate
tacticians, able to adapt their plan of action to the successive
objectives for which they are making. The final aim was
always the same : total equality of rights between Patricians
and Plebeians, as a counterpart and legitimate compensation
of their equality of duties. That principle grew more

unassailable as the external needs of the State compelled the Patricians to call upon the Plebs for greater and greater military and financial sacrifices. So the needs of the public safety gave the Plebeian opposition a first-class weapon, a strike of tax-payers and soldiers, and if need arose it would not scruple to use it. One must add, to complete the picture, that the leaders of the movement were not always guided by purely unselfish motives. In the course of the struggle of the two orders, there were several attempts at tyranny in the Greek manner. Spurius Cassius and Spurius Mælius, two Plebeians ambitious on their own account, tried in succession to fish in troubled waters and to seize the power with the support of the people.

The struggle of the orders was not only political and judicial; it also presents a topographical character which especially deserves attention. The two opposed parties, Patriciate and Plebs, corresponded, within the city itself, to distinct geographical groups. The Patriciate was the population of the old Latin villages of the Seven Hills, that of the Palatine, Cælian, Velia, and Esquiline; the Plebs dwelled in the new quarters colonized by the Etruscan Kings, such as the Aventine and Velabrum, or annexed by them, like the Quirinal, Viminal, and Capitol. In these circumstances, the conflict of the two orders was accompanied by a rivalry of districts, which was to jeopardize the unity of the State and the very existence of the nation. One day, the old Sabine population of the Quirinal started out for the country of its origin, and there was the Secession to the Sacred Mount, a halt by the Via Nomentana, along which they were returning. Another time, the Plebs concentrated on the Aventine, the centre and stronghold of its urban activity. In the course of the fifth century B.C., the central government succeeded, by a series of compromises, in preventing a break-up and saving the principle of the State, which had so nearly perished directly after the Revolution of 509; but for over a hundred years that dreadful menace continued to hang over Roman politics, and more than once the political unification effected by the Etruscans came near to going under altogether in the turmoil.[1]

Yet, in spite of winds and waves, the Roman State came

[1] **XIII,** Eng. pp. 129–52.

through that terrible crisis. For, stubborn as it was, the conflict of the orders was not, we should note, a fight to the death. For this fact, apart from the political sense which always preserved the Romans from desperate solutions and held them back at the very edge of the abyss, there were two essential causes, one internal, one external.

At the beginning of the Republic, the Patriciate was a survival from the past, representing a complete social and political organization, against which the Plebs was still only a confused, inorganic mass. In the Plebs, two elements, with divergent interests and tendencies, found themselves side by side—rich men, who chiefly wanted civil and political equality with the Patricians, and poor men, whose social and economic aspirations were chiefly confined to the improvement of their material position. Between these two sections, whose programmes were so different, the leaders of the Plebs would often have hard work to maintain the indispensable unity of action, and this lack of unity, by favouring the resistance of the Patricians, helped to postpone the final triumph of the common cause for nearly a hundred years (middle of the fifth century to middle of the fourth).

Moreover, during the fifth century the danger from outside strengthened the sense of solidarity of all classes, and the constitutional evolution, which was marked on the one hand by the weakening of the Gens, the great germ-cell of particularism, and on the other hand, correlatively, by the development of the notion of a State, a unifying tendency, was a reflection and a direct consequence of that general situation. All alike were Romans, in the deep sense of the word, conscious of the community of nation which was gradually supplanting the original community of Gens and imbued with a same love for their common city, and, hard though the struggle was, Patrician and Plebeian alike would, if need be, make the sacrifice needed for the safety of the State. So, as is usual is such cases, the conflict went on in the form of spasms of violence alternating with compromises—the convention of the Sacred Mount in 494, the Laws of the Twelve Tables in 451–449, Leges Valeriæ Horatiæ in 449, institution of the Military Tribunate with Consular Power in 444, Licinian Laws in 367, to mention only the chief of them. And when in the course of the fourth century the day was at last won by the Plebs, in the flower of its youth, it was in a State delivered for ever from the outside menace which had paralysed it for over a century, and ready to start, with the union of Italy, on the glorious career to which it was destined.

To carry through their programme of equality, the leaders of the Plebs followed two tactical methods in turn, first that of separatism, and then that of equalization of rights. The result of the first was the organization of the Plebs as an autonomous body ; the second led to its participation in public life and admission to the citizenship on a footing of absolute equality with the Patricians.

The first objective to be attained was the unification of the Plebs in a solid bloc in opposition to the governing party. The fact that the leaders of the Plebs clearly perceived this does the greatest honour to their political wisdom. To solve this preliminary problem, they skilfully made use of the organization of the city itself and exploited both the situation abroad and the social crisis through which the Rome of the fifth century was painfully struggling.

Already in Royal times, the population of the town of Rome had been distributed in four Tribes, Suburane, Palatine, Esquiline, and Colline, territorial divisions in which, on the principle of domicile alone, the Patricians with their Clients and the Plebeians were incorporated side by side. At that time the innovation was confined to the town itself, for the decisive reason that the Plebeian element was then almost entirely urban. Later—tradition gives the date as 495—for reasons which were in essence administrative, and above all military and financial, the system was extended to the rural population by the creation of seventeen new tribes, the Rustic Tribes. At the head of each Tribe was a Tribe-leader, or Tribune (*tribunus ærarii, curator tribunus,* Greek φύλαρχος), who kept registers of persons and goods and had certain administrative powers in matters of finance (taking of the census of landed property, collection of *tributum*), 'of the army (levy of the contingent due from each Tribe), and probably also of justice, at least in certain minor cases. This organization, then, which, it must be repeated, was essentially administrative in character, and therefore applied equally to all citizens, both Patricians and Plebeians, but contained a large majority of the latter because of their actual numbers, provided the Plebeian element with a framework, the Tribes, and its first leaders, the Tribunes.

The creation of the Rustic Tribes entailed a second consequence of great constitutional importance, which, with the legal organization of the Plebs, would very soon make itself evident. In a total of twenty-one Tribes, the seventeen Rustic Tribes would have an overwhelming majority. So there would be, in contrast to the previous situation created by Etruscan ideas, an assured preponderance of the countryside and the end of the political privileges of the town. The State of the Tarquins, with its centre in the town, would give place, and for centuries to come, to a State of peasants.

Once the Plebeians were organized for the conflict, the social situation gave the revolutionary impulse which decided the day. The poorer of them were faced with a most precarious economic situation; they suffered from material needs which must be met at once. For them there were three vital questions, of the kind which brooks no delay and absolutely must be answered—the questions of debts, land, and the food-supply. Let us say a word about each.

The system of debts bore hard on the mass of small landowners who formed the Plebs of the country. Constant war, devastation by the enemy, and bad harvests compelled them to borrow frequently. Now, the rate of interest was not only arbitrary (before the Law of the Twelve Tables there was no legal rate) but very high; the subsequent legislation of the Decemvirs, which represented a considerable improvement in this respect, fixed the rate at one-twelfth of the capital, that is, $8\frac{1}{3}$ per cent for the year of ten months, or 10 per cent for our year of twelve months. Besides, the legislation regarding debts was particularly severe and the position of the insolvent debtor was appalling. On principle, a man was answerable for his debt with his person. A debtor who failed to meet his liabilities had to continue to work for his creditor until he had cleared himself; in the case of *addictio* he could be sold as a slave or even put to death. Nor was debt the Plebeians' only grievance. The proletariate, faced with an enormous birth-rate, also demanded land and, what especially affected the urban Plebs, distributions of foodstuffs. The plight of the poorer Plebeians was such an urgent problem that somewhat later, in 485 according to tradition, it was exploited by the ambitious Spurius Cassius in an attempt at tyranny.

The leaders of the Plebs found in this serious social crisis a lever by which they might accomplish their projects and enable the Plebs to compel the Patricians to give legal recognition to their constitution as an autonomous organism; this was the famous Secession to the Sacred Mount of 494. The origin of the movement had been purely social, but the leaders of the Plebs cleverly made use of their success to legalize the separate organization which, they thought, should constitute the first step towards the accomplishment of their programme, the establishment of civil and political equality. Their tactics succeeded wonderfully. The separate organization of the Plebs, officially recognized by the State by a solemn convention which was a veritable treaty of peace between two foreign peoples, comprised two essential organs, one executive, the Tribuneship, and one legislative, the Assembly by Tribes.

The Tribunes, two in number (later, in the middle of the century, they were increased to ten), enjoyed exceptional power, that they might perform their office effectively as leaders of the Plebs and its authorized representatives with the State. By the right of intercession, which found practical expression in the institution of the veto, they could oppose the decisions of magistrates and arrest by a single action all the working of the governmental machine. The free exercise of this right was guaranteed by the inviolability of the Tribune, violation of which prerogative *ipso facto* entailed outlawry and death for the offender. A little later, we shall see two new representatives of the Plebs appear, the Ædiles, who were at first subordinate assistants of the Tribunes, but were presently given police-duties as their special office.

The second organ of the Plebs, the legislative organ, was the Plebeian Assembly, *Concilium Plebis*. This assembly, which was composed entirely of Plebeians, in virtue of the principle which had presided over the separatistic organization of the Plebs, had, like the assemblies of the State, electoral, legislative, and judicial powers. It elected the Tribunes, from the Plebiscite of Publilius Volero onwards (traditional date, 471), voted decisions or plebiscites, and judged certain

c

cases, the only reservation being that these resolutions, given by the Plebs alone, held good only for the Plebs, and did not bind the whole State.

So a first result was attained. Henceforward the Plebs had a powerful autonomous organization recognized by the public authorities and placed under the solemn protection of the laws. It was now a state within the State. With the power which it now had, it would be able to start the battle for civil and political equality ; a second phase begins in the history of the conflict of the two orders.

III

THE TRIUMPH OF THE PLEBS

The battle was first waged for civil equality, those rights of which the Plebeians still possessed only one, the right of ownership, *jus commercii*. They reached their object in three big stages.

(i) The State admitted the Plebeians to a certain number of acts—marriage, testament, adoption—relative to civil law. At the beginning of the Roman State, these three were acts of an essentially religious nature. The old marriage, marriage by *confarreatio*, required the presence of the Pontifex Maximus and the Flamen Dialis ; testament and adoption required the intervention of the Comitia Curiata in their religious form (Comitia Calata) under the presidency of the Pontifex Maximus. Being strangers to the religion of the city, Plebeians could not perform these acts in their traditional form. New methods of marriage, testament, and adoption were devised, secular forms, based on a round-about application of the right of ownership, a fictitious sale or *mancipatio*, which were therefore accessible to Plebeians, like the right of ownership itself. Although the Plebeians obtained these first civil rights indirectly, they were theirs for good.

(ii) By the legislation of the Decemvirs the Plebeians obtained the drafting and publication of a code of written laws (451–449). Hitherto Rome had had no written law. There was only custom, which was handed down and interpreted by the Patricians alone, in virtue of their monopoly of government. So the Plebeians were, in legal matters, wholly at the mercy of the Patricians. To put an end to a situation which was so unfair in practice, two reforms were necessary—the drafting of a written code and its publication. The Tribune Terentilius Harsa, in 461 according to tradition, proposed that a commission of ten should be appointed for the purpose and given full powers. The Patricians, who set especial store by their control of judicial matters, resisted tooth and nail. At last, tired of fighting, the Senate consented to the appointment of three commissioners to study the codes of the Greek cities of Southern Italy. On their return, in 451, ten Decemvirs were appointed with unlimited powers to draft a new code. These were the celebrated Laws of the Twelve Tables, of which the first ten, we are told, were published by the first Decemvirs and the two others in the following year by a new board. A certain number of authentic fragments of these laws, revised and modernized by the jurists of the classical Republican period, have come down to us.[1]

Their legislative and juridical work ended, the Decemvirs should have resigned in favour of the regular magistrates, but at the instigation of Appius Claudius, the ruling spirit among them, they held on to their dictatorship. There was a rising in Rome, and after serious disorders, in which the legend of Virginia is the chief episode, the Decemvirs were compelled to give up their power. The normal constitution was restored, and the Twelve Tables, after being turned into laws by a vote of the Comitia Centuriata, came into force. These two institutions, both based on the principle of landed property, the code of the Twelve Tables in the domain of law and the Centuriate system in that of politics and war, were an emanation and perfect expression of the peasant state which Rome had become, in the full sense of the term, in the fifth century B.C.

One last step had still to be taken. The code, being common to all, Patricians and Plebeians, was henceforward

---

[1] The question of the authenticity of the Twelve Tables has given rise in these last years to a particularly heated controversy. See especially E. Pais, in **XXII**, i, 3–179 ; E. Lambert, " La Question de l'authenticité des Douze Tables et les Annales Maximi," in **XLVIII**, 1902, 26, 147–200 ; *id.*, " L'Histoire traditionelle des Douze Tables et les critères d'inauthenticité des traditions en usage dans l'école de Mommsen," in **CV**, 501–627 ; E. Täubler, **CXXXV**, 9 ff.

published. Therefore all concerned knew it. But the forms of procedure (*legis actiones*) and the list of the *dies fasti* on which alone justice could be delivered continued to remain secret. This double defect, which gave undesirable advantages to Patrician caprice, was not remedied until the end of the fourth century, in the celebrated Censorship of Appius Claudius (312–308). They were published by a former scribe of the Curule Ædiles, the Plebeian Flavius.

(iii) The law forbade mixed marriages between Patricians and Plebeians, thus condemning the two rival classes to mututal isolation, and the Patricians, from political interest no less than from pride of caste, were strongly in favour of maintaining this express prohibition. Shortly after the drafting of the code of the Twelve Tables, in 445 according to tradition, a Tribune named Canuleius brought forward a bill for the repeal of the prohibition. In spite of violent opposition from the Patriciate, it was carried through, thanks to the tenacity of its author and the energetic support of the Plebs, and soon mixed marriages became frequent.

At the time when, with community of marriage, the Plebs was at last obtaining full equality in civil matters, the campaign for political equality had already begun. The political demands of the Plebs referred to all three great organs of the State—Comitia, magistracies, and Senate.

The Comitia Curiata, composed entirely of Patricians and their Clients, were, by definition, closed to Plebeians. The Comitia Centuriata, in their original form, allowed them only a limited participation. Lastly, the Assembly by Tribes, which was exclusively Plebeian, had neither the official character nor the privileges of a State assembly. Therefore the Plebeian claims in respect of these three assemblies were different. Admission to the Comitia Curiata, a larger place in the Comitia Centuriata, and recognition of the Assembly by Tribes as a State assembly—such was the political programme of the Plebs in respect of the Comitia.

In the end the Plebs made its way into the Comitia Curiata, we do not know at what date, perhaps not until the end of the fourth century. The part which it played in the Comitia Centuriata extended as the State gave it a larger place in the Centuriate organization in respect of burdens. The final result of the evolution appears in the Centuriate organization of the end of the fifth century and the beginning of the fourth. Being based on the principle of wealth, that organization did not on principle make any difference between Patricians and Plebeians, but skilful arrangement gave the chief influence to the richest, that is, to the Patricians and a minority of Plebeians. This preponderance asserted itself both in the organization of the system and in its working.

In organization, the number of Centuries in a Class was in no way proportionate to the number of citizens to be enrolled in that Class. At the top of the scale there were eighteen Equestrian Centuries. The First Class contained eighty centuries, the Second, twenty plus the two centuries of workmen, the Third, twenty, the Fourth, twenty plus two Centuries of bandsmen, the Fifth, thirty, and lastly, at the bottom of the scale, the Century outside the Classes of proletarians or *capite censi*. Out of a general total of 193 Centuries, the First Class and the eighteen Equestrian Centuries had ninety-eight votes, or an absolute majority plus one vote.

As for the working of the system, the Classes voted, not simultaneously, but in succession. Votes were announced as they were given, and as soon as an absolute majority was reached a stop was made. This being so, the Second Class seldom voted, and the three last Classes and the Century of proletarians were never in practice called to vote, so that their right to do so was purely theoretical. Moreover, the Century which voted first, whose decision was held by the Romans to have the force of a religious revelation, the " prerogative " Century, was always chosen by lot among the eighteen Equestrian Centuries. The part taken by the mass of Plebeians in the activity of the Comitia Centuriata was, therefore, very limited at the end of the fifth century. This legal inferiority was maintained until the great reform of the Comitia Centuriata about the middle of the third century.

Lastly, there was the Assembly by Tribes, for which recognition must be obtained as a State assembly, so that its decisions or plebiscites should be legally valid for all citizens, Patricians and Plebeians, without exception. Several stages had to be passed before the end was reached. A first law, the Lex Valeria Horatia of 449, laid down that plebiscites should have the force of laws, on condition that, like laws properly so called, they were afterwards ratified by the Senate, in virtue of the *Patrum auctoritas*. A second law, that of Publilius Philo of 339, amending the foregoing, provided that the Senate should do this, not afterwards, but beforehand, that is, that plebiscites could not be put to the vote of the people without the express authorization of the Senate. Only at the beginning of the third century (287) did the Lex Hortensia, by simply abolishing the sanction of the Senate, give the Assembly by Tribes a general function and unrestricted legislative activity. A parallel evolution took place in the composition of this Assembly and its mode of working. From the day when it became a State assembly, the Patricians, in order to exert influence in it and to affect its decisions, began to take part in it, and the traditional presidents of the Plebeian assembly, the Tribunes, gave up the presidency to the magistrates of the State. Henceforward the Assembly by Tribes, hitherto exclusively Plebeian, was, by its composition, its working, and the legal validity given to its decisions, a State assembly, which, as such, took the name of Comitia Tributa.

The great magistracy of the State, the Consulship, had since its creation been entirely confined to Patricians. Shortly after the drafting of the Twelve Tables, in 445 according to annalistic tradition, the Tribune Canuleius, who passed the law on mixed marriages, demanded that the Consulship should be shared between the two orders. The Patriciate refused downright, and, rather than yield, preferred to allow the office to lapse for a time. By a compromise between the opposing claims of the two orders, which bears witness not only to the great progress made by the Plebs but to the growing political importance of the army, the Consulship was replaced by the Military Tribuneship with Consular Power (*tribunatus militaris consulari potestate*). The Consular Tribunes, who varied in number (first three, then four, then six), might be chosen from either order. In reality (a fact which shows what a distance there was between constitutional theory and practice in Rome), Plebeians did not obtain the office until nearly fifty years later, in 400 B.C., and we should note that even this late result was not unconnected with the necessities of the war with Veii. But the new magistracy did not take over all the old prerogatives of the Consulship. Its financial and some of its administrative powers (census, public works) were given to new magistrates, the Censors, two in number, who were recruited from the Patriciate alone. Rather later, in 421, the Plebeians gained another advantage in legal admission to the Quaestorship.

In the eyes of the Plebeian leaders, the institution of the Military Tribuneship with Consular Power was only a temporary, opportunistic measure, a precedent on which to base the final solution. After the disasters of the Gallic invasion, they called for the restoration and sharing of the Consulship. This proposal was the object of one of the Licinian Laws, proposed in 376 by the Tribunes of the Plebs Licinius Stolo and L. Sextius. In virtue of this law, the Consulship should be restored and henceforward one of the two annual posts of Consul should be reserved for Plebeians. The Patriciate used every means to prevent the voting of this law—the opposition of the Senate, resort to a Dictator, systematic obstruction. But, as so often happened in the history of Rome, the matter was settled by the exigencies of foreign policy. To cope with a critical military situation, it was necessary to concentrate the supreme authority once more and to re-establish the Consulship. Since the Plebeians had exercised the chief command in practice, in the form of the Consular Tribuneship, the question of principle was settled, and it was impossible, without flagrantly arbitrary action, to keep them out of the Consulship. Re-elected ten years in succession, tradition relates, the Tribunes at last wore out the opposition of the Patricians and the law was passed in 367. L. Sextius, one of the two promoters of the reform, was the first Plebeian Consul. The Patricians once again tried to minimize their defeat by further reducing the functions of the Consul, and creating two specialized magistracies, the Prætorship and the Curule Ædileship. The struggle of the two orders did not end with the partition of the Consulship ; it went on for more than fifty years, but the issue was now certain. In the course of the second half of the fourth century the Plebeians, having been admitted to the Consulship, would win entrance into every other magistracy in turn.

Entrance into the Senate, lastly, must be, and was, for the Plebeians the necessary consequence of admission to the magistracies. Through the Military Tribuneship with Consular Power the Plebeians entered the Senate in 400, and the question of principle being thus settled, the Plebeian minority in that council would henceforward increase steadily.

By the middle of the fourth century, the conflict of the two orders had come to an end, at least in theory. Equality of duties was justified by equality of rights. The fusion of the two elements, so long alien to one another, Plebs and Patriciate, a political and social phenomenon which would develop more and more rapidly, was to have decisive consequences on the subsequent evolution of the Roman constitution. A first result, and not the least, was the formation of the Roman citizen body. The traditional barriers between Patriciate and Plebs were down ; in the eyes of the law, and to an increasing extent, all were Roman citizens. Secondly, the State emerged from the long struggle provided with its essential organs. The Patriciate and the Plebs, those two rival bodies, simultaneously gave it two sets of organs, those of the city—Comitia Curiata and Centuriata, Patrician magistracies (Consulship, Censorship, Prætorship, Curule Ædileship, Quæstorship), and Senate—and those of the Plebs, Assembly by Tribes, Tribunes, and Plebeian Ædiles. In the middle of the fourth century, when the question of the Consulship was finally settled, all the organs of the Republican constitution were, as it were, ready to start work.

But between these organs, the result of different systems and of different needs, confusion and lack of co-ordination still reigned. The Comitia Curiata were based on the principle of birth ; the Comitia Centuriata, on that of wealth ; the Comitia Tributa, on that of domicile. Of the magistracies, some, the Patrician (Consulship, Censorship, Prætorship, Curule Ædileship, Quæstorship), were magistracies of government, and the others, the Plebeian magistracies (Tribuneship, Plebeian Ædileship) were revolutionary, or at least magistracies of opposition. A great task lay before the Roman government. It had to co-ordinate, to harmonize, to perfect. That would be the fundamental achievement of the following period (from 367 to the middle of the third century) and of the governing class which would take the place of the old Patriciate at the head of the State—the Patricio-Plebeian nobility.

CHAPTER III

THE REPUBLICAN CONSTITUTION COMPLETE

BIBLIOGRAPHY.—*Ancient Authors* : Livy, vii–x (to 293 B.C.), and *Periochæ* of bks. ix–xx (cf. Florus, i, 9–21, especially 17 ; Eutropius, ii, 5 to iii, 7 ; Orosius, iii, 4 to iv, 13) ; Dionysios Hal., xiv–xx (in fragments) ; *H.R.F.*, *passim* ; *O.R.F.*, pp. 1–3 ; Dion Cassius, vii, 30 to xii (fragments ; cf. Zonaras, vii, 25 to viii, 20) ; Diodoros, xv, 90 to x, xxi–xxiv (fragments) ; Plutarch, *Pyrrhos, Fabius Maximus, Marcellus* ; *De Viris illustr.*, 26–41.

Inscriptions : Consular *Fasti* in *C.I.L.*, i, 2nd ed., pp. 126–40 ; *C.I.L.*, i, 2nd ed., 2, 6–9 (*Elogia* of the Scipios) ; p. 192, 8 (do. of L. Papirius Cursor), 9–10 (of Appius Claudius Cæcus) ; p. 193, 11 (of C. Duilius).

*Modern Works : **XXIII**, iii, 197–230, 336–50 ; v, 86–102, 177–94, 383–405 ; **XXII**, i, 215–40 ; iv, 263–89 ; **XXIX**, ii, 217–40 ; iii, 327–81 ; **XXI**, 65–7, 83–7, 151–3 ; **II**, 86–134, 190–4 ; **X**, iii, 166–73 (Beloch), 442–7 (Neumann) ; **XXVI**, 387–403, 417–18 ; **IX**, i, 76–86, 93–5, 130–2, 136–40 ; **XXVII**, 27–32 ; **XVI**, i, 229–411 ; **XXXI**, 73 ff. ; **XX**, bk. ii, ch. iii ; **XIX**, ref. as for last chapter ; **XVIII**, i, 51 ff. ; **XIII**, bk. ii, ch. iii ; **LIX**, 113 ff.

I

The Decline of the Patriciate and the Advance of the Plebs

THE period extending from the Licinian Laws (367 B.C.) to the middle of the third century, the sources for which are as poor as its events are complicated, plays a particularly important part in the final shaping of the Roman constitution. The two great factors, external and internal, which we have already seen make their appearance and shall find constantly in what follows, continue to act simultaneously. For it is the period of the subjection of Latium, the conquest of Italy, and the first Punic War, and these external events, which were so decisive for the formation of the greatness of Rome, left a profound stamp on constitutional development. From this point of view, three essential facts appear in the foreground—the decline of the Patriciate, the advance of the Plebs, and the break-up of the old parties and formation of the Patricio-Plebeian nobility.

**See also Supplementary Bibliography with Prefatory Note (p. 405)

(i) *The decline of the Patriciate.* The decline of the Patriciate, which was already perceptible at the end of the Royal period, and gained speed in the course of the struggle of the two orders, became headlong after the passing of the Licinian Laws and the decisive victories of the Plebs. The causes of the phenomenon were both material and moral. (*a*) The material causes took the form of two parallel facts—the disappearance of many Gentes and the splitting up of the rest. The number of Patrician Gentes known, which was originally seventy-three, fell to twenty-four at the time of the Licinian Laws and to twenty between 367 and 210 B.C. This decrease weakened the Patriciate in two ways ; not only were there fewer Gentes, but Clients were emancipated as a necessary consequence. Also, the surviving Gentes split up into families which became more and more independent, with the result that the Gens, the germ-cell constituting the Patriciate, gradually disappeared. (*b*) Morally, the Patriciate represented the past ; it was only the survival of a bygone age, and it knew it. Its material weakening was accompanied at an equal pace by its demoralization.

The steady decline of the Patriciate and the corresponding diminution of its influence on general policy are seen very clearly in the composition of the body which had hitherto been its embodiment and stronghold—the Senate. Before 400, the whole Senate had been Patrician. In the fourth century it still contained 130 Curule Patricians as against 65 Plebeians—a big majority. By the end of the third century, in 216 B.C., the Patricians had lost even that majority ; there were 73 Curule Patricians as against 75 Plebeians, and the difference must have been still greater for the non-Curule Senators. The movement became still more rapid in the last years of the third century and the first years of the second ; in 179 B.C. the Patricians held only 88 seats in the Senate, as against 216 Plebeians.

(ii) *The advance of the Plebs.* The Plebs continued to advance all through the second half of the fourth century and the beginning of the third. Like the decline of the Patriciate, and for similar reasons, its progress was both material and moral. (*a*) Materially, the Plebs increased in numbers. This was due to external and internal causes. The great annexations of territory of the fourth century and the beginning of the third, following on the subjection of Latium and the unification of peninsular Italy, led to a considerable extension of the citizenship and the creation of many new citizens, whose numbers automatically went to swell the ranks of the Plebeians. Nor was this all. After the conquest of Italy, which was the great event of foreign policy of the time, the town of Rome grew more and more important. Men went and settled there, trade developed ; and so the Plebs received a second stream of reinforcements. In the economic struggle the Patriciate was hampered by the rigid, obsolete organization of the Gens. The Plebs was free from all such impediments. It was a class which grew constantly richer, and its influence developed naturally with its prosperity. (b) Moral progress : in the constitutional struggle, the Plebs had the impetus usual in victorious parties, and the prestige of the successes which it had gained drove it on invincibly in pursuit of others. The gradual conquest of Italy increased the power of the army inside the Roman State, and therefore that of the Plebeian element, which was the backbone of the army and was definitely preponderant in it.

This state of things had two important consequences from the constitutional point of view. The Plebs finally won complete political equality ; and the influence of the Comitia Tributa increased.

By a series of laws ranging from 366 to the end of the fourth century, under the leadership of men, many of whom played a chief part in the unification of Italy, like M'. Curius Dentatus and C. Fabricius, the Plebs won complete political equality. Tradition gives us facts and dates, but one must not trust it blindly, especially in the matter of chronology. 364, admission of Plebeians to the Curule Ædileship, which office they held every other year, alternately with Patricians ; 356, admission of ˙Plebeians to the Dictatorship ; 351, admission of Plebeians to the Censorship ; 342, a law by which both Consuls could be Plebeians, a purely theoretical ruling which was not carried out till long afterwards, in 172 ; 339, a law of Publilius Philo providing that one of the two Censors must be a Plebeian ; 337, admission of Plebeians to the Prætorship ; 300, the same for the priesthoods (Lex Ogulnia).

Thenceforward the Patricians, save for the possession in practice of one of the Consulships, which they kept till 172, retained only a few constitutional prerogatives, most of which were of no real importance—the exclusive provision of Interreges, of the King of Sacrifices, of the Major Flamens (those of Quirinus, Mars, and Jupiter), of the Palatine and Colline Salii, and probably of the Arvals and Vestals down to the *Lex Papia* of 65 B.C., which introduced a new method of recruiting, and, lastly, the privilege of being entered in the Senatorial " album " above Plebeians, so that they provide the *Princeps Senatus*, or leader of the Senate. But the Plebs also kept a very important political privilege, the Tribuneship, which, except by the round-about procedure of *transitio ad Plebem*, was always, by its very definition, strictly closed to Patricians.

The increasing influence of the Comitia Tributa in this period was expressed alike in legislation, elections, and the law-courts. The evolution is particularly important in respect of legislation. The *Lex Valeria Horatia*, which tradition places in 449, had endowed the plebiscites of the Comitia Tributa with full legal validity, provided that they were afterwards ratified by the Senate (*auctoritas Patrum*). One of the laws of Publilius Philo, in 339, confirmed this concession, but made the sanction of the Senate preliminary instead of subsequent. Finally, the *Lex Hortensia* of 287 drastically settled matters by simply abolishing the need of the *auctoritas Patrum* for plebiscites. The Comitia Tributa, which had hitherto been a legislative assembly subordinate to the Comitia Centuriata, came more and more to the front. In practice, the Comitia Centuriata now retained the right of voting only on a few laws, although these were particularly important ones—decisions of war, peace, and alliance, and laws conferring the Censorial office.

In the matter of elections there was a similar and symmetrical development. The Assembly by Tribes, which had elected the Tribunes and Plebeian Ædiles since 476 (traditional date), obtained the right to appoint the Quæstors (447), the Curule Ædiles (365), who were six (362) and then sixteen (311) in number, and the twenty-four (from the third century) regular Military Tribunes, *Tribuni Militum Comitiati* or *a Populo*, while the Tribunes of supplementary legions,

Tribuni Militum Rufuli) were still chosen by the Consuls or other army-commanders.

Lastly, the Assembly by Tribes was given jurisdiction in all cases likely to involve a large fine. The *Lex Aternia Tarpeia*, which tradition places in 454, had laid down the maximum fine (*multa suprema*) which the senior magistrates could impose at two sheep and thirty oxen, an amount which the *Lex Julia Papiria* of 430 converted into 3,020 *asses* in coin. All higher fines were referred to the judgment of the people, that is, to the Comitia Tributa.

II

THE REDISTRIBUTION OF PARTIES AND THE FORMATION OF THE PATRICIO-PLEBEIAN NOBILITY

The decline of the Patriciate and the advance of the Plebs had two consequences, one negative, the break-up of the old parties, and one positive, the formation of the Patricio-Plebeian nobility, which would replace the old Patricians at the head of the Government.

Hitherto, the Patricians on one side and the Plebeians on the other had, on the whole, formed two opposing blocs. Directly after the passing of the Licinian Laws, and as a result of the new political situation created by that decisive act, the two parties, victors and vanquished alike, began to split up. Each contained a right wing and a left wing, an uncompromising section and an opportunist section. Among the Patricians there were extremists, the right wing of the party, who did not resign themselves to defeat and the concessions which the Plebs had snatched from them, and a liberal element, the left, who accepted the situation whole-heartedly and showed themselves ready to work with the richer and more conservative section of the Plebs. The leaders of the uncompromising Patrician group, the " die-hards " of the fourth century and the beginning of the third, were Appius Claudius, who was Censor in 312, and L. Postumius Gemellus, Consul for the first time in 305, again in 294, and a third time in 291. The leaders of the moderate section were P. Valerius Publicola, Consul in 352, and, above all,

Q. Fabius Rullianus, who was Consul five times, in 322, 310, 308, 297, and 295.

A similar process was taking place in the Plebs. The rich, the right wing of the party, who had won political equality with the Patriciate and were now *beati possidentes*, asked for nothing more. For the poor, on the other hand, the left wing, the conquest of political equality was only a prelude to further developments and even, for many of them, to social revolution. So there were two sections with definitely divergent political and social tendencies. So far, by mutual concessions, they had managed to work together more or less successfully. Of the three Licinian Laws, one, the sharing of the Consulship, was to the advantage of the rich Plebeians, while the two others, the abolition of debts and the agrarian law, had been put forward for the sake of the poor. During the years which followed, the social demands of the Plebs became more numerous and more exacting. In 359 a rising of the Plebs seemed imminent. By a plebiscite proposed by the Tribunes M. Duilius and C. Menenius, the provision of the Twelve Tables regarding the legal rate of interest was confirmed. In 352, the Consul C. Marcius Rutilus carried a law which set up a board of five members which should mitigate the position of debtors by various measures. In 347, the legal rate of interest was reduced to $4\frac{1}{6}$ per cent (*fœnus semunciarium*) for the year of ten months, and payment was distributed over four terms, the first on account and the three others in the form of annual instalments.

In spite of these palliatives, the question of debt was as acute as ever, and usuary continued to rage as in the past. The result was the mutiny of the Roman army in Campania in 343. The army, which was full of heavily involved debtors, marched on Rome. The Dictator M. Valerius Corvus had to make concessions, and, besides certain provisions regarding the debt-regulations, granted that no soldier might be dismissed from the service without his own consent. In the following year, the Plebiscite of Genucius pronounced further penalties on usury and, thanks to these repeated palliatives, the Plebeian agitation at last quieted down.

This movement, no longer political, but purely social, had been, as such, directed against all rich men without distinction, whether Patrician or Plebeian. The logical consequence was that all those affected united and the moderate sections of the Plebs and Patriciate combined for common action. This coalition of material interests adopted a very definite programme, containing three fundamental articles : unreserved acceptance of the situation as it was, an agreement to wield the power between them, and government against the two extreme sections, the reactionaries of the Patriciate and the proletarians of the Plebs. The leaders of this policy were remarkable men—P. Valerius Publicola and Q. Fabius Rullianus on the Patrician side and, among the Plebians, Q. Publilius Philo, four times Consul (in 339, 327, 320, and 315), Dictator, and Censor, P. Decius Mus, Consul in 340, who was to fall in the battle of the Veseris, his son P. Decius Mus, Consul four times (312, 308, 297, 295), who was killed at Sentinum, C. Marcius Rutilus, four times Consul (357, 352, 344, 342) and Dictator, and M'. Curius Dentatus, three times Consul, the illustrious vanquisher of Pyrrhos.

In the interests of the country Plebs, which chiefly wanted material betterment, the nobility in power took very effective measures. In 326 a *Lex Pœtelia Papiria*, put forward by the Consuls C. Pœtelius Libo and L. Papirius Cursor, ordered the abolition of seizure of the person (*nexus*) and the liberation of men imprisoned for debt. Many colonies were founded, chiefly for the benefit of the rural Plebs. Some were Latin colonies, in which, however, there were a large number of Romans—314, Luceria in Apulia ; 313, Suessa Aurunca, Saticula in Samnium, and Pontia on the island of the same name ; 312, Interamna Lirinas ; 303, Sora and Alba Fucensis ; 299, Narnia in Umbria ; 298, Carseoli among the Æqui ; 291, Venusia in Apulia ; 289, Hatria in Picenum. Others were colonies of citizens ; 296, Minturnæ and Sinuessa in Campania ; 286, Sena Gallica in Umbria and Castrum Novum in Picenum. Lastly, the long wars by which Italy was in the end united gave rise to many abundant distributions of booty. All these were wise measures which won over the mass of the rural Plebs to the cause of the governing nobility.

But, right and left of the Patricio-Plebeian nobility, there were still two active elements of opposition, the extreme conservatives of the Patriciate and the ever-increasing urban proletariate. So long as they remained divided, these two sections were powerless against the Patricio-Plebeian nobility which held the power. The situation changed at the end of the fourth century. A man of genius, Appius Claudius, succeeded in combining them for common action, and this unforeseen coalition gave them, at least for a time, control of affairs.

III

The Censorship of Appius Claudius

Appius Claudius, a Patrician of very good birth, was one of the most eminent and curious characters of his age. His political career was especially brilliant; he was Military Tribune three times, Quæstor, Curule Ædile twice, Prætor three times, Interrex three times, Consul twice (in 307 and 296), Dictator, and Censor. He was not a soldier, like his contemporaries P. Decius Mus, Q. Fabius Rullianus, C. Fabricius Luscinus, and M'. Curius Dentatus, but a great statesman, a remarkable administrator, and a highly cultivated man, far ahead of his time and his fellows in the intellectual domain. Politically, he was a Patrician of the right wing, an extreme conservative, the stubborn opponent of the Patricio-Plebeian nobility which had been in power for half a century. Separate, the two extreme elements, Patricians of the right and Plebeians of the left, could do nothing. The great idea of Appius Claudius, his idea of genius, was to unite them, and so to meet the coalition of moderates with a coalition of extremists.

Circumstances abroad, the influence of which on the development of the Roman constitution cannot be emphasized too often, gave Appius Claudius an exceptionally favourable opportunity to carry through his programme. The beginning of the great Italian coalitions in 310—Samnites, Etruscans, Umbrians, Gauls—demanded of Rome sacrifices in men and money which the traditional constitution, based solely on landed property, was unable to furnish. But the cure existed by the side of the evil. Agriculture had already long ceased to be the one and only foundation of Roman economy. By the development of trade and industry, movable wealth had come into being, and the recruiting and budget of Rome could, or rather must, henceforward take it into account.

It was enough to make room in the constitutional machinery
for this new element, in order to obtain the extra soldiers
and taxpayers who were made absolutely necessary by the
last great assault of almost the whole of Italy on the Roman
State.   So, for Appius Claudius, foreign policy and home
policy had to meet the same needs, and in practice converged
towards the same end.

It was chiefly during his Censorship, from 312 to 308, the
crowning period but not the end of his long career, that
Appius Claudius strove to put his political ideas into practice.
His colleague was an insignificant person named C.
Plautius Venox, who was content to follow in his wake and
do nothing on his own account, so that he was able to carry
out his programme freely and without impediment.

At the time when Appius Claudius entered office, the
Patricio-Plebeian nobility had had an absolute monopoly
of government for half a century ; it had a secure hold of all
the organs of the State, Senate, Comitia, and magistracies.
By systematic and skilful use of his Censorial powers, Appius
Claudius worked to take these away from it.   In the Senate
he dealt it two blows :   he excluded some of the most
influential members from that council, and he opened its
doors to sons of freedmen, who might, by allying themselves
with the extremists of the right, form a new majority. The
magistrates, being appointed by election, were naturally
of the same character as the Comitia which elected them ;
therefore Appius Claudius made a direct attack on the
composition of the Comitia. Livy [1] summarizes his political
action in this matter concisely and accurately when he
says, " By distributing the *humiles* among all the Tribes he
corrupted the Forum and the Campus Martius—*humilibus
per omnes Tribus divisis, Forum et Campum corrupit.*" Appius,
then, distributed the *humiles* among all the Tribes, and the
result of this measure, according to the Roman historian, was
to corrupt the Comitia Tributa on the Forum and the Comitia
Centuriata on the Campus. This statement is perfectly
justified, but needs some words of comment.

These humble ones, *humiles*, whom Appius Claudius spread
among all the Tribes without distinction, comprised two
chief categories, quite distinct. Some were *humiles* by their

[1] ix, 46, 11–12.

poverty—the proletarians or *capite censi* who had not the minimum property required for the Fifth Class—others by their birth—the *libertini* or freedmen. Many of these freed-men were well-to-do or even rich, but only in movable wealth, and they were therefore excluded by the constitution from the five Classes. These two kinds of *humiles* received special treatment in the Comitia Centuriata and in the Comitia Tributa. In the former, all alike were lumped in a single Century, that of the proletarians, which in theory voted last, and in practice, since the votes of the Classes were taken in succession, was never called to vote at all. In the Comitia Tributa, by a similar arrangement, all the *humiles* were placed in the four Urban Tribes, and excluded from the thirty-one Rustic Tribes. The means were different, but the political result in both cases was the same—the *humiles* were almost entirely without influence. Appius Claudius took two decisive steps in their favour. In the Comitia Centuriata, where classification was henceforward based on movable property as well as on the traditional landed property, the *libertini* were assigned to the Class and Century to which their wealth entitled them, just like other citizens. In the Comitia Tributa, the *humiles*, whether proletarians or freed-men, were distributed without reservation among the thirty-five Tribes, Rustic no less than Urban. The consequence of this two-fold innovation, and it was the object at which Appius Claudius was aiming, was to shift the majority in the Comitia in favour of the extreme Patricians and to the disadvantage of the Patricio-Plebeian nobility.

The policy of Appius Claudius, clever and marvellously conceived, both in its principle and in its means of applica-tion, dealt a very severe blow to the governing nobility; it was their great ordeal, before their triumph in the third century. But though hard hit, they did not despair, and stood up to the storm with energy. The two Consuls of 311, C. Junius Bubulcus and Q. Æmilius Barbula, who were stout supporters of that party, refused to recognize the Senate as reconstituted by Appius Claudius, and, treating the Censor's innovations as null and void, simply convoked the previous Senate. The new organization of the Comitia, on the other hand, was left in its entirety, and the Censors of 307, C. Junius Bubulcus and M. Valerius Maximus, dared not

or could not tamper with it. The conflict was only postponed ;
three years later the nobility, recovering from their surprise,
resumed the offensive with vigour, and obtained the Censorship for their two leaders, the Patrician Q. Fabius Rullianus
and the Plebeian P. Decius Mus. So far as the external
difficulties of the State allowed, that Censorship constituted
as complete a reaction against the work of Appius Claudius
as possible. The Senate was severely purged, and in the
Comitia Tributa the proletarians and *libertini* were once more
relegated to the four Urban Tribes, by which measure landed
property again became the centre of gravity of that assembly.
Only the new Centuriate organization, in which the monopoly
of landed property was broken and a place was given to
movable wealth, survived intact, for it had become a necessity
to the State, and therefore could not be touched.

Still later, however, we find Appius Claudius back at his
work of leading the extreme Patrician opposition. In 300 B.C.
he combated the voting of the *Lex Ogulnia*, which opened the
priesthoods to Plebeians ; in 297, he again fought his old
opponent, Q. Fabius Rullianus, who was trying for a fourth
Consulship ; in 296 he engaged battle with his Plebeian
colleague, L. Volumnius. As Prætor in 295, he had further
skirmishes with Fabius, but henceforward they were only
unimportant episodes. The political achievement of Appius
Claudius had received its death-blow in the Censorship of
304, and the conflict ended in the final victory of the Patricio-
Plebeian nobility over the two extreme elements, the conservative Patricians and the proletarians of the Plebs, which
for a moment had combined to rob it of its monopoly of
government.

IV

THE GREAT CONSTITUTIONAL REFORMS OF THE THIRD CENTURY

The Patricio-Plebeian nobility had won a great victory,
but they made the mistake, common in political life, of
thinking it more complete than it was, and of showing that
they thought so. Their success over the coalition formed
by Appius Claudius was due to the loyal support of the
middle classes, and above all to the small country land-

owners, who formed its big battalions. After the victory
they thought that they could now neglect their recent allies
—a bad tactical blunder. The awakening was rude, and
came soon. The question of debts, alleviated for a moment
by palliatives, but always latent, revived suddenly in an
acute form. A new movement, not of the urban proletariate
this time, but of the country Plebeians, the small land-
owners, who were the chief victims of the system of debt,
broke out in 287, and the Plebs seceded to the Janiculum, as
they had formerly done to the Sacred Mount. Q. Hortensius,
who was appointed Dictator, had to grant important concessions and caused the Comitia Centuriata to vote the
celebrated laws which bore his name. Besides an amnesty
and an alleviation of debts, both emergency measures, the
most important of them was a constitutional law of
the first order, by which plebiscites no longer required to
be ratified by the Senate. Henceforward plebiscites passed
by the Comitia Tributa were legally valid for all citizens,
and the Senate had no say in the matter. Shortly afterwards a plebiscite proposed by one Mænius ordered that
in elections the sanction of the Senate, *auctoritas Patrum*,
should be given before the election, thus robbing it of all
practical importance.

These were very great constitutional innovations, which
seriously damaged the governmental prerogatives of the
Patricio-Plebeian nobility and its chief organ, the Senate.
By the experience which it had gained and its wise policy,
and thanks to the great events abroad which tempered the
heat of party strife in the third century, the nobility was
able to prevent these legislative novelties from taking full
effect, but it is none the less true that the laws of Hortensius,
by giving the Comitia unrestricted influence, dealt a first
blow, and a very severe blow, to the constitutional fabric
which had been built up by two centuries of experiment and
effort.

In internal politics, the chief fact of the period between the
voting of the Licinian Laws and the second Punic War
(367–218) was the government of the Patricio-Plebeian
nobility, the heir and supplanter of the old Patriciate. But
that nobility did not work for itself alone ; with patriotism
and foresight, it also worked for the State. While it

established itself in power, it also set itself to co-ordinate and harmonize the various organs of the constitution. Those organs, as we have seen, all existed already under the rule of the Patricians, but the Patricio-Plebeian nobility, treating the institutions of the past in that conservative, traditionalistic spirit which was always a fundamental characteristic of the Roman genius, made it their task to co-ordinate and perfect the disparate and often antagonistic elements which they had inherited from the past. The good balance and easy working which mark the Roman constitution of the third century are in great part the conception and achievement of these men.

The work of harmonization was applied to the three great organs of the Roman State—Comitia, magistracies, and Senate. Let us try to determine their essential features.

I. The Comitia.—All three organizations, Comitia Curiata, Centuriata, and Tributa, were taken in hand, in respect both of their composition and of their powers. The Comitia Curiata, by tradition, were open only to citizens belonging to a Gens, that is, to Patricians and their Clients. The Comitia Centuriata and Tributa comprised all citizens, Patricians and Plebeians alike, but the preponderant element differed in the two assemblies; in the Comitia Centuriata the majority was held by the rich, the eighteen Equestrian Centuries and the whole of the First Class, whereas in the Comitia Tributa it belonged to the middle classes, the small country land-owners who predominated in the thirty-one Rustic Tribes. No change was made in the composition of the Comitia Tributa established after the failure of Appius Claudius, but the Comitia Curiata and Centuriata were both remodelled.

In the Comitia Curiata, the Plebeians were admitted by the side of the Patricians. The exact date of the innovation is not known, but it was certainly before the last years of the third century, for we find a Plebeian holding the office of Chief Curio in 209.

For the Comitia Centuriata, there is no doubt that the constitutional reform was effected in the middle of the third century—probably, but not certainly, in the Censorship of C. Aurelius Cotta and M. Fabius Buteo in 241. It was a systematic, complex reform, affecting both the composition and the working of the Comitia. In their composition two very important innovations were made.

First, the flagrant inequality between the numbers of Centuries in the various Classes was abolished. Under the previous system, there were eighteen Equestrian Centuries, eighty Centuries in the First Class, twenty each in the Second, Third, and Fourth, and thirty in the Fifth, with two centuries of workmen attached to the Second Class and two centuries of bandsmen attached to the Fourth ; lastly, outside the Classes and at the bottom of the scale, there was one Century of proletarians or *capite censi*. By the new regulations all were levelled up, each Class containing seventy Centuries, two to a tribe (35 × 2 = 70), one of Seniors and one of Juniors ; the eighteen Equestrian Centuries, the two of workmen, the two of bandsmen, and the one of proletarians or *capite censi* were left unchanged. This reorganization had two results : the total number of Centuries was increased from 193 to 373, i.e. nearly doubled, and the majority shifted considerably. Hitherto, with the eighteen Equestrian Centuries, the First Class alone had had an absolute majority, 98 out of 193, and, save in the exceptional case of dissension within that Class, the right of the other Classes to vote was usually purely theoretical. After the reform, if a majority was to be formed, that is, 187 voting units out of 373, it was necessary, whatever happened, even if the higher Classes voted unanimously, to go down as far as the Third Class, inclusive. The first consequence of the reform, then, was the increase of the necessary majority, and therefore of the number of men who were called to vote.

Secondly, this reform tended to harmonize the two systems, that of Centuries and that of Tribes, which were the constitutional bases of the two great assemblies of the State. Appius Claudius's reform of the Centuries, by the new place which it gave to movable property, had broken the traditional relationship which bound Classes and Tribes. The reform of the third century restored it, since every Class now contained seventy Centuries, two to each of the thirty-five Tribes (one of Seniors and one of Juniors), and, since the Censors of 304, undoing the work of Appius Claudius, had excluded citizens who had no landed property from the thirty-one Rustic Tribes and crowded them all into the four Urban Tribes, landed property, mainly embodied by country land-owners, great and small, gained considerably more influence in the Comitia Centuriata. So it was that, in the end, it was the rural element, the sound, traditional backbone of the Roman State, which chiefly benefited by the new organization.

The reform of the working of the Comitia Centuriata contributed to the same result. Previously in virtue of the system of the " prerogative ", the eighteen Equestrian Centuries exercised a direct influence, material and still more moral, on the voting of the following Centuries. Henceforward the Century chosen to vote first, the " prerogative " Century, was taken from the whole of the First Class, excluding the eighteen Equestrian Centuries and the Seniors. The reform did not go further. After the " prerogative " Century, the eighteen Equestrian Centuries were called to vote, and then the other Classes, downwards, until the legal majority was obtained.

The reform of the Comitia Centuriata did not make the composition of that assembly absolutely democratic (all possessing less than the 50,000 *asses* required for the Third Class were in practice excluded, so that the majority was left in the hands of the rich and the middle classes), nor even place it on a level with the Comitia Tributa in this respect, but, as Dionysios of Halicarnassos very rightly says,[1] it made it " more democratic than it had been before ". By guaranteeing the vote of the Third Class in all circumstances, it ensured the middle classes, that is, the rural democracy, a much larger effective share in voting than they had enjoyed in the past. Now, these rural middle classes, who ruled the thirty-one Rustic Tribes, already predominated in the Comitia Tributa. So the reform of the Comitia Centuriata tended to give the preponderance to the same electors, those of the middle classes, in both assemblies. It was, therefore, one of the great achievements in the direction of constitutional harmonization which we find in the internal policy of the fourth and third centuries.

The competence of the Comitia was subjected to a parallel process of co-ordination. The constitutional distinction between Comitia Curiata and Centuriata had been established in the first century of the Republic. The Comitia Centuriata had attracted all electoral, legislative, and judicial powers to

[1] iv, 21.

themselves, while the Comitia Curiata kept only the right to vote the law conferring *imperium* on a magistrate, *Lex Curiata de Imperio*, and that vote had now become a pure formality, in which the thirty lictors and three augurs were enough to represent the legal assembly of the thirty Curiæ. But, if the Comitia Curiata were of little account, the Comitia Centuriata had seen a new assembly arise by their side, the Comitia Tributa, which were more and more tending to supplant them. In the presence of this growing competition, the need for a definite line of demarcation soon made itself felt in the whole sphere of action of the Comitia Centuriata, in legislation, election, and jurisdiction.

(*a*) *Legislation.*—Until the middle of the fourth century, the Comitia Centuriata had been the great legislative assembly of the Roman people. But soon the Comitia Tributa claimed for their plebiscites the legal force which the constitution conferred on the laws of the Centuries. This validity was granted by the *Lex Valeria Horatia* of 449 and the *Lex Publilia Philonis* of 339, the *auctoritas Patrum* still being required, first afterwards and then beforehand, and was finally guaranteed unconditionally by the *Lex Hortensia* of 287, a signal victory for democracy in general and the peasant democracy in particular. From the middle of the fourth century onwards, bills brought forward by the Prætors were usually submitted to the Comitia Tributa, and after the *Lex Hortensia* those proposed by the Consuls went through the same channels. Thenceforward the legislative powers of the two assemblies were clearly divided. The Comitia Tributa took the place of the Comitia Centuriata as the great legislative assembly of Rome, except for two classes of laws which remained entirely within the competence of the latter—laws concerning the declaration of war, the signing of peace, and the conclusion of treaties, and the *Lex de Censoria Potestate* which invested Censors with their powers.

(*b*) *Elections.*—A similar division of powers was made in the electoral domain. The Comitia Centuriata elected the higher magistrates, Consuls, Censors, and Prætors, while the Comitia Tributa elected the lower magistrates, Quæstors, Curule Ædiles, the twenty-four Military Tribunes of the normal legions, and, of course, the purely Plebeian magistrates, Tribunes and Ædiles of the Plebs.

(c) *Jurisdiction.*—In this competency was divided between the assemblies according to the nature of the case. All capital criminal cases went before the Comitia Centuriata, as in the past. On the other hand, all cases involving a fine higher than the *multa suprema* of 3,020 *asses* laid down by the *Lex Aternia Tarpeia* of 454, the Decemviral Law, and the *Lex Julia Papiria* of 430, went to the Comitia Tributa.

II. THE MAGISTRACIES.—The magistracies stood in as urgent need of co-ordination as the Comitia. Two things had to be done. The Patrician magistracies had to be co-ordinated among themselves; they had been created without any general plan, according to the needs of the foreign situation and of party politics. Also, the Patrician and Plebeian magistracies had to be brought into line; some were mutually antagonistic (the Patrician magistracies and the Tribuneship), and the rest (the Curule and Plebeian Ædileships) merely duplicated one another.

The harmonization of the Patrician magistracies was effected in respect of three points—pluralism, renewal, and conditions of age. (a) *Pluralism.*—A plebiscite of 342, the author of which is unknown, forbade the holding of two magistracies in the same year. But this prohibition did not apply to the extraordinary magistracies, those of Dictator, Master of Horse, and Censor. (b) *Renewal.*—This might be in either of two forms—immediate continuation (*continuatio*) or renewal after a certain interval (*iteratio*). Another plebiscite of 342 forbade the renewal of one same magistracy within a period of ten years, and a law of 265 provided that no citizen could be elected Censor twice. (c) *Conditions of age.*— In the third century Curule magistrates were forbidden to canvass for another Curule magistracy while they held their office. In the first years of the second century, this regulation was extended to all magistracies without exception. The matter was, no doubt, the subject of a series of laws and customs of which we do not know the details. All that we know is that they were finally codified by the *Lex Villia Annalis* of 180, and we do not know how far this law introduced anything new, if at all. Livy defines it as follows : " The ancients gave the name of *Lex Annalis* (Age Law) to the law determining the age of admission to a magistracy." This *Lex Villia* contained a certain number of exact clauses regarding the holding of the various magistracies. First, it laid down the age at which a man might first enter upon the *cursus honorum*. As a preliminary condition, he had to have served in ten complete campaigns (*stipendia*). Therefore, since military service began at the age of 17, he could not canvass for the lowest magistracy, which was the Quæstorship, until he was 28. Then it established the order in which magistracies were held, the *cursus honorum*, the *certus ordo magistratuum*, of which Cicero spoke later.[1] That official career comprised three ordinary magistracies, Quæstorship, Prætorship, and Consulship, going upwards. The Curule Ædileship, which was not strictly obligatory for the politician, came between the Quæstorship and Prætorship if it was held at all. By the side of this scale there were the extra-ordinary magistracies, the Dictatorship and Censorship, which were only open to former Consuls, and therefore could only be obtained after the Consulship. A legal minimum interval was required between the holding of two regular magistracies, two years (*biennium*) for magistracies properly so called and one year for the Plebeian magistracies. Lastly, the legal age for admission to the various magistracies was twenty-eight for the Quæstorship, forty for the Prætorship, and forty-three for the Consulship.

At the same time legislation brought the two sets of magistracies, Patrician and Plebeian, into co-ordination. The Plebeian magistracies came into the series of public magistracies with the conquest of political equality by the Plebs. The Tribune, who originally stood higher than the Ædile, was given a position, at least as a general rule, between the Quæstor and the Ædile, and the Plebeian Ædile was equalized with the Curule Ædile and placed between the Tribune and the Prætor. What was more, the Tribuneship, the great Plebeian magistracy, was gradually assimilated to the magistracies of the State in respect of relations with the Senate. The Tribunes were given the right to convoke the Senate, to preside over it, and to call for its vote ; but they were not yet officially entered on the list of Senators, a final step which was not taken until the following period. Lastly, the Plebeian magistracies were made subject to conditions of holding similar to those of the State magistracies ;

---

[1] *De Lege Agr.*, ii, 9, 24.

pluralism was forbidden, and there had to be an interval of one year between two successive magistracies.

III. THE SENATE.—A last measure of this kind was the regulation of the recruiting of the Senate. During the first centuries of the Republic, that body had been recruited by the Consuls or the extraordinary magistrates (Dictators, Decemvirs, Military Tribunes with Consular Power) who took their place in various circumstances. These magistrates acted entirely at their own discretion ; they took the new Senators either from retired Curule magistrates or from plain citizens. Their choice was subject to one single condition : before 400, Patrician rank was essential. After that date, when there were in practice Plebeian Military Tribunes with Consular Power, the Senate was open to all Roman citizens, Patricians and Plebeians alike. The question was taken up again and settled in a systematic manner at the end of the fourth century, about 312, by the Ovinian Plebiscite, which laid down the following two constitutional principles. Henceforward the recruiting of the Senate was to be done by the Censors ; so the operation became five-yearly, like the Censorship itself, instead of annual. Secondly, the Censors had to take the Senators from among the magistrates who had resigned office since the last recruiting, their only obligation being to choose the worthiest. This important law had three results. It regularized the recruiting of the Senate, which had hitherto been loose and irregular, it raised the level of that body, and it kept it in close contact with the Comitia, making it a regular emanation of the Roman electorate by a sort of selection in two stages.

The great constitutional reforms of the third century— the *Lex Hortensia* of 287 and the reform of the Comitia Centuriata—representing the triumph of the peasant middle classes, launched the Roman State in the direction of a regime of rural democracy, the logical expression of a peasant society, whose original character had been constantly reinforced by many annexations of territory through more than a century. In spite of the stubborn resistance of the governing nobility, the movement went on, slowly but relentlessly, all through the twenty-three years (241–218) which lay between the first and second Punic Wars, a period of which we know little (Livy fails us) but sometimes see the main lines sufficiently exactly. The peasant element had a capable leader, not at all a revolutionary, but patriotic and liberal-minded and in virtue of these two qualities the perfect embodiment of rural democracy—C. Flaminius, whose fifteen years of political life (232–217) were one long fight with the Patricio-Plebeian nobility which had a firm hold of the power.

As Tribune in 232, C. Flaminius crossed swords on the land question. He saw the salvation of Roman society in the prosperity of the farmer, and tried to carry out his programme by an extensive policy of colonization, which should infuse generous new blood into the already anæmic class of the small land-owners. He therefore proposed that the public land in Picenum which had been conquered in the past from the Gallic Senones should be divided into allotments and distributed to the poor citizens. The nobility who intended, by right of occupation, to keep the enjoyment of this land to themselves, put up a desperate resistance. When Flaminius placed his proposal before the Senate, they refused to hear a word of it, and when, ignoring the Senatorial veto, the Tribune took the matter before the Comitia, his own father dragged his refractory son from the platform in the name of his paternal authority. The law, which was a first serious encroachment of the sovereignty of the people on the financial monopoly of the Senate, a first blow at the privileges of the aristocracy embodied by that council, was passed, to the horror of the aristocracy, which afterwards stigmatized this dangerous precedent as the beginning of an era of disorders and of a reign of demagogy, " the beginning of degeneration for the Roman constitution," as Polybios said.[1] Five years later, when, in the capacity of Prætor, Flaminius was governor of Sicily, he acquitted himself of his task most creditably, and—too rare a phenomenon in the annals of the Roman governors—he was long remembered among his subjects with esteem and gratitude.

In 223, after the great victory at Telamon, we find Flaminius again as Consul, commanding in the war against the Cisalpine Gauls. He defeated the Insubres, but new

[1] ii, 21, 8.

quarrels with the Senate prevented him from getting all the results from his victory which he was entitled to expect. He was recalled on the ground of some informality in his election, and had to resign before his command expired. The great popularity which he still enjoyed among the people, especially in the countryside, gave him the Censorship in 220. In that office, the highest to which a citizen could rise, he displayed his habitual qualities of liberalism and far-seeing patriotism. He was opposed to excessive democratic demands, and did not hesitate, like the Censors of 304, to restrict the influence of freedmen by putting them back in the four Urban Tribes. The *Lex Claudia*, proposed by the Tribune Q. Claudius and passed under the influence of Flaminius, was, no doubt, a party law, but it was even more a measure of general interest ; it forbade Senators to engage in overseas trade on a large scale, thus effectively preserving the financial impartiality and moral conduct which were required by the position of the Senate at the head of the State.

But the same years brought upon Rome the hurricane of the second Punic War. Re-elected Consul for 217, and entrusted with the superhuman task of arresting Hannibal in his victorious advance, Flaminius, lacking military genius, at least died bravely in the butchery of Lake Trasimene. It was a first blow dealt to the reforming party, for which the war had many others in store.

V

THE REPUBLICAN CONSTITUTION ON THE EVE OF THE PUNIC WARS

" Cato," according to Cicero,[1] who transmits his testimony to us, " used to say that the reason of the superiority of the constitution of our city to that of other states was that the latter almost always had their laws and institutions from one single legislator—Crete from Minos, Sparta from Lycurgos, Athens, whose constitution was so often changed, first from Theseus, then from Dracon, then from Solon, then from Cleisthenes, then from many others, until at last, when it was fallen and almost lifeless, it was held up by the cultivated Demetrios of Phaleron. Our Republic, on the other hand, was not made by the genius of one man, but of many, nor in the life of one, but through many centuries and generations. For, Cato

[1] *Rep.*, ii, 1, 2.

said, there has never been one man of such genius that nothing could escape him, nor have the combined talents of one age been able to look forward so as to embrace all things without the lessons of experience and time."

And Polybios,[1] in his turn, taking up the same observation of Cato, declares :

" Although the Romans came in the end to the same result (as Lycurgos) in respect of their constitution, they did not do it by mere thinking, but after many struggles and difficulties, always choosing the best course after actual experience of misfortune ; so they have arrived at the same end as Lycurgos, the best of the constitutions of our time."

Indeed, the Roman constitution, as we find it at the height of its development at the end of the third century, has two distinctive characteristics. It is not a written constitution, and it is not the work of a single intelligence or the expression of a single will. It is not without interest that a man like Cato, a contemporary and an authority on constitutional matters, should have remarked on this with pleasure. The product of a long series of centuries, the Roman constitution was the combined result of many varied experiments. The Romans were always conservative in spirit ; their great desire, the inmost tendency of their national genius, was never to break with even the most distant past. So their constitutional development, although it went on without interruption, was always very slow. Towards the end of the third century, when it was provided with all its basic organs, it reached a state of equilibrium, at least temporary. This is the moment to bring out its distinctive features and its spirit in a few lines.

The organic cell of the Roman City, as of every ancient city, is the citizen, *civis Romanus,* but not all Roman citizens are citizens to an equal extent. First we must distinguish between two main categories of citizens.

(i) Full citizens (*cives optimo jure*) possess, and alone possess, all civil rights (of marriage, *connubium* ; of owner-ship, *commercium*) and all political rights (of election, *jus suffragii* ; of office, *jus honorum*). They alone, by definition, are fully citizens of Rome.

(ii) Less full citizens are again divided into two categories : (*a*) citizens without suffrage (*cives sine suffragio*), who enjoy

[1] vi, 10, 13–14.

civil rights but not political; (*b*) freedmen (*libertini*), emancipated slaves, who are citizens with limited rights. The freedmen have the civil right of *commercium*, but not that of *connubium*, with full citizens—a disadvantage which distinguishes them from all citizens of free birth, whether *optimo jure* or *sine suffragio*. In respect of political rights, they do not possess *jus honorum*, and so are excluded from the magistracies, priesthoods, and Senate, and even their power of election is limited by the secondary place, given to them in the Comitia, where they are crowded into the four Urban Tribes and systematically excluded from the Rustic Tribes.

How does one become a Roman citizen? Citizenship can be obtained in two ways—by birth and by subsequent conferring. (*a*) In respect of birth, two conditions are necessary and sufficient; you must be the son of a citizen father, and by a regular marriage. (*b*) There are two categories of non-citizens—free men, alien to the Roman city (*peregrini*), and unfree men, slaves. Both can rise to the citizenship, *peregrini* in virtue of an express law and slaves by liberation (*manumissio*). They can obtain a more or less complete form of citizenship, *optimo jure* or *sine suffragio*. The liberated slave, the *libertinus*, as we have seen, only enjoys incomplete citizenship, both in civil and in political matters; he is not eligible for the magistracies, the Senate, or the various priesthoods. Only in the second generation (and that only from the second century onwards) do the sons of freedmen obtain the full citizenship and all the civil and political privileges which it involves. In all cases, full citizenship is the final civic state into which the incomplete citizen, *peregrinus* or slave, may develop.

The official characteristic of the full citizen, the necessary and sufficient warrant of his legal status, is inscription in a Tribe. Down to 241 B.C., the Tribe was a continuous territorial district, a ward. After that date, no new Tribes were created. New citizens are attached to the old Tribes, and in consequence the Tribes cease to be territorial districts of the old type. A citizen is entered in a Tribe, not on account of the property which he may own in it, but on account of his domicile. The Tribe is therefore personal, and so hereditary. The total number of Tribes was finally fixed in 241 at thirty-five, and they fall into two main categories—the four Urban Tribes (Suburane, Palatine, Esquiline, and Colline), the oldest of all, and the thirty-one Rustic Tribes, the two last of which, Belina and Quirina, were created in 241. The interest of this division is not merely statistical; it has very important political consequences. The Rustic Tribes are more highly esteemed, and enjoy a privileged position as such; it is a degrading penalty for a citizen to be transferred from a Rustic to an Urban Tribe. Lastly, to protect old citizens against excessive intrusion of new ones, the inscription of the latter in the Tribes is not done indiscriminately, after 241. *Peregrini* or half-citizens, when promoted to full citizenship, are inscribed in a minority of the Rustic Tribes (thirteen or fifteen out of thirty-one), and freedmen, still less favoured, go into the four Urban Tribes.

We know the numerical strength of the Roman citizen body from the five-yearly census, the official statistics of which are preserved by tradition. For the third century B.C., the period of the full development of the Republican constitution, the figures are as follows [1] : —

B.C.			Citizens.
294	.	.	. 262,321
290	.	.	. 272,000
280	.	.	. 287,000
276	.	.	. 271,224
265	.	.	. 292,234
252	.	.	. 297,797
247	.	.	. 241,712
234	.	.	. 270,713
209	.	.	. 237,108
204	.	.	. 214,000

Let us stop at this last date, observing that the figure of 300,000 citizens, almost reached in 252 with 297,797, was not exceeded until 169, when the census gave a total population of 312,885 citizens.

What do these figures represent? The ancient texts, and particularly Polybios's statement [2] about the male population of Italy mobilizable for the year 225, leave no doubt of their exact significance. They cover only the male citizens, and, of them, only those who can be mobilized, that is, the male population aged from seventeen to sixty,

[1] **LIV,** 343–6.   [2] ii, 24.

without any political or social distinction. When we add the male citizens aged over sixty, who, being no longer mobilizable, do not appear in the statistics of the census, we get, for the whole citizen body of Rome, about the middle of the third century, a rough total of 350,000 citizens.

From the political point of view, the male citizen population comprises, as we have seen, two distinct categories—full citizens (*optimo jure*) and incomplete citizens (*minuto jure, sine suffragio*). The numerical proportion of the two kinds is not yet known exactly, since the statistics of the census do not give it, but we can get it at least approximately from two series of indications, one of a territorial character, the general distribution of areas populated by full or incomplete citizens, and the other numerical, such as Livy's [1] information about the Campanian contingent which was mobilizable for 216 B.C. Roughly two-thirds of the total number of citizens are full citizens and one-third are incomplete citizens, or about 180,000 and 90,000 men respectively, for the mobilizable contingent, and, if we add the men aged over sixty (a fifth of those totals, by analogy with the statistics of France and Italy to-day), 216,000 and 108,000 citizens.

These last figures enable us to determine nearly enough the total citizen population, men, women, and children. An interesting passage of Dionysios of Halicarnassos [2] tells us that that total was four times the figures of the census, but he includes domiciled aliens and slaves, whose numbers we do not know. Comparison with modern statistics leads us, for Rome in the third century B.C., to a total citizen population of about a million.

The official figures of the census not only give us the mobilizable strength of the city in static form, that is, at a series of fixed dates representing successive Censorships, but allow us, by putting them together, to determine, at least in its main lines, the general movement of the population. First, there is a very important phenomenon. On the whole, the citizen population shows a considerable rise. From 165,000 in 340, it rises to 312,805 in 169, a total increase of 147,805, or 89 per cent. But this figure only represents a general average. In the course of the third century the

[1] xxiii, 5. [2] ix, 25.

D

number of citizens goes through a series of large and varied fluctuations. From 280 to 276, it falls by 15,776 ; from 276 to 252, it rises by 26,573; from 252 to 247, a fall of 56,085 ; from 247 to 234, a rise of 29,001 ; from 234 to 204, a fall of 56,713 ; from 204 to 169, a rise of 98,805. The three periods of decrease correspond to the three great external crises of the third century—the war against Pyrrhos (280–275), the first Punic War (262–241), which was especially costly to Rome in the Sicilian operations of 255 onwards, and the second Punic War (218–201), during which losses in the field were so great as to paralyse the growth of the mobilizable citizen population for more than a hundred years ; the figures of 280 were not again reached and passed until thirty years after the war, in the census of 169. As soon as the causes of stagnation and retrogression due to the great wars cease to act, at once and automatically the rising movement recommences ; from 272 to 252 there is an increase of 26,573 ; from 247 to 234, an increase of 29,001 ; from 204 to 169, an increase of 98,805. This regular increase is due to two main causes, one natural, the normal excess of births over deaths, and one artificial, the conferring of the citizenship, which turns a varying number of non-citizens, *peregrini* or slaves, into new citizens. In what proportion did these two causes operate ? Having no exact statistics of naturalization, we cannot exactly determine the influence of each.

So the census-statistics reveal one first phenomenon of a general kind—a total increase of the citizen population between the end of the fourth century and the first third of the second. By the side of this first phenomenon a second may be observed, not quantitative but qualitative—the steady increase of the number of full citizens compared with that of citizens without suffrage. On this point the ancient texts give us, not concrete numerical data, but at least some definite statements. They mention, for example, in a certain number of cases, the conferring of full citizenship on towns which had previously only had incomplete citizenship—on the towns of the Sabine country in 268, on Picenum, Velitræ, Privernum, and the Hernici in 241, and on Arpinum, Fundi, and Formiæ in 188—and this political advancement of places distant from Rome implies that the nearer towns— at least, the greater number of them—had already received the full citizenship at an earlier date. Another characteristic indication, at least down to 241, is the gradual constitution of new Tribes answering to the creation of a large number of full citizens. From 340 to 241, eight new Tribes appear in succession—Mæcia and Scaptia in 332, Oufentina and Falerna in 318, Arnensis and Teretina in 299, Velina and Quirina in 241. After 241, no more Tribes are created ; new citizens are inscribed in the old Tribes, and with this new system we lose all means of checking the number of citizens. The general results of the development, so far as we can see them, are as follows. First of all, in the second half of the fourth century and at the beginning of the third, the number of incomplete citizens increases considerably in proportion to the total citizen population (15 per cent about 340, 45 per cent about 328, 47 per cent about 296). Then, with the third century, the promotion of incomplete citizens to full citizenship grows more rapid, and the proportion of incomplete citizens to the total decreases correspondingly (40 per cent about 246, 33 per cent between 240 and 230). The movement continues afterwards, as is proved by the conferring of full citizenship on Arpinum, Fundi, and Formiæ in 188, but from then onwards it is impossible to give figures, for lack of sufficient data. Only towards the middle of the second century does it slow down, to cease almost entirely, and this exclusive policy, growing narrower and narrower, provokes a reaction in the great demands of the Italians.

Every Roman citizen has, in relation to the State, a set of duties and a set of rights. His duties and rights correspond to his position in the political and social scale, and the rights, at least, are subject to a number of very important limitations.

The duties of the citizen are of two kinds, military and financial.

(a) *Military duties*. All citizens without exception are liable to compulsory personal service, but in forms which vary according to their wealth or to the type of citizenship (full or incomplete) which they enjoy.

Full citizens. In virtue of the principle that every citizen must serve the State with his person, but only in accordance with his means and his civic position, full citizens serve in conditions which vary according to their fortune. The original military organization of the Republic, known as the Servian organization, was based strictly on this correlation and the timocratic principle. Under the pressure of new tactical problems, it had been necessary to give an ever larger place to personal capacity, to the experience and courage of the individual soldier. After the reorganization effected at the beginning of the fourth century and ascribed to Camillus, all difference of armament had been abolished between the citizens of the heavy infantry of the legion, which is henceforward divided into three bodies—*Hastati*, *Principes*, and *Triarii*—solely according to age. But there is still a differentiation based on wealth. The cavalry is recruited entirely from the richest citizens—the *Equites equo publico* of the eighteen Equestrian Centuries and the *Equites equo privato* of the First Class. The light infantry of the Velites comprises the poorest citizens of the lowest Class legally mobilizable, the Fifth. The citizens excluded from the Classes, the proletarians or *capite censi*, are not liable to regular military service. They only serve in case of exceptional danger and levies in mass. Provision for this eventuality is made in peace-time, and these men appear on the census-lists as mobilizable in case of need. The same is the case with the freedmen, the *libertini*, who can, if needed, be enrolled in the crews of the fleet or even in the legions.

Incomplete citizens. Citizens without suffrage are liable to military duty like the rest, but fall into two classes in respect of the manner in which they perform it. Those who belong to *municipia* which have preserved their local self-government simply serve in the normal legions ; the others are organized in special legions. As the Italian *municipia* are raised to the full citizenship, this type of legion tends to disappear. Becoming citizens *optimo jure*, the men of the *municipia* then serve in the regular Roman legions.

(*b*) *Financial duties.* Citizens of all kinds, full and incomplete, pay tax in two forms, a direct tax on property (*tributum*), and the costs of their equipment for the army. These two obligations have already been discussed, and we need not return to them here.

Now for the rights of the citizen. The full citizen, in addition to the civil rights of marriage and ownership which he shares with the incomplete citizen, has all political rights. He takes part in the meetings of the Comitia, Centuriata or Tributa as the case may be, for elections, direct (for the magistracies), or in two stages (for the recruiting of the Senate), the voting of laws, and the trial of serious cases. He can himself be elected to the magistracies (those of Quæstor, Curule Ædile, Prætor, and Consul, and, provided that he is a Plebeian, those of Plebeian Ædile and Tribune of the Plebs), and by that channel he can enter the Senate. In these two ways he can exercise influence on the Comitia, the magistracies, and the Senate, the three great organs of the Republican government.

As it appears at the height of its development, towards the end of the third century B.C., the Roman constitution presents the fundamental characteristics of the ancient city.

(i) The political system is one of direct sovereignty, where the citizen exercises his rights, personally and directly, in the popular assembly, the Comitia. The law requires that he should exercise these rights on the spot, at the very seat of the city, in Rome, and at the exact place consecrated by the constitution, in the Forum, as a rule, for the Comitia Tributa, and on the Campus Martius for the Comitia Centuriata. Consequently, citizens who happen to be away from Rome for any reason, or live outside, can only perform their duties as citizens if they go to the Comitia in person.

(ii) Powers are not separate. There is no independent military authority, or judicial authority, or religious authority, and the mere notion of the separation of powers familiar to modern States is as alien to Republican Rome as to other ancient cities. The Comitia are at once political and judicial assemblies. The same magistrate has administrative, judicial, and religious functions in the civil domain, and, in virtue of the concept of the complete *imperium*, some of them, the chief —Dictators, Consuls, and Prætors—also have military competence.

(iii) The notions of State and government are completely merged. The personnel of the State and the political personnel are usually the same men. One of the fundamental prerogatives of the modern State, the delivering of justice, is in Rome the affair of a party, just like the other branches of government.

But, if the constitution of the Golden Age of the Republic

presents the essential characteristics of the ancient city, it is distinguished from it by two fundamental differences, one quantitative and one qualitative. Numerically, Rome was a city such as the Græco-Italian world had not yet seen. By the conditions necessary to its existence and working, the ancient city was condemned to a small size. Sparta never had more than 8,000 citizens. Athens, the greatest city of Greece, even at her height had no more than about 30,000. Now, Rome had in the third century 350,000 male citizens, with a total citizen population of about a million. Secondly, the Roman constitution is marked by its wise spirit and the general harmony of all its parts. It was a harmony of two kinds—both between the social classes which shared in the government and between the public powers which were its expression. It rested on the law and on manners, a double base which ensured its stability. The monopoly of initiative enjoyed by the magistrates and the permanent control of these latter by the Senate, which usually reduced them to the position of mere executive agents, guaranteed the system against the invasion of a democracy of the Greek type and the constitutional adventures which might have ensued from such a change. The people, traditionally and temperamentally respectful of the social scale and inured to political discipline as to military discipline, readily left the management of current business to the Patricio-Plebeian nobility which had succeeded the old Patriciate, only reserving, in case of need, its supreme right of control and correcting the policy of the government when the time came.

But we must not imagine that the admirable political equilibrium reached by Rome in the third century meant constitutional stagnation. It was only a phase in which the tendencies of a vanishing past and those of an approaching future counterbalanced one another. Such phases are short in the life of a people, even of one so well balanced and conservative by nature as the Romans. Two great causes, the same as had conditioned the constitutional development of Rome in the first part of the third century, continued to act. One cause was external—the steady expansion of the Roman State, first in Italy and then, after the first Punic War, in the Western Mediterranean, with the gradual widening of the old constitution as a necessary corollary. Hitherto the government had managed, somehow, to put off that dreaded eventuality by resorting to such devices as occurred to it—for example, by extending the term of the old magistracies. But this expedient had soon proved insufficient. As early as 267 B.C., the unification of Italy had led to the creation of four new Quæstors, and about 227 it was necessary, for the administration of Sicily and Sardinia, the first two provinces, to double the number of Prætors, with the consequent multiplication of the junior administrative staff—the nucleus of the future corps of officials. So the contrast between the life of a great state, such as Rome had become, and the obsolete system of the ancient city becomes more and more glaring and irreducible.

There was also an internal cause. The agrarian democratic party, which inspired and chiefly benefited by the great constitutional reforms of the third century, the *Leges Hortensiæ* and the reform of the Comitia Centuriata, pursued its political activity and had not spoken its last word. It found a capable and energetic leader in the person of C. Flaminius. This democratic evolution had its effects on foreign policy. In the first part of the third century, it was not the Senate—as formerly in the fourth century and later from the second Punic War—which had the supreme direction of foreign policy, but the people, won over to warlike tendencies and ideas of expansion. The first Punic War began and ended with characteristic examples in this respect : in 264 the breach with Carthage was decided by the initiative of the Comitia, and in 241 the same Comitia rejected the proposed treaty drawn up by Lutatius Catulus after the victory of the Ægates Islands and ratified by the Senate.

Under the pressure of these two causes, external and internal, different in origin but convergent in effect, the balance of the Roman constitution began to sway and presently collapsed. The crisis of the second Punic War, by the intensity and long duration of the ordeal to which it subjected the Roman State, dealt it the finishing blow. Oligarchy was on the march, and it would not halt.

CHAPTER IV

THE GENESIS OF OLIGARCHY

BIBLIOGRAPHY.—*Ancient Authors* : Livy, xxi–xlv (to 167 B.C.) ;
Periochæ of bks. xlvi–lii (cf. Florus, i, 22–33 ; Eutropius, iii, 8 to
iv, 14 ; Orosius, iv, 13–23 ; and the new data given by the *Epitome*
of Oxyrrhynchos for the period 150–146, in *Klio*, Beih., ii, 1904,
ed. K., pp. 21–5, and ed. R., pp. 131–7) ; *H.R.F.*, *passim* ; *O.R.F.*,
esp. the oratorical frags. of Cato, pp. 5–162 ; Velleius Paterculus,
i, 9–13 ; Dion Cassius, xiii–xxi (frags. Cf. Zonaras, viii, 21, to ix, 31) ;
Diodoros, xxv–xxxii (frags.) ; Plutarch, *Fabius Maximus, Marcellus,
Flamininus, Cato the Elder, Æmilius Paullus* ; Cornelius Nepos,
Cato ; *De Viris illustribus*, 42–56.

Inscriptions : Consular *Fasti* in *C.I.L.*, i, 2nd ed., pp. 140–8 ;
C.I.L., i, 2nd ed., 2. 10 ff. (*Elogia* of the Scipios) ; p. 193, 12–13
(do. of Q. Fabius Maximus) ; p. 194, 14 (do. of L. Cornelius Scipio
Asiaticus), 15 (of L. Æmilius Paullus) ; p. 195, 16 (of Ti. Sempronius
Gracchus) ; p. 201, 37 (of Scipio Africanus) ; p. 202, 43 (of Cato the
Elder) ; No. 581, letter of the Consuls *ad Teuranos de Baccanalibus*
(186 B.C.).

Modern Works.—**XXIX**, iv, 1, 486–516 ; **XXI**, 153–6 ; **II**, 135–90,
195–201 ; **IX**, i, 186–8, 193–203 ; **XXVII**, 48–51 ; **XVI**, i, 412–608 ;
XXXI, 73 ff. ; **XX**, bk. iii, ch. xi–xii ; **XIX**, see ref. to chap. ii ;
XIII, Eng. pp. 245–332.

I

THE FORMATION OF THE CAPITALIST CLASS

THE stability of the Roman constitution, as we find it
in the third century B.C., was above all based on the
equilibrium of institutions and the harmony of classes.
Government was in the hands of an aristocracy, the Senatorial
nobility, supported by the Knights (the Equestrian order)
and by the mass of the middle classes, mainly rural. Should
these two stays fail the ruling class, the equilibrium would
break down and the very principle of the constitution would
be jeopardized. That is exactly what happened in the first
half of the second century, and its direct consequences were,
first, the advent of oligarchy and, still far off, that of the
rule of one man.

How and why did these two supports, the Equestrian
order and the middle classes, the fundamental conditions
of the success and very existence of the Roman constitution,

*See also Supplementary Bibliography with Prefatory Note (p. 405)

suddenly fail the ruling aristocracy ?   While the result was the same, we find on examination that the cause and manner of the phenomenon were quite different in the two cases. The Equestrian class failed to maintain the balance of the constitution because it gradually broke loose from the Senatorial order and finally became its opponent ; the middle class did so because decay took hold of it and it was doomed to disappear.

The development of the power of Rome after the Punic Wars and the increasing exploitation of the Mediterranean basin which ensued resulted in the creation of Italian capitalism on a big scale, by which new fields of action were opened to the Equestrian class and its economic activity was developed beyond all bounds.   The three main branches of that activity—the farming of taxes, the adjudication of public works, and banking—thus steadily increased in importance. First, let us consider the farming of taxes, in Italy and in the provinces.   In 199, the Censors P. Cornelius Scipio and P. Ælius Pætus farmed out the customs of Capua, Puteoli, and Castrum to publicans.   In 179, the Censors M. Æmilius Lepidus and M. Fulvius Nobilior established other such dues. The creation of the first provinces—Sicily in 241, Sardinia and Corsica in 237, the two Spains in 197, Macedonia in 148–147, and Africa in 146—led to the creation of new customs-lines, to the great profit of the publicans of the Equestrian class who generally farmed them.   It was usually the same with the pasturage-dues (*scriptura*), tithes, and customs established in Sicily in 241.

Secondly, with the extension of Roman power and the gradual enrichment of the treasury, the State engaged in many undertakings, especially great public works, which the Knights took on by adjudication.   During the third Macedonian War, we find the Prætor C. Sulpicius giving an order for 6,000 togas, 30,000 tunics, and the requisite number of horses on this system.

Lastly, the increasing size of the State gave the Knights an opportunity to extend their banking operations.   In the comedies of Plautus, at the beginning of the second century, we already find the banking world at work and flourishing.

The advance of the Roman power at the end of the third century and in the first half of the second and the consequent introduction of capitalism on a large scale therefore resulted in a great development of the activity and social influence of the Equestrian class.

This social development soon made itself felt, as was inevitable, in a parallel advance in respect of politics, a consequence which the timocratic character of the Roman constitution made even more perfectly logical than it would have been elsewhere. A few definite episodes of the junction of the third and second centuries illustrate the fact fully. The first occurred at the time of the second Punic War. Two publicans, M. Postumius of Pyrgi and T. Pomponius Veientanus, who had taken an order for war supplies and transports, had a clause inserted in their contract to the effect that all sea risks must be borne by the State. After filling their ships with goods of no value, they sank them on the high seas, and then, in accordance with their contract, demanded a large compensation from the State. The question came before the Senate. That body, fearing to bring the very powerful Equestrian class down on it, since it needed its support at the moment, allowed the matter to drop. But it was taken up by two Tribunes of the Plebs, who carried it to the popular assembly and proposed that the guilty parties should be sentenced to a fine of 200,000 *asses*. The publicans managed by violence to prevent a vote from being given. The Tribunes did not give in. They brought a capital charge against Postumius and his accomplices. Most of them judged it prudent to forestall the sentence and retired into banishment.[1]

In 184, Cato, as Censor, had to farm out the collection of taxes and great public works, according to the regulations. He acted in the best interests of the treasury, getting the maximum price for the taxes and giving the minimum price for the public works. This way of doing things did not at all suit the publicans, as may be imagined. They took steps with the Senate, and succeeded in having the contracts cancelled. Certain Tribunes, won over by the Equestrians, even took the remarkable step of summoning Cato before the people to give account of his action.

Fifteen years later, in the Censorship of C. Claudius Pulcher and Ti. Sempronius Gracchus (169), another affair

---

[1] Livy, xxv, 3–4.

occurred, as symptomatic as those mentioned above. The Censors excluded from the offers of public contracts all who had had a share in those of the previous Censorship, by which, it seems, they had made exorbitant profits. The excluded publicans were furious, and caused one of the Tribunes, P. Rutilius Rufus, who belonged to their order, to take action. A charge was brought before the people against the two Censors, who, although they had such a good case, only just managed to escape condemnation.

The result of the increasing importance of the Knights in Roman society was that they gradually began to aim higher. In the first half of the second century, they felt justified in demanding a political influence in the State proportionate to their increased economic power and new social position. Now, just at the time when the Equestrian class was beginning to ask for more, the Senatorial aristocracy, marching straight towards an oligarchical system, was closing its ranks and showing itself more and more jealously exclusive in the political and social spheres. By the time of the second Punic War, the split between the Senatorial and Equestrian classes was preparing. A decisive event, which happened about the middle of the second century, made the split inevitable and final. The Senatorial nobility, which, in addition to the Senate, its stronghold, held all the magistracies and consequently the command of the army, succeeded in laying hands on the last organ of the State which it had not yet appropriated, the judicial power.

By the traditional constitution, the higher criminal courts were held by the Comitia Centuriata or Tributa, according to the importance of the case—by the Centuriata for capital charges and by the Tributa in the case of fines exceeding the *multa suprema* of 3,020 *asses*. But this arrangement had soon proved unpractical, in respect both of speed, for the procedure was slow and clumsy, and of competence, for the people was hardly capable of dealing with complicated and special cases. It was therefore decided to have special criminal courts (*quæstiones*), which should be entrusted with the trial of certain cases by express delegation from the people and in the name of the people. One of these exceptional courts (*quæstiones extraordinariæ*) is already found in 413, when, according to tradition, it tried the murderers of

M. Postumius, and they came into common use at the beginning of the second century.

Somewhat later, in the middle of that century, in·consequence of the increase of business due to the uninterrupted extension of the Roman State, the exceptional courts began to be transformed into permanent courts (*quæstiones perpetuæ*). The first of these permanent courts, created in 149 on the proposal of the Tribune L. Calpurnius Piso, was the court which dealt with the exactions of provincial governors, *Quæstio de Repetundis*. Later, others appear—about 145, the court which dealt with crimes against the person, *Quæstio de Sicariis et Veneficis*; in the second century, the *Quæstio de Ambitu*, for cases of illicit canvassing for office; and, in the beginning of the first century, the *Quæstio de Peculatu*, for misuse of public funds. From the purely administrative point of view, the establishment of permanent criminal courts was an advance, and a great advance, upon the previous organization of justice. But this was not the respect in which it interested public opinion, still less the governing circles. What mattered to them was the choice of judges, a problem which the nobility settled very simply by claiming it all for themselves. The ordinary courts, like the extraordinary courts in the past, had to be recruited entirely among the Senators.

By thus appropriating the judicial power, the nobility made its control of the government complete. Its political monopoly was finally established, to the great disgust of the Knights, as can be imagined. The fact was a sore blow to that class, hitting it in its political aspirations and, what was still more serious, in its material interests. For the growing tension between the two classes, which is the main characteristic of their relations from the end of the third century, did not manifest itself only in the political domain; it also, and chiefly, appeared in the financial domain, for it affected the sphere of activity and very conditions of existence of the money-making Knights. A characteristic symptom of their rivalry had already appeared on the very eve of the second Punic War. The Claudian Plebiscite, warmly supported by the Equestrian class, forbade all Senators and sons of Senators to fit out a ship of more than 300 amphoras burden. The result would be that the Senatorial nobility would be excluded from big business and the Knights would have an absolute monopoly of trade. The Senate did not give up this important source of profit without a fight, but it had to surrender and the law was passed. All that the Senators could now do was to evade it, and this they did by joining as sleeping partners and shareholders in joint-stock companies, the official representatives of which were Knights. But, in spite of this expedient, the result was none the less disagreeable to the interests and self-esteem of the Sentatorial order.

A second conflict occurred between the two orders in 167, in connection with the Macedonian mines. It was a question of settling the status of Macedonia after the defeat of Perseus, and, in particular, of establishing the system of the mines, one of the chief sources of wealth of the country. The Knights hoped that these would be farmed out to themselves, a certain source of large profits, but the Senate refused downright.

> " It was decided," Livy says,[1] " to abolish the farming of the Macedonian mines, which constituted a very large revenue, and also that of the public lands, for this system could not be carried out without the assistance of the publicans, and to have resort to them was either to compromise the rights of the State or to sacrifice the liberty of the allies."

It must have been a very hard blow for the Equestrian order, and without a doubt it helped greatly to increase its discontent.

But the decisive point, both in finance and in politics, was the question of the law-courts. In the provinces, Senators and Knights entered upon a veritable competition of violence and pillage, the former as governors and the latter as tax-farmers, public works contractors, and bankers. Those who suffered were the provincials. If there was a complaint, the competent organs were the newly created permanent criminal courts (*quæstiones perpetuæ*). So the composition of the jury meant everything to Senators and Knights alike. We have seen the simple fashion in which the Senatorial nobility settled the question. By that Draconian measure, the Knights were delivered over, purse and person, to the judgment and caprice of the Senatorial class. They were struck, not only in their political pretentions or even in their pride of caste, but in their speculations, profits, and very life. The question of the courts was the last straw, which

[1] xlv, 18, 3–4.

brought about the irremediable breach between the rival orders. With the defection of the Equestrian class, the Senatorial government lost, from the middle of the second century onwards, one of its two indispensable supports.

II

THE RUIN OF THE MIDDLE CLASS

The great phenomenon, from the social point of view, which marks the Roman world of the first half of the second century is the disappearance of the middle class, the ancient and traditional mainstay of the Roman constitution. In the third century, that class was chiefly composed of small country land-owners. At the end of that century its ruin began, and grew more and more rapid in the following years.

Appian,[1] in a celebrated passage in the first book of his *Civil Wars*, demonstrates the fact fully, and exactly describes its profound effects on the very destinies of the State :—

" The Romans," he says, " in the course of the gradual conquest of Italy, took possession of part of the land. There they founded towns or else sent settlers of their own nationality into towns already existing. These colonies were conceived by them in the form of garrisons. Of the territory conquered in war, they at once distributed the cultivated portion among the new settlers, selling it or letting it out ; as for the very large uncultivated portion, they did not trouble to distribute it by lot, but proclaimed that anyone might work it, on payment of a tax on the yearly produce—a tenth for corn and a sixth for fruit. In addition, those who engaged in stock-breeding were subject to a similar tax on large and small livestock. By these measures they wished to provide for the development of the Italian population, of whose endurance they had had experience, and so to procure trustworthy auxiliaries for themselves in the country itself.

" But the result was just the contrary. The rich, having occupied the greater part of these unassigned lands, trusting that as time went on no one would ever take them away from them, had turned to the small neighbouring estates held by the poor, and, taking them either by private purchase or by force, had, instead of fields, enormous domains to cultivate. To exploit these, they made use of slaves as cultivators and herdsmen, fearing that if they employed free men these would be taken away for military service. Besides, the system was very profitable to them, since the slaves, being free from military service, had a high birth-rate. So they accumulated great wealth, and the number of slaves in the country multiplied. The Italians, on the other hand, suffered from depopulation and shortage of men, exhausted as they were by poverty, taxation, and military

[1] *Civil Wars*, i, 1, 7–8.

service. If they ever enjoyed a relaxation of these evils, they were corrupted by idleness, since the land was in the hands of the rich, who used slaves instead of free men to cultivate it.

" The people was, therefore, disturbed both by the possibility that Italian contingents might not be forthcoming when needed and by the danger which such a large number of slaves might mean to its empire. But, finding no remedy, for it was neither easy nor quite fair to turn so many people out of properties which they had occupied for a long time and had enriched by plantations, buildings, and improvements, they ended by voting a law on the subject, proposed by the Tribunes of the Plebs. No one should have over 500 *jugera* of colony land, or graze over 100 head of large cattle or 500 of small there. They must employ a certain number of free men, who should supervise work and render account of it to the owner. The law was made the subject of an oath, and a fine was laid down for offenders. It was thought that in consequence the rest of the land would at once be sold in small portions to the poor. But neither laws nor oaths had the least effect ; those who appeared to take them seriously ceded the land in question to their own relations, and most treated the law with open contempt."

This striking and illuminating passage is confirmed and illustrated by a number of contemporary facts of a highly symptomatic kind. In the year 104 B.C., the Tribune L. Marcius Philippus proposed a land-law to solve the almost hopeless difficulties which the recruiting of the army encountered, and in connection with it he made a sensational declaration in the midst of the Comitia : " There are not in the city two thousand citizens who own property—*non esse in civitate duo millia hominum qui rem haberent.*" [1]

But the evil was of much older date. Livy and Polybios tell us that, as early as 180, it had been difficult to find in the citizen body enough eligible men to make up the strength of the legions. Before the middle of the second century, to obtain the recruits needed, the State had to reduce the minimum of property required for the Fifth Class (the lowest legally mobilizable) from 12,500 or 11,000 *asses* to 4,000—that is, by two-thirds. C. Gracchus, in the course of his office, carried a law forbidding the enrolment of youths aged less than seventeen—a proof that in the preceding years the authorities had not scrupled to allow it, doubtless to an abusive extent. In 131, the Censor Q. Cæcilius Metellus Macedonicus cold-bloodedly proposed the most heroic of remedies—compulsory marriage. This concordant evidence cannot be disputed. But must we conclude from their

[1] Cic., *Off.*, ii, 21, 73.

unanimity, as might as first sight seem necessary, that there was a serious decline in the citizen birth-rate ? Not at all. The shortage indicated referred, not to the whole number of citizens, but only to that of legally mobilizable citizens, that is, to land-owners, the middle class.

Of this fact we have irrefutable proof in the official figures of the census for the second half of the third century and the whole of the second.[1]

Censorship.	Eligible male population.	Censorship.	Eligible male population.
252	297,797	169	312,805
247	241,712	164	337,452
241	260,000	159	328,316
234	270,713	154	324,000
209	237,108	142	327,442
204	214,000	136	317,933
194	243,704	131	318,823
189	258,318	125	394,736
179	258,794	115	394,336
174	269,015	86	463,000

If we neglect a few temporary fluctuations, we see that the total of eligible male citizens, those physically fit for mobilization, fell, between 252 and 204, from 297,797 to 214,000, the decrease being the direct consequence of the Punic Wars. But in the second century the figures go up from 214,000 in 204 to 463,000 in 86. It follows from these statistics, which, it must be repeated, are official, that in the period between the second Punic War and the Gracchi, the very time in which we see the serious difficulties of recruiting mentioned above manifesting themselves, the Roman State had a larger citizen population than in the preceding century, when difficulties of that kind were still unknown. In 104, the very year in which the Tribune Philippus raised the cry of alarm by his declaration that Rome had only two thousand citizen land-owners, the official number of eligible citizens recorded by the census was near 400,000, almost double the figure for 204, and eighteen years later, in 86, the same Philippus, now Consul with M. Perperna, entered a total of 463,000 in his records. So two movements were going on in the citizen body, one upwards—the increase of the total number of citizens—and one downwards—the decrease of citizens owning land, the

[1] LIV, 343–8.

middle classes which constituted the bulk of the contingents legally mobilizable and the majority of the population voting in the Comitia Tributa and, since the reform of the third century, in the Comitia Centuriata.

These facts could not be clearer. What were the underlying causes to which we must ascribe this gradual disappearance of the middle class ? Such a continuous and relentless process must be due to many causes. Two played a particularly important part, one military and one economic.

The chief military cause may be summed up in one word—war. War followed war almost without interruption all through the third century—conquest of Italy and Samnite Wars, Gallic Wars, war with Pyrrhos, Punic Wars—and the first part of the second—Macedonian and Asiatic Wars, third Punic War, wars in Spain—and these continual campaigns hit the middle class which supplied the whole strength of the legions in two ways. At Trasimene, 15,000 citizens were left on the field, and at Cannæ nearly 50,000, half of whom were citizens. The Eastern wars, on the whole, involved few losses (we are told that the decisive victory of Magnesia cost the Roman army only 300 infantry and 24 horse), but this was not the case with the two Macedonian Wars, especially the second, or the third Punic War, or the unending butchery of the wars in Spain.

But men killed in the field were not the only loss incurred by the middle class in the wars of the third and second centuries. Those who came through were kept a very long time away from their homes by compulsory service, and were accordingly lost to civil life. The legal term of service in the active army, as a Junior, was twenty-nine years (from the age of seventeen to forty-six) ; at forty-six, you went into the reserve, the Seniors, until you were sixty, and you could only be called up, if needed, for territorial service, to defend the city itself. No doubt, you could be transferred to the reserve before the age-limit of forty-six, but only if you had done a certain number of campaigns, from sixteen to twenty for the infantry and ten for the cavalry. No doubt, too, the years during which the citizen was liable to service in the active army were not all years of actual service in the field. The fact remains that the burden which lay especially on the middle class was very heavy, and Appian, as we have seen, expressly says that rich occupiers of public land had recourse to slave-labour in order that they might have employees exempt from it.

Livy,[1] writing of the third Macedonian War, brings on to the stage, in a concrete and picturesque manner, a typical specimen of the middle class whose sons were the backbone of the legions. It is the year 171 B.C., and war has just been declared on Perseus. The Senate, to give the Roman army of operations the stiffening which it needs, has ordered that a certain number of old centurions should be called up again, provided that they are not over fifty years of age. Some of these centurions, twenty-three in all, have answered the summons, but demand at least that they should have their old rank, and have appealed to the people, which has the final voice in these matters. The meeting opens, and one of the protesters, Spurius Ligustinus, a small country land-owner, speaks for his comrades. The text is so definite and so racy that it must be given in full.

" I am Spurius Ligustinus, of the Tribe Crustumina, and I come from the Sabine country. My father left me a *jugerum* of land and a little cottage, in which I was born and brought up ; I live there now. As soon as I was old enough my father gave me his brother's daughter for my wife, who brought nothing with her but her freedom and her respectability, and with them a power of bearing children which would be enough for a rich man's house. We have six sons and two daughters, both now married. Four of my sons have the man's toga ; the other two are still in their lad's togas. I became a soldier in the Consulship of P. Sulpicius and C. Aurelius. I was in the army which sailed to Macedonia, and I served in the ranks against King Philip two years. In the third year T. Quinctius Flamininus promoted me to tenth-rank spearman for courage. When Philip and the Macedonians were beaten and we were brought home to Italy and released, I at once went to Spain with the Consul M. Porcius as a volunteer. Of all the Generals living there is not a better for seeing and judging merit, as everyone knows who has had much experience of him and of other leaders. This General thought me fit to have the rank of First Spearman of the First Century.

" A third time, again, I enlisted as a volunteer in the army which was sent against the Ætolians and King Antiochos. M'. Acilius made me First Princeps of the First Century. When we had driven out Antiochos and put down the Ætolians, we were brought back to Italy ; and since then I have twice done annual service in the legion. Then I served twice in Spain, once under Q. Fulvius Flaccus and again under the Praetor Ti. Sempronius Gracchus. I was among the men that Flaccus took from the province with him for his triumph, for their courage, and I went back to the province at the special request

[1] xlii, 34.

of Ti. Gracchus. I was Primipilus four times in a few years, and thirty-four times I received rewards for courage from Generals, and I got six civic crowns. I have served in twenty-two annual campaigns with the army, and I am over fifty. Even if I had not done all this service and had not reached the age for retirement, yet, since I can give you four soldiers instead of my one self, it would have been right to dismiss me.

" I hope that you will accept what I have said for myself ; but for my own part, so long as anyone enrolling an army thinks me fit for service, I shall never try to back out. What rank the Military Tribunes think I deserve, is for them to decide ; I shall see that no one in the army fights better, as I have always done, as my Generals and the men who have served with me can bear witness. And you, too, mates, even if you use your right of appeal, when you were young you never did anything against the authority of the magistrates and Senate, and it is right that to-day you should put yourselves at the disposal of the Senate and Consuls, and have all the honourable posts, in which you will fight for the Republic."

Whether he is historical or not, this old soldier is typical of a class and is valuable as a symbol. He has escaped the blows of the enemy, and come home to his bit of land in the Sabine country ; but all were not so lucky as he, nor so fond of their native soil. Many, attracted by the easy life and the hope of making their fortunes, settled in the country where the chances of war had taken them, without intending to return, and there were so many more gaps in the middle class, so many more losses for the country life and agriculture of Italy.

Economic causes acted as effectively and continuously as military causes. First, there was the development of the large estate in Italy. Before Italy was united by Rome, it had been essentially a land of small farms. The result of the conquest and the ensuing confiscation of all or part of the land of the conquered, had been the formation of a State domain (*ager publicus*), which grew larger and larger. The State exploited this domain in various ways. It sold part of it to private individuals. It disposed of some of it in favour of the citizens, either collectively, by founding colonies, or individually (*viritim*). The remainder left in the hands of the State after these transfers, the *Ager Publicus* in the narrow sense, which generally consisted of uncultivated or uncultivable land, was given to the first man who occupied it (*agri occupatorii*), on terms, not of complete ownership *ex jure Quiritium*, but of mere enjoyment against legal payment of an annual *vectigal*. In practice the nobility, who ran the government, profited by this to appropriate all the *Ager Publicus*, bit by bit, and, in addition, found a means of escaping the *vectigal*. The middle classes protested violently against a practical monopoly which was obviously unfair and also greatly injured their material interests. As early as 367, the second of the Licinian Laws had limited the occupation of *Ager Publicus* by formally prohibiting the possession of more than 500 *jugera* of public land and the pasturage on it of more than 100 large cattle or 500 small. But these legal stipulations, as Appian very clearly shows, soon fell into disuse and the abuses which they were intended to abolish reappeared in a worse form than ever. As successive conquests gave them the means (first the conquest of Latium and then the unification of Italy), the rich occupied more and more of the State domain, and, forgetting that the law allowed them only the use of it, came to regard it as their permanent property.

A second economic cause, contemporary with the first, was the transformation of Italian agriculture. Italy had always been a corn country. Corn was the basis of the Roman's food. Therefore the government, careful of the interests of the consumer, at an early date took pains to keep the sale-tariff as low as possible. First, it encouraged the importation of foreign corn, which competed with Italian corn on the spot and kept down its price, and then, when the overseas provinces were created, which had to pay their tribute, at least in large part, in corn, the State, having considerable supplies at its disposal, instituted public sales of corn at reduced prices. This inverted protectionism naturally suited the consumer, and in this respect the measures were a complete success, but corn-growing became less and less profitable to the Italian producer, and was therefore gradually abandoned all over the country. It gave place to more remunerative crops, in particular vine, olive, garden-produce, and grass. Unfortunately, these new crops were delicate and costly, and did not as a rule suit the system of small farms, and two of them, vines and above all pasturage, found their best possible conditions in the big estate. The great Italian estates, therefore, were turned mainly into pasture land, which gave considerable returns. They were an ideal field of exploitation for the new capitalism, while the case of the small farm with its traditional methods of working grew steadily worse. Another fact, also a result of the conquest, further aggravated the already critical position of the small land-owner. The cost of living rose constantly, just at the time when his crops were becoming riskier and their produce less remunerative. The costs of victory fell on him, while, by a distributive justice the irony of which did not appeal to him, others, the Senatorial class, the Knights, even the proletariate, got almost all the benefits.

Faced with an increasingly precarious economic situation, many small land-owners gave up the struggle and left the countryside. Others, more obstinate, tried to hold out. They borrowed, hoping for better days to come, but the rate of interest was very high. Their land was security for the payment of the debt, and in the end it usually fell into the creditor's hands, by agreement or by force. This gradual dispossession of the small farmer is painted to the life, in all its heartrending brutality, by Sallust and by Horace after him.

" Victorious generals," says the former, " shared the fruits of conquest with a few others ; meanwhile, the parents or children of their soldiers, if they had a powerful man as neighbour, were driven from their homes." [1]

And Horace : " What shall I say of you, who tear up the landmarks of your neighbour's field and spring over your Clients' boundaries in your greed ?   Man and wife are driven out, she carrying at her breast the household gods and their ragged children." [2]

The damning words of the Tribune Philippus in 104 record a result of significance in this respect.

Evicted from the land of his fathers, the small farmer was left only the strength of his arms, but in the country he found no employment for them. Labour in the country was gradually given over entirely to slaves, who, in addition to other advantages, cost the master much less and were more manageable than free workers. The first Servile War, a startling manifestation of the social change which had taken place, presently broke out in Sicily (136). The small rural land-owner, ruined, helpless, at bay, had only one resource, the same as in all countries and all times—the town, Rome. He poured in in his masses, and in the last century of the Republic Varro shows us him in his new surroundings :—

---

[1] Sall., *Jug. War*, xli, 8–9.   [2] *Odes*, ii, 18, 23–8.

" Since, in our time, almost all fathers of families have left sickle and plough to migrate into the walls of Rome, and would rather employ their hands in clapping at the theatre and circus than in working on their fields and vineyards, we have to pay for corn to be brought from Africa and Sardinia to feed us, and load our ships with the vintage of Cos and Chios." [1]

It was all very well to come to Rome, but what was there to do there ? No doubt, there were plenty of ways of making a living in Rome ; unfortunately, they were not suited to the social position or the professional capacity of the ruined countryman. Moreover, all domestic service and small trade and industry were, here again, taken up by slaves and freedmen. In the face of this universal, overpowering competition, the small farmer had no more chance of doing well in Rome than in the country. But he came to Rome all the same, and in crowds, for many reasons. First, life in Rome, with its entertainments and shows and bustle, offered many attractions to the countryman who had lost his old position, and, secondly, if there were few creditable sources of livelihood for the ruined farmer, there were a good many others—government food-doles, the charity of rich individuals, the sale of his vote to the highest bidder. So, driven from their land and unable to carry on the fight, the rural middle classes abandoned the countryside more and more and crowded into Rome, where they constantly swelled the ranks of an idle and demoralized town populace. This was the second great cause of the collapse of the old constitution. The party of government lost the Equestrian class, which was breaking away from it, and the middle class, because, in the first half of the second century, that class was being drained of its healthiest elements and was making, with giant strides, for complete disappearance.

III

THE SECOND PUNIC WAR AND ITS CONSTITUTIONAL CONSEQUENCES

The second Punic War, by the political consequences which it brought after it, marks a capital date in the history of the Roman constitution. But it was not, at its very

[1] *De Re Rust.*, ii, pr. 3.

beginning, a radical breach with the past. All Rome lined up against the Punic invader, but the appearance of Hannibal on the soil of the peninsula did not put an end, as with the wave of a magic wand, to party struggles, and the sacred union of all parties—a fact which cannot be emphasized too strongly, especially in a patriotic and disciplined people like the Romans—only took shape after a time, in the face of the imperative necessity of national defence.

The parties which had been in conflict since the first Punic War—the governing aristocracy and the peasant democracy—continued to fight for the power, but, as a result of the new circumstances, the conditions of the conflict had changed. The crisis, by its unprecedented intensity and the extraordinary ordeal to which it subjected the men and institutions of old Rome, was peculiarly favourable to the aristocratic party, and that in two ways. First, there was the very nature of the second Punic War, a struggle in which the unity of Italy and the very existence of Rome were at stake. Unlike the first encounter between Rome and Carthage, this deadly duel was fought on Italian soil, with all the anxieties and destruction which such a situation entails. The war lasted long in time, and went on spreading in space until it covered the greater part of the Mediterranean basin. Left to his own devices, Hannibal tried to force an issue by reviving the war in Sicily, and Syracuse joined the Carthaginian cause. He made an alliance with the King of Macedonia, Philip V, who was to create a diversion in the east of Italy, which he hoped would be decisive.

Rome replied to this series of actions by a vigorous counter-offensive. In 212, Syracuse was stormed by Marcellus, and two years later the Carthaginians had to evacuate the island for good. Spain was systematically conquered in four years of hard fighting (210–206) by Scipio, the future Africanus, and in 206 Gades, the last Carthaginian possession in the peninsula, capitulated. In the East, to paralyse Philip's offensive on the Adriatic and to secure Italy against any danger of his intervention, Rome, aided by her Ætolian allies, kindled a war in Greece which went on for seven years (212–205). In 204, at last, she dealt the knock-out blow, the great counter-offensive in Africa, which, by the victory of Zama, brought Carthage to her knees. As the theatres of operations became more numerous and more extensive, men were fighting not only in Italy, but in Sicily, Sardinia, Spain, Illyria, Greece, and Africa. Roman diplomacy was equally active, and little by little extended its sphere of action to every part of the Mediterranean basin.

Such vast military operations and such a complicated diplomacy as these require, in the power which attempts them, a consistency of programme and a continuity of effort of which the traditional organs of the Roman State were not usually capable. The Comitia lacked the necessary permanence and competence ; the magistracies were hampered by the two sacrosanct principles, those of annual office and of the college, which had governed their constitutional activity from the earliest times. Only one body in Rome presented, in the matter of foreign policy and provincial administration, the conditions of stability and practical power required by the situation—the Senate. As far back as one could go into the past, that council, the only abiding element in a constitution in which everything else was mobility and change, appeared as the legal guardian of the Roman people—witness the traditional formula, *Senatus Populusque Romanus*, the official expression of the State— and the recognized keeper of the national tradition. " *Res ad Patres redit*," " *Auspicia ad Patres redeunt*," two forms of one same truth—that was what was said when there was an interregnum, even in the Royal period, and the Republican constitution had made no change in that ancient legal truth. The introduction of the principles of annual office and the college when the magistracies were first created, and, later, a series of successful encroachments in politics, administration, and finance, ratified by public opinion and made into integral parts of the constitution as precedents, had gradually strengthened the position of the Senate and given it an influence over the conduct of affairs which, if not always legitimate, was at least decisive in fact. Now, the body which thus combined the advantages of life-membership and very important functions constituted the very stronghold of the aristocratic party in the Roman constitution. So the exceptional situation created by the second Punic War, by enhancing the importance of the Senate, affected the mutual relations of the two great historical parties and definitely favoured the aristocratic faction at the expense of its rival.

Secondly, while the aristocratic party was thrust to the fore by circumstances, the democrats, during the war, were less fortunate in the choice of their leaders. Whether from military incompetence or from bad luck, C. Flaminius, M. Minucius Rufus, and C. Terentius Varro hardly did it credit. After the defeats of the Ticinus and Trebia, for which the generals of the nobility, P. Cornelius Scipio and L. Sempronius Longus, were held responsible by public opinion, the people conferred a second Consulship on C. Flaminius, the man whom it trusted. On this occasion again, in spite of the very serious danger, we find Flaminius at loggerheads with the Senate as usual, and, if the assertions of the aristocratic party are true (and they are perhaps only calumnies in the circumstances), the popular Consul neglected some necessary formalities when he took up office. The question is really of very minor importance ; what mattered was that Flaminius was utterly defeated by Hannibal on the field of Trasimene, and the party had to bear the responsibility for the disaster as least as much as its leader.

After the defeat, Q. Fabius Maximus, the celebrated temporizer, a leader of the aristocratic party, was made Dictator, contrary to traditional usage, by a formal vote of the people, and, that there might be continuity of command in the hands of the most competent men in the presence of the enemy, a law was passed provisionally suspending the plebiscite of 342 which forbade re-election to the Consulship within ten years. In virtue of this legal dispensation, in the course of the Punic War, apart from their pro-magistracies, Q. Fabius Maximus, who had already been Consul twice, in 233 and 228, held the office three times (215, 214, 209), M. Claudius Marcellus four times (215, 214, 210, 208), and Q. Fulvius Flaccus twice (212, 209). By his unforgettable services Fabius Maximus justified the exception made in his favour, but presently the party struggles recommenced, and the very method by which the Dictator saved Rome inspired the liveliest dissatisfaction in popular circles.

By the side of Fabius Maximus was another man who became involved in these political passions, his Master of Horse, M. Minucius Rufus. The Tribune M. Metilius proposed, in flagrant violation of constitutional precedent, that both men should be given full powers. The proposal was carried, but Minucius, in whose favour the extraordinary innovation was made, had little cause to congratulate himself on it. Having got himself into a difficult situation through his own misjudgment, he quickly waived his new prerogatives and spontaneously placed himself under the command of his former chief. It was a second discomfiture for the democratic party, and it was not to be the last.

For that party, in spite of its two unfortunate attempts, did not give up the struggle. At the elections for 216 it secured the Consulship for a new man, C. Terentius Varro. Varro, a man of humble origin, being the son of a wealthy butcher, had in the past shown himself a faithful supporter of the democrats, and he came to the highest magistracy with a very definite programme of opposition. The aristocracy, which had been unable to prevent his election, at least succeeded in giving him as a colleague one of its most eminent members, L. Æmilius Paullus, who had already been Consul for the first time in 219. But the result was deplorable—the disaster of Cannæ, the bloodiest defeat which the Roman State had ever written down in its annals. After that immense catastrophe, the lesson was learned, and through the last fifteen years of the war the people, at last abandoning party strife, entrusted the aristocracy with the whole conduct of operations. By its energy, its patriotism, and, one should add, its capacity, the aristocracy showed itself worthy of that confidence. Fabius Maximus, the true head of the government, and his fellow-workers, Marcellus, the conqueror of Syracuse, M. Livius Salinator and C. Claudius Nero, the victors of the Metaurus, and Scipio, the triumphant hero of Spain and Africa, all men of the nobility, delivered the soil of their country and made an end of the Carthaginian peril for ever.

The Republican constitution very soon felt the effects of this state of things, and in twofold form—the dictatorship of the Senate and the advance to oligarchy, which were connected and complementary phenomena. The suspension of the plebiscite of 342 had, as the re-elections turned out, given the monopoly of the Consulship to a limited circle of aristocratic families. For more than a century to come, new men would be elected only by a sudden recrudescence of the opposition, and, as the influence of the Senate grew, the Consuls gradually became mere instruments of that body. Only one constitutional obstacle was left on the path of the Senatorial aristocracy—the Tribuneship. The aristocracy did not commit the incredible blunder of trying to break the Tribuneship ; with greater shrewdness, it nullified it, and, as it were, absorbed it. It made it a mere step in the *cursus honorum*. The Atinian Plebiscite, which may have been passed at this time, or perhaps only later, provided that all Tribunes of the Plebs, and probably also Plebeian Ædiles, should henceforth have the official rank of Senators. Flaminius and his party had striven to save the Plebeian magistracies from the clutches of the nobility ; favoured by circumstances in the duel for power, the aristocratic party ended by securing the advantage in full. Only with the Gracchi did the Tribuneship, after being domesticated by the governing nobility for three-quarters of a century, return to its origins and revive the tradition of the distant past. The development revealed itself in material form in the domain of outward distinctions ; the Censors of 194, S. Ælius Pætus and C. Cornelius Cethegus, decided that seats of honour should be reserved for the Senators at the Roman Games. A movement towards oligarchy, then, was the first great constitutional result of the second Punic War.

But there was a second consequence, no less important. Just as the external crisis had led to the unity of direction which was the basis of the political influence of the Senate, so it had demanded, no less imperatively, unity of execution, in the form of the great military commands. The military power, being constitutionally bound up with the chief magistracies of the City—Dictatorship, Consulship, Prætorship—was hampered by the double impediment of annual tenure of office and the collegiate system to which they were subject. Against these two fundamental disadvantages, the various expedients devised in succession—separation of spheres of action, alternation of command, extension of office—had been little more than opportunistic solutions. Unity and permanence of command were especially necessary in distant theatres of operations, over which the Senate could only exercise a remote and too often intermittent control.

A flagrant example occurred in Spain in the second Punic War. In 212, P. and Cn. Scipio had fallen on the field of battle. Without waiting for new generals to be sent from Rome, the soldiers, gathering in military Comitia, took it on themselves to confer the chief command on a plain Knight, L. Marcius Septimus, who by his energy and success had made himself worthy of the honour. Although the circumstances of the moment somewhat excused this spontaneous intervention of the troops, it none the less had its grave side. The Senate did not ratify the election, and hastened to restore a legal situation in the army in Spain by giving it a new commander-in-chief in the proper manner.

Another fact, similar and still more significant in respect of the man in question and of the consequences which ensued, was the career of Scipio Africanus. In 211, young Scipio, then aged barely twenty-four, presented himself before the people, and, although he had so far only held the Ædileship, canvassed for the command of the army in Spain. The people granted it to him, in an exceptional form and with the title of Proconsul. In 210 he arrived in Spain, and, under the legal form of extension of office, kept his command without interruption for five years (210–206). As Consul in 205, he prepared for the counter-offensive against Carthage and conquered Sicily. From 204 to 202, he conducted the war in Africa, and on the conclusion of peace he returned to Rome to hold his triumph in 201. It was a new fact in the annals of the Roman State—a single man, Scipio, acted as commander-in-chief without interruption for ten years running (210–201), first in Spain, then in Italy and Sicily, and lastly in Africa.

Like oligarchy, and parallel with it, and for the same reasons, military power, thanks to the second Punic War, had advanced with giant strides, and already threats of dictatorship were taking shape in the distance. The old constitutional balance of the third century had ceased to exist, and the old party of the peasant democracy, the embodiment of the voice of the people and the supreme gurantee of control, was only a memory. Oligarchy or dictatorship ? That was the new form which the constitutional problem would take as Rome emerged from the great crisis.

IV

Oligarchy or Dictatorship? Scipio and Cato

Immediately after the second Punic War, Scipio held a position without equal. After a brilliant triumph, he was given the high-sounding surname of Africanus. He was the idol of the people, which decreed statues and extraordinary honours to him. In 199 he was elected to the Censorship, and soon afterwards, as Princeps Senatus, he became moral director of the Senate. All these distinctions had been earned by the vanquisher of Hannibal by his deathless services, but it was none the less true that the career of this man under forty, both for the rapidity and for the many irregularities of his advancement, was regarded as a permanent challenge to the old Roman constitution. Contrary to usage, he had sought and obtained the Ædileship in 213 at the age of twenty-two ; contrary to usage, the people had elected him Proconsul and given him the command of the army in Spain in 217 ; contrary to usage, again, in 206, when he was twenty-nine years old, he had been elected Consul for the following year and the Senate had willy-nilly authorized him to carry the war into Africa. His political methods, his boundless prodigality, and his persistent seeking after popularity, all so unlike traditional ways, had soon, notwithstanding his legitimate renown, inspired the mistrust and then the sarcasms of the Senatorial aristocracy. Old Fabius Maximus had, in a moment of ill-temper, gone so far as to remind him that the Consul was elected, not for his own benefit, but for that of the State, and had protested against the over-royal manner—*regius mos* [1]—in which Scipio, after his election to the Consulship, claimed to dispose of his army as he pleased.

In spite of all, Scipio's prestige rose steadily. After Zama, the people had in its enthusiam wanted to make him Consul and Dictator for life, that is, to establish in his favour the personal power which was to be realized by Cæsar a century and a half later. Scipio had refused, but the danger of dictatorship was still in the air, and the oligarchy, threatened in its privileges, jealously watched for its moment. But, just when oligarchy and personal power seemed at the point

[1] Livy, xxviii, 42.

of coming to grips over the ruins of the old constitution, for the inheritance of which both were striving, events suddenly took an unexpected turn. A new man, Cato, stepped on to the stage.

M. Porcius Cato was a new man in the full force and with all the Roman exactness of the term. Born at Tusculum, in 234, of a family of farmers, he had reached man's estate in the very middle of the second Punic War, and had distinguished himself in it by his courage as a soldier and his abilities as a leader. He had been Military Tribune in 207, Quæstor in 204, and Plebeian Ædile in 199. In the following year he obtained the Prætorship. He was starting on a political career which was to last half a century. In spite of variations inevitable in a public life of that length and of such changes in tactics as might be imposed on him by the variety and number of his successive opponents, Cato may be described in one word—he was a constitutionalist, in the traditional sense of the term. The constitution of the third century, with the permanent system of popular control which it implied, and the important, if not preponderant, part which it gave to the influence of the rural middle class (his own class), was to him an ideal which he must save at all costs, and when its decay became too apparent he tried to restore it to life. That traditional constitution had two enemies, which the second Punic War had turned into two serious, permanent menaces—oligarchy and personal power. As champion of the old constitution, as a survivor from a past which he had seen in his earlier years and which was rapidly fading away under the pressure of circumstances, Cato fought both enemies and brought every political conviction and personal quality which he possessed to the implacable conflict.

When Cato entered public life, the great danger to the constitution was Scipio Africanus and the menace of personal power which the conqueror of Hannibal embodied. So it was he that Cato and his party first attacked, in a duel lasting eleven years, full of incidents and victories on one side or the other, in which, as was to be expected, the defender of the constitution did not fail to find active and valuable allies among the oligarchy.

Cato and Scipio were no longer unknown to one another.

Cato had been Scipio's Quæstor in Sicily before the African expedition, and had considered it his duty to make remarks to the commander-in-chief regarding his excessive and unreckoning prodigalities. The haughty aristocrat had taken the remonstrance in very ill part, and we are told that Cato returned in dudgeon to Rome, to bring an accusation against Scipio in proper form. But after Zama Scipio was far too popular for an unimportant person, as Cato then was, to venture to attack the hero of the day. If he wanted to carry out his purposes, he must grow bigger. His advance was rapid. In 195 he rose to the Consulship. His victorious campaigns in Spain won him great prestige, and brought him definitely before the public eye as a man apart. But Scipio was still master of the situation. In 195, in spite of Cato's personal intervention, the people voted for the repeal of the *Lex Oppia*, a sumptuary law. In 194, after the legal interval, Scipio obtained election to his second Consulship. In 193, the Senate entrusted him with a diplomatic mission in Africa, to settle difficulties outstanding between Carthage and the Numidian King Massinissa, and two of his friends, L. Cornelius Merula and Q. Minucius Thermus, were elected Consuls. But in the next year he failed to obtain the election of his cousin P. Cornelius Scipio Nasica and his friend Lælius, who were defeated by Lucius, the brother of Flamininus, and Cn. Domitius Ahenobarbus.

The war against Antiochos, which broke out in 191, gave Scipio the opportunity to restore his influence, which for a moment had been shaken. He obtained the Consulship of 190 for his brother Lucius and his friend Lælius, and, by a family arrangement which was quite understood, caused the former to be given the command of the war. Lucius Cornelius Scipio was quite incompetent, and everybody in Rome knew it, but Africanus had offered to accompany him as Legate, and he would be the real leader of the expedition. The victory of Magnesia raised the glory of the Scipios to their summit. Of course, there were discordant voices, and the word " corruption " began to be breathed among their enemies, but no one dared show his hand and attack the conquerors of the day. The conflict was only postponed. In the next year, the open attack began.

In 191, the Consul P. Cornelius Scipio Nasica, Africanus's

cousin, had beaten the Boii of Cisalpine Gaul and had compelled them to sign peace. He asked for a triumph. Cato
and his supporters tried to cause it to be refused. They
failed, but presently they took their revenge by depriving
Q. Minucius Thermus, the Consul of 193, who was a friend of
Scipio, of the same honour (191). In 190, elections for the
Censorship were to be held. Cato was a candidate, with his
old friend L. Valerius Flaccus, and, at the same time,
P. Cornelius Scipio Nasica and M'. Acilius Glabrio, the victor
of Thermopylæ, who were both backed by the party of the
Scipios, and also the famous Flamininus and M. Claudius
Marcellus. Cato made a direct attack on M'. Acilius Glabrio,
who was the most dangerous of them all, and caused him to
be accused of peculation. The accusation was not followed
up, but Cato attained his object. M'. Acilius had to withdraw
his candidature, but at least had the consolation of seeing
his opponent fail. Flamininus and M. Claudius Marcellus,
the two most independent candidates, were elected. Somewhat later, Cato tried to cause Scipio Asiaticus to be refused
a triumph, but without success. Scipio Africanus won the
day again (189). But bad days were coming for Scipio,
and Cato's hour was at hand.

So far, the two adversaries had confined themselves to
indirect attacks, or at least to mere skirmishes. In 187 the
decisive battle began. Two Tribunes of Cato's party, the
two Q. Petillii, proposed to the Senate that Lucius Scipio
should be asked to account for the 500 talents received by
him as a first payment of the indemnity owed by Antiochos.
The books were brought out, but Africanus tore them up.
Upon this ill-advised exhibition, the Petillii, still at Cato's
instigation, took the matter before the Comitia and proposed
that an extraordinary commission of inquiry should be
appointed to clear it up. Two Tribunes of Scipio's party,
Q. and L. Mummius, opposed their veto. Cato persuaded
them, by his personal intervention, to withdraw it.
Another Tribune, C. Minucius Augurinus, then brought
an accusation against Lucius Scipio and tried to have him
sentenced to a fine. He was very nearly dragged off to jail,
and, without being actually prosecuted, Africanus himself
seems to have come in for his share of discredit. Both were
saved by the intervention of the Tribune T. Sempronius

Gracchus, the father of the famous Gracchi, and the matter was dropped so far as the courts were concerned. But, in this implacable conflict of two parties, what matters is the practical result. The political fortune of the Scipios had received a deadly blow, from which it would never recover. Scipio Africanus saw this clearly enough ; he knew that his public career was over, and retired from Rome to his estate at Liternum in Campania. There he died four years later (183). With his great opponent removed from public life, Cato triumphed all along the line.

With the person of Scipio, one of the two dangers which threatened the old constitution, that of military dictatorship, had disappeared. There remained the second—the movement towards oligarchy. Cato was to devote the last thirty-nine years of his life to fighting it (187–149). In 185 he offered himself for the Censorship of the following year, once again with L. Valerius Flaccus, and, as in the previous Censorial elections, he collected against him both the remains of the party of the Scipios—P. Cornelius Scipio Nasica and Scipio Asiaticus—and the champions of the oligarchy—M. Fulvius Nobilior, Cn. Manlius Vulso, L. Furius Purpurio, Ti. Sempronius Longus, and M. Sempronius Tuditanus. But Cato was at the height of his popularity and of his political fortunes, and triumphed over them all with L. Valerius Flaccus. He made use of his high office to expel seven eminent members of the oligarchical party from the Senate, with L. Quinctius Flamininus, the brother of the great Flamininus, and L. Furius Purpurio at their head (184).

Four years later, in 180, the *Lex Villia Annalis* was passed at Cato's inspiration, laying down the exact conditions of obtaining honours—age, succession, and probably also the obligation of having served in ten campaigns before approaching the lowest step of the *cursus honorum*, the Quæstorship—and thus raising serious obstacles to ambitious young nobles who were in a hurry to pass through the stages. In the following years Cato went on indefatigably attacking the supporters of the oligarchical system. In 179, he attacked the Censors M. Fulvius Nobilior, an old enemy, and M. Æmilius Lepidus ; in 178, the Consul A. Manlius Vulso, the brother of the conqueror of the Galatians ; in 172, M. Popilius Lænas, the Consul of 173 ; in 171, M. Titinius,

M. Furius Philus, and M. Matienus, all former governors of Spain ; and in 149, Ser. Sulpicius Galba, the butcher of the Lusitanians. This last blow was the final effort of the old fighter, who died some months later (149).

But, successful or otherwise, all these actions of Cato were only of secondary importance, and could not be anything else. The inexorable necessities of foreign policy required in the Government an ever closer concentration of purpose and an ever completer unity of action. That vital problem could not be solved by the traditional constitution of the City. So the progress towards oligarchy, which had begun at the end of the third century and had been hastened by the second Punic War, went on relentlessly. Of popular control there was no longer any question, except by fits and starts, in an almost revolutionary form. Dead bodies cannot be brought to life, and the Republican constitution was certainly dead. There was only one question—oligarchy or dictatorship ? *Sic vos non vobis* . . . by striving to avert personal power, Cato, far from saving the traditional constitution, had only hastened the advent of oligarchy.

BOOK TWO

FROM OLIGARCHY TO MILITARY RULE

CHAPTER I

THEORIES AND REALITIES

BIBLIOGRAPHY.—*Ancient Authors*: Polybios, vi (frags.), 3–18 ; Cicero, *Republic*, i, 26, 29, 35, 45–6 ; *Laws*, iii, 2–5.
Modern Works: **X**, iii, 447–51 (Neumann) ; **XXVII**, 51–4 ; **XIX**, see ref., p. 24 ; **CXLI**, i, 303–80, and ii ; **XIII**, bk. iii ; **LXXVII** ; **LXXII**, Eng. vol. i, 18–43.

I

POLYBIOS ON THE ROMAN CONSTITUTION

THE Romans, being practical-minded men, lending a readier ear to the teaching of facts than to the charm of theories, did not begin to study their constitution until very late. Only in the second part of the second century B.C., when the system was showing marked signs of decay, did they make their public law a subject of speculation. C. Sempronius Tuditanus, the Consul of 129, an enemy of Tiberius Gracchus, and C. Junius Gracchanus, a supporter of the policy of the Gracchi, set forth the theory of the magistracy, the former in his *Libri Magistratuum* and the latter in his *Libri de Potestatibus*, both of which works are lost. But we have a precious though fragmentary document in the evidence of Polybios. The Greek historian, exiled in Italy, lived long in Rome. There he saw Roman institutions at work before his eyes, and his close connection with governing circles, particularly that of Scipio Æmilianus, gave him special advantages for making observations and conclusions. His opinion, which has mercifully been saved from the wreckage of his historical work, being the opinion of a contemporary, an eye-witness, and a specialist, is of the utmost interest to the historian of the Roman constitution, and deserves a place of honour.

First, then, let Polybios speak :—

" Of the Greek states, which have so often risen to greatness and so often suffered a change of fortune in the other direction, expositions about the past and predictions about the future are easy.

*See also Supplementary Bibliography with Prefatory Note (p. 405)

For it is easy to recount what is known and to foretell what is to come by drawing inferences from what has previously happened. But in the case of the Roman State, it is not at all easy to describe the present situation, since the constitution is very complex, or to speak of the future, since we know little about its special features, in public and in private affairs, in the past.   Great attention and consideration are therefore needed if one would obtain a clear view of its peculiar characteristics.

" Most of those who try to discuss these matters methodically speak of three kinds of state, which they call kingship, aristocracy, and democracy. Now, it seems to me that one might well ask them whether they mean that these three are the only kinds, or the best. In either case I think that they are wrong ; for it is plain that the best state would be one combined of all these three varieties. We have proof of this, not only in theory, but in fact ; Lycurgos was the first to establish the constitution of the Spartans on this method.[1] . . . He, perceiving by some process of reasoning from what source and in what manner each system came about, established his constitution without mishap. But, although the Romans came in the end to the same result in respect of their constitution, they did not do it by mere thinking, but after many struggles and difficulties, always choosing the better course after actual experience of misfortune ; so they have arrived at the same end as Lycurgos, the best of the constitutions of our time." [2]

" The three forms of government of which I spoke above were combined in the Roman constitution, and the share of each was so fairly and appropriately laid down and maintained that no one, even a Roman, could say definitely that the whole system was aristocratic or democratic or monarchical. This was only natural. For if one looked at the power of the Consuls it seemed to be entirely monarchical and royal ; if at that of the Senate, aristocratic ; and if one considered that of the masses, it seemed quite clearly to be democratic. The attributions of each of these parts were at that time, and still are on the whole, as follows :—

" The Consuls, before they lead out the armies, stay in Rome and are at the head of all public affairs. All the other magistrates except the Tribunes are subordinate to them and obey them. It is they who introduce embassies to the Senate. In addition, they consult the Senate on urgent matters and promulgate *Senatus consulta*. They also deal with all matters which are settled by the people ; they summon the Assembly, present bills, and carry out the decisions of the majority. In everything concerning the preparation of war and the conduct of operations their power is almost absolute. It is their business to say what contingents shall be furnished by the allies, to appoint military tribunes, to make levies, and to choose the men who are fittest for service ; moreover, they have the right, when in the field, to punish anyone as they see fit. They are at liberty to spend as much of the public funds as they wish, being accompanied by a Quæstor who at once carries out all their orders. If one considered only this part of the constitution, one might reasonably say that it was purely monarchical and royal. If, in the institutions which I have described or am about to describe, any change should be made, now or later, it would in no way affect my present remarks.

[1] vi, 3, 1–9.   [2] vi, 10, 12–14.

"The first function of the Senate is to administer the public treasury, for it controls all revenue and expenditure. The Quæstors cannot take out the smallest sum for public purposes without a decree of the Senate, except for the Consuls. Even the heaviest expenses of all, those incurred by the Censors every five years for building and repairing public works, come under the Senate, which gives the Censors the necessary authority. [All crimes committed in Italy which call for public action, such as treason, conspiracy, poisoning, and murder, are within the competency of the Senate. If an individual or a city in Italy has a dispute to settle, deserves punishment, or needs help or protection, it is always a matter for the Senate. Even outside Italy, if an embassy has to be sent to settle a disputed claim, to transmit an exhortation or an order, to receive submission, or to declare war, the Senate does it. So, too, when embassies come to Rome, the Senate considers how they should be received and answered. The people has no say in any of these matters. So, if one goes to Rome when the two Consuls are away, the constitution seems to be purely aristocratic. This, indeed, is the opinion of a great many Greeks and kings, since it is almost always the Senate that deals with their affairs.

" After this, one may naturally ask what share in the constitution can be left to the people, since the Senate has all the prerogatives which I have just mentioned, the chief being complete control of revenue and expenditure, and the Consuls have full powers in respect of the preparation and conduct of war. All the same, the people has a share, and the most important share, since it alone in the State can confer honours and inflict punishment, and these are the things which hold kingdoms and republics and, in short, all human life together. Where this manner of distinguishing between men is unknown, or is known but abused, it is impossible to conduct any undertaking in a reasonable way. How could it be otherwise, if the good and bad are held in equal honour ? So the people has its jurisdiction. It deals with offences punishable by a heavy fine, especially when the accused has held the higher magistracies. It alone can pronounce sentence of death. In this respect there is in Rome a very praiseworthy custom which is worth mentioning : in any capital case, the accused is allowed, while the trial is still in progress and so long as one of the voting Tribes has not given its vote, to leave the City openly. In this way he condemns himself to voluntary banishment, and finds a safe refuge at Naples, Præneste, Tibur, or some other allied city. Moreover, it is the people that confers office on those who deserve it, the greatest reward which can be given to virtue in a state. It has the power of adopting or rejecting laws and, most important of all, it deliberates on war and peace. Alliances, peace-terms, and treaties are ratified or rejected by the people. So one might reasonably say that the people has the greatest part in the government and that the Roman constitution is democratic.

" Having stated how the government is shared between these three orders, I shall now show how they can work against or with one another. When the Consul, invested with the authority which I have described, sets out at the head of the army, he certainly seems to have absolute power to carry out what plans he has in view. But he needs the people and the Senate ; without them, he cannot bring his operations to a successful conclusion. For it is clear that the troops constantly need supplies ; but without a decision of the Senate they cannot get food or clothing or pay. So their leaders are helpless if the Senate is ill-disposed or obstinate. It also depends on the Senate whether the plans of generals shall be fully carried out or not, for after a year it can replace them in their command or maintain them in it. It can, at its pleasure, glorify and make much of their successes or belittle them and diminish their lustre, for the ceremonies which the Romans call " triumphs ", in which generals bring their exploits before the eyes of their fellow-countrymen in material form, cannot be held with all the necessary pomp, nor, indeed, at all, if the Senate does not give its authorization or grant the necessary funds. The Consuls also have great need of the people, however far from Rome they may be, for it is the people, as I said before, that ratifies or rejects peace-terms and treaties. Lastly, and most important of all, when the Consuls lay down their office it is to the people that they have to give account of their doings. Therefore, the Consuls cannot with any safety neglect the feelings of the people or of the Senate.

" The Senate, for its part, powerful though it may be, must first of all, in all public affairs, consult the people and take its opinion into account. It cannot pronounce judgment on the more serious and important legal cases, nor on crimes against the State punishable with death, unless the people ratifies the decisions submitted by it. The same is true of matters directly affecting the Senate ; for if anyone introduces a law tending to diminish the traditional power of the Senate, or to limit the honours and prerogatives of Senators, or even to take part of their property from them, the people alone is empowered to adopt or reject the proposal. Last, but not least, if one single Tribune uses his right of veto, the Senate cannot carry out its decision, it cannot even meet and hold a sitting. Now, it is the Tribune's duty to do always what pleases the people and to conform to its wishes. For these reasons the Senate is afraid of the people and treats it with consideration.

" Similarly, the people has to depend on the Senate in public and private affairs. All over Italy many public works are given out on contract by the Censors—the repair and construction of public buildings, almost more than one can count, and the working of the countless waterways, harbours, gardens, mines, lands, and, in short, everything which comes under Roman rule. All these matters are undertaken by the mass of the people, and one might say that every-body has a share in the contracts and profits which they involve. Some make contracts with the Censors, others join these as partners, others stand surety for them, and others, in their name, pledge their own property to the State. Now, all these operations are under the supreme control of the Senate. It can grant an extension of time, release a man from part of his obligations in the case of an accident, or, if the work proves quite impossible, cancel the contract altogether. There are, therefore, many circumstances in which the Senate can do serious injury to public works contractors, or, on the contrary, can favour them, since in all cases reference is made to it. Most important of all, in most public and private trials the judges are taken from among the Senate, when the case is a serious one. So everyone is dependent on the Senate ; since no one can foresee whether he will have need of it some day, no one dares to resist or disobey its orders. For a like reason men hesitate to oppose the will of the Consuls, since in the field all, as individuals and as a mass, come under their authority.

" Since the three orders can thus hamper or support one another, their working gives the best results in all circumstances, and it is impossible to find a more perfect form of government than this. When common danger threatens the Romans from abroad, compelling them to think and act in complete unity, the strength of the constitution becomes so great that no necessary measure is neglected, for all are determined to deal with the situation and decisions which are taken are carried out without delay, since all combine, collectively and individually, to accomplish the object which they have undertaken. That is how Rome is indebted to her constitution for her invincibility and her successes in everything which she undertakes. When, on the other hand, all fear from outside is removed, and the Romans have nothing to do but to enjoy the prosperity and wealth earned by their victories, and, allowing themselves to be corrupted by flattery and softness, fall, as usually happens, into insolence and pride, then, above all, we see their constitution deriving from itself a remedy for their ills. For, suppose that one of the three orders presumptuously tries to encroach on the rights of the two others and to become too predominant, since none of them is wholly independent, as we have seen, and the action of anyone can be checked and hampered by that of the others, none will go too far in pride and arrogance. Each keeps its own place, either because the others oppose its efforts or because it is too much afraid of their intervention to make the attempt at all." [1]

Although Polybios's account is fragmentary—a fact too often forgotten—it has the form of a thesis with complementary and logically co-ordinated divisions. It contains two essential propositions. One is general : there are three fundamental kinds of government, kingship, aristocracy, and democracy, and the most perfect government is that in which they are combined in the most harmonious proportions. The other is particular : this is exactly the case with the Roman constitution. Then comes the demonstration in three points : (a) the Roman constitution is not a form of exclusive government ; (b) it contains the three fundamental principles, kingship, aristocracy, and democracy ; (c) these three principles are mingled and balanced in it in the most satisfactory manner. Lastly, the conclusion : this constitutional system has the happiest effects for the Roman State.

The more especially theoretical part of the thesis—the ideal of good government—is of only accessory interest to us here. Let us merely note in passing that it is neither

[1] vi, 11, 11 to 18, 9.

new nor peculiar to Polybios. It was familiar to Greek philosophy, which had already acclaimed its supposed realization in the constitution of Sparta, and it is found in particularly definite form in Aristotle's *Politics*.[1] Polybios took the idea from Aristotle, probably through his friend the philosopher Panætios. The second part of the thesis, on the other hand, the application of the principle to the Roman constitution, was a new idea, which enjoyed great and lasting popularity in Republican Rome. The thesis of Polybios, accepted by government circles, soon became the official theory. We shall find it again, greatly developed, in Cicero.

II

Cicero's *Republic* and *Laws*

Cicero treats of the question in the two great systematic treatises which he especially devotes to the study of constitutions, the *Republic* and the *Laws*. He makes no pretence of stating original views of his own. In the *Republic*,[2] in which his mouthpiece is Scipio Æmilianus and the scene is laid in the summer of 129 B.C., he expressly places his theory under the patronage of Polybios.

> " Lælius : (If I have come to you) it is not only because it is right that the first citizen of the State should talk about the State, but also because I remember that you have often discussed these matters with Panætios in the presence of Polybios, two Greeks with the greatest knowledge of political matters, and that, after comparing many facts, you decided that far the best constitution was that which our fathers have left to us."

In Cicero we shall certainly find the thesis of Polybios once more, but with a fuller development and new determinations of detail.

Cicero's account, like that of Polybios, contains two fundamental points : (*a*) the definition of the best form of government ; (*b*) the application of that general principle to the particular case of the Roman constitution.

> (*a*) *The Best Government.*—There are three essential forms of government. " Government may be placed in the hands of a single man, or of a few chosen ones, or of the mass and all men. When the

---

[1] ii, 3, 10–11 (1266*b*).   [2] i, 21, 34.

sovereignty is held by one man, we call that man a king, and the state of his polity a kingdom. When it is held by chosen men, then that state is said to be ruled by the decision of the aristocracy. Popular government exists where all power lies with the people. Any one of these three kinds, if it maintains the bond which first held men together in a society, can become, not perfect, nor in my opinion the best possible, but at least tolerable ; and one or another may be preferable according to the circumstances." [1] But the best form of constitution results from a right modification of the three kinds. " Therefore, I think that the fourth kind of government is most to be approved, which is a combination and mutual modification of the three which I mentioned before." [2] Or, again, Scipio says, " I do not approve of any of the three alone and in itself, and I place that which is a combination of all three above any one." [3] Lastly, " Royal government is far the best of the three first kinds ; and far better than royalty itself is a moderate combination of the three best kinds in fair proportion. For I would have something pre-eminent and royal in a state, another part given to the authority of the leading men, and certain things reserved for the desire and judgment of the mass." [4]

(b) *Application of the Principle to the Roman Constitution.*—Now, the ideal of government thus defined is realized in full by the Roman constitution. " I perceive, I feel, I affirm, that there is none of all the forms of government to compare, for constitution, organization, or discipline, with that which our fathers received from their for-bears and left to us. And, since you would hear from me what you already know yourselves, I shall tell you what it is like, and that it is the best ; and having described our Republic as an example, I shall, if I can, refer to that example all that I have to say about the best form of government." [5]

" CICERO : Since, then, we are legislating for free peoples and have already said what we think about the best form of government in six books, to-day we shall adapt our laws to the government which we prefer.

" Well, then, we need magistrates, for without their wisdom and diligence there can be no State, and an account of them gives the whole economy of the State. We must prescribe not only the manner in which they shall command, but that in which the citizens shall obey. For a man who commands well must some time have obeyed, and a man who obeys with docility shows himself worthy to command some time. So the man who obeys should have the hope that he will one day command, and he who commands should reflect that in a short time he will have to obey. But we must prescribe, not only that the magistrates shall be treated with submission and obeyed, but that they shall be revered and loved, as Charondas did in his laws. Our Plato calls those men Titans, who oppose the magistrates as the Titans did the race of heaven. And now let us go on to the laws themselves, if you approve.—ATTICUS : For my part, I approve that, and your arrangement.

" CICERO : The power of the magistrate shall be just, and the citizens shall obey it with docility and without dispute.—The magistrate shall constrain the rebellious and guilty citizen with fine, imprisonment, or flogging, unless this is opposed by an equal or

---

[1] i, 26, 42.   [2] i, 29, 45.   [3] i, 35, 54.
[4] i, 45, 69.   [5] i, 46, 70.

higher authority or by the people, to whom there shall be right of appeal. When the magistrate has tried the case and given his verdict, the discussion of the penalty or fine shall lie with the people.—In war there shall be no appeal from him who is in command, and what the man who is conducting the war commands shall have the force of law.—Junior magistrates, who have only partial authority, shall be numerous in the various offices. In war, those who have received orders shall command, and they shall have Tribunes. At home they shall guard the public treasury ; they shall watch over the prisons ; they shall punish capital crimes ; they shall sign bronze, silver, and gold ; they shall try lawsuits ; and they shall do whatever the Senate decrees.—There shall be Ædiles, to take care of the city, the corn-supply, and the festival Games, and that shall be the first step to the higher honours.—Censors shall take the census of the age, number of children, number of slaves, and property of the people ; they shall look after the temples of the city, roads, water, treasury, and taxes ; they shall divide the various parts of the people in tribes, and then distribute them according to their property, age, and order ; they shall keep a record of the children of men of the cavalry and infantry ; they shall forbid celibacy ; they shall control the morals of the people ; they shall allow no infamous person to remain in the Senate. They shall be two in number, and hold office for five years. The other magistrates shall be annual, but the authority of the Censors shall be permanent.—There shall be a Prætor, an arbitrator in justice, who shall try private suits or order them to be tried ; he shall be the guardian of civil law ; there shall be as many officials, equal to him in power, as the Senate shall decree and the people order.

" There shall be two magistrates with royal power, who shall be called Prætors, Judges, or Consuls, according as they command, give justice, or consult.—In war, they shall have sovereign authority and take orders from no one. For them the safety of the people shall be the supreme law.—No one shall hold the same magistracy a second time until ten years have expired.—They shall observe the age-regulations of the Annal Law.—But in the case of a dangerous war or civil strife, a single man shall hold the same power as the two Consuls, if the Senate so decrees, for not more than six months ; and if the auspices are favourable to his appointment he shall be the Master of the People. To command the cavalry he shall have under him one equal in authority to the Prætor. . . .

" The auspices shall belong to the Senate, which shall transmit them to the man who can create the Consuls in the Comitia, and according to the rites.—Those who hold *imperia, potestates,* or *legationes* shall, on the decree of the Senate and the order of the people, go out of the City ; they shall wage just wars justly, treat the allies well, control themselves and their subordinates, increase the glory of their people, and return home with honour.—No man shall be given a mission with a view to his personal interests.—The Plebs shall have the ten Tribunes whom it has created to protect it from violence. Their veto and their proposals to the Plebs shall have the force of law. They shall be sacrosanct and the Plebs shall never be left without Tribunes.—All magistrates shall have their auspices and their jurisdiction. The Senate shall be formed of them. The decrees of the Senate shall have the force of law. If no equal or higher authority forbids, *Senatus consulta* shall be kept in the records. That order shall be without stain ; it shall be a model to the others.— Appointments of magistrates, judgments of the people, and orders or prohibitions, when they proceed from the suffrage, shall be known to the great and free to the Plebs.

" If something arises which is outside the competence of the magistrates, the people shall create one to deal with it, and shall give him the right to do so.—The right of dealing with the people and Senate shall lie with the Consul, the Prætor, the Master of the People, the Master of Horse, and the magistrate whom the Senate delegates for the nomination of Consuls. The Tribunes whom the Plebs has appointed shall have the right to deal with the Senate, and they shall convey to the Plebs what needs to be told to it.—Moderation shall be observed in speeches made before the people and the Senate.— A Senator who is absent shall present a reason or be censured.— Senators shall speak in their place and with moderation ; they shall maintain the causes of the people.—There shall be no violence in the people. An equal or superior authority shall have the greater weight. If a proposal causes disturbance, the blame shall lie with the promoter. He who opposes a bad proposition shall be counted a good citizen.—Those who speak shall observe the auspices. They shall obey the auguries of the people. They shall only make their proposals after promulgating them, putting them forward, and publishing them in the Treasury. They shall not discuss more than one subject at a time. They shall explain their intentions to the people. They shall themselves allow magistrates and private persons to speak of them.— No privileges shall be conferred. No sentence shall be passed on the life of a citizen except in the Great Comitia and before those whom the Censors have admitted into the Classes of the people.—No gifts shall be given or taken, before, during, or after the holding of an office. If anyone infringes any of these laws, the penalty shall be equal to the offence.—The Censors shall hold the laws in their keeping. Magistrates who have returned to private life shall give account of their office to them, without being thereby exempted from legal action.

" The law is read. Take notice of the question and proceed to the ballot.

" QUINTUS CICERO : What a succinct account you have given us of all the magistracies, Marcus ! But, save for a few small additions of your own, it is almost a description of our own Republic.— CICERO : You are quite right, Quintus. For this is the well-balanced Republic which Scipio praises in our books and prefers. It could not be put into effect without that organization of magistracies. For a state is contained in its magistrates and those who rule over affairs, and the nature of a state can be recognized from the way in which they are organized. Since these matters were arranged with the greatest wisdom and moderation by our ancestors, I found nothing, or very little, to change in their laws." [1]

---

[1] *Laws*, iii, 2, 4 to 5, 12.

III

FROM WORDS TO FACTS

What is the value of the theory of Polybios and Cicero, when applied to the Roman constitution of the second century B.C. ? Apart from the fact that a thesis stated in that absolute form is always in danger of distorting and more or less contradicting the complex reality of things, both passages make one statement as an axiom and base their whole argument on it—that the Roman constitution did not change.

> Polybios writes [1] : " The attributions of each of these parts (Consuls, Senate, and people) were at that time, and still are on the whole, as follows." Cicero says [2] : " There is none of all the forms to government to compare, for constitution, organization, or discipline, with that which our fathers received from their forbears and left to us."

That the constitution remained outwardly " on the whole ", as Polybios says, the same as in the third century, there is no doubt ; only the contrary would surprise us in a people so attached to tradition and conservative, especially in the matter of forms, as the Romans. Thus, in particular, the legislation of the third century, which had shown a perceptible progress towards democracy—the *Leges Hortensiæ* and the reform of the Comitia Centuriata—was maintained. But if the appearance was unchanged, the spirit and practice of the constitution were considerably altered. The Roman constitution was not a written constitution (that was one of its fundamental characteristics), but was chiefly based on a long past of experience and a very ancient series of precedents. Polybios himself,[3] speaking of Crete, notes that " every constitution is based on two principles . . . customs and laws ". In the absence of formal texts, by which difficulties of application might be avoided or settled, realities—things and men—were called to play a part of the first importance, whether they belonged to the past, as traditions and precedents, or to the present, such as the recruiting of the government personnel, political habits, social transformation. Outwardly, things were on the whole the same, as is usual among conservative peoples, but the

[1] vi, 11, 13.   [2] *Rep.*, i, 46, 70.   [3] vi, 47, 1-2.

old constitutional fabric now housed a new political life ; oligarchy had taken possession and had adapted it for its own benefit. The dogmatic thesis of Polybios and Cicero, the now specious, rigid thesis of the constitutional equilibrium, must be supplemented and corrected by a concrete examination of the facts.

The sovereignty of the people in its Comitia, which was the basis of direct government in Rome as in other ancient cities, may, in the last analysis, be embodied in the double principle that all are eligible and all are electors. If we consider only the theory of the constitution, all Roman citizens in the full sense of the term—*cives optimo jure*— in so far as they could take part in the Comitia in person and were not debarred from all effective part in political life by living far from Rome, had the two prerogatives of eligibility [1]—*jus honorum*—and election—*jus suffragii*—both expressly implied by the very fact of citizenship. To what did these two rights come in practice, and how far did the reality correspond to the principle ?

I. *Eligibility.*—Standing, as we now do, on the ground of practice, we are faced with one hard fact. Public offices, far from being open to all, were the privilege of a small minority, and that minority, in the constitution of the second century, was a minority of nobles. New men who attained to the Consulship were exceptions, and are mentioned on account of their very rarity—Cato in 195, P. Pompeius Rufus in 141, Marius in 107, and, at the beginning of the next century, T. Didius in 98, C. Cælius Caldus in 94, and Cicero in 63.[2] One should note, too, that most of these belonged by birth to the Equestrian order, and that two of them, at least, Marius and Cicero, were no ordinary men in respect of their character and services.

" I did think," says Cicero in his speech for Murena, " that thanks to my labours lowness of origin would no longer be considered a disability in so many excellent citizens. It was in vain that they used to quote the example of new men who had done valuable services— such men as Curius, Cato, and Pompeius in the past and more recent instances like Marius, Didius, and Cælius. But when at last, after a long time, I had broken down that barrier of birth, so that henceforward the Consulship was open, as it was in the days of our ancestors, not only to blood but to merit, I little thought that when

[1] Except in the case of freedmen, as has been seen above.
[2] **LXXVII,** 40–1.

a Consul designate, of an old and distinguished family, was defended by a Consul, the son of a Roman Equestrian, his accusers would talk about the newness of his origin." [1]   Sallust, too, writes : " The nobility passed on the Consulship from one to another. Any new man, however he might have distinguished himself and whatever great deeds he might have done, was considered unworthy of the honour, and as if sullied by the taint of his birth." [2]

The causes of this systematic exclusion of new men and monopolization of the government by a few nobles were manifold.   First of all, in virtue of the old principle inherent in the ancient city-system, that the holding of public office was not a burden but an honour, no pay was attached to the magistracies ; what was more, vast sums had to be spent in various distributions to the citizens, feasts, games, etc., in order to obtain an office and to conduct it in the proper way.   You could not pass straight into the higher magistracies ; you had to go through the regular channel, the *cursus honorum*, the first step on which, the Quæstorship, was accessible at the early age of twenty-eight.   Now, a new man, entering public life late (as he usually did, by definition), was often too old to begin the whole *cursus honorum* to any purpose.   Moreover, the Senatorial nobility, whose caste-spirit had grown stronger and stronger since the end of the third century, systematically rallied together to keep out new-comers, however rich they were, who did not belong by birth to the narrow circle of the governing oligarchy.   Public spirit in Rome encouraged this selfish attitude, for the lower classes, brought up to respect social privileges, provided that their own material needs were properly satisfied, regarded it as quite natural that the magistracies should be reserved for the upper classes.   Since the Senate was open only to retired magistrates, access to it was governed by the same conditions as that to the magistracies, and the question was indeed one and the same.

So the magistracies, and therefore the Senate, were the monopoly of an aristocratic minority.   The principle that all men were eligible (except freedmen of the first generation), solemnly inscribed on the front of the constitutional edifice, was in practice purely figmentary.

II.   *Election.*—In theory, every Roman citizen *optimo jure* was an elector.   What became of his privilege in practice ?

---

[1] *Pro Mur.*, viii, 17.   [2] *Jug. War*, lxiii, 7.

The real result of the elaborate organization set up by the constitution was flagrant inequality in suffrage and even, for many citizens, complete nullification of the right to vote. In Rome there was never individual, direct, equal voting as in the Greek democracies, but only group-voting, by Curiæ, Centuries, or Tribes, which was, therefore, based on a suffrage in two stages.

Of the three great Republican assemblies in which the elector might vote—Comitia Curiata, Centuriata, Tributa—the first, the Comitia Curiata, had become in the third century a mere ghost or formality. Let us consider the two others, the Comitia Centuriata, and the Comitia Tributa, the two real and truly living expressions of the sovereignty of the people.

For the Comitia Centuriata, we have to consider two things, their composition and their working.

(a) *Composition.*—Before the reform of the middle of the third century, the inequality of the value of the vote was due to two things—age and the different number of Centuries in the various Classes. The Seniors, though naturally less numerous than the Juniors, made up almost as many Centuries in the five Classes as the latter. What was still more important, there were eighteen Equestrian Centuries, eighty Centuries in the First Class, twenty-two in the Second, twenty in the Third, twenty-two in the Fourth, thirty in the Fifth, and a Century of proletarians or *capite censi* outside the Classes. Thus the Knights and First Class together had ninety-eight votes out of a hundred and ninety-three, an absolute majority. The legal majority was in the hands of a very small minority of electors.

The reform of the middle of the third century maintained the privilege of age intact, but at least abolished the inequality between the number of Centuries in the different Classes ; every Class alike henceforward contained seventy Centuries, that is, two, one of Seniors and one of Juniors, to each of the thirty-five Tribes. But, in spite of this move towards general equalization, we still see a glaring inequality between the different electors, if we consider the number of men in each Class, since, in accordance with the usual distribution of wealth, the Classes were far more crowded as they stood lower in the social scale.

Let us try to establish some figures, at least of an approximate kind. The strength of the eighteen Equestrian Centuries is known exactly ; there were in Rome, at the beginning of the second century B.C., 1,800 Knights *equo publico*.[1] The strength of the First Class can also be deduced from the fact that at the end of the third century it all served on horseback. According to Polybios the whole of the mobilizable Roman cavalry in 225 numbered 23,000 Roman and Campanian horse, which number comprises three distinct elements—the eighteen Equestrian Centuries of cavalry *equo publico*, the Roman cavalry of the First Class, and those of the citizens *sine suffragio*, among whom were the Campanians. We know that there were 4,000 Campanian horse. The general proportion of citizens *sine suffragio* to citizens *optimo jure* gives a total of 6,000–7,000 non-Campanian cavalry *sine suffragio*, that is, a total of 10,000–11,000 mounted citizens *sine suffragio*. There remain, therefore, 12,000 or 13,000 men for the whole of the cavalry *optimo jure*, that is, the Equestrian Centuries and the First Class. If we subtract from this total the known number of cavalry *equo publico*, 1,800, we get an approximate total of about 10,000 men for Roman cavalry other than *equo publico*, that is, for the mobilizable total of the First Class.

There remain Classes Two to Five and the Century of proletarians or *capite censi* outside the Classes. Dionysios of Halicarnassos [2] says that in the time of Servius Tullius there were as many *capite censi* as citizens owning land. To apply this estimate to the distant days of Servius Tullius is mere anachronism, but the fact is doubtless true of a later period, that in which the so-called Servian organization, the Centuriate system, was fully developed, the end of the fifth century, and the beginning of the fourth. But one observation must be added. Those whom Dionysios calls proletarians are those who, in the Servian organization, have not the minimum of wealth needed in the Fifth and last Class, 12,500 *asses* according to Dionysios and 11,000

---

[1] Livy, i, 36, 7, and Cic., *Rep.*, ii, 20, 36, give for the Royal period the figure of 1,800 knights, and the latter makes Scipio Æmilianus add " a custom which has been maintained to our own day ", and therefore, at least, to the time which we are discussing here. Cato, in a speech in the Senate (H. Jordan's ed., p. 66, lxiii) had unsuccessfully tried to have their strength raised to 2,200. On the question, see **XIX**, vi, 119 (and n. 2), 120, 293–4.

[2] vii, 59.

according to Livy. If the proletarians were already half of the whole citizen body in the Centuriate organization of the fifth century, their preponderance must have been infinitely greater in the middle of the second century, when the middle class had so much decreased. The fact is certain, but we have no means of translating it into exact figures. We must therefore start from another side.

The Tribune Philippus declared, as we have seen, in 104 B.C., that there were not 2,000 land-owners in the Roman citizen body. Now, at that time the census of mobilizable citizens gave about 394,000 citizens (394,736 in 125 and 394,336 in 115). There were, therefore, in fact, practically only proletarians left, and we have direct confirmation of this in the fact that in order to obtain the contingents wanted for the legions Marius had to incorporate these men in masses. A situation of this kind is due to remote political and economic causes, and does not arise in one day. C. Gracchus had to forbid enlistment under the age of seventeen. In 151, L. Licinius Lucullus had serious difficulty in recruiting his army for Spain, and earlier still, in 180, a similar fact is reported. At that same date—a most important piece of information on account of its exactitude—there was great difficulty in making up nine legions. Now, apart from cavalry, nine legions, with an average of 4,200 infantry in each (for the legion of 6,000 men only began to appear in the war with Perseus), represent a total infantry strength of about 37,800 men.

What total of available legionary infantry, that is, of citizens of Classes Two to Five, does this figure imply? The mobilizable citizen is liable, according to Polybios, to sixteen campaigns (*stipendia*) in all. The normal levy only covers those citizens aged between seventeen and forty-six, the Juniors. The minimum number of mobilizable Juniors, therefore, if the nine legions are to be brought up to establishment, is about 70,000. But the Classes do not contain only the mobilizable Juniors; we must add the Juniors who are unfit for service and all the Seniors, that is, citizens aged over forty-six. According to the usual statistics of population, these two elements are to the total of fit Juniors in a proportion of 57 to 100, that is, in the present case, about 40,000 men. Conclusion: to maintain nine legions at their normal strength Classes Two to Five had to contain at least 70,000 mobilizable Juniors or 110,000 men aged over seventeen.   Now, this minimum was not reached, or, at least, it was only reached with great difficulty, since, in 180, it was extremely difficult to make up nine legions. In the middle of the second century, with the middle class rapidly disappearing—once more, let us remember the words of the Tribune Philippus in 104—there can be no doubt that the shortage was still greater.

So, about 180 B.C., the approximate total of mobilizable citizens aged from seventeen to sixty, the Juniors of the active army and the Seniors of the territorial force, were at the very most about 100,000 men, confined to the four lowest Classes.   To obtain the number of full citizen electors, we must deduct the total of citizens without suffrage and add citizens *optimo jure* aged over sixty.   Before the second Punic War, about two-thirds of the citizen body were full citizens, while one-third were citizens *sine suffragio*. If we assume that the proportion was the same at the beginning of the second century, we get a maximum of 70,000 full citizens who are mobilizable (i.e. aged between seventeen and sixty) for Classes Two to Five.   To these we must add the men over sixty, not mobilizable but entitled to vote ; according to the usual proportion (one-fifth of all adults), these must be 14,000 to 15,000 men.   Therefore Classes Two to Five must have contained about 85,000 electors all told.   So we get : Knights *equo publico*, 1,800 ; First Class, 12,000 ;   Classes Two to Five, all together, 85,000 ; proletarians or *capite censi*, at least 130,000 ;   such are the general statistics which one can make out of the electoral body of Rome in the first quarter of the second century B.C.

If these figures are accepted, how were votes distributed within the Centuriate organization ?   If the numbers of men in the different Classes were unequal, with 12,000 in the First Class and an average of over 20,000 in Classes Two to Five, the inequality of the numbers of electors in the different Centuries was even more glaring, in spite of the reform of the third century.

Equestrian Centuries.—$\frac{1,800}{18}$, or 100 electors to a Century.

First Class.—Here a new factor comes in—that of age.

In this and the four following Classes we must distinguish between Centuries of Seniors and those of Juniors. If we accept the usual proportion of men between seventeen and forty-six to those over forty-six, we get the following figures : about 5,000 Seniors, with an average of $\frac{5,000}{35} = 142$ electors to a Century ; about 7,000 Juniors, with an average of $\frac{7,000}{35} = 200$ electors to a Century.

Classes Two to Five.—Total, 85,000. Average number of electors in a Class, 21,000. Seniors, $\frac{9,800}{35} = 280$ electors per Century ; Juniors, $\frac{11,000}{35} = 320$ electors per Century. But it should be remembered that we do not know the strength of these four Classes individually, and that the lower ones were certainly very much larger than the higher, as their members were poorer.

Proletarians or *capite censi*.—One century of about 130,000 electors.

From these figures one may draw two conclusions regarding the composition of the Comitia Centuriata in the final shape given to them by the great constitutional reform of the third century.

1. The votes of individual electors were very unequal in value. The inequality was due to two things—to differences of wealth, as is obvious when one compares the 100 electors of the Equestrian Century with the 130,000 (at least) in the Century of proletarians or *capite censi*, and to difference of age, since the Centuries of Seniors were smaller than those of Juniors, yet they carried equal weight in voting.

2. In virtue of the strict constitutional principle by which all voting was in groups, in this case the Classes and Centuries, the legal majority did not correspond to the numerical majority. Legally, since the reform of the third century, a majority could be reached with the vote of the Third Class. The total number of Centuries was 373. The absolute majority was 187. The total number of Centuries, down to and including the Third Class and the two Centuries of workmen, was 230, i.e., a majority, if the eighteen Equestrian Centuries and the first three Classes all voted unanimously. But this legal majority actually represented 1,800 electors in the Equestrian Centuries plus 12,000 in the First Class plus a maximum of 42,000 in Classes Two and Three, in all 55,800. The minority, the Fourth and

Fifth Classes and the proletarians or *capite censi*, represented at least 42,000 electors in Classes Four and Five plus 130,000 in the Century of proletarians, that is, over 170,000 men, and in reality far more, and the disproportion increased all through the second century. The hard fact was that the legal majority of the 230 top Centuries represented less than a quarter of the electorate. For that legal majority to correspond to the numerical majority, it would have had to exceed 115,000 electors, that is, all the rest of the citizens, Fourth Class, Fifth Class, and proletarians, would have had to be called to vote, and that was never done in practice. So wealth and age both acted in the same direction, towards conservatism.

(b) *Working*.—The votes of the Comitia Centuriata were not all given at once. The Classes voted in turn—first the " prerogative " Century, which was one of the Centuries of Juniors in the First Class, drawn by lot, then the eighteen Equestrian Centuries, and then the other Classes downwards. The president of the Comitia stopped voting as soon as the majority was reached ; if the Equestrian Centuries and first three Classes agreed, there was an absolute majority and no more votes were taken. The Fourth and Fifth Classes and the Century of proletarians did not vote. If there was disagreement among the higher Classes, as but rarely happened, the Fourth Class might be called to give its vote, but in practice it was never necessary to go lower. Therefore for the electors of the lower units—the Fifth Class and the proletarian Century—the vote was not merely of less value, it was non-existent save in theory ; and so it was usually for the Fourth Class.

Let us now consider the second of the great Roman assemblies, the Comitia Tributa. In composition and working they did not show the great inequalities inherent in the Comitia Centuriata. In composition, there was no discrimination of age. The same is true of their working. Votes were not given in succession, as in the other assembly, but simultaneously. In consequence, contrary to what happened in the Comitia Centuriata, in the Comitia Tributa all citizen electors voted in all circumstances.

Does this mean that we should find in the Comitia Tributa the strict equality of votes of which there was not even a remote possibility in the Comitia Centuriata ? The question will be answered by the facts.

Since 241 B.C., when the last two Tribes had been created, Velina and Quirina, there had been thirty-five Tribes, and this number was maintained. If the whole citizen body about the beginning of the second century contained about 230,000 electors, there was an average of over 6,500 citizens to a Tribe. But the real strength of the Tribes was far from being equal. We have not the exact statistics by which to confirm the differences in the strength of all the various Tribes, but there is one striking fact—the enormous difference in strength between the four Urban Tribes and the thirty-one Rustic Tribes. At the beginning of the second century, the population of the town of Rome was at least 150,000 (we do not know the exact figure), so that there must have been about 40,000 urban electors. These urban electors were divided among the four Urban Tribes, so that there were on an average 10,000 citizens in a Tribe. Moreover, there were two classes of citizens—freedmen and proletarians—who automatically went into the four Urban Tribes, wherever their domicile might be. Appius Claudius, in his famous Censorship, had distributed them among all the Tribes, Urban and Rustic, without distinction. Q. Fabius Rullianus and P. Decius Mus, the Censors of 304, put them all back into their four old Tribes. A similar step was taken by the Censors of 220, L. Æmilius Papus and C. Flaminius. Later, the Censors of 169, Ti. Sempronius Gracchus and C. Claudius Pulcher, acted still more drastically, crowding all freedmen, not merely into the four Urban Tribes, but into a single one of them, which was chosen by lot, the Esquiline Tribe. An exception was made in favour of freedmen who had a son aged over five or landed property worth more than 30,000 sesterces ; this exception considerably mitigated the severity of the measure.

If we subtract the 40,000 urban electors, freedmen, and proletarians, belonging to one or other of the four Urban Tribes, we are left with a maximum of 100,000 electors for all the Rustic Tribes, or an average of about 3,000 ($\frac{100,000}{31}$) to a Tribe. So the value of any one vote was at least ten times as great in the Rustic Tribes as in the Urban. Now, at the beginning of the second century, the mass of the urban electors were proletarians, for non-proletarian urban electors had their names put on the Rustic Tribes in which they had property. So, though the process was not the same as in the Comitia Centuriata, the result was the same in practice ; the value of the poor man's vote was very much reduced, and the preponderant influence was given to the possessing classes, the rich men and the middle classes who made up the mass of the Rustic Tribes.

Finally, if we would obtain an exact opinion of the working of the Roman constitution in the second century, there is a last factor, not least in importance, which we should take into account. The citizen, who had a portion of the popular sovereignty, had to exercise his rights in person, in the centre of the City, the town of Rome, at the actual seat of the Comitia, the Forum or Campus Martius as the case might be. The result of this absolutely rigid condition was that the greater number of those who had the right to vote were unable to do so, since they were now distributed all over Italy, and some of them even in the provinces, and could not make the journey, except in very rare cases. Even citizens living in the surrounding countryside, for whom the problem of distance was not insurmountable, were restricted by one of the *Leges Hortensiæ*, by which no Comitia could be held on market-days, the very days on which the countryman usually went to Rome on business.

By the force of circumstances, the Comitia, Centuriata and Tributa alike, came to include only those citizens who were on the spot, those of the town. It is true that the constitution set up safeguards against this unfair and dangerous monopoly. Legally, the rural element had a crushing majority—310 Centuries of Rustic Tribes out of a total of 373 in the Comitia Centuriata since the reform of the third century, and 31 votes of the Rustic Tribes out of a total of 35 in the Comitia Tributa, one single elector being in theory enough to represent a Century or a Tribe, since no quorum was required. But in practice these scattered representatives of the legal majority, lost among the masses of the urban electorate, were exposed to every method of intimidation and pressure, as may be imagined where the numbers were so disproportionate, and by the very nature of things the urban proletariate, the dregs of the citizen population, came, especially in the Comitia Tributa, which had become the most important of all, to exercise a preponderant and sometimes exclusive influence which was as undesirable as it was unjustified.

IV

THE ROMAN OLIGARCHY AND ITS MONOPOLY OF GOVERNMENT

In the third century, popular sovereignty and republican equality had really become only appearances in the Roman constitution. The real goverment was in the hands of an aristocracy, the Senatorial nobility, which wielded the power and was bent on keeping it to itself. But since that time a double phenomenon had taken place, which had precipitated the tendency and had, in reality, turned the old constitution into something quite new ; this was the gradual disappearance of the middle class and the condensation of the aristocracy into an oligarchy. Behind the constitutional forms of the second century the government was held by an oligarchy which grew steadily closer and more exclusive, and this new fact was to have immense and lasting consequences for the Republican constitution.

The formation of the governing oligarchy, as we find it complete at the middle of the second century B.C., took place in two phases. First, the power was concentrated in the hands of the Senate, a process the causes and essential stages of which have been described. Then, within that aristocracy, a narrow oligarchy was formed of the small circle of Consuls and Consulars, which gradually appropriated all dignities and power to itself.

What were the distinctive characteristics of this oligarchy ? From the political point of view, it comprised the aristocratic families—Patrician or Plebeian, it does not matter which—which supplied most of the higher Curule magistrates, the Censors and Consuls. Let us recall Sallust's bluntly descriptive phrase,[1] " The nobility passed on the Consulship among themselves from hand to hand—*Nobilitas consulatum inter se per manum tradebat.*" Socially, they had the money, but they were not alone in this for, as we have seen, since the second Punic War a powerful class of capitalists had grown up, the Knights. But the fact remains that, since the official career entailed enormous expenditure, it was quite impossible

[1] *Jug. War*, lxiii, 6-7.

to belong to the oligarchy unless one was rich. The oligarchy enjoyed outward distinctions in common with all the Senatorial aristocracy, the *jus imaginum*, or right to exhibit in public the images of ancestors who had held a Curule magistracy, and the gold ring. Lastly, in practice if not by right, it obtained a prerogative which, with its exclusive policy, played a chief part in making it a closed caste, the system of hereditary succession. Men inherited honorary distinctions, such as the right to show images, the broad-bordered tunic, the gold ring, and they inherited magistracies and the Senatorial dignity. The sons of Senators were regarded as destined for the Senate by right of birth, and went to the Senate House and listened to debates to familiarize themselves with the conduct of business ; in the eyes of public opinion it was quite natural that they should one day succeed their fathers. An exclusive nobility, possessing wealth, outward marks of distinction, and hereditary privileges, in a word, a real political and social monopoly without a legal basis, an aristocracy which had become a caste, such, in its essentials, was the Roman oligarchy of the second century B.C.

Favoured by the sovereign necessities of the policy of conquest, which more and more required the concentration of power in the hands of a few, the oligarchy made itself mistress of the whole State ; government, diplomacy, war, finance, in the end it managed them all.

Government, first. The Senate, whose constitutional rôle, under the inexorable pressure of external circumstances, had steadily increased for a century, was the very stronghold of the oligarchy. The Consulars, the most influential element in the Senate, belonged to the oligarchy, and, by the jealous watch which it kept on the Consulship, which was strictly closed to new men, the oligarchy protected itself against disagreeable surprises and consequences. It kept to itself the magistracies, at least the higher Curule magistracies, and, consequently, the pro-magistracies and provicial governorships. No doubt, it could still meet with opposition in the exercise of its governmental monopoly from the Comitia, recalcitrant magistrates, and the Tribunes, but thanks to the change which the constitution had in practice undergone since the third century, it had more than one way of defeating any such resistance.

The gradual disappearance of the rural middle class had emptied the Comitia of their soundest element and transferred the preponderance in elections from the country Plebs to the town Plebs. Now, this latter could be managed by various means—corruptions, illegal canvassing, largesses, shows—and the facts, particularly the two Consular laws on illegal canvassing, *Lex Cornelia Bœbia* of 181 and *Lex Cornelia Fulvia* of 159, prove that these were not neglected. Against obstructive and intractable magistrates who by some chance had managed· to obtain office the oligarchy had the Senate and the many weapons which the old constitution placed in its hands. Ambitious men could be restrained by a natural anxiety about their future career, and, if grand methods were necessary, resort could be had to the Tribune's veto, a supremely efficacious instrument for reducing recalcitrant magistrates to a desirable submissiveness.

Lastly, the Tribuneship, the orthodox opposition magistracy, had lost its traditional character, and since the third century, except in a few cases like that of Flaminius, which shocked opinion, the aristocracy had completely neutralized it by incorporating it, like the Plebian Ædileship, in the *cursus honorum.* As early as 294, Livy [1] shows us the Tribunes of the Plebs turned into an obedient instrument of the nobility, *mancipia nobilium.* Afterwards the movement became even more marked. Perhaps as early as the time of the second Punic War, the Atinian Plebiscite conferred the official rank of Senators on the Tribunes, and doubtless also on the Ædiles of the Plebs. By the *Lex Villia Annælis* of 180, the Plebian Ædileship was introduced into the *cursus honorum.* Lastly, about 154, the *Leges Ælia* and *Fufia* completed the neutralization of the Tribuneship by the governing oligarchy. Among other clauses regarding the observation of auspices, they provided that in future the *obnuntiatio* (declaration that the omens were unfavourable to holding an assembly) of the Tribunes should be accepted against that of the Consuls, and vice versa. Equitable as this regulation might seem, in practice it favoured only the Consuls. The Tribunes, who already had a traditional right of veto, gained nothing by the further privilege of *obnuntiatio*, while the Consuls, who had been helpless against the

[1] x, 37, 11.

Tribunician veto, received a similar means of action, and especially of protection, against the legislative prerogative of the Tribunes.   So, through the Consuls, the Senatorial oligarchy recovered, in indirect but effective form, the veto, the *auctoritas Patrum*, of which the *Lex Hortensia* had deprived it.   The domestication of the Tribuneship, which had been pursued so long and with such patience, was at last complete. The Tribunes did not return to their old tradition and recover their voice until the Gracchi came.

But here again it is in foreign policy, in the actual needs of conquest and administration, that we must look for the underlying reasons of the constitutional change in the second century which was so profitable to the oligarchy. The advance of imperialism in that century and the extraordinary strain in military, political, and administrative matters which the conquest and the organization of the Mediterranean basin put upon the old Roman constitution had the result of placing new weapons and more powerful means of action at the disposal of the oligarchy.   The great instruments of imperialism—diplomacy, the army, finance— were so many levers of which it had complete control, and if, on the whole, it served the interests of Rome well, it was careful (charity beginning at home) not to neglect its own. The facts are there, to give us many proofs of it.

In accordance with the general dogma of the sovereignty of the people, which was the very foundation of the Roman constitution, the great official acts affecting the foreign policy of the State were ordered directly and solely by the people, assembled in its Comitia, that is, in the Comitia Centuriata.   The people declared war, ratified treaties, and concluded alliances.

" The people," says Polybios,[1] " has the power of adopting or rejecting laws and, most important of all, it deliberates on war and peace.   Alliances, peace-terms, and treaties are ratified or rejected by the people."

But if, in this particular case, the supreme decision lay with the people, there was another body in Rome which had its word to say, and that was the Senate.

Declaration of war, first.   In practice, by the rules of custom (*mos majorum*) in force, the initiative in declaring war lay

[1] vi, 14, 9–12 ; xxi, 30, 16 ; Cic., *Pro Balbo*, xv, 34.

with the Senate. It considered whether the breach should be proposed to the people, and, if it decided that this should be done, it caused a proposal to that effect (*lex de bello indicendo*) to be placed on the agenda of the Comitia Centuriata by the presiding magistrate. If the Senate objected to a breach proposed in the Comitia themselves, it easily found a magistrate who was ready to interpose his veto. As a general rule, the people confined itself to ratifying the opinion of the Senate. But there is at least one example to the contrary, which occurred on a memorable occasion. In 200, the Centuries almost unanimously rejected the proposal of war with Philip of Macedon presented by the Consul P. Sulpicius Galba.[1] But the Senate would not allow itself beaten ; it caused the proposal to be placed on the agenda again, and in a second vote the people acquiesced.[2] Once a declaration of war was legally valid, it was usually conveyed to the foreign sovereign or people concerned by a Senatorial commission specially appointed for the purpose.

Conclusion of peace.[3] The general in immediate charge of operations received the proposals of the enemy, and he could accept them as preliminaries and sign them, but only provisionally and subject to ratification by the Senate and people.[4] He granted an armistice, during which he transmitted the proposed terms to the Senate. The Senate might reject these without more ado, and in that case the people had no say in the matter ; if, after discussing them, it accepted them, it requested the Tribunes of the Plebs to have them ratified by an express vote of the people, a law or a plebiscite. When that general ratification was obtained, the general, assisted by a Senatorial commission of five, or more often ten, members, settled points of detail and disputed questions on the spot. If there was serious difficulty, the matter was referred to the Senate, which settled it in the last resort. When agreement was reached, the foreign ruler or people sent an embassy to Rome for the final exchange of ratifications.

International treaties, lastly. All proposals of international treaties or conventions were referred to the Senate, which examined them and, if necessary, amended them. Then two cases might arise. The most important of these acts,

---

[1] Livy, xxxi, 6, 3.   [2] Livy, xxxi, 8, 1–2.
[3] **CXLI**, ii, 472–9 ; **CXXXIV**, i, 44–157.   [4] **CXXXIV**, i, 29–44.

treaties of offensive or defensive alliance properly so called (*fœdera societatis*), had to receive the ratification of the people. Others, such as treaties of friendship (*fœdera amicitiæ*) or mere renewals of previous treaties, did not require this formality and were made valid by a simple *Senatus consultum.*

The declaration of war, the conclusion of peace, the signature of treaties are manifestations of international activity which, although they may be important, and, indeed, because they are important, are only exceptions in the life of a people. Its ordinary life is taken up with the many actions which go before them, accompany them, and follow them—the preparation of war and peace, the execution of treaties, negotiations regarding the conclusion of alliances, or, in brief, the whole domain of diplomacy.

The direction of the foreign policy of a country, in all times and in all places, requires two first qualities in the body which undertakes it—permanence and capacity. In the absence of a special diplomatic corps like our own, which the ancients in general did not possess, that vital function could not be entrusted to the Comitia or to the magistrates, for neither had the permanence or capacity needed for the successful conduct of affairs. Moreover, the chief magistrates of the State, the Consuls, were too often absent from Rome, being called or kept away by their duties, to give the necessary attention to international questions, which had to be dealt with in the capital itself. Nor had they the necessary staff. That being so, only one organ in the Roman constitution was available—the Senate. Normally, the Senatorial office was held for life. The Senate was composed of retired magistrates, the oldest and most influential of whom had gone through the whole *cursus honorum* and acquired, or had the opportunity to acquire, indisputable competence in the conduct of the highest offices. The Senate, by the very nature of its functions, was always present in Rome. In virtue of the number and the past experience of its members, the Senate, and the Senate alone, was always able to form a diplomatic corps, at least for any particular occasion. The work of diplomacy which contributed to making Rome the mistress of the Mediterranean basin was prepared within the Senate and carried out by the Senate.

The Senate concentrated the direction of Roman diplomacy in its hands.

" If one goes to Rome when the two Consuls are away," says Polybios,[1] " the constitution seems to be purely aristocratic. This, indeed, is the opinion of a great many Greeks and kings, since it is almost always the Senate that deals with their affairs."

The Senate showed itself very strict and exclusive in this matter. In 169 B.C., it caused a *Senatus consultum* to be read publicly in all the cities of the Peloponnese, to the effect that the allied peoples owed no assistance or service to Roman generals unless the Senate had decreed it expressly,[2] and it carefully made it an absolute rule never to use agents or intermediaries who were not members of its own order. Apart from the general direction of foreign policy, the diplomatic activity of the Senate took two forms—the reception of foreign embassies and the sending of Roman embassies abroad.

When a foreign embassy came to Rome for any purpose— to ask for help, to offer submission, to appeal to arbitration, to make various complaints, or as a mere act of courtesy— its first act was to request an audience of the Senate. The latter might grant it or refuse it. In case of refusal, the embassy had to leave Italy within a determined time, which varied in length, being a month at the most but usually less. A *Senatus consultum* of 166 [3] even forbade kings to appear in Rome, on principle, and Eumenes of Pergamon, who had landed at Brundusium at the time when it was being passed, had to depart forthwith. But this was a personal measure, taken for the particular case, and it was soon allowed to lapse. If the Senate granted an audience, it first saw to the lodging of the embassy, in the Villa Publica on the Campus Martius or in the city itself, according as the embassy came from enemies or friends. During their stay on Roman territory foreign ambassadors enjoyed the privilege of inviolability. Then the Senate gave them audience, in the form of a full sitting or, if there were a great number of embassies or for some other reason, of a sitting of a committee. These committees, which were appointed by the Senate or left to the president to appoint, heard the embassy and then

[1] vi, 13, 8–9.   [2] Livy, xliii, 17, 2–3 ; Polyb., xxviii, 16, 1.
[3] Polyb., xxx, 19, 6–7.

made their report. In 193, an embassy came from Antiochos to ask for the alliance of the Roman people, and was referred by the Senate to a committee of ten, which presented its report the next day.[1] In 183, four Lacedæmonian embassies were heard in the same conditions.[2] In 170, a deputation from the town of Thisbe in Bœotia presented itself to the Senate on the 9th October and asked to be allowed to set forth its grievances without delay. The Senate ordered the presiding Prætor to appoint a committee of five to hear it and draft a reply. The audience was held, and the report was submitted and ratified at a full sitting of the Senate on the 14th October. To judge from the minutes, the text of which is preserved in the *Senatus consultum* from Thisbe, the Senate was not in the habit of allowing urgent matters to accumulate in its files.[3]

Secondly, the Senate sent commissions abroad for various diplomatic purposes—the delivery of ultimatums (the mission to Carthage in 218 before the second Punic War), the renewal of alliances and friendships (172 to Macedonia, 173 to Ptolemy VI Philometor), the settlement of disputes (193 to Africa, 186 and 174 to Macedonia, 155–154 to Cyprus and Asia), requests of assistance (192 to Greece, against Antiochos, 171 to Massinissa, Carthage, Crete, and Asia, against Perseus), the execution of treaties (196 to Greece, 189 to Asia Minor, 167 to Macedon and Illyria), to make complaints (218 to Hannibal in Spain and to Carthage, 203 to Philip of Macedon, 195 to Carthage, 183 to Prusias and to the Gauls, 172 to the Illyrians), or simply to investigate, *ad res inspiciendas* (208 to Gaul, 173 to Macedon, 172 to Asia, Crete, and Rhodes, 171 to Greece). The appointment of a Roman embassy abroad lay with the Senate, and the Senate alone. The *Senatus consultum* which ordered that it should be sent also laid down the number of its members and sometimes, too, the categories of Senators from which they should be drawn. The number of members usually varied with the importance of the mission—they might be two, three, four, five, and in especially important cases ten. They were not all of equal rank ; commissions of two generally consisted of a Curule Senator (a Consular or Prætorian) and a *Pedarius* (inferior Senator), while those of five contained three or four

[1] Livy, xxxiv, 57, 1–4.   [2] Polyb., xxiii, 4, 1–8.   [3] *I.G.*, vii, 2225.

Curule Senators, and those of ten, six Curule Senators. The man who was highest in the Senatorial scale presided, and, in the case of equality, the senior man in his category. Appointment by the Senate, being safest in all respects, was usual, especially when the business was very serious, but sometimes the Senate left it to the president, or even to lot.

Whatever their nature, numbers, and composition might be, these Senatorial commissions all had two characteristics : they were composed entirely of Senators and, what was very important, they gave a very large place to specialists in the various matters in question. The magistrates (Consuls or Prætors), or pro-magistrates (Proconsuls or Proprætors) employed outside Rome, and their staffs (Legates and Military Tribunes), being constantly renewed by the operation of the principle of annual office, easily furnished the diplomatic personnel needed. Let us take a few definite instances. In 196, a commission of ten was sent to Macedon and Greece to execute the peace-treaty concluded with Philip ; of the six members known to us,[1] two, the most influential, namely P. Sulpicius Galba and P. Villius Tappulus, both of them Consuls, the former in 200 for the second time and the latter in 199, to whom we should doubtless add Flamininus's brother Lucius, had had direct experience of Eastern affairs. In 193, a Senatorial deputation was sent to Antiochos [2] ; the three members composing it, P. Sulpicius, P. Villius, and P. Ælius, had already taken part in the conferences of Corinth or in those of Lysimacheia in 195. In 193, the commission which gave audience to the envoys of Antiochos was identical with the commission of ten of 196, and Flamininus, one of the chief experts in Greek and Eastern affairs, was given the charge of answering them.[3] In 183, the Senatoral commission set up in Rome to hear the Lacedæmonian representatives contained three members, Flamininus, Q. Cæcilius Metellus, and Appius Claudius Pulcher, all of whom had already served on Roman embassies in the Peloponnese.[4]

This constant effort to maintain continuity in the conduct

[1] Polyb., xviii, 48, 2–4 ; Livy, xxxiii, 24, 7 ; 35, 1.
[2] Livy, xxxiv, 59, 8 ; xxxv, 13, 6 ; M. Holleaux, in **XLV**, 1913, 12 ff.
[3] Livy, xxxiv, 57, 1–5.   [4] Polyb., xxiii, 4, 7.

of foreign policy was obviously to the interest of the State as a whole, but the oligarchy, which supplied the senior personnel, also benefited immensely by it as a caste.

After diplomacy, we come to the army. In virtue of the fundamental conception of the ancient city, which admitted no distinction between civil and military powers, the chief magistrates of the City were, by definition, the commanders-in-chief of the civic body when mobilized, that is, the army. So the oligarchy had in addition to its political privilege a military privilege, or rather, it was one single prerogative seen in two aspects. Since the disappearance of the Dictatorship during the second Punic War, the higher military command had belonged to the Consuls. Each, by the constitutional rule, was entitled to a Consular army (*exercitus consularis*), consisting of two Roman legions and the corresponding corps of allies. But since Rome had won preeminence in the Mediterranean basin two high commands were not enough. Moreover, the creation of the provinces had led to the institution of a certain number of permanent commands outside Italy—two (Sicily and Sardinia-Corsica) in the third century and four more after the conquest of Spain (197, Hither Spain and Further Spain), Macedonia (148–147), and Carthaginian Africa (146), or six in all. This need of more high commands was met in two ways, one extraordinary, the extension of the period of office of Consuls and Prætors, and one ordinary, the creation of new Prætors. In both cases the result was the same. Bound to the Consulship and Prætorship, in whatever form it might be, the chief military commands were in the hands of the governing oligarchy.

This was not all. Every commander of an army was aided by lieutenants, Legates, placed under his orders, who were drawn from the Senate and were appointed by the Senate itself on the recommendation of the commander-in-chief. Every legion was under six Military Tribunes, who took duty in turns, monthly or daily. Since 207 B.C., the twenty-four Tribunes of the normal number of legions had been elected by the Comita Tributa (*Tribuni Militum a Populo*), while the Tribunes of the supplementary legions (*Tribuni Militum Rufuli*) were appointed by the general commanding the army. Now, in the constitutional system of the Republic, these Military Tribuneships were not a purely military grade, but a mere stage preliminary to the *cursus honorum*. In exceptional cases, when there was a particularly difficult war to be waged, like the third Macedonian War or the Spanish Wars, they might be chosen from among men of experience, Ædiles, Prætors, or even Consuls ; but usually they were beginners who took this post as a preliminary to a political career. Scipio Africanus and Flamininus, in the second Punic War, held the Military Tribuneship, the former at the age of twenty and the latter at eighteen. Commanders-in-chief, Legates, Tribunes, all the higher grades were for the greater part provided by the oligarchy and, in practice, these posts were monopolized by it.

One should add that the Senate, the great organ of the oligarchy, had complete control of the chief military commands. It determined their number and their nature, it distributed the land and sea forces, it established military budgets, it supervised army-commanders, it co-ordinated operations, as became more and more necessary as Roman policy extended its field of action, and, when the campaign was over, it had a supreme voice in deciding what rewards should be given to generals and to men.

Lastly, the third great instrument of the Roman conquest was finance. Down to the formation of the first provinces in the third century, the financial system of Rome was based on three kinds of revenues—direct taxes, indirect taxes, and the revenues of State land and monopolies. The direct tax was that laid on a man's whole capital (*tributum ex censu*). Indirect taxation took two chief forms—customs (*portoria*) and the tax of a twentieth on the emancipation of slaves (*vicesima manumissionum*). The revenues of State land and monopolies, lastly, comprised the tax on leased-out State lands (*vectigal*), the pasture-due (*scriptura*), and the salt-monopoly. The traditional system of taxation may not have undergone any great change by the third century, but at least its returns had increased in proportion to the objects taxed—the tax on capital with the increase of those liable to it, that is, of citizens, and of their wealth, customs with their transference to the boundaries of the Italian peninsula, and the revenues of public domains with the extension of the conquest.

But these revenues by themselves would have been insufficient to support the great policy which Rome had begun to conduct in the second third of the third century. A new idea took form. War must support war. Countries first defeated and then conquered must pay (in three chief forms, war-contributions, booty, and provincial tax) not only the costs of the war but those of the permanent administration which victory imposed on the conqueror.

Whether exceptional or permanent, the exploitation of the conquered countries supplied the treasury with means to cope with a financial task which the constant extension of Roman policy had increased beyond all bounds, and the result was the creation of a true imperial budget. Not only did the rest of the world come to pay the costs of its conquest, but a time soon came when the State was able to relieve the fiscal burdens of its own citizens. After the triumph of Æmilius Paullus in 167, the tax on capital, the keystone of the old financial system, ceased to be collected in practice. It was not declared abolished by law, and, indeed, the need for such a measure did not make itself felt. Since the tax on capital had never been regarded as a regular, permanent tax, it did not need to be abolished. It was enough to refrain from ordering it to be collected, except when the new resources should prove insufficient, when the ancient tradition could be revived. In fact, this case never arose during the Republic, and, down to the death of Cæsar, the tax on capital was relegated to the company of ancient practices which, very naturally, nobody wanted to see restored. This year of 167 was a turning-point in the history of the Roman State, for it saw the consecration of a financial system, arising from the conquest, under which the City paid as little as possible and the balancing of the budget depended almost entirely on the methodical exploitation of the conquered peoples.

Now, both for its general drawing-up and for its principal subdivisions, this imperial budget was under the sole and direct control of the oligarchy. The great organs of financial administration in the Rome of the second century were, in the first place, the Senate, and after it the magistrates. Polybios [1] defines the financial competence of the Senate exactly :—

[1] vi, 13, 1–4.

" The first function of the Senate," he says, " is to administer the public treasury, for it controls all revenue and expenditure. The Quæstors cannot take out the smallest sum for public purposes without a decree of the Senate, except for the Consuls. Even the heaviest expenses of all, those incurred by the Censors every five years for building and repairing public works, come under the Senate, which gives the Censors the necessary authority."

The Senate was, then, the highest financial authority in Rome ; with it lay both the management and the general supervision of Roman finances.

Of the magistracies, two in particular are concerned— the Censorship and the Quæstorship. Every five years the Censors made up the budget of receipts (*vectigalia*) and expenditure (*ultro tributa*). Under the heading of receipts, they farmed out the taxes to the highest bidder, and under that of expenditure they made contracts for military supplies, the building and upkeep of public works, and so on. The two Urban Quæstors had charge of the treasury (*ærarium Saturni*). Under their control, the sums taken or paid out by the treasury were entered in the official books by scribes. In the provinces, there were Quæstors attached to the governors who held a similar office.

Lastly, to complete the picture, let us recall what was said in connection with the struggle between the Senatorial and Equestrian orders, that at the middle of the second century, in virtue of the *Lex Calpurnia de Pecuniis Repetundis* of 149, the oligarchy definitely laid hands on the judicial power, the last and not the least of its great constitutional conquests. The extraordinary advance of Roman power in the first half of the century, the satisfaction which it gave to the national pride, the advantages which it brought to the population as a whole, all contributed to establishing its authority and enhancing the Senate's prestige. The Roman State belonged to it, and it did not hesitate to deal with it accordingly.

" At home and abroad," Sallust says in his *Jugurthine War*,[1] " everything was done at the bidding of a few men. Theirs were treasury, provinces, magistracies, glory, triumphs ; the people bore military service and poverty." One must give the original words : " *Paucorum arbitrio belli domique agitabatur. Penes eosdem aerarium, provinciæ, magistratus, gloriæ, triumphique erant ; populus militia atque inopia urgebatur.*"

[1] xli, 7–8.

That is the formula of the whole oligarchical system. It was a political, military, financial, and judicial monópoly, which was imposed on Rome by the prodigious extension of her conquest and the creation of the Mediterranean State and was accepted by a public spirit broken in to discipline and traditionally respectful of social superiority ; but it was a monopoly which the very conditions of the general situation condemned to instability and precariousness. In the last analysis, the whole constitutional development of Rome is seen to be a faithful reflection of her external history. The acquisition, administration, and unification of that vast empire demanded and produced an ever closer concentration in the organs of government. Oligarchy, Principate, and " Dominate " would be the three great stages of that long evolution. The first solution of the problem, the oligarchical formula, having no deep roots in the constitution, would soon prove inadequate and incomplete, at the rude contact of experience. With the Gracchi the constitutional crisis begins. The knell of oligarchy will soon be rung.

CHAPTER II

THE DECLINE OF OLIGARCHY AND THE FIRST *COUPS D'ÉTAT*

BIBLIOGRAPHY.—*Ancient Authors* : Livy, *Periochæ* of bks. liii–cxvii (cf. Florus, i, 33–40 ; ii, 1–11 ; and, especially for the anarchy, ii, 12 ; Eutropius, iv, 15 to vi, 10 ; Orosius, v, 8, 24 ; and the new data given by the *Epitome* of Oxyrrhynchos for the period 149–137, in *Klio*, Beih., ii, 1904, ed. K., pp. 21–33, and, for the commentary, pp. 104–110, and ed. R., pp. 131–45) ; Sallust, *Jugurthine War*, *Catiline*, *Histories* (frags. : speeches of M. Æmilius Lepidus, L. Philippus, Licinius Macer, C. Aurelius Cotta, Pompey's letter to the Senate) ; Velleius Paterculus, ii, 1–30 ; Dion Cassius, xxii–xxxv frags.) ; Diodoros, xxxiii–xxxix (frags.) ; Appian, *Civil Wars*, i, 1–121 ; *H.R.F.*, *passim* ; Plutarch, *Gracchi*, *Marius*, *Sulla*, *Sertorius*, *Lucullus*, *Pompey*, *Crassus*, *Cæsar*, *Cicero*, *Cato the Younger* ; *O.R.F.*, pp. 162 ff. ; Cicero, *Pro Quinctio*, *Pro Roscio Amerino*, *Verrines* ; Zonaras, x, 1–2 ; *De Viris illustribus*, 57–76.

Inscriptions : Consular *Fasti* in *C.I.L.*, i, 2nd ed., 2, pp. 148–55 ; p. 195, 17 (*Elogium* of Q. Cæcilius Numidicus), 18 (of C. Marius) ; 196, 20 (of Sulla) ; 199, 30 (of M. Livius Drusus) ; No. 582, Law of Bantia (between 133 and 118 B.C.) ; No. 583, *Lex repetundarum* (123 or 122) ; No. 585, agrarian law of 111 ; No. 587, *Lex Cornelia de XX Quæstoribus* ; No. 638, inscr. of P. Popilius Lænas, Consul in 132 B.C. ; Nos. 639–45, terminal *cippi* of the Gracchi.

Modern Works : **XXI**, 169–207 ; **III**, 201–99 ; **XXVI**, 453–75 ; **X**, iii, 177–82 (K. J. Beloch) ; **XVI**, ii, 3–210, 241–84 ; **XXVII**, 55–79 ; **IX**, i, 225–355 ; **XXXI**, 73 ff. ; **XIX**, see ref., p. 24 ; **XX**, bk. iv, chs. ii–iv, vi–vii, ix ; bk. v, chs. i–iii ; **CIX**, 11–36 ; **LX** ; **LXX**, v, 163–209 (Cato), 230 ff. (Cicero) ; **CXXVI**, 266–81 ; **LXXII**, Eng. vol. i, 44–105.

I

THE DECLINE OF OLIGARCHY. SYMPTOMS AND PHASES

THE decline of the Roman constitution, in the century which extends from the Gracchi to the final establishment of personal government (133–131 B.C.), and the constitutional crisis which was the immediate result of it, is manifested by three fundamental, parallel symptoms :—

(1) There was no longer a majority for the government.

(2) The constitution was perverted by the exclusive preponderance of the Comitia Tributa.

(3) Public morals broke down.

On this triple phenomenon we must dwell for a moment.

*See also Supplementary Bibliography with Prefatory Note (p. 405)

The old government majority of the third century, based mainly on the aristocracy and the middle class, had been gradually destroyed by the split between the Senatorial and Equestrian orders and by the gradual disappearance of the middle classes. Caius Gracchus put the finishing touch to the work of time, and the traditional majority, receiving its death-blow, would soon be a distant memory.

Caius Gracchus, with his clear head and his iron will, knew where he was going. He destroyed only in order to re-build. His object was to replace the old majority of the right by a new majority of the left, formed of the Equestrians, the Plebs, and, if possible, the Italians. But, while he succeeded in the negative part of his work, he utterly failed in the positive part. After him, there was never a permanent majority of the right, nor one of the left either ; there were only coalition majorities, brought about by special circumstances. Socially, the Senatorial and Equestrian orders, being both parties of the rich, had common interests, and in this domain they tended to come together ; politically, the Knights, as the rivals of the Senatorial aristocracy, found a natural ally in the Plebs. As a result, two coalition majorities were possible. In the social domain, it would be a majority of the right, of the Senatorial and Equestrian orders against the Plebs ; in the political domain, it would be a majority of the left, of the Equestrian and Plebeian orders against the Senatorial aristocracy. Even the third possible coalition majority, that of the extremes, Senatorial nobility and Plebs against Knights, was once achieved, but without lasting success, by the great reformer Livius Drusus.

The constitutional history of the second century and the first half of the first is simply the successive rise and fall of these various coalition majorities. Let us recall the principal episodes. 122–108, *right majority* (Senate and Knights) directed against the social policy of the Gracchi, and chiefly the agrarian law, which was its keystone. Failure of Caius Gracchus to obtain a third Tribuneship (122). Death of Caius Gracchus (121). Gradual destruction of the agrarian legislation (121–111).—108–100, *left majority*. Marius elected Consul (108). Military reforms of Marius. Sixth Consulship of Marius. Laws of Saturninus and Glaucia.—100–91, *right majority*. Murder of Saturninus and

Glaucia. Effacement of Marius. Aristocratic reaction.— 91–89, *Coalition majority of the extremes*, Senatorial nobility and Plebs against the Equestrian order. Laws of Livius Drusus. Judicial law of 89.—88–83, *left majority*. Legislation of Sulpicius Rufus. Marian party in power (87–83).—70–63, *left majority*. Reaction against Sulla. First Consulship of Pompey and Crassus. *Leges Manilia* and *Gabinia*. Recall of Lucullus.—63, *right majority* against the threat of social revolution. Consulship of Cicero. Suppression of Catiline's conspiracy. At this date we may stop. The advent of military power is near. Immediately after the triumph of Cicero, the man of the conservative coalition, the First Triumvirate was formed, and two years later the victor himself sadly departed into banishment.

The second phenomenon was that the constitution was perverted by the exclusive preponderance of the Comitia Tributa. Since the third century, the Comitia Tributa had become the great legislative organ of the State, the Comitia Centuriata having preserved nothing of their old monopoly but the voting of two particularly important kinds of laws, those regarding peace, war, and treaties, and those investing Censors with their office. The *Leges Hortensiæ* had given the Comitia Tributa complete sovereignty in legislation ; henceforward, plebiscites automatically had the full force of laws, and the Senate, in losing its right of veto, had lost the means to prevent their being voted or even to amend the text. By doing away with the *auctoritas Patrum*, the only legal check on the legislative omnipotence of the Comitia, the *Lex Hortensia* had dealt a very serious blow, the first, at the ancient equilibrium and scientific harmony of the Roman constitution.

Nevertheless, as was natural with a people so attached to tradition as the Romans, the disastrous consequences of this innovation did not appear at once. Although there was no legal check, the legislative power of the Comitia Tributa was limited in two ways. First, there was their composition. The majority was held by the middle class of small country land-owners, that is, by the peasant element, always slow-going and well-balanced, while the mass of the proletarians and freedmen, being confined to the four Urban Tribes, at the most could raise four votes out of 35, a very small minority. Secondly, there was political tradition, and, in particular, there was the great moral authority of the Senate. Magistrates who, in accordance with the terms of the *Lex Hortensia*, ventured to take their legislative proposals before the Comitia Tributa direct, without first obtaining the opinion of the Senate, were exceptional down to the middle of the second century. They were regarded with disfavour by the public, as free-lances and revolutionaries. But before the end of the second century the development began to take on speed. By the gradual alteration of the composition of the Comitia Tributa, on the one hand, and by the introduction of new political morals on the other, the last restrictions to which the legislative potentialities of that assembly were in practice subjected disappeared one after another.

The result of the increasing ruin of the middle class was that the Comitia Tributa were drained of their sound, well-balanced element. Besides, citizens living in the outer environs of Rome, and still more those of the rest of Italy, did not put themselves out, or only did so exceptionally, to come to the meetings of the assembly, and in the face of that practical abstention, which was due to material difficulties and was a fatal consequence of the ancient city-system, the government was powerless. The law merely required the real presence of the thirty-five Tribes at the meeting-place, without specifying any quorum. Thirty-five voters in the Comitia Tributa, and three hundred and seventy-three (one per voting unit) in the Comitia Centuriata, were legally sufficient to represent the whole civic body of Rome. So the Tribes gradually gave place to skeleton Tribes [1] composed of professional electors, recruited in Rome (and not for nothing) among the urban populace, absurdly small voting units, which we shall find again in the first century of the Empire in the degenerate form of corporations of poor men. These professional electors had no other means of livelihood than electoral corruption, and were ready for any vileness, and, if need arose, any violence, provided that they were paid for it. For them lawfulness and constitution were obsolete notions, words without meaning.

[1] Cic., *Pro Sest.*, 109 : " I come to the Comitia, whether they are electing magistrates or passing laws. We often see many laws passed. I say nothing of those which are passed when each tribe is represented by five voters, and even they belong to another Tribe."

With the transformation of the Comitia Tributa went a
change in political traditions. The magistrates gradually
broke loose from the moral authority of the Senate. From
the Gracchi onwards, they took to informing the people of
all important matters direct. Presently they went so far as
to attack the sphere of competence which had always been
reserved for the Senate by the constitution—foreign affairs.
In 108 B.C., the Senate had extended Metellus's term of
governorship in Africa, that he might continue the war
against Jugurtha. Marius, elected Consul, appealed to the
popular Comitia. He was given Africa by a plebiscite, and
by this procedure the *Senatus consultum* was simply set aside.
The precedent was not forgotten, as we shall see ; in the course
of the first century, it was the Comitia Tributa that invested
ambitious men—Pompey, Crassus, Cæsar—with the high
commands to which they aspired, and so were wholly
responsible for the power of the generals, the origin of personal
rule and the Imperial system.

Being the stronghold of the oligarchy and the store-house
of tradition, the Senate did not passively allow the Comitia
Tributa to rob it of the legitimate interests which it had held
for centuries. In law, it had been helpless since the *Lex
Hortensia*. Sulla, in the course of his Dictatorship, restored
its old right of veto, but it was only for a short time. In 70,
that prerogative, revived for a moment, vanished with
the rest of Sulla's constitution. But, although the Senate
had no direct control, it could fight the Comitia in a round-
about way, by skilful use of the auspices. Two laws, the
Leges Ælia and *Fufia*, passed about 154, had determined the
value of the auspices in the hands of the different magistrates.
The Tribunes had been given the right of *obnuntiatio* as against
the Consuls ; in practice, this simply gave a religious form
to their legal veto, without in any way increasing their power.
At the same time, the Consuls had been invested with
exactly the same prerogative respecting the Tribunes ; this
was a most important innovation (and the true motive of the
two laws in question), for it gave them a right of veto against
the Tribunes which they had not had before. The result of
the *Leges Ælia* and *Fufia* was a considerable increase of the
influence of the Consuls and, still more, of the Senate, of
which those magistrates were as a rule the traditional mouth-

pieces and representatives. By attacking the Tribunes'
right of initiation, the measure also struck the Comitia
Tributa, the source of their power and the principle of their
authority. Thus the Senate recovered, in an indirect form,
the right of veto which the *Lex Hortensia* had taken from it
a hundred and thirty years before.

Between the furious attacks of the democrats and the
equally energetic defence of the Senatorial aristocracy, the
Leges Ælia and *Fufia* were maintained for nearly a century.
In 58 B.C., the Tribune Clodius obtained their abolition.
No doubt, the legality of the law by which this was done
was contested, but the result was attained. The laws went,
and with them the power of the Senate. In the last years
of the Republic, the Comitia Tributa, or rather the grotesque
caricature of them which survived, enjoyed a legislative
monopoly in the State without bound or restriction.

A last phenomenon, the most characteristic of all, for it
was their combined result—*quid leges sine moribus ?*—was
the collapse of public morals. This manifested itself mainly
in two things which went together—the part played by money,
corruption, and that played by force, riots.

Electoral corruption had become a chronic evil, displayed
without pretence. The days of reservations and indirect
ways were past. Men were no longer content with largesses
in some disguised form. Votes were bought at open bureaux,
and candidates showed an ever greater ingenuity in obtaining
at any price (in the full sense of the term) the victory on which
their political future would depend. In vain, laws on illegal
canvassing were passed one after another—*Lex Cornelia
Bœbia* in 181, *Lex Cornelia Fulvia* in 159, *Lex Cornelia* in 81,
Lex Calpurnia in 67, *Lex Tullia* in 63, *Lex Licinia* in 55, *Lex
Pompeia* in 52—and their very number gives striking proof
of their complete ineffectiveness. In this respect the
elections of 54 deserve special mention in the constitutional
annals of the Republic. The electoral Comitia were turned
into a battlefield ; on the Forum and the Campus Martius
rival parties were now in the habit of coming to blows.
Already candidates whose prospects were doubtful, such as
Glaucia in 100, had cleared the way for themselves by the
simple device of assassinating their rival. The final crisis
was clearly at hand ; the symptoms which precede collapse—

demoralization, disorder, riot—grew more numerous and more acute. A little more, and the day of anarchy would arrive.

The decline of the traditional constitution, officially represented by the oligarchical system, was due, as we have seen, to two fundamental causes—the split of the ruling aristocracy into two classes, Senatorial and Equestrian, henceforth distinct and presently actively opposed, and the disappearance of the middle class, the essential element of equilibrium and the backbone of the army and Comitia. The only possible cure for this situation was a return to the harmony of the classes which was so characteristic of public life in the third century, and which seemed to have been destroyed for ever by the conquest of the Mediterranean world. That return to the past seemed both desirable and necessary from the constitutional point of view ; but could it be brought about, or must it be relegated to the realm of vain dreams ?

A first element in the problem was the reconstitution of the old aristocratic *bloc*. The conflict dividing the two kinds of nobility, Senatorial and Equestrian, doubtless took the form of caste-rivalry, but, what was much more serious, it was above all a question of material interests, or, to put it plainly, a matter of money. That rivalry was aggravated more and more every day by the increasingly intensive exploitation of the Mediterranean domain of Rome. To restore the old governmental *bloc* and to give the Roman constitution its lost stability, the Senatorial nobility would have had to give up its exclusive attitude and the Equestrian nobility its love of money, that is, it would have been necessary to change the mentality of the ruling classes with a wave of a wand. It was only a dream, pursued by liberals like Scipio Æmilianus and Cicero after him, and destined, like all such Utopias, to come into conflict with human passions and to be shattered against merciless realities.

A second element was the restoration of the middle class, a much more serious problem than the other, for not only home politics were involved. The disappearance of that class, which supplied the legions with their best men, meant the drying-up of the very source of military recruiting, and so imperilled the power and national life of the State itself. Among a patriotic people like the Romans, only one consideration ought to matter in this question. Here, therefore, the reformers found themselves on surer ground, and Tiberius Gracchus, who was fully aware of it (as Appian says expressly),[1] did not fail to make foreign policy a chief point in his argument.

The problem of the reconstruction of the middle class allowed of a definite solution, and, indeed, of two. At home, the Roman civic body showed no lack of men, witness the official statistics, and to make land-owners of them it was only necessary to give them land. Or a solution could come from outside : the new land-owners needed for the normal working of the constitution could be taken from outside the Roman civic body, among the Italians, on whom it was only necessary to confer the citizenship. These two solutions, internal and external, the agrarian solution and the Italian solution, were to find in Rome clear-sighted statesmen to perceive them and bold reformers—the Gracchi, Livius Drusus—to attempt them.

These two were the only solutions which might have saved the Roman constitution, if it could be saved, and, by widening it, have restored the admirable equilibrium of the past. The first, the agrarian solution, was successfully knocked on the head by the ruling oligarchy after the fall of the Gracchi ; and all parties in Rome, in spite of the outcome of the Social War, combined to nullify the second, the Italian solution, and to rob it of all practical effectiveness. The old constitution had failed to scrap its obsolete machinery when the time came, to abandon the antiquated system of the City, and to accept in its laws, as it already did in fact, the unescapable formula of the future, the formula of the State. From that moment republican government was doomed irretrievably and the way lay open to monarchy. Rome would proceed along it at a full speed, but she would only enter port after a half-century of bloody trials and frightful anarchy.

The failure, one after the other, of the great agrarian and Italian reforms sealed the fate of republican government. The political life of a nation lies essentially in the conflict of parties within the framework of the constitution. Now, in the middle of the first century B.C., the old constitution

[1] *Civil Wars*, i, 9.

was evidently quite worn out and decaying fast. We have seen this in the case of the organs of government. The same was true of the two great historical parties, the *optimates,* or government, and the *populares,* or opposition. When Sulla placed the oligarchy back in the saddle, it was dazed by its triumph and could not ride ; it lacked both men and political sense. A few years later military power, the new force rising on the horizon, would deal it its death-blow.

The opposition showed itself even more powerless, for many and various reasons. The oligarchy, which controlled the Senate, the only permanent organ of the Roman constitution, like the Conservative party in the British House of Lords, did not fight the democratic opposition on equal terms. The Comitia and the magistrates, the only legal weapons at the disposal of the opposition, were powerless against the action, or, still more, the inertia of the Senate, in consequence of the irregular manner in which the Comitia were held and the fact that the magistrates were hampered by the two fundamental restrictions, the principles of the college and annual tenure, to which their office was subject. The democratic magistrate came up against the right of intervention (*par potestas*) of his colleagues, and, since under the existing laws he could not hold office for a long continuous period, he had to bring off his reforms in a very short time— with a rush, as it were—and often, therefore, in a revolutionary manner. The failure of the Gracchi, in particular, made this quite plain. Moreover, the democratic party, since the disappearance of the old agrarian element which was its backbone and the vain efforts of the Gracchi to restore it, had been without cohesion, programme, or leaders. The urban proletariate which was henceforward the most active nucleus of it, being without convictions or patriotism, ready to answer the call of money or of an ambitious general, had made the political fortune of the big capitalist and was now about to forge military dictatorship with its own hands.

This state of political and social decomposition, the final result of the Roman conquest, which attacked organs and parties alike, found concrete expression in two phenomena which went together and were equally symptomatic—conspiracy and street-fighting. Contemporaries, with Sallust and Cicero at their head, give us full information about both.

The governmental machine seemed worn out beyond repair. The constitutional development of the Republic ended in complete shipwreck, by which government and opposition suffered equally.   Restored by Sulla and provided with powerful weapons, the Senatorial oligarchy, lacking men and political sense, collapsed less than ten years after the Dictator had gone.   The democratic opposition, having no exact object or definite programme, drained by the disappearance of the country middle class, reduced to an unorganized, poverty-stricken urban proletariate, and bound, since the time of the Gracchi, to the service of the big capitalists, whose humble servant and passive tool it had become, could create nothing but disorder, and surrendered to the military power, which made use of it without reserve or scruple in its advance to personal government.

For the inevitable conclusion it is best to go to the writers of the time.

> " O Pomponius," Cicero writes to the faithful Atticus, " we have lost not only all the sap and the blood, but even the colour and old appearance of the City. There is no longer a Republic which delights me or in which I can find rest." [1]
> " You see," he says in a letter to his brother Quintus, " that there is no Republic, no Senate, no dignity in any of us." [2]

Non mos, non jus, as Tacitus would say,[3] with his usual conciseness. The funeral oration which the famous historian, though little suspect of hostility to the old government, felt compelled to pronounce over the grave of the Republic may be translated in one word, which sums up and explains everything—anarchy.

II

THE FORMATION OF MILITARY POWER

The gradual, incurable decay of the republican constitution had, by an inevitable process, brought Rome first to civil disorders and finally to anarchy. In the second century B.C. the traditional machinery of government had shown itself obsolete.   In the hands of a decrepit and jealously exclusive oligarchy, the State no longer had the instruments required by its needs, and its growing expansion made the

---

[1] *Ad Att.*, iv, 18, 2.   [2] *Ad Quint.*, iii, 4, 1.   [3] *Ann.*, iii, 28.

incongruity more marked every day. But to confine oneself to this negative conclusion would be to see only one face of the truth, one wing of the diptych. By the side of what was perishing, something was growing up. The collapse of the traditional institutions of the City had a counterpart, which was positive—the birth of a new idea, the monarchical idea, at first dim and veiled, but destined, through a century of civil dissension, to emerge gradually and, with the clear genius of Cæsar, to take the form of a systematic conception and a concrete programme.

Caius Gracchus had for a moment built up on the Tribune-ship a personal power, an autocracy like that of Pericles ; it was an attractive but unstable system, and events, with their usual brutality, had very soon revealed how perishable it was. The short-lived success and spectacular downfall of Caius Gracchus had taught one great lesson—that the means which he had used were fundamentally insufficient. The Tribuneship, although enlarged, and even transformed, could not, by reason of the constitutional limitations of collegiate system and annual tenure which hampered its action, be a sound, permanent instrument of government. Another factor, far younger and more vigorous than that venerable but worn-out magistracy, was about to enter on the scene—military power, which, from advance to advance and from victory to victory, would come in the end, by the logic of things, to personal rule and the Empire.

Among the Romans, a people of soldiers and conquerors, military power had its roots in a very distant past. But two elements played a chief part in its development and growth—the high idea which the Romans had of the supreme magistracy, in the extraordinary form of the Dictatorship or in the ordinary form of the Consulship, and the policy of conquest adopted by the Roman State, in fact if not in theory, as early as the fourth century B.C.

The Roman kingship, as embodied by the Etruscan rulers, had always been mainly, if not wholly, military in character, and when it became a pure tyranny with the last of them that original quality had been still more marked. After the Revolution of 509, the royal power was replaced by two new magistracies, one regular, the Consulship, and one extraordinary, the Dictatorship. But a double series of restrictions ensured the security of the Republican constitution and guaranteed the State against a return to the offensive on the part of personal power. The Consulship was limited by the two sacrosanct principles of annual tenure and the college, and the Dictatorship by the legal term of six months and the obligatory presence of the Master of Horse by the Dictator's side. The Dictatorship had become obsolete and discredited by the time of the second Punic War, and disappeared at the end of the third century ; the Consulship, on the other hand, remained the supreme magistracy of the State down to the end of the Republic, but never succeeded in emancipating itself from the legal limitations which the Republican constitution had placed on the exercise of its authority from the very beginning. For the military power, which was to be the origin of the Imperial system, to be able to establish itself right in the midst of the constitution, something else was needed. So we come to the second of the two elements mentioned above, the policy of conquest.

The extension of the conquest and the widening of the zone of the armies which it entailed resulted in longer and more distant campaigns. The principle of annual office, jealously maintained in respect of the army leaders in their capacity as Consuls or Prætors, was prejudicial to the successful conduct of military operations. Moreover, since the middle of the third century, the State had had possessions outside Italy to manage, in the form of provinces. These two new needs led to two constitutional innovations of great importance—the former to the system of extension of office and the latter to the creation of provincial governors.

In 327 B.C., at the beginning of the Samnite Wars, Q. Publilius Philo, as Consul for the second time, was besieging the Greek city of Naples in Campania. At the end of the year the campaign was not over and the besieged still held out. Accordingly, in order to ensure continuity in military operations, the Senate resolved on the unprecedented step of maintaining the general in his command for another year, and caused the Tribunes to propose a plebiscite to this effect. In this way the practice of extending office started, and thereafter it gradually became the rule for Consuls retiring from office. The same procedure was extended, at the middle of the third century at the latest, to the junior colleagues of the Consuls, the Prætors. At first extension was granted by a plebiscite especially passed by the people for the particular case, at the proposal of the Senate ; later, from the second Punic War onwards, the people ceased to take any action, and the Senate granted it by a simple *Senatus consultum*. The length of the extension varied according to the circumstances ; usually it was for one year, but it might be for two, three, or even, in exceptional cases, four or five years. Thanks to this arrangement, there were in the Roman State—a very serious innovation from the constitutional point of view—military leaders who kept their powers, whether as magistrates or as pro-magistrates, for several years on end.

About 227 B.C., in consequence of the annexation of Sicily, Sardinia, and Corsica and the formation of the two provinces of Sicily and Sardinia-Corsica, the number of Prætors was doubled and two of these magistrates were given the administration of the new provinces. From the beginning, these military leaders had two immense advantages over the other magistrates, the non-provincial Consuls and Prætors. As the sole representatives of Rome, without any colleagues to hamper them, they exercised almost monarchical authority in their district, and, in addition, their distance from Rome gave them a practical independence unknown to their fellows who served in Rome or even in Italy. Even more than the system of extension of office, therefore, the creation of the provincial governorships represented a decisive stage, a great step towards the formation of military power. That there was in this a danger to the future of the constitution, everyone in Rome, and especially the governing nobility, was perfectly well aware. But however real the danger might be, it was still remote. There was no lack, in the constitutional armoury and elsewhere, of machinery carefully devised to keep provincial governors in check and to prevent them from becoming too dangerous to the institutions of the State.

The many checks by which the ambition of military leaders might be restrained if necessary were of two kinds, legal and practical. Let us glance at both.

There were two precautions of a constitutional kind by

which the road leading to high commands could be closed to
a dangerous magistrate, or one regarded as such. There
was, first, the part taken by the Senate in the allotment
of ordinary and extraordinary provinces ; the Senate
decided which should go to pro-magistrates and divided the
others into two classes, Consular provinces and Prætorian
provinces. It made this classification after the Consular
elections—that is, when it already knew who the Consuls
would be. It might, therefore, if it saw fit, give them less
important provinces, and so refuse a man the high military
command to which he aspired with a view to greater things.
Secondly, at least in the case of the Prætorian provinces,
it could dispense with the practice of drawing the Prætors
by lot, and itself place some Prætor in charge of a certain
province, in particular of the City provinces (Urban and
Peregrine), and could even, when they had been drawn by lot,
order the transfers which it considered necessary by a
Senatus consultum.

But suppose that a dangerous magistrate managed to secure
a high command in spite of these precautions. The Senate,
if it could not stop the appointment without more ado, had
three ways of reducing him to impotence, or at least of
hampering his activity very seriously. The Senate controlled
the supply of troops and held the purse-strings. Every magistrate or pro-magistrate invested with a provincial governorship received from the Senate, by a special *Senatus consultum*
(*ornatio provinciæ*), the men and money needed for the
exercise of his mandate. According to custom, the normal
contingent of a Consular army consisted of two legions and a
corresponding force of allies, but the Senate could always
grant or refuse an increase of strength and of financial
allowance. Secondly, the provincial governor could not
declare war, nor make peace, nor conclude an alliance,
all these rights being expressly left to the sovereign decision
of the people, nor could he substitute himself for the Senate
in the conduct of the diplomatic negotiations preceding or
following those constitutional acts. Thirdly, when a magistrate or pro-magistrate in command of an army had finished
his term of command, it was the Senate, and the Senate alone,
which, by the legal method of extension, could maintain him
for a longer or shorter time in his office.

In addition to these constitutional checks, there was, in the domain of fact, the great check of the civic nature of the army, with its passionate devotion to the Republican government and its readiness to do its duty against the attempts of ambitious men and the manœuvres of adven-turers.

This combination of various powerful barriers which law and custom had set up against the unwholesome aspirations of generals retarded the advance of military power, but only for a time, and could not put an end to it. As early as the middle of the second century, the circumstances abroad following on the conquest compelled the ruling oligarchy to make a series of symptomatic and disturbing concessions. The Spanish Wars,[1] in particular, by the extraordinary strain which they put upon the army and by the technical knowledge which they required of the chief command, were a turning-point in this respect. The oligarchy betrayed its growing incapacity. The principle of annual office, one of the constitutional pillars of the system, had to be abandoned in favour of two-yearly commands, and the circumstances made it necessary, in practice, to give up the renewal of the effectives every year and institute a standing army. Long commands and a professional army were the two essential bases on which, in the following century, military dictatorship and its logical corollary, personal rule, were founded. Once started, under the action of causes of increasing potency, the movement never stopped. In the course of the eighty years between the Tribuneship of the Gracchi and the triumph of Cæsar, the checks imposed by the constitution and custom on the aspirations of military leaders collapsed one by one under the repeated attacks of ambitious generals and their willing or unconscious allies at home.

Even in the time of the Gracchi a first barrier fell. By a law of Caius Gracchus, the *Lex Sempronia de Provinciis*, which was the chief ruling in the matter until the *Lex Pompeia* of 52, the Senate had to indicate the Consular provinces of the following year before the Consuls who would get them were elected, and, to ensure the execution of this clause, the Tribunes of the Plebs were deprived of the right of veto against the *Senatus consultum* by which the provinces

---

[1] The fact is well brought out by A. Schulten in **CXXVI**, 266–81.

were allotted. Therefore, when the Senate allotted the
provinces, it did not yet know who would receive them. It
could not, therefore, take such precautions as it might,
rightly or wrongly, deem legitimate and necessary. Its
traditional weapon was thus broken in its hands.

A second constitutional check disappeared fifteen years
later, at the time of the famous election of Marius to the
Consulship (108). It was customary, as we have seen, for
the Senate to indicate the two classes of Consular and
Prætorian provinces beforehand, the Consuls and Prætors
afterwards arranging matters among themselves in their
respective categories, either by mutual agreement (*com-
paratio*) or by drawing lots (*sortitio*). In practice, the people
had no say in the matter. No doubt, in virtue of its ultimate
sovereignty, it had the right, in theory, to make a special
appointment to an army command or to a provincial
governorship. During the second Punic War and in the course
of the second century the people had more than once appointed
men to high military commands. In 205 Scipio Africanus
had threatened that if the Senate did not give him the province
of Africa he would take the matter to the people. In 147,
Scipio Æmilianus had been given the command of the army
of operations against Carthage by a plebiscite. But in all
these cases the situation was extraordinary and the exceptional
action taken did not, in the eyes of the ruling oligarchy,
in any way legalize a violent infringement of traditional
usage. When in 108 Marius, being appointed Consul,
demanded to be allowed to conduct the war against Jugurtha,
which the Senate had already been careful to assign to
Metellus, his action was regarded by the governing class
as outrageous. He stood his ground, however, and the
command which he wanted was conferred on him, in frank
defiance of the previous *Senatus consultum*, by a plebiscite
passed by the Comitia Tributa at the proposal of the Tribune
T. (or C.) Manlius Mancinus (107). Now that the precedent
was established, ambitious men had a legal means of obtaining
the military commands which they desired, and, being masters
of the Comitia, they did not hesitate to use it. In 88, Marius,
once more, secured the conduct of the war against Mithradates
by the same procedure, and then came the Plebiscites of
Gabinius (67), of Manilius (66), of Vatinius (59), and of

Trebonius (55), and the *Lex Pompeia Licinia* (55), the first
two in favour of Pompey, the third and fifth in favour of
Cæsar, and the fourth in favour of Pompey and Crassus,
and some others as well.   This was not all; these holders of
extraordinary commands had under them Legates who, by
their title and by their functions, were the ancestors of the
Legates *pro Prætore* who governed the Imperial provinces
under the Empire.

With the loss of its power of disposing of military commands,
the Senatorial oligarchy lost its strongest weapon.   The
Gracchi had failed because without the army no success
could be real.   The lesson was taken to heart, and the crisis
was at hand.

The last checks of a constitutional kind—the sole right of
the Senate to extend the term of a command and to grant
the necessary means of action, military and financial—
disappeared in the first century.   The plebiscite which gave
a general his command at the same time laid down the length
of his office, and that length, in formal violation of tradition,
ceased to be confined to one year.   The Plebiscite of Gabinius
made it three years ; those of Vatinius and Trebonius and
the *Lex Pompeia Licinia* made it five years, and this latter
in the end became the normal term.   Moreover, to crown
the series of acts by which the people had encroached—or
recovered its own—on the competence of the Senate, the
people itself gave the generals whom it had appointed the
means of action which they needed.   The Plebiscite of
Gabinius is the first instance of a procedure which, in subsequent plebiscites, became the rule.

Lastly, the very great practical check which an ambitious
general might encounter in the national character and civic
recruiting of the Roman army disappeared in the general
collapse of constitutional traditions.   When, after the
plebiscite had given him the command of the war against
Jugurtha, Marius proceeded to raise the necessary troops in
the usual way, he met with two serious difficulties.   Hitherto
the normal legions had been recruited only from the Classes
of the census, but the gradual disappearance of the middle
class had long made these resources inadequate.   On the
other hand, citizens excluded from service by lack of the
legal minimum of property swarmed in the Century of

proletarians or *capite censi* outside the Classes, which had
never been called up save in exceptional circumstances.
This was not all. In this matter, as in so many others, it is
in the demands of foreign policy that we must look for
the causes of a military transformation which was to have
such profound influence on the development of the Roman
constitution. Between the object to be attained—the completion of the conquest—and the instrument available for
the purpose—the civic army—there was now no proportion
at all. Rome no longer had the military instrument adequate
to her ambitions, or even to her needs. The traditional system
of the annual levy was of no use for distant wars or for the
permanent occupation of lands beyond the sea. These things
could only be effected by a professional army. By an innovation of capital importance, Marius called upon the proletarians,
but, in respect for the letter of the law, he enrolled them as
volunteers, not on a principle of compulsory service. In
any case, the result was the same. Military service became
less and less a civic duty, and more and more a profession,
and the army gradually lost its character as a national army
and became a professional one.

Although Marius's reform of the army was essentially
military in principle, it had very important consequences
of a political and constitutional kind. The soldier might
be a citizen the day he joined up, and a citizen when he
returned to his home, but the mere length of his service
made him a mercenary, knowing nothing of civil life and
having no interest outside the army. Legality and constitution
were only meaningless words to him ; the only thing round
which he rallied was something military—the common
standard, the eagle of the legion.

In addition to this disadvantage there was another, yet
more serious. This army, strongly organized in itself and
completely detached from civil institutions, had chiefs,
who were absolute chiefs. Soldiers entered the service
because they liked it, and, still more, because they had to.
They hoped for loot, allotments of land, and, with luck,
promotion. Who could give them these different privileges ?
The general. So there grew up between general and men a
close association (one might almost call it complicity) based,
not on the old discipline, nor even on the religion of the

standard, but on mutual interests and greed. The men expected everything from their general ; the general might, if he paid for it, get anything from his men. The whole mighty machinery of the Roman army was thus at the sole and complete disposal of a single man, who throughout his command had unlimited authority.

There might, no doubt, have been a remedy for such a situation. As has been the case in modern states, when the Roman army became a professional army it might have been commanded by generals who likewise were purely and simply professionals. But that transformation would have entailed a very serious revolution—the abolition of the close bond which existed in the ancient city between civil institutions and military organization. That connection was logical so long as the army retained the character of a national army, but ceased to be so as soon as it became, whether in fact or in theory, entirely an army of mercenaries. In Rome, even after the reform of Marius, the commanders of the army continued to be, as in the past, the supreme magistrates of the City, Consuls, Prætors, Proconsuls, Proprætors. To their hand there lay a formidable instrument which they might use as they pleased to bring pressure upon the constitution and to obtain dictatorship. Soldiers on active service and retired veterans, all trained to passive obedience by the iron discipline of the Roman army, were all equally interested in seeing their general of to-day or yesterday become the head of the State, and so able to dispose of the treasury, lands, posts, and a thousand other good things in favour of the men who had raised him to power.

Moreover, since military leadership was not a career, there were in Rome as many generals as there were higher magistrates or pro-magistrates (except the Censors). Of these generals, some were more restrained or miserly, others more enterprising or lavish. They competed one against another, being followed by their troops with an enthusiasm proportionate to the hopes which might be placed in them. The army, now an instrument of despotism against the City, was ready to sell itself, body and soul, to support the projects of the ambitious. This consequence has been noted by a contemporary, Sallust,[1] with his usual sure and vigorous touch.

[1] *Jug. War*, lxxxvi, 1–3.

" Others put his action down to ambitious calculation ; for that class of the people had been the chief source of Marius's popularity and rise to office. Moreover, needy men are the most useful supports of one who seeks power, for they have nothing to lose and whatever pays is honourable in their eyes—*omnia cum pretio honesta videntur.*"

Above the strife of parties a new idea henceforward floated in the air, the eternal obsession of ambitious men—the army as an instrument of power and a means of domination. The reform of Marius was the prelude to the first *coups d'État.* A few years more, and they would begin.

As the action of a well-constructed play proceeds methodically from act to act, military power continued to advance, steadily and relentlessly. In 107, Marius had forged the instrument, the professional army. In 88 and in 83–82, by two successive *coups d'État,* Sulla taught the method. In 70, before the combined efforts of the democratic opposition and factious generals, the Sullan constitution, the last effort of an oligarchy at bay, fell like a house of cards. The way was now open to militarism. The fates would soon be accomplished.

CHAPTER III

IN SEARCH OF A NEW FORMULA. THE PRINCIPATE OF POMPEY AND THE MONARCHY OF CÆSAR

BIBLIOGRAPHY.—*Ancient Authors* : Livy, *Periochæ* of bks. xcvii–cxvi (cf. Florus, i, 41–7 ; ii, 12–13 ; Eutropius, vi, 12–25 ; Orosius, vi, 4–17) ; Cicero, *Pro Fonteio, Pro Lege Manilia, De Lege Agraria, Pro C. Rabirio, Catilinarians, Pro Murena, Pro Sulla, Pro Flacco, Post reditum in Senatu, Post reditum ad Quirites, Pro Domo, De Haruspicum responsis, Pro Sestio, In Vatinium, Pro Cœlio, De Provinciis consularibus, Pro Balbo, In Pisonem, Pro Plancio, Pro C. Rabirio Postumo, Pro Milone, Pro M. Marcello, Pro Q. Ligario, Pro Rege Deiotaro, Brutus, Ep. ad Familiares* (62–43 B.C.), *to Atticus* (68–44 B.C.), *to Quintus* (60–54 B.C.) ; *H.R.F., passim* ; *O.R.F.*, pp. 358–443 ; Cæsar, *Gallic War, Civil War* ; Velleius Paterculus, ii, 31–57 ; Suetonius, *Twelve Cæsars* ; Dion Cassius (complete from 68 B.C.), xxxvi to xliv, 21 ; Diodoros, xxxix, 20 to xl (in frags.) ; Appian, *Civil Wars*, ii, 1–117 ; Plutarch, *Lucullus, Pompey, Cæsar, Crassus, Cicero, Cato, Brutus, Antony* ; Zonaras, x, 3–11 ; *De Viris illustribus*, 77–86.

Inscriptions : Consular *Fasti* in *C.I.L.*, i, 2nd ed., 1, pp. 154–8 ; *Elogium* of M. Valerius Messala, *ibid.*, 2, p. 201, 40 ; *Lex de Gallia Cisalpina* (49 B.C.), *ibid.*, No. 592 ; *Lex Julia Municipalis* (45 B.C.), No. 593 (*I.L.S.*, 6085) ; *municipal law of the Colonia Genetiva Julia Urso*, No. 594 (= *C.I.L.*, ii, supp. 5439 ; *I.L.S.*, 6087).

Modern Works : **CIX**, 3–316 (Principate of Pompey), 319–542 (monarchy of Cæsar) ; **XXI**, 216–56 ; **II**, 318–30 ; **X**, iii, 182–5 (Beloch) ; **XXVI**, 475–91 ; **IX**, i, 355–69 ; ii, 1–92 ; **VII**, i, 15–21 ; **XXVII**, 80–111 ; **XVI**, ii, 211–544 ; **XIX**, see ref. on p. 24 ; **XX**, bk. v, chs. iii, v–vi, viii–xi ; **LXX**, ii, 172–313 (P. Clodius) ; iii, 125–827 (Cæsar) ; iv, 84–127 (Crassus), 332–561 (Pompey), 164–209 (Cato), 230–697 (Cicero) ; **CVIII** ; **LXXVI** ; **CIII** ; **LXXII**, Eng. vol. i, 106 to end, and vol. ii ; Ett. Païs, " L'Aspiration de César à la royauté et l'opposition tribunicienne en 45–44 av. J.-C.," in **XXXIII**, Apr.-May, 1914 ; R. Heinze, " Ciceros *Staat* als politische Tendenzschrift," in **XXXVI**, lix (1924), 73–94.

I

THE PRINCIPATE OF POMPEY

IN the face of an anarchy which the failure of attempts at reform had made henceforth incurable, Rome could no longer choose. The constitution was now but a corpse ; but the empire, born of the conquest, was a very living reality, and meant to live. The system of the ancient city, as conceived and practised by the oligarchy of the second

*See also Supplementary Bibliography with Prefatory Note (p. 405)

century with its antiquated principles, its meagre framework, and its primitive administrative organs, had been unable to reform itself as was necessary. The concession of the citizenship to the whole of Italy, the growing importance of the part played by the provinces, and the whole world asking to be protected and governed made it absolutely necessary to adopt a new constitutional formula, wider, more comprehensive, and more fruitful—that of the State. This formula could now be supplied by personal rule alone.

But, while the vital necessities which the State had to face at home and abroad and the defects of the oligarchical system, congenital and acquired, made that solution inevitable in the immediate future, at least there were two alternative forms in which it might be adopted. It was possible to imagine a compromise, in which foreign affairs and war should be left to the sole and permanent direction of one citizen, a first citizen (*princeps*), with the appropriate legal powers, while internal administration remained in the hands of the traditional organs, Comitia, magistrates, and Senate. This arrangement, based on the loyal collaboration of the old and new powers, would reduce the constitutional innovations needed to a strict minimum. On the other hand, one might prefer a more thorough reform, which would completely wipe out the past and build up personal power, in the full force of the term, in its place. The first system was that of Principate ; the second was absolute, hereditary monarchy of the Hellenistic type. Pompey personifies the first, Cæsar the second.

The idea of Principate was in the air, and, that being so, Pompey did no more than appropriate it to his own advantage. The great political theorist of the day, Cicero, though an ardent champion of the traditional constitution, for which he lived and died, did not hesitate to speak in defence of Principate—less from personal conviction than under the inexorable pressure of circumstances. In his treatise *On the Republic*, written in 54 B.C. and published three years later, he defined, still in a veiled form (such ideas are long in taking shape) and with the reservations imposed by the general state of affairs, the rôle of the " first citizen " in any well-organized state, and in the Roman State in particular.

" As the grieve knows the nature of the soil, and the house-steward is acquainted with letters, but both turn from the pleasures of knowledge to the usefulness of doing their work, so this guide of ours (*noster hic rector*) will no doubt have studied the laws, and will indeed have examined their very sources, but he must not fill up his time with giving consultations and reading and writing, so that he is unable to manage the Republic as a house-steward or grieve. He will have a great knowledge of justice in the higher sense, for no one can be a just man without it, and some acquaintance with civil law, but only in the same way as a navigator knows the stars or a physician drugs ; for each of these makes use of them for his art, without being kept from doing his work." [1] " I spend my whole time," he says in a letter to Atticus, in which he quotes his own words, " meditating on the character of the man of whom I drew a portrait in the *Republic* which you thought fairly successful. Do you remember the object which we wanted that director of the State (*moderator Reipublicæ*) always to have before his eyes ? If I remember right, this is what I make Scipio say in the Fifth Book : ' As the object of the navigator is a safe passage, and that of the physician is health, and that of the general is victory, so our director of the Republic aims at the happy life of the citizens, that it may be secure in its resources, rich in wealth, distinguished in fame, and honest in virtue ; for I mean him to be the accomplisher of this task, which is the greatest and noblest among men.' " [2]

This chief he designates by various terms—*rector rerum publicarum, rector patriæ, gubernator, moderator Reipublicæ, tutor et procurator Reipublicæ*—and when, at the end of the same treatise, he speaks of the God who moves the world, he uses the characteristic word *princeps*—*ille princeps deus*.[3]

But we find the clearest expression of the idea in the speech which Cicero made for Marcellus in 46, when Cæsar was Dictator. Here Cicero gives a complete definition of the nature and objects of a Principate.

" Is anyone so ignorant of everything, so raw in political matters, so utterly unused to thinking of his own security and that of the State, that he does not understand that his security is bound up with yours, Cæsar, and that the life of all of us depends on yours ? I, for one, who think about you day and night, as I should, am in dread even of the ordinary dangers of mankind, the accidents of health and the weakness of our common nature, and deplore the fact that a Republic which should be immortal must depend on the life of one mortal man. But if to ordinary dangers and the accidents of health there are added crime and conspiracy, what god could, if he wished, save the Republic ?

" It is for you, Caius Cæsar, to raise up everything which you see lying, shaken and thrown down by the impact of war. You must set

---

[1] v, 3, 5.   [2] *Ad Att.*, viii, 11.
[3] *Rep.*, frags. of bk. v ; vi, 1–2 and 26 ; **CIX,** 181–3 ; H. Dessau's important observation in **VI,** 61, n. 2 (cf. R. Heinze, " Cicero's *Staat* als politische Tendenzschrift," in **XXXVI,** lix (1924), p. 77, n. 2).

up the law courts, restore confidence, put down licence, revive the birth-rate, and tighten up by severe laws all that has dissolved into chaos. In such a great civil war and in all that frenzy of feeling and clash of arms, the shaken Republic could not but lose, whatever the outcome of the war might be, many ornaments of its dignity and mainstays of its stability, and it was inevitable that both leaders did many things as soldiers which they would not have allowed as civilians. All these wounds of war have now to be healed by you, for no one but you can heal them.

" So it was with sorrow that I heard you pronounce those wise and splendid words, ' I have lived long enough for nature and for my glory.' Perhaps long enough for nature, if you will, and I shall even add for your glory, if it pleases you ; but not long enough for your country, and that is what matters. Therefore do not, I beg, indulge in the philosopher's wise contempt of death ; do not be wise to our peril. For I have more than once heard that you too often make that same remark, that you have lived long enough. I believe it ; but I should accept it only if you lived for yourself alone, or were even born for yourself alone. To-day, when the safety of all citizens and the whole Republic are bound up with your deeds, you are so far from the completion of your immense task that you have not yet laid the foundations which you have in mind. Is this a time to decide the length of your life, not by the safety of the Republic, but by the moderation of your own spirit ? " [1]

" However great an achievement may be, it is too little if there is more to be done. If this were the end of your immortal deeds, Cæsar, to crush your opponents and to leave the Republic in its present state, consider, whether your divine worth would not win more wonder than glory, if glory is indeed the illustrious and widespread report of many great services done to one's kin, to one's country, and to all mankind.

" This, then, remains for you to do . . . Give a constitution to the Republic, and be the first to enjoy its benefits in all leisure and tranquillity. Then, if you will, when you have paid your debt to your country and have satisfied nature herself with the number of your years, say that you have lived long enough." [2]

" Now all dissension has been broken down by the arms and dispelled by the justice of the victor. What is wanted is that all men with any wisdom or even common sense should desire one same thing. Unless you live, Cæsar, and continue in the sentiments which you have shown in the past and more than ever to-day, there can be no life for us. So all of us, who want these things to be saved, beg and beseech you to take counsel for your life and safety ; and, since you think that there is a danger, we all—I say for others what I myself feel—are ready to protect you with guards and with the strength of our own bodies." [3]

Cicero's speech had only one fault, that it came a little late, at a time when the idea of Principate was already considered out of date, and the victory of Cæsar established, or seemed to establish, the triumph of monarchy. But at

---

[1] *Pro Marc.*, vii, 22 to viii, 26.
[2] viii, 26 to ix, 27.   [3] x, 32.

least the idea had already been realized, more or less completely, in the past. The career of Pompey is the proof.

As always in Rome, the new political system was born, not of an *a priori* conception, but of the facts. As early as the second century B.C., there had been men in the State who, by their merits and services, had come to hold an exceptional position. Scipio Africanus and Scipio Æmilianus, in particular, had enjoyed recognized pre-eminence in the domains of home and foreign politics, and Cicero actually calls the latter " *Princeps Rei Publicæ* ".[1]

Pompey in his turn dreamed of holding this high position, but in the form of a regular, legally conferred office, and this idea, which was at first vague, but grew more and more definite as time went on, until at last it triumphed with Augustus, was the ruling principle of his whole political career.

Pompey, the old supporter of Sulla, had risen to greatness on the fringe of the law. Twice already—in 77 when he commanded the Spanish expedition and in 70 when he was elected Consul—he had been raised to high military posts, in defiance of the constitution, with the help of the all-powerful army. The method had served him so well in the past that it was natural that he should adhere to it in the future.

On retiring from the Consulship, he did not take the province which the constitution allotted to him, but remained in Rome, where, in accordance with his programme, he hoped to continue to direct policy in general. He was speedily disillusioned. Without a military command, at a time when the army was everything, he soon found himself powerless. At least he had one consolation ; his old opponent Crassus was in the same boat. Once again, as before 70, they both set out to look for an army and a war. This time again circumstances were kind to Pompey, who reached his object the first.

The development of piracy in the Mediterranean had made the provisioning of Rome increasingly difficult, and the cost of living went up considerably. The succession of generals who had attacked the pirates had not managed to put down the plague. The people, hungry and discontented, called for a decisive effort. Pompey, who had kept his eyes open,

[1] *Rep.*, i, 21, 34.

hastened to seize upon this windfall. In 67, a Tribune of his following, A. Gabinius, brought forward a bill regarding the suppression of piracy. He proposed that an exceptional military command should be instituted, to make an end of the matter once and for all. The general who received this command should, with the title of Proconsul, have supreme command all over the Mediterranean and fifty miles inland. He should have fifteen Legates under him, should have complete freedom in raising the forces which he needed, and should have 200 ships and a credit of 6,000 talents on the treasury. Pompey was not named in the bill, but everybody in Rome knew quite well that no other could be meant. Before this revival of the military danger, the oligarchical party, in the person of its leaders Catulus and Hortensius, set up a stubborn opposition; despairing of success, they resorted to their old tactics of using the Tribunician veto. A Tribune named L. Trebellius placed his veto on the bill, but Gabinius quietly revived the procedure of Ti. Gracchus, and Trebellius, seeing himself about to be deposed by the vote of the people, gave way. The bill found an enthusiastic supporter in Cæsar, who was not sorry to see Pompey depart or to create a precedent which would be useful to himself in the future. The law was passed, and a second vote invested Pompey with the chief command. To punish the oligarchs for their opposition, the people took delight in still further increasing his forces, and he was given 120,000 infantry, 5,000 horse, 500 ships instead of 200, twenty-four Legates of Senatorial rank instead of fifteen, and two Quæstors. The authority thus bestowed on Pompey represented, and in legal form, a personal power such as Rome had not seen before; in all but name it was monarchy, and no one in Rome, supporter or opponent, had any illusions about it.

With these overwhelming forces and this assured unity of command there could be no doubt of the issue of the war. Besides, Pompey showed real organizing capacity. He divided the whole seaboard of the Mediterranean into thirteen sectors, each under a Legate, while he himself, at the head of a flying squadron and landing-troops, methodically swept the sea from west to east. Driven back everywhere and finding all the coasts strictly guarded, the pirates had to withdraw to Asia, chiefly to Cilicia, where their principal nests were.

Pompey hunted them out, destroyed their forces when they emerged, and compelled them to surrender. In three months the war was over. At once food came pouring into Rome and prices came down with a run. Pompey's popularity grew in proportion. He and his friends hastened to make the most of the situation. When the war with the pirates was ended, Pompey should have laid down his command and returned to private life, but that was exactly what he did not want to do. He wanted another war, longer, more glorious, and more profitable. Such a war was in progress, the war against Mithradates which Lucullus, a leader of the oligarchy, had been carrying on for seven years, and which must necessarily be followed by the complete reorganization of the East. In Pompey's absence his supporters in Rome were working to have Lucullus removed from his post and Pompey made commander in his place. The last act of the reaction against the Sullan constitution was beginning.

Once again, Pompey was well served by fortune. In 67 things began to go badly in Asia Minor. M. Fabius Hadrianus, a lieutenant of Lucullus, was defeated by Mithradates at Cabeira, and two legions refused to follow Lucullus himself in Armenia. The Equestrian order, which was on the watch, took advantage of these reverses to excite public opinion against Lucullus. Gabinius, Pompey's spokesman, who had been standing by, brought forward a new bill, by which Lucullus's command was split up, that general only retaining the province of Asia, while Bithynia and Pontus were given to another general, the Consul M'. Acilius Glabrio. Glabrio was quite incapable, and this was exactly why the Knights had picked on him, in the certainty that Pompey would presently be summoned to take his place. But Pompey was in a hurry to get his war, and did not even allow Glabrio time to show his incompetence. At the beginning of 66, another Tribune, one Manilius, also a man of straw, proposed the *Lex Manilia*, by which the chief command of the provinces of Asia, Bithynia, and Cilicia and the conduct of the war against Mithradates should be transferred to Pompey. Pompey was also to retain the powers all over the Mediterranean conferred on him by the *Lex Gabinia*, although the disappearance of piracy removed their object. Thus Pompey's extraordinary command was territorially extended over the

G

whole East, and this time no exact time-limit was specified. The bill was combated by the oligarchs and, once again and for the same reasons, supported by Cæsar, and also by Cicero, who was at that time making his appearance in public life. In spite of the active efforts of Catulus, the oligarchical party was beaten again and the law was passed by a considerable majority.

The laws of Gabinius and Manilius were above all the expression of the external necessities which were pressing on the Roman State and which could not be met by the Republican constitution with its superannuated system of local Comitia and annual magistrates or governors. In practice, they constituted a first legal realization of the theory of Principate, in favour of Pompey. The traditional organs of the City continued to direct home policy, while foreign policy, in the form of diplomacy, army, and navy, was concentrated in the hands of a new organ, the " first citizen ", the Princeps, who could ensure the unity of views and continuity of action necessary to the successful working of the State. But the compromise was precarious, and for two reasons. First, it was limited in space (the Mediterranean seaboard and the East) and in time (three years, by the *Lex Gabinia*; until Eastern affairs were completely settled, by the *Lex Manilia*). Secondly, it only worked successfully because of a chance circumstance—the distance lying between Pompey and his opponents, which kept them out of immediate contact and prevented conflicts. What would happen when he returned, and what would become of the new system ? It was an anxious question, the solution of which was not brought about, but delayed for five years, by Pompey's long absence in the East (66–62).

While in Rome the conservative coalition which gathered round Cicero averted the danger of social revolution by crushing Catiline, Pompey, at the head of his victorious army, was completing the reorganization of the East. Everyone knew that when he came home he had but to say the word and personal government would be established. Friends and foes alike waited impatiently for the day on which the fate of the old Republican constitution would be decided. The year 62 went by amid these anxieties, and not until the last days of it did Pompey land at Brundusium at the head of his legions. Then came a surprise for everybody.

As soon as Pompey set foot on Italian soil, he declared his troops disbanded. In the circumstances his conduct was absolutely constitutional, and his predecessors had always acted in the same way, but it was so little expected—such progress had the idea of military monarchy made in men's minds—that there was general stupefaction. No one would believe that Pompey, with the State in his hands, was of his own free will giving up his exceptional position and returning to legal Republican ways as a private citizen. When he at last arrived in Rome, alone and without the army, people had to believe their eyes. How can we explain Pompey's conduct in those decisive circumstances? Constitutional scruples, no doubt—it is a fair explanation, but insufficient. Pompey wanted personal power, but, according to his conception of Principate, that power must be accepted by the traditional organs, not imposed by force. In reality, on the day when Pompey dismissed his troops, he remained true to his political ideal; he showed that he wanted no *coup d'État*; he gave a pledge to the Senatorial oligarchy in the hope of being paid back. But that party would not have personal power at any price, even in the mild form of a Principate; it only resigned itself to the system, under Augustus, after thirty years of fighting and in the face of an accomplished fact. When the first moment of surprise was over, party struggles were at once resumed.

The situation soon became very difficult for Pompey. One would suppose that the oligarchy ought, for whatever reason, to have given Pompey credit for the constitutional correctness of his action. It did nothing of the kind. The Senate seemed to have only one concern—one which says little for its political wisdom—to avenge itself on Pompey for the apprehension which his return had caused it. The democratic party now followed Crassus and Cæsar. On the side of Pompey there was only the Equestrian order, which could not constitute a majority by itself. Pompey was driven by the nature of things to seek support either in the Senate or in the leaders of the democrats. In spite of the repeated warnings of Cicero and the moderate fraction, who wanted to maintain the conservative coalition of 63, setting Pompey at the head of the State in the capacity of Princeps, the Senate, led by the extremist section, especially Cato,

obstinately repelled his advances. No affront was spared him.
He was made to wait six months for his triumph, the ratification of his measures in the East was delayed a year, and
the distribution of land to his veterans was refused. Scorn-
fully rebuffed by the Senatorial oligarchy, Pompey had no
choice ; he was compelled to turn to the democratic party
and its leaders, Cæsar and Crassus. Here he found a very
different welcome. Cæsar, who had been Proprætor of
Further Spain in 61, had just returned to Rome, and he had
not concealed his intention of trying for the Consulship of 59.
He knew that the Senatorial party would fight him tooth
and nail. The success of his election therefore depended
on the Equestrian order, which obeyed Pompey. So Pompey
and Cæsar needed one another, and they drew together.
To strengthen their alliance, Cæsar also reconciled Pompey
with Crassus, his old enemy. The result of these skilful
and complicated manœuvres was the formation of the First
Triumvirate of 60 B.C.

In virtue of their agreement, Pompey, Cæsar, and Crassus
pooled their influence and resources in the interest of their
various aspirations. Pompey brought the support of the
Knights, Cæsar, that of the democrats, and Crassus, that of
his vast wealth and the many connections which it had
earned him. In exchange for his contribution, each of the
three associates would get definite advantages from the
agreement. Cæsar, the promoter and soul of the Triumvirate,
was naturally to be the most favoured of the three ; he was to
have the Consulship of the following year and, when he laid
it down, an important military command. Pompey would
have all his measures in the East ratified and land would be
given to his veterans. As for Crassus, we do not know exactly
what his two allies promised him, but it was quite certain
that that able man of business would, when the time came,
get his share, and a big one, even if he had not done so
beforehand. The three accomplices had only one thing to
fear, the opposition of the Senatorial oligarchy ; and that,
thrown on its own resources by the defection of the Equestrian order, was doomed to impotence. Of the result there
could be no doubt ; the agreement of 60 rang the knell of
Republican government and proclaimed the undisguised
arrival of personal rule.

In March, 58, Cæsar, after a Consulship which was most obnoxious to the Senatorial oligarchy, set out for Gaul, and commenced its conquest. Left in Rome with Crassus, who was once again the associate of his disillusionment, Pompey could give himself up to bitter reflections. His beloved system of Principate had failed, in 61, before the refusal of the Senate. At a time when military force was certainly everything, he had no army, while Cæsar had one. Faithful to his political ideal, he at least hoped that fear of Cæsar would be a beginning of wisdom for the Senate, and that at last, with its help or at least its resigned acceptance, he could establish that Principate, the fickle mirage which he had hitherto pursued so obstinately and so vainly.

Once again, he took the first steps and gave pledges. He broke with Clodius and brought about the recall of Cicero, who returned to Rome on the 4th September, 57, amid extraordinary enthusiasm. The policy of conservative union at which Pompey was once more aiming was, *mutatis mutandis*, the traditional policy of Cicero. Both from conviction and from gratitude, the orator resumed it with fresh ardour. The Senate had caused it to fail a first time in 60 by the bungling of the extremists, and so had brought about the formation of the Triumvirate. Cicero might hope that, enlightened by the consequences of its mistake, it would show more sense this time and would not unceremoniously reject the hand held out to it by Pompey. No doubt, Pompey stated terms, and those terms had not changed—the Principate in the future, and in the meantime, as an indispensable preliminary, a military command for himself similar to Cæsar's. But the proofs which he had given of his respect—at least, his apparent respect—for legal methods ought to dispel the doubts of the Senate. Besides, the Senate had no choice. To fight the danger of military monarchy which, in the person of Cæsar, was rising on the horizon, the Senate needed Pompey. It was therefore reasonable that it should pay him for his services, as Cicero proposed.

A first opportunity for the Senatorial oligarchy to show its intentions presented itself in 57, a few days after Cicero's return. The Tribune C. Messius, a tool of the type of Gabinius and Manilius, proposed that Pompey should be entrusted with the general management of the corn supply, and that for this purpose he should be given a great military command, with an army, a fleet, free disposal of the treasury, fifteen Legates, and an *imperium* superior to that of governors of provinces—in short, a renewal, in more extensive form and for five years, of the power which had been conferred on him by the laws of Gabinius and Manilius.   Combated by the Senatorial party, the bill had to be withdrawn, and in the end was only passed in the form of a Consular law—*lex modesta*, Cicero calls it [1]—without any of the military provisions which, for Pompey, made its whole value.   He himself, as his political system of the Principate required, pretended to be quite satisfied.   But it was a hard lesson, and soon he was to receive a harder.

Ptolemy Auletes, King of Egypt, being driven out by his subjects, had taken refuge in Rome, and asked the Senate to restore him to his throne.   Such an expedition would be the great command of which Pompey had dreamed for years. He ardently desired to obtain it, and the Senate knew it. Unfortunately, once again the extremists, who, as so often happens in history, had learned nothing and forgotten nothing, carried the majority with them.   The matter was adjourned, and, after one delay and another, finally buried (January, 56). The management of the corn-supply (*cura annonæ*) for five years was, it is true, one of the constitutive elements of the Principate which Augustus appropriated in 22 B.C., but in the cut-down form which the law had given it it was far from answering to the hopes which Pompey had originally placed in it.   Repelled by the Senate, he had only one safeguard left, the Triumvirate.   So, condemned to be for ever rolling a stone of Sisyphos, he tried to obtain from that side what the Senatorial oligarchy had twice refused him.

Pompey's political change of direction was to bring about consequences which were all the more important because, at that very moment, Cæsar had urgent need of him.   His enemies were openly calling for the annulment of all his measures of 59, including the *Lex Vatinia*, the most important of all, by which he held his military command.   All his legislative work and all his projects for the future were thus threatened.   Common necessity drew Pompey and Cæsar together.   In April, 56, the Triumvirs met at Luca.   Each

Ad Att., iv, 1, 6.

had brought his political following and his chief officers. In addition, a great number of political men—magistrates, two hundred Senators, governors of provinces, Knights— had come to hear the news or to pay court to the masters of to-day and to-morrow ; a hundred and twenty lictors with their bundles stood at Cæsar's door.

Cæsar wanted to guarantee the measures of his Consul- ship against any possibility of annulment and to have his military command, which would presently expire, extended for a further period. Pompey and Crassus, taught by the methods of their associate and determined not to be left helpless against him, as in the past, wanted a second Consul- ship, at the end of which each should at once receive a long and important military command. Each Triumvir thought only of his personal interests, but, since each needed his colleagues in order to advance them, they ended by agreeing, as is usual. It was agreed that Cæsar should obtain the exten- sion of his powers, and that Pompey and Crassus should be elected to a second Consulship the next year and receive a big command when it ended. These were, no doubt, great concessions on the part of Cæsar, but, with the opportunism which always marked him, he did not think them too high a price to pay for the certainty of keeping his army and, with it, the means to realize his hopes when the time came.

In spite of their precautions, Pompey and Crassus were not elected to the Consulship without difficulty, and only achieved their object by terrorizing the Comitia. They were compelled to use violence to dispose of the Senatorial candidate, L. Domitius Ahenobarbus. Cato, who was trying for the Prætorship, was removed by the same methods, and the candidates of the party of the new Consuls were elected to the other magistracies by large majorities. Pompey and Crassus then set themselves to carry out the programme drawn up at Luca. They caused the Tribune C. Trebonius to propose a law regarding the allotment of the provinces. Pompey was to receive Spain and Crassus Syria, but on special terms in respect of duration and competence ; they were appointed for five years, they could raise whatever troops they pleased, and they had the right of declaring peace and war, which, under the old constitution, belonged to the people

and Senate alone. By another law, presented by the two
Consuls, Cæsar's governorship of Gaul was extended for the
same period. The two chief articles of the programme of
Luca having been thus carried out, the Consuls caused certain
secondary measures to be passed—a law which increased the
penalties for illegal associations, and a law on the courts of
justice which, in the state of complete decomposition into
which the Republican constitution had fallen, could hardly
produce any useful result.

When Pompey and Crassus concluded their Consulship
they should, according to the constitution, have departed to
their provinces, like Cæsar. Crassus left Rome, but Pompey,
reviving his tactics of 70, ever in pursuit of his political
ideal, managed, on various pretexts, to stay in the capital
and allowed his Legates L. Afranius and M. Petreius to
take his place in Spain. Being thus free of his fellow
Triumvirs, with Cæsar in Gaul and Crassus in Syria, he hoped,
with favourable circumstances, to oust them both and remain
sole master. Of the Principate of his dreams he already had
two essential elements, the Proconsular *imperium*, wielded
in Rome itself, contrary to the law, and the supreme control
of the corn-supply, which he had kept in his hands since 57.
In fact, from this year of 54 onwards, not only did Pompey
have, at least in rudimentary form, the powers of a Princeps,
but contemporaries were beginning to call him by that name.
Certain passages written at that time are characteristic in
this respect.

> In September, 54, Cicero wrote to his friend Lentulus : " Since
> Pompey was Princeps in the Republic—*cum autem in Republica Cn.
> Pompeius Princeps esset.*" [1] In the same year, he said in his speech
> for Plancius : " Should I not support in Pompey the man whom all
> allow to be Princeps in the Republic ?—*quem omnes in Republica
> Principem esse concedunt.*" [2] Lastly, on the 27th February, 49, in
> a letter to Atticus, after defining the Princeps, he adds : " Our
> Pompey has always failed to understand this task, and now more
> than ever. Mastery was what both sought (*dominatio quæsita ab
> utroque est*) ; the object was not that the State might be happy and
> virtuous." [3]

Moreover, Pompey distrusted Cæsar, whose ambition he
knew, and he did not despair of one day obtaining from the
Senate the supreme power of a legal kind, the full Principate,
which he had always pursued and never reached, and to which

---

[1] *Ad Lent.*, i, 9, 11.   [2] xxxix, 93.   [3] *Ad Att.*, viii, 11, 2.

he always remained attached, in spite of many disillusion-
ments. The utter anarchy to which Rome was a prey in 54
and 53 suited his purposes admirably.

Amid the general disorder, Pompey, armed with Proconsular power and commanding several legions, represented
the only existing authority ; but he took care not to interfere,
and did his best to encourage the anarchy, in the hope that
the Senate, driven by necessity and not knowing where to turn,
would throw itself into his arms and at last give him the
legal power, the Principate, which was always the objective
of his policy. In the Senatorial camp, Cicero, after being
taken aback for a moment by the agreement of Luca,
advocated this course with all his might. Circumstances
did the rest. Julia, the daughter of Cæsar and wife of
Pompey, died in 54, and so an intimate bond between the
two chief members of the Triumvirate was broken. In
the following year, Crassus was defeated by the Parthians
at Carrhæ and treacherously killed during an interview.
Pompey and Cæsar were now left alone, face to face, and,
sooner or later, a conflict between them was inevitable.

It began to dawn upon some of the Senate that henceforward their choice lay, not between Republic and personal
government, but between two forms of the latter—Principate
with Pompey or monarchy with Cæsar. So everything
conspired to bring Pompey and the Senate together. Only
the extremists of that body, with the narrowness of mind
which was their most marked characteristic, still showed
reluctance, but circumstances, stronger than their will-
power, in the end compelled them to go with the rest, whether
they liked or not. In the face of the frightful anarchy
which broke out in Rome at the beginning of 52, the Senate
passed the *Senatus consultum ultimum,* and entrusted Pompey
with the restoration of order. But this temporary, limited
mission did not satisfy Pompey. He wanted more, and,
until he got it, he remained inactive. The Senate, knowing
that it could not do without him, had to resign itself to voting
him exceptional powers. Pompey was appointed sole Consul,
being forbidden to choose a colleague for himself for two
months. The appointment bristled with illegalities. The
existence of a single Consul was absolutely contrary to the
con stitution and to its whole spirit. Under the laws

governing the *cursus honorum*, Pompey, having been Consul
in 55, could not hold the office again three years later. Lastly,
by definition, no man could be a Consul and a Proconsul
at once. But in the Rome of the end of the Republic one
illegality the more mattered little, and at least, by giving
Pompey, in this form, what was really a dictatorship, the
Senate was able to limit its duration. After all, if Pompey
obtained, from the Senate itself, the legal power to which
he had always aspired, he only received it temporarily.
For him it was only a partial victory, perhaps a stage,
certainly not his goal.

Nevertheless, Pompey set himself seriously to his task
of restoring order. First, he caused four important laws
to be voted—a law on illegal canvassing, which increased
the existing penalties, a law on violence, setting up a special
court for such cases, a law on magistracies, regularizing the
manner in which they should be obtained and conducted,
and a law on the provinces, which provided for an interval
of five years between the holding of a magistracy and that
of the provincial governorship to which it entitled its holder.
The laws on canvassing and violence were strictly enforced.
The chief incident was the trial of Milo, the murderer of
Clodius, who, in spite of Cicero's defence, had to go into
exile. The disturbers of the peace who had set the Senate
House on fire during Clodius's funeral were likewise prosecuted
and sentenced. The gangs which had been terrorizing Rome
for some years disappeared, and, under the rough but salutary
treatment of Pompey's soldiers, general order was at length
restored. So far, Pompey had worked in the public interest.
When the object was reached, the Senate had only one desire
—to see him retire into private life as quickly as possible.
But Pompey was not to be fooled again. He took care not
to forget his own interests. In virtue of his law on the
provinces, he obtained an extension of his governorship of
Spain for five years.

In spite of this very relative improvement, the old constitution was dead. The hard facts consisted of two military
leaders, Pompey and Cæsar, both equally ambitious, and
aiming, in the different forms of Principate and monarchy,
at one same object—personal power. The one who should
succeed in keeping his military command longer than the

other, for however short a time, must *ipso facto* remain master of the State. Therefore everything had been settled in minute detail among the Triumvirs so that their various commands might all expire simultaneously. But the further extension which Pompey—not without definite intention—had obtained for himself upset the whole situation. Cæsar's command was to terminate at the end of 51 ; Pompey's, by the recent law, would last until the end of 46. Thus armed, Pompey had only to wait for his colleague to retire into private life, when he, left alone of the great military leaders, would at once, without contest, take the chief place in the State. Pompey's plan was admirably designed, and, moreover, it was clothed in the legal form for which he had always had a preference. He therefore believed himself sure of success. A little patience, and the Principate could not escape him.

But Pompey had reckoned without Cæsar, who was not easily duped, and, in spite of Pompey's precautions, saw through his game clearly. Cæsar asked Pompey for an extension of command like his own. Pompey, without refusing it categorically, took steps that it should be refused. Cæsar then altered his plan. He asked for a second Consulship for the year, which would follow the expiration of his Proconsulship, hoping to profit by it to obtain a long and important military command as he had done in 59. But this procedure presented one grave difficulty. By Sulla's law on the magistracies, which was still in force on this point, at least ten years must elapse between two successive tenures of one same office. So, having been Consul in 59, Cæsar could not hold the office again until 49 at the earliest, that is, should he be elected, become Consul designate before the middle of 50. Therefore, since his command expired at the end of 51, six months would pass between that moment and the Consular elections at which, by the law, Cæsar could enter himself as a candidate. During those six months, Cæsar would be a private citizen, without an army, and would be exposed to all the attacks of his enemies, who, as he knew, would only wait for the first opportunity to take their revenge. To forestall this danger, he had asked for leave to canvass for the Consulship while absent from Rome, and therefore to keep his command until his election, that is, until the day when his opponents, because of that election, could no longer touch him.   Pompey, on his side, had been careful, in his law on the magistracies, to renew the clause excluding absentees, and, to give Cæsar at least apparent satisfaction, he had afterwards simply added to the text an exception in his favour which, in view of the irregularity of the procedure, was of no legal value.   From the legal point of view, the situation was quite clear.   Pompey had his command for certain until the end of 46 ; Cæsar would lose his on the 1st January, 50.   Pompey's plan seemed to triumph.   To be rid of Cæsar, he had only to wait on the events which would soon automatically make him the supreme head of the State.   Moreover, Cicero's policy had in the end prevailed.   After so many vain attempts Pompey and the Senate had at last come together.   The cause of Pompey was henceforward regarded as that of the Republic and constitution themselves.   The two objects of Pompey's whole career seemed to have been reached ; he held the supreme power and he wielded it with the consent of the organs of the constitution.   In both its fundamental articles, for the first time in Pompey's political life, the formula of the Principate was realized in full.

II

The Monarchy of Cæsar

So the monarchical idea, which had been progressing since the end of the third century, and had been realized for a moment in civil form by Caius Gracchus, at last received from Pompey the concrete form of the Principate.   But, if the Republican past furnished anticipations of the Principate as early as the second century, it also presented, at a later date, another type of personal government in the form of the monarchical power which was for a moment realized by Sulla.   Sulla, the first monarch of Rome, had doubtless been a monarch in spite of himself, and without the intention of remaining such ; but his example none the less survived, a permanent danger to the Republican constitution which he had tried to restore and a constant object of meditation for reformers with pure intentions and, still more, for men ambitious for power.   Marvellous as his intuition in political matters may have been, Cæsar would not have been a Roman if he had not observed for years and retained much. The example of Sulla had shown him what could be done with military power, and that of Pompey, still more instructive, had shown him the joints in the harness of a Principate. He had learned, and would not forget, that the Senatorial nobility would never resign itself, unless compelled, even to the modified form of personal government represented by Principate. Pompey, in spite of his repeated advances and the many pledges which he had given to the constitution, had not been able, even in 54 and after, to establish it more than incompletely and temporarily, and Cicero himself, who was not one of the extremists of the Senate, would, immediately after Cæsar's death, jettison the programme which he had so obligingly expounded in the *Pro Marcello*.

Pompey's Principate, Cæsar's monarchy—the difference between the two conceptions appears both in the method of acquisition and in that of exercise. Cæsar did not hesitate to use force if necessary—the crossing of the Rubicon and the Civil War are proof enough of this—and, secondly, he used his personal power without respect for the old authorities and constitution. Twice in his political career he had the opportunity to apply his methods—during his first Consulship of 59 and, still more, from 49 to 44, during his Dictatorship. In the course of those two decisive stages on the road to monarchy the statesman in him was fully revealed.

In 60 Cæsar formed the Triumvirate with Pompey and Crassus. The first step towards the execution of the agreement was the election of Cæsar to the Consulship. In the exceptional circumstances in which the election was held, there was no doubt of the result, even among his adversaries. Being unable to prevent his success, the oligarchy sought at least to paralyse him by giving him one of his political enemies as a colleague. For want of a better, since able men were not abundant in the party, it cast eyes on M. Calpurnius Bibulus, an insignificant person, but obstinate, and—his chief claim to attention—a staunch opponent of Cæsar. Opposed by the combined forces of the Triumvirate, Bibulus only secured election by corruption. Cæsar came to the Consulship with a very definite programme, in which the public good played a purely subordinate part. What he chiefly expected from it was, when it was over, a big military command, which would enable him to aim still higher in the future. That command he counted on obtaining, like Marius and Pompey before him, by a vote of the people. He must, then, before all, secure the support of the people. Consequently, as soon as he took up office, he brought forward an agrarian bill.

The new bill reproduced in its main lines that which Rullus had presented four years earlier, at the beginning of Cicero's Consulship. All State land in Italy, and other land specially bought for the purpose with the resources of the treasury, particularly the money brought by Pompey from the East, should be distributed in allotments to poor citizens, and especially to Pompey's veterans. For twenty years those who received these allotments should not be allowed to sell them. A full commission of twenty members and an executive commission of five should be entrusted with its application. By proclaiming the principle that no one should be obliged to sell his land, Cæsar's bill removed the chief cause of complaint which had been found in the agrarian law of Tiberius Gracchus ; it also prevented the executive commission having the excessive powers which it was given by the bill of Rullus. Altogether, it appeared as moderate as it was well conceived, and it did not seem that either the principle or the wording of the various articles would arouse any serious opposition. Lastly, in an excess of caution and tactfulness towards the aristocratic party, Cæsar was so conciliatory as to submit his bill beforehand to the Senate. There was no declared opposition, but Cæsar's opponents held up the bill by systematic obstruction. Cato spoke for a whole day. At last Cæsar lost patience and had him taken off to jail. The entire Senate followed him, and Cæsar was left alone in the chamber. The ill-will of the Senate was obvious. Cæsar withdrew his bill and presented it direct to the Comitia.

With the people, where the Triumvirs held the majority, there was no doubt of the success of the agrarian bill. The oligarchy did not attempt open fighting, and revived its tactics of obstruction in another form. Three Tribunes interposed their veto, and Bibulus, in virtue of his Consular prerogatives, blocked progress systematically. He made great play with the auspices, and declared that he was watching the sky for favourable omens. Cæsar, knowing his obstinacy, decided to take things by storm and ignore him. He placed the bill on the agenda of the Comitia. The democratic gangs were mobilized, and the army, represented on this occasion by Pompey's veterans, stood by, ready to act at the first summons. On the day of the voting, Bibulus started obstructing again ; the people hurled him from the top of the steps of the Temple of Castor and the law was carried as if nothing had happened. Cæsar had won the day, but only by violence and a grave breach of the constitution. The infringement of the *Leges Ælia* and *Fufia* regarding the right of auspices constituted a defect in form which might later entail the annulment of the law. But for the moment, at any rate, Cæsar's victory was complete. Bibulus, to show his disapproval, ceased to take part in public affairs. He retired to his house, where he continued his legal obstruction, informing Cæsar that the auspices were unfavourable on every occasion. This attitude might create difficulties for the future, but at present Bibulus's voluntary retirement made Cæsar's task very much easier. Henceforward he systematically ignored his colleague, just as he had already ignored the Senate. For him the constitution was now a dead letter, and he did not even trouble to save its face. In spite of his subsequent advances, the governmental oligarchy never forgot it or forgave it.

Meanwhile, Cæsar, with the opportunism which was second nature in him, made full use of the advantageous situation and continued to carry out his programme by passing various laws—on the courts of justice, on peculation, on the ratification of Pompey's measures in the East. But he really regarded all the acts which he rushed through in this rapid way as mere preliminaries. The essential article in his programme was the law which should give him, when he laid down his office, a solid army and a good command, that is, the means to make a big place for himself in the State at some later time. The Senate, knowing his intentions, had taken precautions before he became Consul, giving the Consuls of his year quite unimportant governorships.

This was not what Cæsar wanted. Already, with his usual foresight and discernment, he had laid claim to Gaul. The conquest of that country would be a long task, which would give him time to collect and maintain a large army. All the same, he did not want to be too far away from Rome, where he knew that his opponents, and even his colleagues of the Triumvirate, would not waste time in his absence, and he meant to follow events there from close at hand. He therefore wished to have not only Transalpine Gaul, or Gaul properly so called, but Cisalpine Gaul, or the whole of Northern Italy down to the Arno and Rubicon. This admirably conceived plan of Cæsar for the first time combined two advantages which had hitherto been incompatible— a big provincial command and the holder's presence in Italy, at the very gates of Rome.

To execute his plan, Cæsar had only to use the method established by Marius and afterwards followed by Pompey— voting by plebiscite on the proposal of a Tribune. The Tribune P. Vatinius presented a bill granting Cæsar the province of Cisalpine Gaul with an army of three legions for a period of five years. The proposal, which might seem comparatively moderate—many scruples in this respect had vanished in the last century—was passed without great difficulty. But for Cæsar it was only a beginning. The sequel soon came. Cæsar asked the Senate to add Transalpine Gaul to his government, with a fourth legion. The Senate only yielded to intimidation, and made the formal reservation that Cæsar should have Transalpine Gaul for one year only. The main thing for Cæsar was to have won his case in principle ; for the actual term, he had only to obtain an extension by engaging in a big war and so forcing the hand of the recalcitrant Senate.

He had won a complete victory on the very point which meant most to him, for his whole later career depended on it, but he had no illusions about its precarious nature. The Senatorial oligarchy was beaten for a moment, but it was only waiting for his departure to take its revenge. Even his fellow Triumvirs, Pompey and Crassus, were beginning to see that he had obtained the most immediate and certain profits from their association. Therefore Cæsar, before his departure, took minute precautions to protect his work in his absence against both his opponents and his allies. He found the instrument which he needed in a young Patrician without convictions or scruples, ready for anything if it was profitable, named Clodius. Cæsar had him transferred into the Plebs and elected Tribune for 58 B.C. On entering office Clodius caused four laws to be passed—a corn-law instituting free doles instead of sales at reduced prices, a law on the colleges, re-establishing the associations put down in 64, a law limiting the prerogatives of the Censors, and, lastly, a law on the observation of the omens, which did away with the political importance of the auspices.

These laws were merely so many preparatory measures intended to strengthen the democratic majority in the Comitia ; the great object of Clodius and his backer Cæsar was to strike Cato and Cicero, the two men in the Senatorial party who were most to be feared. Clodius presented two bills which, without mentioning them expressly, were aimed at each of them. The first ordered that Cyprus should be made a Roman province, while the second dealt with men who had caused Roman citizens to be put to death without trial. The first law was passed, and Cato was appointed to go to Cyprus, to settle its annexation on the spot. The voting of the second allowed of no doubt. Cicero, directly threatened, went into voluntary exile. A special law, again passed at the proposal of Clodius, exiled him to a distance of 400 miles from Rome, under pain of death in case of non-compliance for himself and for those who sheltered him, and further ordered the confiscation of his goods. In the hope of a speedy change for the better, Cicero left for Macedon and Greece. Cæsar had taken his precautions wisely. The leaders of the Senatorial party, Cato and Cicero, were out of the way, at least for some time. His allies, Pompey and Crassus, who would both remain in Rome, would watch and neutralize one another. Clodius, the trusty watch-dog, would protect his work. In March, 58, Cæsar could start for his province with an easy mind.

Nine years later, at the beginning of 49, we find the glorious conqueror of Gaul at the head of his army. Condemned to conquer or to disappear from the political scene, he has just crossed the Rubicon ; in a lightning offensive, which might appear madness and is really supreme wisdom, he marches

on Rome, where, after Pompey's departure for the East,
he takes possession of the government. When Italy is
conquered, the turn of the provinces comes—in 49, the
conquest of Spain, where Pompey's lieutenants, Petreius
and Afranius, are reduced to surrender ; in 48–47, the
conquest of the East, following on the victory of Pharsalos
and the death of Pompey ; in 46, Thapsus and the conquest
of Africa ; in 45, a second conquest of Spain, where the
reconstituted Pompeian forces are finally crushed at Munda.
The reconquest and pacification of the Roman world, was,
therefore, a long task, interrupted, no doubt, by sojourns
of varying length in Rome, and it kept Cæsar for over four
years. The last victory, that of Munda, was won less than
one year before the bloody scene of the Ides of March.

In these conditions of space and time, Cæsar's wars and
internal reforms were necessarily carried out side by side.
The fact that he was doing two things at once and his
premature death explain why his internal reforms look like
sketches, although they are characteristic enough to allow
us to determine both the method and the guiding idea which
lay behind that immense constitutional transformation.

A first characteristic is that Cæsar, like Sulla, seized
the power by force, and thereby was obliged, whether he
liked it or not, to establish a military government. But,
unlike Sulla, he looked not to the past but to the future ;
he wanted not to restore but to innovate, and to give the
Roman State the constitutional structure which was now
necessary to its development and to its very life. Suetonius
quotes a significant remark of his on this matter :

> " He said that if anything happened to himself the Republic
> would enjoy no peace, but would relapse into civil war under worse
> conditions than ever—*Rempublicam, si quid sibi eveniret, neque
> quietam fore, et aliquanto deteriore conditione civilia bella subituram.*" [1]

Republican government no longer suited the Roman State.
Rome needed a leader and a master. The example of Pompey
had proved that, in the face of the obstinate, rancorous
ill-will of the Senatorial oligarchy, the system of Principate
was hardly possible. Cæsar, with his clear, logical mind,
now taught by the experience of the past, without hesitation
and without vain illusions, marched straight for his goal,

[1] *Julius,* 86.

absolute, hereditary monarchy of the Hellenistic type, the perfect pattern of which was furnished by the East and had been offered to his own eyes by the Lagid kingdom. The democrat of a few years ago, the party man, gave place to the head of the State, who by his victory had won the power to act and would be capable of assuming the consequent responsibilities.

Apart from the high-handed way in which he had seized the power, Cæsar's monarchical tendencies are shown in two correlative things—his organization of the government and his attitude towards the old authorities.

Raised to supreme power by the army, the leader of the democrats brought with him a definite idea, which would govern his whole policy—that the Republican constitution was dead and military monarchy had become a necessity. In 49, he entered Rome, and stayed there only a week. His Proconsulship of Gaul had expired. Legally, he was nobody, but by a succession of offices which were conferred on him he concentrated in his own hands the personal power which he wanted and considered necessary to the salvation of the State. During the first Spanish War, a law made him Dictator; he took up the office when he returned to the capital, and kept it only eleven days, until he had obtained election to the Consulship of the following year. In 48, he was Consul with P. Servilius Vatia Isauricus, and it was in this capacity, as lawful and official head of the Roman State, that he waged war on Pompey. After the victory of Pharsalos, which finally decided the conflict in his favour, he was given a whole series of prerogatives of various kinds—the right to present himself for the Consulship five years running, to declare war and make peace without the intervention of the people or Senate, to assign the Prætorian provinces without any drawing of lots, and to indicate the candidates whom the people should elect to the various magistracies, except the Tribuneship and Plebeian Ædileship. He was given Tribunician power for life. Lastly, a law invested him with the Dictatorship, but a wider Dictatorship of the Sullan type, with powers to form a constitution (*dictatura Reipublicæ constituendæ*) and without any fixed time-limit. In 46, he held the Consulship for the third time; after Thapsus, he was made Dictator for ten years ; he was given Censorial power, without a colleague, for three years, with the title of Prefect of Morals (*præfectus morum*) ; and he was empowered to designate men direct for all magistracies, ordinary and extraordinary.

In 45, he was Consul for the fourth time, but this time without a colleague, and he held the office simultaneously with the Dictatorship, which he retained. In the same year, after Munda, the Senate conferred the title of Imperator on him permanently, and the people decided that he alone should have the right to command armies, levy troops, and dispose of the resources of the treasury. He was authorized to assume the Consulship for ten years, and to appoint all magistrates without election, but these prerogatives he refused. In the same year he was made Prefect of Morals for life, and was given Tribunician inviolability, not only in Rome and within the constitutional radius of a thousand yards, but all over the Roman State. In 44, he was Consul for the fifth time, and shortly before his death his ten years' Dictatorship was made a life-office. He appointed the magistrates who dealt with the allotment of lands to soldiers all over Italy, had complete control of the provincial governorships, and had a seat on all the religious colleges. We should add that since 63, as Pontifex Maximus, he had been the head of Roman religion and exercised all the material and moral privileges which that high office conferred.

These practical powers were accompanied by corresponding outward honours, which were heaped on him, year after year, by the growing adulation of the public. In 46, after Thapsus, he was given the right to sit in the Senate on a curule chair between the two Consuls at any time when he was not a Consul himself ; to give the signal for the Games in the Circus in the place of the Consuls ; to have his statue borne on a ceremonial chariot with the inscription, " To the Demigod " ; to have an escort of seventy-two lictors in his triumph. In the following year he was voted further honours : he could appear at the Games in his triumphal robe, with the laurel wreath of the triumphant general and the red boots of the ancient Kings of Alba ; statues were set up to him, one in the Temple of Quirinus, with the inscription, " To the Unconquered God—*Deo*

Invicto," and one on the Capitol, near those of the Kings ;
the anniversaries of his victories were declared holidays.
Somewhat later, the Senate went still further : he was ordered
to wear the triumphal robe and sit on the curule chair at
all times ; he was given the title of Father of his Country,
with the right to place it officially on coins after his names
and other titles ; his statues were set up in every temple
in Rome and in all the *municipia* ; *spolia opima* were offered
to Jupiter Feretrius in his name ; and an annual festival
was held to celebrate his services. At last, in 44, the Senate
authorized him to wear the costume of the ancient Kings ;
his curule chair was replaced by a golden throne ; prayers
were ordered for Cæsar and his welfare ; a third brotherhood
of Luperci, the Luperci Juliani, was created in his honour ;
the fifth month of the year, in which he was born, was called
Julius ; it was decided, as a solemn and unprecedented
honour, that he should be given a tomb inside the Pomœrium ;
a temple was voted to him under the name of Jupiter Julius,
an honour which made him the incarnation of the chief god
of the State, and a special Flamen was attached to his
worship. Cæsar was not only a master ; he was beginning,
even in his lifetime, to be venerated as a god.

By the side of this monarchical system, which was being
built up in its entirety by the deliberate will of Cæsar, in
conformity with his political programme, the traditional
institutions were in theory maintained. The old authorities,
Comitia, magistracies, Senate, survived, but, emptied of all
reality, they lost all effective meaning and in practice were
reduced to complete nullity.

The Comitia, which, as in the past, embodied the popular
sovereignty, made use of their electoral and legislative
powers only so far as Cæsar condescended to allow them.
In 48 there were no elections for the following year, except
of the Tribunes, and in 47 Rome had only one Curule
magistrate, the Master of Horse, Antony. Cæsar decided
on peace and war and alliances, and, in virtue of his capacity
as Dictator with power to establish the constitution, he
himself promulgated whatever laws he pleased. It was the
same with the magistracies. In 48, Cæsar had the right to
designate men for all magistracies except the Tribuneship
and Plebeian Ædileship, and to present himself for the

Consulship five years running. In 47, the Consuls Q. Fufius Galenus and P. Vatinius were appointed only for the last three months of the year; in 45, a substitute Consul, C. Caninius Rebilus, was in office for one day. In the same year, Cæsar replaced the Prætors, Ædiles, and Quæstors by a number of extraordinary magistrates—six deputy Prætors and Ædiles and two Prefects of the City (deputy Quæstors), whom he appointed himself and placed under the orders of his Master of Horse, Lepidus. In 44, before leaving Rome, he chose P. Cornelius Dolabella to take his place in the Consulship. The nomination was doubly illegal, for Dolabella was not old enough and had not been through the preliminary stage of the Prætorship. Cæsar did not scruple to encroach on the constitutional functions of magistrates : in 45, in a series of important lawsuits, he took the matter out of the hands of the Prætors on his own responsibility, and tried the cases in their place, with the aid of a council.

The Senate, lastly, the great organ of oligarchical government, fared no better. Cæsar struck both at its recruiting and at its competence. He recruited it himself and alone, in virtue of his Censorial power, and was revolutionary in his selection of new Senators. He introduced not only provincials—a very defensible action answering to a definite political idea—but the sons of soldiers and of freedmen. Still more unscrupulously, without regard for the ancient prestige of the body, he reinstated former Senators who had been expelled for notorious bad conduct. He increased the numbers from 600 to 900, a perfect mob, from whom no serious work could be expected. Inside the Senate, he established ranks arbitrarily, without respect for rules and usages. The ten Prætors of 46 were authorized, by a stroke of the pen, to wear Consular insignia, and even non-Senators were admitted to a like privilege by the device of *adlectio*. In practice, the Senate no longer played any legislative part in the working of the government. Cæsar settled current business with a small council of political friends, on which the most prominent figures were L. Cornelius Balbus, C. Oppius, C. Matius, A. Hirtius, and C. Vibius Pansa, and the Senate confined itself to passively ratifying their decisions. Moreover, even in matters of foreign policy, Cæsar did not hesitate to ignore it when it showed opposition ; for example, he conferred the title of King on certain foreign rulers contrary to its recommendation.

This was not all. Not only did Cæsar set aside the old authorities in practice ; what was still more symptomatic, he disdained them as the useless organs of a dead past and an ancient but obsolete constitution.

This system of government, in which Cæsar exercised the powers of a master, and of an absolute master, and the magistrates were merely officials under his orders, and the only rôle of the Senate and Comitia seemed to be to heap titles and honours on the master's head, could only be called by one name, monarchy, *dominatus*, and Cicero frankly gave it that name, more than once.[1] Monarchy after Principate, *dominatus* after *principatus*—that was the fundamental characteristic of the new order.

For this democratic military dictatorship to attain its complete form, kingship of the Hellenistic type, only two attributes were needed—the hereditary system and the title of King. That Cæsar wanted both there can be no doubt. In respect of the former, there are significant indications. After Munda, in April, 45, Cæsar caused the Senate to give him the title of Imperator, with the right to pass it on to his descendants. So the transformation of monarchy held for life into hereditary monarchy was beginning to be envisaged officially. A little later, it was requested that one of his sons, natural or, failing that, adoptive, should be appointed Pontifex, and when Cæsar himself was nominating a number of Patricians in 45 he was careful to include on the list his grandnephew C. Octavius, the future Augustus. In 47, the same C. Octavius had been Prefect of the City, and in that capacity had presided over the Latin Holidays. In 45, he joined Cæsar on the second Spanish expedition. At the beginning of 44, when he assumed his fourth Dictatorship and fifth Consulship, Cæsar decided that when his master of Horse Lepidus went to his province Octavius should take over his office. Lastly, a still more characteristic symptom, Cæsar adopted his grandnephew in his will and made him his heir.

Nor can there be any doubt about the royal title. In

---

[1] *Ad Fam.*, iv, 8, 2 ; cf. *Phil.*, ii, 27.

the triumph after Thapsus, the soldiers escorting Cæsar's chariot sang : " You'll be King if you do right, and if you don't, you won't ! "—*Rex eris, si recte facies ; si non facies, non eris !* " Among the people, the Dictator was now always called the King. Of the opinions of the person most interested, every one in Rome knew what to think. Kingship—in name as well as in fact—was regarded as the necessary culmination of the new political order. Cæsar had taken for his political ideal the absolute world-monarchy of Alexander, and he meant to realize it in its two constitutive elements. He would make it a world-monarchy by subduing the Parthian Empire, the last independent state left in the world by the side of the Roman Empire ; he would make it absolute by changing his power into a monarchy pure and simple.

His sayings were quoted (one day he had said that for him the word " Republic " was meaningless),[1] and, still better, his actions had been seen. In 44 somebody—an enemy, it was maintained—placed the diadem of Eastern kings on his statue on the speakers' platform. Two Tribunes, C. Epidius Marullus and L. Cæsetius Flavus, took it upon themselves to remove it, and summoned an assembly, at which they declared, to the credit of Cæsar, that he had no wish for power of that kind. Cæsar was displeased with their action and with their comment, and did not conceal the fact. Shortly afterwards, when Cæsar was returning on horseback to Rome after celebrating a minor triumph, some of the bystanders hailed him with the title of King. The Tribunes sent the first man who had uttered the cry to prison ; the matter was referred to the Senate and the people voted that the magistrates in question should be dismissed from office. Then Cæsar, in virtue of his Censorial powers, struck their names from the list of Senators and caused them to be superseded in their post. Lastly, in the theatrical manifestation which was the beginning of the tragedy, the famous scene of the Lupercalia, when Antony repeatedly offered him the royal diadem, Cæsar doubtless rejected his offers, but only because he saw that the people was not favourable and the decisive moment was not yet come. At least, he took care that the Consul's offer and his own refusal should

---

[1] Suet., *Julius*, 77.

be officially recorded. In his mind, the necessary act was only postponed. The triumph over the Parthians for which he hoped would, he thought, by arousing patriotic feeling, disguise the constitutional gravity of the innovation and, with the aid of national enthusiasm, break down the last resistance.

That day Cæsar would never see. Fortune, which had showered favours on him all through his career, did not allow it. But was fortune really to blame ? Whether from political miscalculation, infatuation, sickness, or perhaps all three, the fact remains that Cæsar, in the last years of his life, made one blunder after another, especially blunders of form, which men are least ready to forgive, and with his own hands made the conspiracy which killed him. Looking with clear vision into the far future, he had been the first to see definitely the mission of Rome and the political system under which alone it could be fulfilled. But the time was not yet ripe for absolute monarchy. Public opinion, even among the lower classes, which were most ready to accept the new necessities, from natural bent and interest alike, would not admit the name, even though it accepted the reality. Cæsar had seen rightly, but—and it is the great defect in his political system, a mistake for which he paid with his life—in the history of a people one cannot hurry over intermediate stages with impunity. In the last analysis, the tragedy of the Ides of March was only one more illustration of that elementary, eternal truth. Cæsar had fallen, but the monarchical idea still stood and there were men there, preparing to take advantage of it. With the Empire, Cæsarism and bureaucracy, the two great parallel creations of the Imperial system, would attain their full development and, in the course of a constitutional evolution lasting five centuries, find their final formula.

BOOK THREE

CÆSARISM: PRINCIPATE AND "DOMINATE"

CHAPTER I

AUGUSTUS AND THE PRINCIPATE

BIBLIOGRAPHY.—*Ancient Authors* : Livy, *Periochæ* of bks. cxvii–cxlii (to 9 B.C.) (cf. Florus, ii, 14–34 ; Eutropius, vii, 1–10 ; Orosius, vi, 17–19) ; Tacitus, *Annals*, i, 1–5 ; Velleius Paterculus, ii, 58 ; Cicero, *Philippics, Letters to Brutus* (43 B.C.), *to Atticus*, xiv–xvi (44 B.C.), *ad Familiares* (the latest, 44–43 B.C.) ; *H.R.F.*, pp. 252–61 ; *O.R.F.*, pp. 443–551 ; Dion Cassius, xliv, 22 to lvi, 30 ; Appian, *Civil Wars*, ii, 118 to v ; Nicolaos of Damascus, *Life of Augustus*, i–xxxi, in *F.H.G.*, iii, 427–56 ; Plutarch, *Cicero, Antony, Brutus* ; Suetonius, *Twelve Cæsars (Augustus)* ; Aurelius Victor, *De Cæsaribus*, 1 ; *Epitome*, 1 ; Zonaras, x, 12–39.

Legal Documents : Especially in the *Digest*.

Inscriptions : Consular *Fasti* in *C.I.L.*, i, 2nd ed., pp. 158–66 ; *C.I.L.*, ii ff., *passim*, especially vol. vi, 873–901 ; 3745–8, 31188–97 (cf. *I.L.S.*, 75–143, 8893–7).—*Res Gestæ Divi Augusti* (Will of Augustus, or Monument of Ancyra), in *C.I.L.*, iii, pp. 769–99, 1054, 1064, suppl. 2328 (57) (for editions, see below, pp. 377–8) ; *I.G. ad R.R.p.*, iii, 159.—*Lex de Imperio Vespasiani*, *C.I.L.*, vi, 930 ; *I.L.S.*, 244. For the names and titles of the Emperor, cf. **III**, 157–74.

Coins : H. Cohen, **IV**, i.

Modern Works : **VI**, i, 1–359, 453–84 ; **XXI**, 256–304 ; **I**, 7–75 ; **X**, iii, 185–7 (Beloch), 457–61 (Neumann), 210–16, 274–81 (E. Kornemann) ; **VIII**, i ; **XXVI**, 491–507 (R. Poehlmann) ; **XXX**, i, 3–248 ; **XXVII**, 111–17 ; **XIX**, v, and vii, 484–505 ; **IX**, ii, 93–206 ; **XVI**, ii, 545–673 ; **XXXI**, 421 ff. ; **XVIII**, i, 233 ff. ; **LXXV** ; **LXX**, i, 9–17 (Lepidus) ; ii, 42–484 (Antony) ; iv, 258–309 (Octavian) ; **LXXII**, Eng. vols. iii–v ; **VIII**, *passim* ; **XCV** ; **CIII** ; **CXXIX** ; **LVII** ; **CX** ; **CXXXIII** ; **LXXI** ; **XCVII** ; H. Dieckmann, " Die effektive Mitregentschaft des Tiberius," in **XXXVIII**, xv (1918), 339–75 ; A. von Domaszewski, " Die Konsulate der römischen Kaiser," in **L**, 1918, vi. Abh. ; L. Homo, " Les Privilèges du Sénat romain sous l'Empire et leur disparition graduelle au cours du III⁰ siècle," in **XLVII**, 1921 (cxxxvii), 161–203 ; (cxxxviii), 1–52 ; E. Kornemann, " Zum Streit um die Enstehung des Monumentum Ancyranum," in **XXXVIII**, v (1905), 328 ff. ; W. Kolbe, " Das Zweite Triumvirat," in **XXXVI**, 1914, 273–95 ; A. Bauer, " Der Staatsstreich des Octavianus im J. 32 v. Chr.," in **XXXVII**, 1917, 11–23 ; H. Dessau, " Der Staatsstreich des J. 32 v. Chr.," in **XLII**, 1925, 1017–23 ; U. Wilcken, " Der angebliche Staatsstreich Octavians im J. 32 v. Chr.," in **LI**, 1925, 66–87.

I

THE ORIGINS OF IMPERIAL GOVERNMENT

" After the battle of Actium," Tacitus writes at the beginning of his *Histories*,[1] " government by one man became the condition of

[1] i, 1.

*See also Supplementary Bibliography with Prefatory Note (p. 405)

peace " ; and Dion Cassius,[1] still more categorically, adds, " At this time the government assumed a better and more salutary form, for it was quite impossible for the Romans to save themselves with the Republican constitution."

Personal government was the result of distant causes and deep-seated necessities. They may all be summed up in one word—the conquest. A time came when Rome, the city which, by a unique destiny, had conquered a world, had to choose between maintaining her traditional institutions and keeping her empire. It was one of those problems before which peoples never hesitate ; on the day when the question was asked—and that was early—the Republic was doomed and the constitutional crisis had potentially begun. But such complete changes take a long time, and, though the development was inevitable, the solution was only reached after a century of civil war.

The idea which was to give birth to the Imperial system was slow to emerge. It was a product of facts much more than a source of them, as was natural in a people whose dominant quality was not imagination, and which always looked to experience for the guiding principles of its action. The Gracchi, Marius, Sulla, the forerunners of the new age, had felt much more than reasoned out how the Roman State would develop. Pompey, between 52 and 49, had obtained a supremacy in fact, but had not succeeded in finding an exact formula to express the constitutional problem which Rome had to solve at all costs. The lucid genius of Cæsar was the first to pierce the mists of the future and to discover in the Hellenistic type of monarchy the inevitable end of an evolution which had been going on for three hundred years.

Late though the idea may have developed, the instrument by which it was put into effect had been made ready at an early date. The Romans, with their will-power and their capacity for realizing their ideas, had always had a very high conception of the executive power, in the successive forms of the Kingship and the Consulship. The development of the policy of conquest, with the practical institutions— extension of office and provincial governorships—which inevitably followed from it, still further reinforced that

[1] liii, 19

traditional principle. But they had not been blind to the dangers to which such a state of affairs might expose Republican institutions, and law and custom had set up against the holders of the public authority powerful barriers, which should support them in their functions and also confine them to their constitutional position.

The appointment of the Dictator for six months only, with a Master of Horse attached to him, and the appointment of the Consul for one year only, with a colleague, were precautions intended to hold difficult men in check. Provincial governors, in addition to the fact that their very numbers were a great safeguard for Republican institutions, were closely dependent on the Senate, in other words, the aristocracy, for the provinces allotted to them, the resources placed at their disposal, and the period for which they held their office. Last but not least, military leaders found an obstacle in the army serving under them, a citizen army which would have allowed no antics at any price, and would still less have favoured ambitious projects.

The dissolution of the city system, which began in the third century B.C. and ended with the establishment of the Empire, was the result of a double evolution—the gradual decline of the traditional political institutions and the steady development of military power. Even at the time of the Punic Wars, the Golden Age of the Roman constitution, Scipio Africanus had thrown over citizen equality and claimed to set himself up above the laws. A century later, the exception which had created an outcry had become the rule, and the barriers erected against military power fell one after another under the assaults of generals, each more powerful than the last. In 108, when the Senate, in virtue of its traditional prerogatives, gave Metellus an extension of his governorship of Numidia, the Consul Marius appealed to the Comitia, which passed a plebiscite in his favour overruling the Senate's decision.

The precedent was established. Pompey and Cæsar obtained by the vote of the people (the Plebiscites of Gabinius, 67 ; of Manilius, 66 ; of Vatinius, 59) the great military commands which set them on the path to power. It was the people, too, in its complete sovereignty, which determined the length of the command, and granted the military and financial resources needed for the work in hand—two more blows at the rights of the Senate, two more barriers down.   At the same time, the army underwent a great change.   The reform of Marius turned it into a professional army, a faithful instrument in the hands of leaders who could or would use it.

In the last century of the Republic, the long evolution was completed.   Sulla, during his Dictatorship, and Pompey, in 67 and 66, were really emperors.   Only the rivalry of the great military leaders delayed the inevitable fall of the Republic and the final establishment of personal rule.   The elimination of Crassus and Pompey created the monarchy of Cæsar.   The example had been given and the method found ; Octavian had only to follow the one and apply the other.

II

The Principate : Theories and Realities

Monarchy had become a necessity for the world.   What form would it be given by Octavian, the heir of Cæsar, when the victory of Actium rid him of his last rival, Antony ? First Cæsar, and then Antony in the East,[1] had thought that the absolute monarchy of the Græco-Asiatic type offered a complete solution of the problem.   The idea was right, and would be justified by the future, but the Roman people was not yet ripe for it, and it had suffered the fate of all premature conceptions.   Both men had failed, thereby delaying by three hundred years the victory of a political formula which the Roman Empire was bound to adopt sooner or later, and the lamentable end of both must have inspired wholesole reflections in their successors.   Octavian, like them, was well aware that henceforward monarchy was the only possible form of government for the Roman State, and his whole political system was based on that guiding idea.   Created by the army, forged on the battle-field, the Empire was a military monarchy, and so it always would be. But not all truths should be told, especially in the sphere of politics.   The murder of Cæsar, the Republican reaction

[1] H. Jeanmaire, " La Politique religieuse d'Antoine et de Cléopâtre," in **XLIV**, 1924 (1), 241–61.

which followed his death (striking evidence of the vitality of the old Roman aristocracy, even in its decay), the attitude of Italy when Octavian was entering the arena, in short, the whole experience of the last twenty years proved with overwhelming force that the past was far from dead. For reasons both of general policy and of personal prudence, Octavian had every interest in saving appearances and draping a constitutional cloak over the crude nakedness of things. The substitution of the Roman formula of Augustus for the Græco-Asiatic formula of Cæsar had no other meaning or purpose.

For any great constitutional innovation to last, it must be a compromise between two primary considerations— what is wanted and what is possible—and it was to forgetting that elementary truth, in the last analysis, that Cæsar owed his ultimate failure. Military monarchy, which had become a necessity to Rome, could only take root there at the price of a constitutional fiction, and that fiction Octavian found in the Principate. Was the idea original? No. Even before Cæsar attempted to carry out his programme of monarchy, Pompey had endeavoured to bring about the inevitable advent of personal rule by another system. His policy was, to reconcile the ancient traditions of the Senatorial aristocracy, the traditions of Rome herself, with the necessity of single control in the hands of a master, or at least of the most eminent of the citizens. The very name of the new organ, *Princeps*, was in existence, and Cicero several times uses that significant term to describe the pre-eminent position held by Pompey in the State in 52 and after. Octavian, thorough realist and subtle psychologist that he was, took up this notion of Principate, bequeathed to him by the Republican past, but, while he played with the word like a political juggler, he changed the thing profoundly. Conservative peoples—and such was the Roman people—are often more sensitive to appearances than to realities. The oligarchy had kicked against the Hellenizing monarchy of Cæsar and Antony. Octavian broke completely with the political system of Cæsar, and performed his supreme feat of cleverness by causing personal government to be accepted under the decent veil and innocent name of a Principate. Of that

H

constitutional fiction, the Roman formula of personal power as opposed to the Græco-Oriental formula of Cæsar, the principles are summarized in the Will of Augustus, while the manner in which it was carried out can be gathered from the nature of his powers.

The Will of Augustus, for all its pragmatic air and pretence of objectivity, is a pure defence of the Imperial policy. The whole argument is based on one fundamental thesis— that the Emperor's power has always had a strictly legal basis, but the form of that legality has not always remained unchanged. Two periods must be distinguished—the period of formation (43–27 B.C.), during which the Imperial power, although wearing a legal character as the result of a free devolution by the Roman Senate and people, was still an extraordinary power ; and the organic period (27 B.C. to A.D. 14), in which the State had returned to complete constitutional legality, and the legal organs, Comitia, magistracies, and Senate, had recovered full possession of their traditional prerogatives. So much for the principles. Let Augustus himself demonstrate them.[1]

I.   *Period of Formation* (43–27 B.C.)

§ i [1] 1–4. At the age of nineteen, by my own counsels and at my own expense, I raised an army, with which I liberated the Republic, oppressed by the domination of a faction (43 B.C.)—4–5. In return for this service, the Senate by decrees of honour admitted me to its ranks by *adlectio* and conferred on me Consular dignity, the right of voting, and the *imperium* (same date).—6–7. The Senate requested me in the capacity of Proprætor, simultaneously with the two Consuls, to take steps that the Republic should suffer no detriment (same date).—8–9. In the same year, when both Consuls fell in war, the people made me Consul and Triumvir for making the constitution— *IIIvir Reipublicæ constituendæ.*—[2] 10–12. Those who killed my father, I drove into exile, punishing their crime by a legal trial, and afterwards when they waged war against the Republic I defeated them twice in battle (43–42 B.C.).

§ v, 4–6 [25]. All Italy took the oath to me spontaneously and demanded me as leader in the war in which I won the battle of Actium. The provinces of the Gauls, the Spains, Africa, Sicily, and Sardinia took the same oath (32 B.C.).—§ vi, 14–15 [34]. When I had put an end to the civil wars, having taken control of everything by the consent of all. . . .

In every line Augustus shows his constant anxiety to legalize the irregularities of the brilliant career which had

---

[1] The quotations refer to the edition of R. Cagnat and G. Lafaye, in *I.G. ad R.R.p.*, iii, No. 159, pp. 65–95. [The more usual numbering of English editions is given in square brackets.—TRS.]

raised him to the supreme power. There was irregularity in his admission to the Senate at the age of nineteen, without having first held a magistracy, and in the conferring of Consular rank, right of voting, and *imperium*, but they were legal because the Senate had taken the initiative in the matter. There was irregularity in his election to the Consulship and Triumvirate, but it was legal because it was done by the people. There was irregularity in his taking over of the government in 32 B.C., but it was legalized by the universal approval. These were extraordinary powers, no doubt, but they were legal powers. The theory is as absolute as it is definite.

II. *Organic Period* (27 B.C. to A.D. 14).—For this period, the thesis is based on two chief arguments : (*a*) that Augustus has systematically refused all unconstitutional functions ; (*b*) that the only powers which he has kept in the State have been strictly constitutional powers.

(*a*) Refusal of all unconstitutional functions.

§ i [5] 32. The Dictatorship was conferred on me, in my absence and in my presence, by the People and Senate in the Consulship of Cn. Marcellus and L. Arruntius, and I did not accept it (22 B.C.).— 36. The Consulship for the year and for life was given me at the same date, and I did not accept it (same date).—§ iii [6] 11–21 (Greek text, the Latin passage being lost). Three times, in the Consulships of M. Vinicius and Q. Lucretius (19 B.C.), of P. Cornelius and Cn. (Cornelius) Lentulus (18 B.C.), and of Paullus Fabius Maximus and Q. (Ælius) Tubero (11 B.C.), when the Senate and People of the Romans agreed to confide in me, alone and with unlimited powers, the *cura legum morumque*, I accepted no function contrary to the usages of our fathers ; and the administrative work which the Senate expected of me, I carried out in virtue of my Tribunician power.— 21–2 (Greek text, the Latin being lost). In this office I took a colleague, for whom I asked the Senate five times.

§ ii, 23–9 [10]. When the people offered me the position of Pontifex Maximus (which my father had held) in the place of a colleague who was alive, I refused it. I did not hold that priesthood until some years later, on the death of the man who had taken advantage of the civil wars to secure it . . . in the Consulship of P. Sulpicius and C. Valgius (12 B.C.).

(*b*) The powers of Augustus were of a strictly constitutional kind.

§ vi [34] 14–15. In my sixth and seventh Consulships (28–27 B.C.), when I had put an end to the civil wars, having taken control of everything by the consent of all . . .—14–27. In my sixth and seventh Consulships (28–27 B.C.) . . . I transferred the government of the State from my hands to those of the Senate and Roman People. In return for this service, I was given the title of Augustus by a *Senatus consultum*, the door-posts of my house were adorned with laurels in the name of the State, a civic crown was placed above my door, and a golden shield was placed in the Curia Julia, with an inscription on it stating that it was given to me by the Senate and Roman People for my virtue, clemency, justice, and piety. Since that time I have been above all in authority (*auctoritate*) [1] but have had no more power (*potestatis*) than those who have been my colleagues in magistracies.—24–7 [35]. During my thirteenth Consulship, the Senate and Equestrian Order and whole Roman People gave me the name of Father of the Country, and decreed that that should be inscribed in the fore-hall of my house and in the Senate House and in the Forum of Augustus, under the chariots which were set up in my honour by a *Senatus consultum* (2 B.C.).

In this *apologia*, two sentences deserve special mention, both for their general import and for their definite language. " I transferred the government from my hands to those of the Senate and Roman People." " I accepted no function contrary to the usages of our fathers."

That was the theory. What are we to think of it ? After words, let us look at facts. An examination of the political career and the legal powers of Augustus will supply us with material for an answer.

In spite of ambiguities and pretences, Octavian, like Cæsar, and even more than Cæsar, had had a revolutionary political career, in which the last word had always lain with force, whether admittedly or otherwise. He was a revolutionary in his first Consulship of 43 B.C., which was doubly illegal, for he did not fulfil the required conditions of eligibility and he had recourse to the army to obtain it. He was a revolutionary in forming the Triumvirate, an association of three military leaders who covered themselves with Cæsar's name in order to pool their resources and to carry out their ambitious plans. He was a revolutionary in the decisive events of 32 B.C., which led up to the breach with Antony and received their sanction in the final establishment of personal government.[2] When the Triumvirate expired on the

---

[1] The restoration *dignitate*, proposed by Mommsen and generally accepted after him, must, on the evidence of one of the new fragments of the Antioch copy (see below, p. 378), be replaced by *auctoritate*. On this point, see especially recent articles by A. von Premerstein, " Zur Aufzeichnung der *Res Gestae Divi Augusti* in Pisidischer Antiochia," in **XXXVI**, lix (1924), 95–107, and by V. Ehrenberg, " Monumentum Antiochenum," in **XXXVIII**, xix (1925), pp. 191, 200–7.

[2] For different opinions on this question, see **XIX**, iv, 431, 443–5 ; **LXXV**, ii, 178 ; **XCVII** ; **CX**, 453–4 ; E. Kornemann, " Zum Streit um die Entstehung des Monumentum Ancyranum," in **XXXVIII**′ 1905, 328 ff. ; W. Kolbe, " Der zweite Triumvirat," in **XXXVI**, 1914, 273–95 ; A. Bauer, " Der

31st December, 38, it was renewed by the Treaty of Tarentum, probably without ratification by the vote of the people, for another period of five years, which should end with the year 33. Legally, if the Triumvirate was not renewed again, it ceased to exist at this latter date, and the two Triumvirs who were left after the deposition of Lepidus—Octavian and Antony—should return into private life. At this moment a breach between Octavian and Antony was bound to come shortly. Antony proposed that the old constitution should be restored. He had on his side the two legal heads of the government, the Consuls Cn. Domitius Ahenobarbus and C. Sosius, who were his declared supporters, and his proposal, which was cleverly conceived, was of a kind to attract the majority of the Senate. It was a very skilful move ; while condemning Octavian to return to private life, Antony kept his exceptional position as a veritable prince-consort in Egypt which he obtained by his marriage with Cleopatra. He broke the political power of his rival and kept his own for all practical purposes. Octavian, left master of the public power in fact, but shorn of all legal title to it, for a moment found himself in a very delicate situation. In this case again, the only way out of his dilemma was to resort to the army, to force. Like a man of decision, he did not hesitate to use it.

Dion Cassius describes the scene [1] :—

" Cæsar trumped up a pretext for absenting himself, both for this reason and in order to be able to think over the news at his leisure and take counsel with himself what he should do. On his return, he collected the Senate, and, surrounding himself with a guard of soldiers and friends carrying concealed daggers, and sitting on a curule chair, between the Consuls, he made a long and moderate speech about himself from his seat, and uttered a lengthy indictment of Sosius and Antony. Since no one else, not even one of the Consuls, dared to open his mouth, he told them to meet again on a fixed day, that he might prove the wrong-doing of Antony by certain writings."

This anticipation of the 18th of Brumaire may have been less violent (Octavian's " Grenadiers " drove no one out of the council-chamber), but the practical results were the same.

Staatsstreich des Octavianus im J. 32, v. Chr.," in **XXXVII**, 1917, 11–23 ; K. Fitzler and O. Seeck, in **XXV**, *s.v.* " Julius (Augustus)," 324–5 ; H. Dessau, **VI**, 24, rem. 2 ; *id.*, " Der Staatsstreich des J. 32, v. Chr.," in **XLII**, 1925, 1017–23 ; U. Wilcken, " Der angebliche Staatsstreich Octavians im J. 32 v. Chr.," in **LI**, 1925, 66–87.
[1] I, 2.

All the opposition, the two Consuls and more than three hundred Senators, fled in a body, and Octavian took care to place no obstacle in the way of their departure. He was left master of the constitutional battle-field; that was the main thing for him.

The *coup d'État* had succeeded. All that had to be done was, as always, to cause it to be ratified, and, still better, if possible, pardoned. Antony's blunders and the publication by Octavian of his opponent's will secured the sanction of public opinion. The difficult corner had been turned, and Octavian had won. With the political adroitness which was one of his chief qualities, he hastened to restore the constitutional bond which for a moment had been broken and to give his power the basis in law which it had lost by the legal expiration of the Triumvirate at the end of 33. While retaining his title of Triumvir by an act of pure usurpation, he made the Senate, people, and Western provinces take a special oath giving him an extraordinary position as legal head of the West,[1] and he himself, in a passage which we have already seen,[2] recalls the exceptional event with a certain pride. So the *coup d'État* received, in the form of a solemn plebiscite with retroactive effect, the legalization of public opinion; as Octavian had wanted, it was both ratified and pardoned. To crown his work, Octavian also assumed the Consulship for the following year, and it was in the capacity of Consul that in 31 B.C. he won the deciding victory of Actium.

It was as a Triumvir that Octavian had laid the foundations of his political fortune. In that capacity he had enjoyed the same extraordinary powers as Sulla in the past, with the sole limitation in practice that he shared the office with two others. But while the position had solid advantages, it had one grave defect : it was an exceptional position, owing its existence to an act of force, and in spite of every possible legalization it bore the indelible taint of its origin. Moreover, this initial character had been further aggravated, and to a disagreeable extent, by two new facts—the elimination of Lepidus and Antony, which reduced the magistracy to the domination of a single man, and the arbitrary extension of the office by Octavian himself at the beginning of 32.

[1] Suet., *Aug.*, 17 ; Dion C., l, 6.   [2] *Mon. Anc.*, § v, 4–6 [25].

Lastly, the supreme command conferred on Octavian by the Western plebiscite of 32 created an unconstitutional position which the head of the State would be wise to abandon, and that as soon as possible. So, being left sole master by the removal of Antony, and desiring to close the period of civil wars by the establishment of a stable government, Octavian set out to wind up his revolutionary past, to bring his power within the framework of the constitution, and to obtain for it, as a supreme safeguard, the permanent consecration of legality.

With kingship, a concept opposed to the very notion of Principate, Octavian, true to the constitutional formula of his choice, would have nothing to do. Nor did he want extraordinary magistracies ; he himself has been at pains to tell us so, and we may well believe him. Dictatorship being thus put out of court, he naturally turned to the Consulship, and it was in the Consulship that, down to 23 B.C., he sought the main legal basis of his authority. But, by a return to the original nature of the office, it was no longer the limited Consulship of the last age of the Republic ; it was a Consulship widened in respect of time, space, and competence. The Republican Consulship was annual and did not permit of immediate re-election ; that of Octavian, in spite of re-election, which was a pure formality, was permanent in conception. He had been Consul as early as 43, but in revolutionary circumstances. He was Consul a second time in 33, ten years later, and then for nine years without interruption, from 31 to 23. Secondly, since the reforms of Sulla, the Consulship had been a strictly Italian magistracy, the provinces being the domain of the pro-magistracies ; Octavian restored to the Consul's *imperium* its old extent in space and its original superiority over that of the Proconsul. Lastly, the Republican Consul had a colleague ; Octavian maintained the principle, but in form only. In all the force of the term he was a " First Consul " ; his colleagues, far from being his equals (whatever he may say), were simply men of straw, appointed by himself and subservient, body and soul, to his all-powerful will.

In spite of these infringements of the old rules, the Consulship, with its annual tenure and its collegiate principle, was an inconvenient and defective instrument of government.

Octavian perceived this, and had to look out for something
else. In 38 at the latest, perhaps as early as 40, he had
assumed the *prænomen* of Imperator, which he inherited from
Cæsar with his other names. This title made its holder, in
a still vague but sufficiently transparent form, the permanent
incarnation of the power of the State, the *imperium*. In 36,
he took another step ; the Senate invested him with the Tribunician privilege of inviolability. So, five years before
Actium, Octavian already held officially two of the fundamental elements of the Imperial power, the *imperium* and
(still in a rudimentary form) the Tribunician authority. In
30, he increased this latter by obtaining the right to give
help (*jus auxilii*). In 28, lastly, he solemnly abrogated the
measures of the Triumvirate. This was the preface to the
re-establishment of legality, the chief act of which was his
renunciation of the Triumvirate, which had been extended
arbitrarily during the last period of five years, and the
supreme command bestowed by the plebiscite of 32. The
ground was now staked out ; the decisive step was taken
in the following year.

On the 13th January, 27 B.C., Octavian proceeded to the
Senate and there made a great speech. His work, he said,
was ended ; his father was avenged ; order was restored.
He had therefore resolved to return to private life, he gave up
his exceptional powers (the Triumvirate and extraordinary
chief command), and he placed the armies and finances once
more at the free disposal of the Senate. The Senate protested,
and implored Octavian to abandon his decision. He refused
to resume all the power, as a burden too heavy for his
shoulders, and then in the end he gave in, but on the express
condition of a twofold limitation, in space and in time.
The provinces should be divided, and the Emperor, in virtue
of his Consular *imperium*, should assume the direct government of certain of them. His functions, thus restricted,
should be limited to a period of ten years. Three days later,
the Senate officially expressed its gratitude to Octavian,
conferring on him the title of Augustus, by which his person
was invested with a sacred character.

The scene was meant to be edifying, but it was all comedy
and make-believe. According to the official account,
Augustus on that day restored the old constitution to force.

The reality was quite otherwise, and clear-sighted historians have not been deceived. Besides, the theory of government did contain an element of truth, and that is just what explains how it was able to come into being and to impose itself. The Emperor's decision consecrated the restoration, not of the old constitution, for that was impossible, but at least of a system of legality, the " semblance of a Republic— *quædam imago Reipublicæ* " of which Tacitus speaks [1] For more than twenty years, Rome had been living under the arbitrary governments which great men chose to give her. The return to a legal order was a real improvement, and one can well understand that it caused general satisfaction. The great actor had once again played his part superlatively well. That was all, no doubt, but it was a great deal.

By the constitutional act of 27 B.C., the Empire, being based in essence on the function of the Consul, ceased to be an exceptional state of affairs and entered on its organic period. But the age of transformations and amendments was not over. Augustus continued to hold the Consulship for another four years (27–23), and during this time the Consular *imperium* remained the chief basis of his legal position. Then, in 23, he suddenly changed his front. He renounced the Consulship for the following year, and after that date he only held the office twice, as an exception, in 5 and in 2 B.C. The reason was that, in spite of the great changes which had been made in it, the Consulship had many disadvantages. The traditional character of the office, which had enabled Augustus to effect the necessary transition from Republican to personal government in Italy, was at once its strength and its weakness. The time had come to reorganize the provinces. Now, the Consulship, in the form finally given to it by Sulla, by its very nature kept the Emperor tied to Rome, and did not allow him the freedom of action needed for the settlement of the fundamental question, that of the government of the world, which, in the coming years, was to rise to the chief place in his cares. The new problem required a new constitutional form. In 23, therefore, when Augustus was about to leave Italy for a long visit to the provinces, he made two fundamental

[1] *Ann.*, xiii, 28.

innovations.   He gave up the Consulship, and, in exchange, he caused the Senate to give him the Proconsulship over the whole extent of the Roman State, Italy and the Senatorial provinces included, in the form of the *imperium majus* (wider both in territorial extent and in competence) which the Senate itself, after the murder of Cæsar, had conferred on Brutus and Cassius for the whole East.   So the Proconsulship, a more practical and infinitely more elastic legal form, took the place of the Consulship as the fundamental and permanent basis of the Emperor's power.   Nor was this all.   At the same time, Augustus obtained a further increase of his Tribunician power, which was made annual as well as perpetual, and henceforward the year was called after it and not, as formerly, after the Consuls.   Next year, he took over the management of the corn-supply.   At the end of 19, the Senate bestowed on him further honours, to have force from the following year, 18—the Consular insignia for life, with the twelve lictors and curule chair— and, in addition, " the right to make what laws he pleased," an extension of the old right of edict (*jus edicendi*) attached to the Republican magistracies, without the restrictions of time and competence to which it was traditionally subject. This privilege, the juridical source of the Imperial " Constitution " (*constitutio Principis*), in practice gave the Emperor unlimited, discretionary power in legislative matters. In 12 B.C., lastly, on the death of Lepidus, Augustus was elected Pontifex Maximus.

From the point of view of legality, then, the Emperor's authority was the result of a series of acts constitutional in form ; but his powers were not constitutional, in the sense of the Republican tradition, in extent, duration, or number. Really, the Principate was not an illegal power, but an extra-legal power ; it was a foreign body which, having become necessary to the very life of the Roman State, had won a place for itself at the point of the sword and had only been reconciled with the old constitution by a succession of ambiguities and compromises.   Augustus affected to be merely the first of the citizens, *princeps civium*, and he makes a point of saying so in his will—" I have been above all in authority (*auctoritate*)." [1]

[1] *Mon. Anc.*, § xviii, 6–7 [and 34] (Greek text).   On the restoration, see above, p. 208, n. 1.

The reality Dion Cassius gives us in his terse and definite way :—

" So it was," he writes of the sitting of the 13th January, 27, " that all the power of the people and Senate passed over to Augustus, and from that day pure monarchy was established." [1]

Augustus was master, and doubly so. He was master in fact, because he was the supreme military chief and army and navy, bound by their oath, were wholly devoted to him ; he was master in law, because his omnipotence was expressed by a collection of exactly defined powers. The source of the ruler's authority lay in the people, which had given up its sovereign rights in his favour and, both by *Senatus consultum* and by popular vote, had conferred on him a legal mandate, that of *Princeps*, by the side and on the edge of the traditional constitution. That theory of the legitimacy of the Emperor's position already appears in the reign of Augustus ; the jurisconsults of the Empire were to develop its principles and give it its final formula.

III

The Empire and the Government of the World

The City of Rome had conquered the world, but it had been unable to organize it in a permanent form, and when the Republic went it left only anarchy behind it. Anarchy in the government—an incapable and discredited Senate, Comitia reduced to a travesty, impotent and unanimously derided magistracies. Anarchy in the administration— a small, narrow-minded staff, routine-ridden and without initiative, law-courts ruled by corruption and intimidation, finances in utter disorder, provinces in which governors and tax-farmers vied in greed and robbery. Anarchy in the streets, which armed gangs turned into daily battle-fields. Anarchy, lastly, in the consciences of men, in which the collapse of old beliefs and traditions had left nothing but chaos or vacancy. The central power had to be re-organized, the administration brought up to date, the fruitful conception of the State set up in the place of the outworn system of the City ; in short, the whole machinery of government had to be transformed and the whole age-old edifice

[1] liii, 17 ; cf. Strabo, vi, 4 (p. 288) ; xvii, 3 (p. 840).

built up again on new foundations. Such was the form
taken at the beginning of the Empire by the problem of
the government of the world. Never had a new-created
system been confronted with a more complex task and more
overwhelming responsibilities.

The very nature of the Principate and the difficulties,
constitutional or other, which it met on its way made its
task still more delicate. The Empire, in the form given
to it by Augustus, was a compromise between old institutions
and new needs, and it was obliged to take both into account.
The government of Rome and Italy was in theory still in the
hands of the old powers, Senate, Comitia, and magistracies,
but the Emperor, in virtue of his Proconsular *imperium*, had
all military, civil, and judicial attributions there as in the
rest of the Empire ; his right of intervention was complete
and permanent there as elsewhere. No doubt, for motives
of prudence which can be understood, the Emperor was
careful to disguise that right, but, for all that, it was revealed
in the administrative domain, even in the reign of Augustus,
by the creation of new organs wholly controlled by the
Emperor—Prefects (of the City, of the Prætorium, of the
Corn-supply, of the Watch) and executive commissions or
curatelæ (water, public buildings, Tiber).

In the provinces, as conquered territory, the Emperor
had a freer hand, but even here Augustus judged it wise to
allow the past its lawful share. Officially, by the allotment
of 27 B.C., the provinces were divided into two classes—
the Senatorial provinces, which by definition were those
already pacified, the administration of which was kept by
the Senate, and the Imperial provinces, those in which troops
were stationed, the government of which the Emperor
reserved for himself, being represented by direct agents,
the Legates. Egypt, as the property of the Emperor,
who enjoyed the absolute power inherited from the Ptolemies
without control, and as the chief basis of his financial power,
had a separate place in this organization. But, if the
Emperor was master in his own provinces, this was not the
case with the Senate. By a formal clause of the constitutional act of 23 B.C., it was laid down that the Proconsular
imperium of the Emperor (the transformation by which his
previous Consular *imperium* had been replaced) should extend

to the Senatorial provinces as to the others. So the Emperor had a right of general supervision which took the form, if need arose, of more or less discreet interference in the choice of governors and, in the domain of justice, of permanent exercise of the right of appeal.

The problem of the government of the world, therefore, presented two aspects from the beginning—one political and one administrative. First, for the political aspect. The Empire was a military monarchy, and, appearances notwithstanding, its strength would always lie in the army ; it was the avowed or concealed action of the army which would gradually drive the Imperial system along the road to military despotism. In Rome, the Emperor was the supreme magistrate in his capacity of " first citizen " (*Princeps*), and as such was subject, at least in theory, to the control of the law. In the provinces, he was the great military chief, Imperator ; in Egypt he was the heir of the Pharaohs, the King. The notion of complete Cæsarism, coming from the provinces, would in the end impose itself on Rome and Italy themselves. When that happened, the Principate would go, without hope of return.

This complicated situation created a permanent danger for the Imperial power, further aggravated by the absence of the hereditary principle. We shall see the disastrous consequences of it in the third century, but the first symptoms of the peril, which was inherent in the system itself, did not wait so long to show themselves. Already the founder of the military monarchy, Cæsar himself, had twice had to deal with dangers of this kind. At the end of 49, the Ninth Legion revolted at Placentia. Two years later, it was the turn of the legions of Pharsalos, which had been brought back to Italy by Antony and were dissatisfied at not getting the distributions of land and money promised them before the battle. Cæsar sent orders from Asia that they should leave Campania and go to Sicily. His emissary, P. Cornelius Sulla, who conveyed the order, was driven away. Then, having murdered two Prætorians, Cosconius and Galba, the mutinous legions marched on Rome and occupied the Campus Martius. Only the personal intervention of Cæsar and his timely use of the word " Quirites " won them over from their insubordination. In A.D. 14, on the death of

Augustus, the armies of Pannonia and Germany both
mutinied; the latter attempted to make Germanicus
Emperor, and only his loyalty averted the danger. In
41, Claudius was proclaimed Emperor by the Prætorians,
and in the following year the Legate of Dalmatia,
L. Arruntius Camillus Scribonianus, revolted and raised
his troops against the new Emperor. There could be no
hope of putting down the military danger. The evil was
inherent in the system itself, and would last as long as it
lasted. At least it was possible to lessen it by seeking
a counterbalance in the civil power. Now, that " civil
façade ", with which the Empire could not dispense if it was
to endure, could only be provided by the Senate, the only
one of the traditional organs which had survived the total
shipwreck of the Republic. In that unavoidable necessity
we must seek one of the chief causes of the conservative
policy of Augustus and some of his successors.

The problem also had an administrative aspect. From
devotion to the traditional system of the city, from lack of
the mere numbers to supply a personnel, or from a selfish
caste-interest which hesitated to extend a profitable
monopoly, whatever the motive might be, the oligarchy
had not been willing (and in any case would have been
unable) to create the administrative and military means
of action—civil service and army—required alike by the
government, defence, and exploitation of the Mediterranean
world. So, in respect of administration, the Republic
bequeathed to the Empire only a rudimentary organization
and an equipment accumulated haphazard—a powerless
and ill-served central authority, no organ of transmission,
and at every stage of the scale an insufficient staff, ill-
equipped for its task. In short, the Roman world had not
the organs suited to its needs. To meet those needs, the
Empire would gradually find itself involved in increasing
centralization, of a Hellenistic and especially Egyptian
type, which could only be effected at the expense of the
Senate and the previous administrative system, that is,
of the national tradition of Rome. The evolution ended
in the Later Empire with the triumph of the Cæsarian
formula in its double form of absolute and centralized
monarchy. But we must not be deceived by appearances

or labels. Even at the beginning of the Empire, in the modest guise of the Principate, the Roman State had a master. Augustus, under the pressure of necessities, judged it right to break with the Cæsarian system; the same necessities compelled him to maintain its spirit. In reality he was as powerful as Diocletian or Constantine three centuries later. The only difference lay in form. The first Emperors, both from general policy and from personal prudence, made a point of disguising their power; the last took pleasure in displaying it. A new master did not appear; an old ambiguity disappeared.

Augustus, with his well-balanced intelligence and practical nature, had wisely thought that each day should bear its own burden, and he had left it to time to complete his work. Peace, order, a programme, a head, a will—such was the blessing which the Imperial system brought to the world. The great problems were stated. It was for the men who should hold the Empire in succession for five centuries to find the solution.

IV

The Emperor. Honours and Powers

Names and Titles.—The dignity of Princeps, a legal office, which made its bearer the first of the citizens, but, by the same definition, a citizen subject to the law like others, was translated in official language by a complicated but precise system of titles, the form of which has been preserved by the inscriptions and coins. Two essential elements must be distinguished—names and titles.

(*a*) *Names.*—The first name is Imperator, which marks the sovereign as the holder of the *imperium*—Consular *imperium* before 23 B.C. and Proconsular after that date—in its civil, military, and judicial aspect. The word, already employed in this sense as a surname by Cæsar and at the beginning by Augustus, afterwards became a generic *prænomen* which replaced the individual *prænomen*, and so came at the head of the official names and titles.[1]

---

[1] One should not, therefore, regard this title of Imperator as an equivalent merely recalling the Imperial salutations, as has been done quite recently in **LXXI**.

Cæsar was originally merely a family-name, the private *cognomen* of the Gens Julia, which was naturally preserved by the Gens when it rose to the Empire and was transmitted by kinship or adoption down to Caligula. Then the word changed in character. The possession of the supreme power by the Gens Julia for nearly a century made it a symbol inseparable from that power. Claudius, the first Emperor unrelated to the family, adopted it, and his successors regularly bore it after him. Under Hadrian, this Imperial *cognomen* acquired a new meaning ; it was conferred on the heir presumptive, as the official mark of his dignity and of his designation to the Empire.

Augustus was a surname of a religious nature, which raised the Emperor above mankind and gave him a sacred character. For a long time it was indivisible, and was first shared in 161, when, by an extension of the system of the college, two Emperors, Marcus Aurelius and Lucius Verus, held the Imperial dignity on equal terms.

(*b*) *Titles.*—Some of the titles expressed the material reality of power, and were at the very foundation of the Emperor's authority. One of these was the Tribunician power, which was both permanent and conferred annually since the constitutional act of 23. Every renewal was numbered, so giving the year of the reign. Another title was that of Pontifex Maximus, which Augustus held from 12 onwards and his successors from the beginning of their reign or thereabouts. The Emperor could also, if he wished, hold some of the old Republican magistracies and bear their titles officially. It was so with the Consulship and Censorship (with the latter twice only—Claudius in A.D. 47–8 and Vespasian with his son Titus in 73–4).

The second class of Imperial titles was purely honorific—Imperator, followed by a figure indicating the number of Imperial salutations which the Emperor had received, and Pater Patriæ (Father of the Country), which was generally conferred late.

The Emperor was not only a master, a man immensely superior to all others. He was more than human ; he tended to become a god, and was paid the honours due to godhead. The Imperial cult contained two principal elements—the worship paid to the dead Emperor and that paid to the living.

After his death, the Emperor could be proclaimed *divus*, that is, if not a god in the full sense of the term, at least a deified man. The title was conferred on him by apotheosis, and the Senate, the legal representative of the Roman people, had sovereign authority in the matter. Promotion to the rank of *divus* entailed a certain number of honours, particularly a temple and a cult served by special priests designated by the name of the dead Emperor, his Flamens, and sometimes, too, by a supplementary religious college, the Sodales. As likely one day to be deified, the Emperor also received especial honours in his lifetime, particularly a worship in the *municipia* and in the provinces, which made him akin to the gods.

Powers.—After the form, the substance ; after honours, realities. The Imperial power, as organized by Augustus in the form of the Principate, in a series of constitutional stages, and bequeathed by him to his successors, was based on three essential and permanent elements—the Tribunician power, the Proconsular *imperium*, and the office of Pontifex Maximus.

Tribunician power.—The Emperor was not a Tribune of the Plebs, and, as a Patrician, born (Augustus and the Julio-Claudian dynasty) or made (all Emperors from Vespasian onwards), he could not be one, but he was invested with the Tribunician power and held it for life. This first basis of the Emperor's power made him the heir of the old Tribunes and gave him all the material and moral prerogatives traditionally attached to the office.

The Tribunes had been created to be the chief leaders and representatives of the Plebs, and accordingly sacred law had invested them with exceptional safeguards in the exercise of their authority. Their principal function, their true *raison d'être*, was the right of giving help (*auxilium*), which in practice took the concrete form of intervention or veto (*intercessio*), at first individual and material and soon after collective and moral. The right of veto was itself guaranteed by the inviolability of the Tribune, which had a political and a religious foundation. The Tribune was sacrosanct, and anyone who dared to lay hands on him was dedicated to the infernal gods and cut off from the society of men. Lastly, he had the right of arrest (*prehensio*) in respect of the magistrates of the City, a sure and expeditious means of obtaining justice for himself. Although it started as an office of opposition, the Tribuneship had soon been brought into the system of Roman magistracies and had thereby acquired a new series of legal rights; the Tribunes now convoked and presided over the Senate and the Comitia, in addition, and sometimes in contradiction, to their former prerogatives.

The Republican Tribuneship, although its constitutional position was strong enough, did not owe all its influence to the extent and complexity of its legal attributions. Memories of the distant past, the illustrious line of its representatives, Licinius Stolo, the Gracchi, Drusus, clothed the old popular magistracy in immense prestige, and when the heirs of the democracy became heads of the State they were resolved to keep and exploit these advantages.

All these traditional privileges were taken over by the Emperor—the veto on decisions of the Senate or magistrates, the sacrosanct character which became the chief safeguard of the Emperor's dignity and person, the right of arrest, the right of convoking and presiding over the Senate and introducing bills there,[1] and the same rights in respect of the Comitia.

Such were the material and moral privileges which the Emperor inherited from the old Tribunes and exercised in virtue of his Tribunician power. But he was not content to take these rights as they were; he transformed and extended them, liberating them from the impediments traditionally attached to the office. Under the Republic, the exercise of the Tribune's authority had been limited in time, in space, and by the principle of the college. His office was annual, and immediate re-election, if not illegal, was at least very disputable from the constitutional point of view. His authority did not reach beyond the town of Rome and the constitutional radius of a thousand yards.

---

[1] These proposals might be made orally, by the Emperor himself or a representative, or in writing, in which case they were read by a magistrate, generally a Prætor. They enjoyed priority, and were automatically placed at the head of the agenda as soon as formulated. There was no limit to the number of oral proposals; written ones were at first limited to one per sitting, and later became more numerous, varying with different Emperors—three under Probus, four under Pertinax, and five under Marcus Aurelius and Severus Alexander (*jus tertiæ, quartæ, quintæ, relationis*).

The college of Tribunes consisted of ten members, all armed with the right of veto against one another and absolutely equal in authority. To this threefold limitation the Tribunician power of the Emperor was not subjected ; in the form given to it by the constitutional acts of 36 and 23 B.C., it was held for life, it was exercised all over the Empire, and, being in essence superior to that of the Tribunes, it was not exposed to their veto.

The Emperor sometimes took colleagues in the exercise of his Tribunician power, as Augustus took Agrippa and Tiberius, but they were subordinates with inferior competence, and, moreover, they were heirs designate to the Imperial dignity, so that there was no possibility of a conflict. In practice, by the abnormal extension of the office, by its permanent character, and by the additional authority given by his other functions, the Emperor was a Tribune such as the Roman world had never seen, nor even imagined. All the advantages without the disadvantages and omissions— that describes the whole advance made on the old Tribune-ship by the new Tribunician power.

Proconsular imperium.—In the Republican period, the *imperium* constituted the essence of the power of magistrates (Dictators, Consuls, Prætors) and pro-magistrates (Pro-consuls and Proprætors). It involved the civil administration of the territory, the command of the troops, and the exercise of justice—in short, all civil, military, and judicial attributions. In the last century of the Republic this traditional conception was very greatly changed by Sulla ; the magistrates in Rome, the Consuls and Prætors, were reduced to purely civil duties, which in practice were strictly confined to Italy, while the pro-magistrates, as governors of provinces, retained their previous position, with the full *imperium*. This Proconsular *imperium* was what Augustus, after laying down the Consular *imperium* which he had held uninterruptedly since 31, finally took over by the constitutional act of 23.

The Proconsular power of the Emperor, expressed in his title by the *prænomen* of Imperator,[1] the symbol of the chief military command, was, therefore, based on the old

---

[1] On the theory recently maintained by D. McFayden in **LXXI**, see above. p. 219, n. 1.

Republican *imperium*, but, like the Tribunician power, it was reinforced and freed of the impediments which hampered its action. The Proconsular *imperium* of the Republic was limited in time and in space. A governor of a province only had it in his own district ; governors of Consular provinces on the one hand and those of Prætorian provinces on the other had an equal and simultaneous *imperium* ; none could exercise it outside his own province, particularly in Italy, which came within the purely civil competence which Sulla gave exclusively to the Senate and the magistrates of the City. Moreover, the *imperium* lasted only one year, unless the holder was granted an extension or recalled before his time expired. In the last century of the Republic this twofold limitation was dropped, and a higher form of *imperium* gradually grew up, the *imperium infinitum majus*, the precedent on which the constitutional act of 23 modelled the Proconsular *imperium* of the new heads of the State.

The Proconsular *imperium* of the Emperor thus conceived had two fundamental characteristics : it was complete and it was universal. First, it was complete, being at once civil, military, and judicial. It is in the special domain of the sovereign, in the Imperial provinces, that we find it in its most perfect form. The governor, the Legate, who exercised the Emperor's Proconsular *imperium* as his deputy, was at once a civil official, a commander-in-chief, and a supreme judge. He governed the district, managing finance (allotment of taxation, centralization of revenues, authorization of expenditure), the food-supply, public works, and posts, and controlling the working of municipal government in the towns. He commanded the land and sea forces, and if necessary led them against the enemy. In the criminal courts, in virtue of the "right of the sword" (*jus gladii*), he had the right of life and death over all the inhabitants of the province ; in the civil courts, he tried all cases which were outside the competence of the municipal magistrates ; the only appeal in either case was to the Emperor.

Secondly, the Proconsular *imperium* of the Emperor was universal. The traditional domain of the Proconsular power was the provinces ; therefore the Emperor governed those allotted to him, the Imperial provinces, in the capacity of

Proconsul, and the governors, the Legates, were merely his lieutenants. But, by the constitutional act of 23 B.C., the Senatorial provinces, in spite of their independent organization, and Italy and Rome itself, in spite of the fiction by which they were still the domain of the City and the annual magistrates, were likewise brought under the Proconsular *imperium* of the Emperor. In fact, Italy and Rome lost their character of unarmed territories (*inermes*). There was a strong garrison in Rome (the Prætorian and Urban Cohorts, the Watch, and various detachments), and outside the capital there were troops in Italy (Prætorian Cohorts and the Misenum and Ravenna fleets), of which the Emperor was the supreme chief. Numerous officials in the country (Prefects of the Prætorium, of the City, of the Corn-supply, of the Watch, and executive commissions) came under his authority direct. In criminal and civil jurisdiction he was a supreme judge both of first instance and of appeal, or, at least, could constitute himself such if he chose.

So the reality is everywhere the same, while the appearances vary ; this contrast need not surprise us and is easy to explain. In his own provinces, the Emperor had a free hand, and could without danger act as an absolute master ; in the Senatorial provinces, on the other hand, and especially in Italy and Rome, where the traditional powers of the Senate and magistrates were maintained and so many Republican memories survived, he was obliged, at least in form, to take certain precautions. This caution in the exercise of his Proconsular *imperium* is shown in various ways. First of all, in the Imperial titles. In Italy, during the first two centuries, the title of Proconsul never appears in official documents ; we do not find it until Septimius Severus, who represents a new spirit. In the exercise of his power, the Emperor handled the traditional authorities, Senate and magistrates, with tact, and was careful to disguise the administrative evolution which had become inevitable under a veil of survivals. Lastly, a very symptomatic precaution, Augustus only accepted the *imperium* temporarily, for a strictly limited period—for ten years in 27, for five years in 18, for five years in 12 B.C., for ten years in A.D. 3, and for another ten years in 13, the year preceding his death.

These various limitations—the periodical extension of the Proconsular *imperium*, the autonomy of the Senatorial provinces, and the privileges of Rome and Italy—gradually crumbled away, the first on the accession of Tiberius and the two others during the crisis of the third century, and, saved by a miracle, the Imperial power was left, standing alone among the scattered ruins of a past which was doomed to oblivion.

The office of Pontifex Maximus.—The third great basis of the Imperial authority, after the Tribunician power and the Proconsular *imperium*, was the office of Pontifex Maximus. The Emperor was the chief pontiff, and as such he presided over the official church and revived in his person one of the highest prerogatives of the old Roman kingship, the mighty union of temporal and spiritual power, of throne and altar. Cæsar had been elected Pontifex Maximus in 63 B.C., and had held the office until his death, when it went to Lepidus, the colleague of Octavian and Antony in the Triumvirate. In spite of his political downfall, Lepidus kept it until his death in 12 B.C. Augustus inherited the function, which henceforward remained inseparable from the Imperial dignity. In conformity with Republican tradition, Augustus had been appointed to the post, on the presentation of the Sacerdotal Comitia (an electoral body of seventeen Tribes chosen by lot), by co-optation of the College of Pontifices. When Tiberius transferred the electoral powers of the Comitia to the Senate, the right of presentation for the office of Pontifex Maximus passed to that body, save for the pure formality of ratification by the people. The office was conferred, at least in the first century, by a constitutional act distinct from and later than that investing the Emperor with his other prerogatives ; this was still the case with the Flavians. Later, this distinction disappeared, and the Emperor on his accession received all the prerogatives making up his power together, the Pontificate among the rest.

The College of Pontifices, the first in dignity of the great priestly colleges of Rome, which, according to tradition, went back to the very beginnings of the City, was the storehouse of the religious traditions of Rome, the official keeper of the national religion. The preservation and interpretation of religious law, the establishment of the calendar, the consecration of public and private buildings, the maintenance of the worships of the deities of the City (Vesta, the Penates, the Capitoline Triad), all came within its competence. These attributions, though common to all its members, were more particularly concentrated in the person of its president, the Pontifex Maximus, the successor of the ancient Kings, both as president of the College and as religious head of the City.

In the capacity of Pontifex Maximus, apart from the moral authority and ancient prestige attaching to the office, the Emperor had a certain number of definite attributions. First of all, he had a say in the recruiting of priests. In Republican times, the priests had been elected by the people (as were the four great colleges, Pontifices, Augurs, Quindecimvirs *Sacris Faciundis*, and Fetiales) or chosen by co-optation (like the Arvales), or appointed direct by the Pontifex Maximus. As Pontifex Maximus, the Emperor intervened in the appointment of all three classes. For the first, he received a right of presentation, even of a number beyond the normal establishment, corresponding to his right of making recommendations for the magistracies; in practice, especially from Tiberius onwards, this was a right of election pure and simple. For the second, the Emperor, being a member of every priesthood and putting members of his family into them as he wished, had the legal means to play a decisive part. Lastly, he appointed a whole series of priests direct—the fifteen Flamens, the three most important of whom (those of Jupiter, Mars, and Quirinus) were nominated on presentation by the College of Pontifices, the King of Sacrifices, the Salii, the lower Pontifices, and the priests of certain Latin towns (Lavinium, Alba, Cænina, etc.) —and presided over the recruiting of the Vestals. He also had a number of administrative powers in religious matters, legislative, judicial, and financial. He could issue edicts, give consultations, and lay down rulings regarding the interpretation of religious law; he had jurisdiction over the priests whom he appointed and over the Vestals, whose guardian and judge he was in virtue of his domestic jurisdiction; and he managed the pontifical funds, a central religious treasury fed chiefly by the proceeds of fines and the inheritances of Vestals who died intestate.

Of all the great dignities attached to the Emperor's office, that of Pontifex Maximus was the last to remain indivisible. In A.D. 161, Marcus Aurelius and Lucius Verus held the Imperial power on an equal footing ; the only exception was the office of Pontifex Maximus, which the former kept to himself in name and fact.   It was the same with Septimius Severus and his sons Caracalla and Geta.   Only when things were on the verge of military anarchy, on the accession of Pupienus Maximus and Balbinus in 238, was the religious prerogative given equally to the two colleagues, and the precedent established on that occasion became the rule for the last centuries of the Empire.

Complementary prerogatives and the law of investiture.— The Tribunician power and Proconsular *imperium* which conferred political and military attributions on the Emperor and the Pontificate which gave him moral and religious authority were the three fundamental elements of his dignity. In virtue of the two first, he was a permanent incarnation of the alliance of the democracy and the military power from which the Empire was born ; by the third, he revived the ancient union of throne and altar which had been destroyed at the advent of Republican government.   But if these were the chief elements of his power, they were not the only ones.   The picture must be completed by two sets of complementary prerogatives.   Of these, some ensued either from special, permanent functions (the Emperor as Prince of the Senate, *princeps Senatus*, and member of all religious colleges) or from the exceptional, temporary conduct of old Republican magistracies, such as the Consulship and Censorship.   A certain number of others did not legally come within any of the previous categories or could only have been connected with them by an effort of arbitrary interpretation, and the conferring of them on the Emperor therefore had to be legalized by definite constitutional measures.   Such were, in the domain of foreign affairs, the right of peace and war ; in that of home policy, the right of presenting candidates for magistracies who would have to be elected (a privilege which might, when necessary, go as far as direct appointment, as in A.D. 7, when, on account of serious disorders, Augustus himself nominated all magistrates), and the rights of conferring the citizenship, founding colonies, and striking coins. All these rights except that of presentation, which was an innovation of the Empire, had in Republican times belonged to the Senate and the people ; in the last centuries of the Republic, pro-magistrates had often used them, by express delegation or by sheer usurpation. All that was needed, therefore, was to make rights of these practices and to confer them legally on the new chief of the executive, the Emperor.

Being the "first of the citizens" (*princeps civium*), according to the official theory of the Imperial system, the Emperor was the authorized and lawful representative of the Roman people, which had given up the whole of its rights in his favour.

" The will of the Princeps has the force of law," writes the jurisconsult Ulpian,[1] " for, in virtue of the *Lex Regia* . . . the people . . . transfers to him all its *imperium* and all its *potestas—utpote cum Lege Regia . . . populus in eum omne suum imperium et potestatem conferat.*" The text appears again, with a slight variation, in the Code of Justinian [2] : " In virtue of the ancient law which was called *Lex Regia*, all the right and all the *potestas* of the Roman people have been transferred to the Imperial *potestas—Lege antiqua quæ Regia nuncupabatur, omne jus omnisque potestas populi Romani in imperatoriam translata sunt potestatem.*"

The transfer was not tacit, nor was it left to chance ; it was operated according to precise rules and a regular constitutional procedure. But the methods by which these rights were conferred were different in the case of the first Emperors, who created the system, and in that of their successors, who found the precedents already created and the system securely established. Augustus, like Cæsar, before him, received his powers gradually, by a series of constitutional acts. Tiberius, being associated with Augustus in the Imperial authority in the latter's lifetime, already had the Tribunician power and Proconsular *imperium* before his accession, and when Augustus died the Senate had only to give him the further powers which he still lacked, such as the Pontificate. The position of the third Emperor, Caligula, was quite different. Tiberius had doubtless appointed him his heir in his will, but only in private matters, and when Caligula assumed the power he had none of the funda-mental prerogatives inherent in the exercise of the Imperial

[1] Ulpian, *Institut.*, i (in *Dig.*, i, 4, pr.) ; cf. *Institut.*, i, 2, 6.
[2] i, 17, 1, 7.

authority, neither the Tribunician power nor the Proconsular *imperium*, in particular.

These attributions, probably from Caligula onwards and certainly from Vespasian, were conferred on the new sovereign at his accession, all together, an infinitely more expeditious method than that of conferring them piecemeal. This was done by a special constitutional act, the law of investiture, which was voted by the Senate in the form of a *Senatus consultum* and then submitted to the Comitia for ratification. This official procedure of giving over the power was still maintained in the third century, when the electoral power of the Comitia was only a dim memory and the vote of the people, reduced to the simple method of acclamation, was a pure formality. Only one of the Imperial prerogatives was, because of its special nature, excluded from this general investiture, and that was the Pontificate, which, down to the end of the first century, was conferred on the Emperor, not on the day of his accession, but shortly afterwards, and was made the object of a special religious act.

The law of investiture, the official formula of the constitutional system of the Empire, is known to us, at least in fragments, from an epigraphic document regarding the accession of Vespasian.[1] The remnants of the constitutional history of the Empire are so rare that we may well reproduce the whole of this unique text.

" (Vespasian shall be allowed to declare war) and to make treaties with whomsoever he will, as was allowed to the Divine Augustus, to Tiberius Julius Cæsar Augustus, and to Tiberius Claudius Cæsar Augustus Germanicus.

" He shall also be allowed to preside in the Senate, to submit proposals to it, to dismiss proposals made by others, to cause *Senatus consulta* to be voted, either consulting the Senators individually or merely ordering those who approve to line up on one side and those of the contrary opinion on the other, as was allowed to the Divine Augustus, to Tiberius Julius Cæsar Augustus, and to Tiberius Claudius Cæsar Augustus Germanicus.

" So, too, when by his desire, authority, or order, the Senate shall have been convoked by his representative or by himself, all that it enacts shall be considered regular and valid, exactly as if the Senate had been convoked and held according to the law.

" Any candidate for an ordinary magistracy, for an office conferring *potestas* or *imperium*, or a special extraordinary magistracy whom the Emperor shall have recommended to the Senate, or to whom he shall have given or promised his suffrage, shall be elected extraordinarily.

[1] *C.I.L.*, vi, 930.

" He shall be permitted to advance or move back the limits of the *pomœrium* when he judges it to be for the good of the Republic, as was permitted to Tiberius Claudius Cæsar Augustus Germanicus.

" He shall have the right and power to take any action which he shall judge to be for the good of the Republic and worthy of the majesty of things divine and human, public and private, as was permitted to the Divine Augustus, to Tiberius Julius Cæsar Augustus, and to Tiberius Claudius Cæsar Augustus Germanicus.

" The Emperor Cæsar Vespasian shall be exempted from the observation of the laws and plebiscites from which the Divine Augustus Tiberius Julius Cæsar Augustus, and Tiberius Claudius Cæsar Augustus Germanicus were formally exempted, and all that those Emperors had the right to do, in virtue of any law or legislative provision (*rogatio*), that shall the Emperor Cæsar Vespasian likewise have the right to do.

" All acts, actions, decrees, and orders emanating from the Emperor Cæsar Vespasian Augustus and whatever shall have been done at his order or by any of his representatives prior to the voting of this present law, all that shall be considered just and ratified as if it had been done by order of the people or of the Plebs.

SANCTION

" If anyone, in conformity with this law, has done or should do anything contrary to laws, provisions, plebiscites, or *Senatus consulta*, and if anyone, in conformity with this law, has failed to do all that he should have done in virtue of a law, provision, plebiscite, or *Senatus consultum*, that shall not be counted against him. He shall owe no sum to the people on account of it. No one may obtain a lawsuit or judgement against him, and no authority shall allow him to be prosecuted for that reason."

The document, in the fragmentary form in which it has come down to us, mentions, in particular, the Emperor's right of compelling the electors to accept his candidates by the process of recommendation (art. 4) (the Consulship was excluded under Augustus and Tiberius ; later it was treated like the other magistracies in practice) ; of extending the bounds of the *pomœrium* of the City when he sees fit (art. 5) ; and of concluding what treaties he pleases (art. 1). Lastly, as a measure of precaution, to make sure that legality is maintained, two articles of the law are intended to cover all possible omissions. Article 7 exempts the Emperor from all legislative acts, laws, or plebiscites, from which his pre-decessors were exempted, and authorizes him to do whatever, in virtue of a law or a *rogatio*, they were empowered to do ; and Article 6, still wider, allows him to take legally " any action which he shall judge to be for the good of the Republic and worthy of the majesty of things divine and human, public and private ". All these authorizations and exemp-tions mean that the practical omnipotence which was the real basis of the Emperor's power received the official consecration of the law.

Lastly, the Imperial power, as emanating, from the people, received its final and supreme consecration in a special oath taken by the inhabitants of the Empire, Roman citizens included, the form of which is preserved in an inscription.[1] The document refers to the province of Paphlagonia in Asia Minor, and belongs to the reign of Augustus, being dated the year 3 B.C.

> " In the name of the Emperor Cæsar Augustus, son of the God (Julius Cæsar), Consul for the twelfth time, in the year 3 (of the Province), on the 6th March, at Gangra, on (the Agora ?), the oath taken by the inhabitants of Paphlagonia and by the Romans doing business among them :—
>
> " ' I swear by Zeus, by the Earth, by the Sun, by all the Gods and Goddesses, and by Augustus himself, to be well-disposed to Cæsar Augustus, to his children, and to his descendants all the time (of my life ?) in word, deed, and thought, regarding as friends those whom they regard as such and regarding as enemies those whom they regard as such. To (defend) their interests, I swear not to spare my body, my soul, my life, or my children, but in every way to meet every danger, to (protect) what belongs to them. If I perceive or learn that anyone speaks, plots, or acts against them (I swear) to denounce and be an enemy to him who thus speaks, plots, or acts. If they regard anyone as their enemy, (I swear) to pursue and punish him on land and sea with arms and iron.
>
> " ' If any of my acts is contrary to this oath or is not in conformity with what I have sworn, I dedicate myself and my body and my soul and my life and my children and all my race and goods to extermination and annihilation down to my last posterity and to that of those who shall be descended from me. And may neither land nor sea receive the bodies of my kin and posterity, and may they give forth no fruits for them.'
>
> " In these terms all (the inhabitants of the country) swore in the Augusteums (established in districts ?), on the Altars of Augustus. In the same manner the Phazimonites, who live in the city now called Neapolis, all swore in the Augusteum on the Altar of Augustus."

An oath of this kind was probably renewed at the accession of every Emperor. The oath to Caligula (A.D. 37), which is mentioned by Josephus [2] for Syria and by an inscription from Acræphia in Bœotia [3] for Greece, has come down to us in two copies, one in Latin, the inscription of Aritium in

---

[1] F. Cumont, " Un Serment de fidélité à l'empereur Auguste," in **XLVI**, 1901, 26–45 ; cf. W. Dittenberger, *I.O.*, No. 532 ; *I.G. ad R.R.p.*, iii, p. 58, No. 137 ; *I.L.S.*, 8781.

[2] *Ant. Jud.*, xviii, 5, 3.   [3] *I.G.*, vii, 2711.

Lusitania,[1] and one in Greek, that of Assos in the Troad.[2] This is how the former runs :

OATH OF THE INHABITANTS OF ARITIUM

" On my conscience, I swear to be the enemy of those whom I know to be the enemies of Caius Cæsar Germanicus. If anyone places or shall have placed his safety in danger, I shall not cease to pursue him with arms in a war to the death by land and sea, until he shall have received his punishment. I shall not hold my children dearer than his safety. Those who shall have shown hostile intentions towards him, I shall regard as my enemies. If wittingly I fail or shall have failed my word, may Jupiter, Greatest and Best, and the Divine Augustus, and all the other immortal gods deprive me and my children of our country, our safety, and all our goods.

" The 11th May, in the city of Old Aritium, in the Consulship of Cn. Acerronius Proculus and C. Petronius Pontius Nigrinus (A.D. 37)."

These various powers were exercised by the Emperor either directly (the conduct of diplomacy, command of the land and sea forces when necessary, right of veto and inter- vention, convoking and presiding over the Senate) or by delegation to intermediate organs which were created one after another—organs of a consultative kind (the Imperial Council), organs of transmission (the secretariat), and the many organs of execution. Of the executive organs, some were ministers of State—the Prefect of the Prætorium and the directors of Finance, the Patrimony, and the Post. Others were : in Rome, the Prefects of the City, of the Corn- supply, and of the Watch and the commissions dealing with water, public buildings, the Tiber, and drains ; in Italy, the roads department, Consulars, Juridici, and Correctors ; and in the provinces the Imperial governors—Legate- Prætors, the Prefect of Egypt, and Præses-Procurators. Lastly, there were the financial staff and the body of officials of all grades who, working in combination with the traditional organs of the City, legislative organs, namely the Senate and Comitia, or executive, namely the magistrates (Consuls, Prætors, Ædiles, Tribunes, Quæstors) and pro-magistrates (Consular or Prætorian governors of Senatorial provinces), represented the central power and embodied its activity all over the Mediterranean world. It is enough here to mention these two types of servants of the Emperor. We shall examine them at greater length when we come to the Imperial administration.

[1] *C.I.L.*, ii, 172.   Ditt., *Syll.* (3), 797.

V

The Problem of the Succession.   Theory and Practice

Legally the Principate was based on an act of delegation by the Roman people, but, in virtue of the juridical principle that the sovereignty could be delegated but not made over, the Romans did not regard this delegation as hereditary, and so the Emperor, whose dignity was personal and lasted during his life, could not transmit his power by right of inheritance nor even by formal designation.   It was, therefore, logically impossible to introduce the hereditary principle of the Oriental type outright, and in any case public opinion would have failed to understand or would have rejected any such system and it would have remained inoperative, a dead letter,   Yet Augustus meant to make his own arrangements for the succession.   He regarded himself as the heir of Cæsar, and the oath taken to the Emperor by the inhabitants of Paphlagonia in 3 B.C. expressly associates his children and children's children with the head of the State himself.   The theoretical difficulties involved made this question of the succession one of the most serious concerns of the reign.   Augustus solved the problem, as he usually did and as so many others have done, by a makeshift. The constitution forbade him to nominate his successor. but at least he was allowed to express a wish and to propose a candidate to the future suffrages of the Senate.   The main thing was that that candidate should be sure of success in advance.   Augustus achieved this object by a double process—adoption and partial association in the Imperial power.   Tiberius, whom he finally chose as his successor, became his adopted son and took his name ; in addition, he was associated in the exercise of the two essential prerogatives of the Emperor, first the Tribunician power and then the Proconsular *imperium*.   On the death of Augustus, his heir designate, his associate of the last years of his reign, became the first man in the Empire.   In these circumstances, the Senate had only one course, and the election of the new Emperor was bound to become a mere formality.   All this policy of Augustus to make up for the absence of the forbidden principle of heirship was as ingenious in its guiding idea as in the means by which he carried it out.   But would it have the only sanction which mattered in the circumstances, that of success ?   Would the decisive scene, which would be enacted in the Senate after Augustus's death, proceed according to the scenario so cleverly devised by the creator of the system ?   The future of his whole work was at stake.

The historians who have related the beginnings of the Empire—Suetonius,[1] Dion Cassius,[2] and above all Tacitus at the beginning of the *Annals* [3]—enable us to reconstruct the scene as a whole in its true character.   Augustus died in A.D. 14 at Nola in Campania.   At once Tiberius, in virtue of his Proconsular *imperium*, gave the word to the Prætorian Cohorts and wrote to the provincial armies advising them of his accession.   In Rome, the Consuls S. Pompeius and S. Apuleius took oath of fealty to him.   Seius Strabo and C. Turranius, who were the Prefects of the Prætorium and Corn-supply, the Senate, the troops, and the people, all in turn took the same oath before the Consuls.

"In Rome," Tacitus writes in his downright way,[4] "Consuls, Senate, and Knights, rushed into slavery.   The higher a man's dignity the more faithless and eager he was."

So far, the play had been acted according to Augustus's programme.   In fact, Tiberius had taken the power and acted as Emperor.

There remained the Senate, which should legally, by the very theory of the Principate, have the official designation of the Emperor.   It was the critical moment for Augustus's scheme for the succession.   Tiberius summoned the Senate, in virtue of his Tribunician power, not in order to proceed to the election of the Emperor, but solely, as the official edict of convocation said, "to consult it on the honours due to his father, whose body he did not leave." [4]   The sitting opened.   First, the will of Augustus was read ; then, in accordance with the agenda, the question of funeral honours was settled and the Senate broke up.   So far there had been no mention of the succession to the Empire.   After the solemn funeral of the late Emperor, there was another sitting, and this was decisive.   They began by winding up the past by conferring apotheosis on Augustus, and after

[1] *Tib.*, 22–5.
[2] lvii, 1–3.
[3] i, 6–13.
[4] *Ann.*, i, 7.

that preliminary they came to the main business, the official investiture of the new Emperor.

" Then," says Tacitus,[1] " they addressed their prayers to Tiberius. He answered with generalities about the greatness of the Empire and his own inadequacy." Everyone was waiting to hear the conclusion. " Only the genius of Augustus, he said, could cope with that huge burden. He himself had been called by him to take on a part of his cares, and had learned by experience how hard and risky was the charge of the whole government. In a State which rested on so many distinguished men, it was not right that everything should be laid upon one. The task of government would be more easily accomplished by several men, combining their labours."

He did not, then, refuse outright to take his share of the power, but he allowed it to be understood that he preferred not to assume it all himself. At bottom, he was thoroughly ambiguous, and meant to be.

In the presence of this enigmatic attitude, as was to be expected, the discussion continued and became more intense. The Senators, who were not deceived by the comedy played by Tiberius but pretended not to understand, renewed their entreaties. " They stretched out their hands to the gods, to the image of Augustus, to Tiberius's own knees." [2] Then Tiberius, in support of his statements, caused the *Breviarium totius Imperii*, written by Augustus's own hand, to be read, and after further supplications he ended by declaring that, " if he was not equal to the whole government, yet he would undertake whatever part of it they should entrust to him." [3] Then he became definite : the Empire could be divided into three distinct parts, and he enumerated these parts—Rome and Italy, the armies, the provinces. More prayers from the Senate that he should accept the whole, followed by another refusal by Tiberius. Then Asinius Gallus, from sheer stupidity or perhaps, rather, in clumsy flattery, asked Tiberius at least to indicate the part which he would consent to take on ; after that, realizing his mistake from the angry expression of Tiberius, he returned to the proposal that he should accept it all. Three other Senators, L. Arruntius, Q. Haterius, and Mamercus Æmilius Scaurus, came to his support, one after another, and took up the same strain.

[1] *Ann.*, i, 11.   [2] *Ann.*, i, 11.   [3] *Ann.*, i, 12.

" ' How long, Cæsar, will you allow the Republic to be without a head ? ' asked Haterius, and Scaurus said that he hoped that Cæsar would not let the prayers of the Senate be unavailing, since he had not used his Tribunician power to veto the discussion opened by the Consuls." [1]

In the face of these repeated entreaties, Tiberius, while pretending to yield only to force, and provisionally, ended by accepting, and that, in spite of his reservations, formally. The Senate proceeded to vote on the proposal of the Consuls, and, doubtless by acclamation, officially invested Tiberius with the Empire. Then the sitting continued and they discussed other matters. The difficult moment was past. The heir of Augustus had obtained from the Senate the vote of confidence and solemn investiture which he wanted. Augustus's system of succession emerged triumphant from the ordeal, a last victory, which, though posthumous, was highly creditable and, what was more important, lasting.

[1] *Ann.*, i, 13.

I

CHAPTER II

FROM PRINCIPATE TO "DOMINATE"

BIBLIOGRAPHY.—*Ancient Authors*: Tacitus, *Annals*, i, 6 to xvi (to A.D. 68); *Histories*, i–v (A.D. 68–70); *Agricola*; Velleius Paterculus, ii, 124–31 (Tiberius); Dion Cassius, lvi, 31 to lx (to A.D. 46), lxi–lxxx (frags., from A.D. 47 to 229; cf. Xiphilinos, *Abridgement*, A.D. 147–357, the reign of Antoninus being almost entirely missing); Suetonius, *Twelve Cæsars* (Tiberius to Domitian); Herodian, *History* (A.D. 180–238); *Augustan History*, from Hadrian to Carus and his sons (the lives from Philip to Æmilianus are missing and that of Valerian is fragmentary); Aurelius Victor, *De Cæsaribus*, 2–38; *Epitome*, 2–38; Eutropius, vii, 11 to ix, 18; Orosius, vi, 20 to vii, 24; Zosimos, *History*, i; Zonaras, xi–xii, 30; Pliny the Elder, *Natural History*; Statius, *Silvæ*, especially iii, 3; Pliny the Younger, *Panegyric of Trajan*, *Letters*.

Legal Documents: Various texts of jurisconsults in the *Digest*, and Imperial Constitutions in the Code of Justinian.

Inscriptions: *C.I.L.*, ii ff., *passim*, especially vol. vi, 902–1115, 3749–86, 31197–380; cf. *I.L.S.*, 144–611, 8898–927; *Lex de Imperio Vespasiani*, *C.I.L.*, vi, 930.

Coins: H. Cohen, **IV**, i–vi.

*Modern Works: **XXI**, 304–80; **I**, 76–187; **VII**, ii, 1 (Tiberius to Vitellius); **X**, iii, 216–30 (E. Kornemann); **XXVI**, 516–48 (R. Poehlmann); **XXX**, i, 249–885; **VIII**, ii; **VII**, *passim*; **IX**, ii, 207–317; iii, 1–159; **CXXIX**; **CXXVII**; **XXXI**, 421–553; **XIX**, v and vii, 484–505; **XVIII**, i, 233–96; **XI**; **CXXV**a; **CXL**; **LXXXIII**; **LXXX**; **LVI**; **LXXVIII**; **XCIX**; **CXXII**; **LXVI**; **LXXIV**; **CXXI**; **LXXXII**; **CXXXVI**; **XC**a; **LXXXVII**; **LXXXVIII**; **LXXIX**; **CXXXVIII**; **CXXXIX**, especially pp. 5–7; L. Homo, " L'Empereur Gallien et la crise de l'Empire romain au IIIe siècle," in **XLVII**, cxiii (1913), 1–22, 225–67; **XCIV**; **XCVIII**; A. Rosenberg, " Ein Dokument zur Reichsreform des Kaisers Gallienus," in **XXXVI**, lv (1920), 319–21.

I

MILITARY DANGER AND ADMINISTRATIVE NEEDS

IN organizing the Principate, Augustus hoped that he was accomplishing something which, if not permanent in form—he had too much good sense to think that—would at least endure for a time.

" May it be allowed to me," he himself said in an edict,[1] " to establish the Republic safe and sound, and from that work to receive the fruits which I desire—to be regarded as the author of its welfare

[1] Suet., *Aug.*, 28.

*See also Supplementary Bibliography with Prefatory Note (p. 405)

and, when I die, to be able to hope that the foundations of the Republic which I shall have laid will remain in their place—*mansura in vestigio suo fundamenta Reipublicæ quæ jecero.*"

But in reality the Principate and the traditional constitution, with the preponderant part which it assigned to the Senate, were irreconcilable things, and, according to the eternal rule, the needs of the hour were soon to dispose of the will of men.

The system of personal government, at its origin, was confronted with two contradictory problems, a political problem, rising from the military character inherent in the new order, and an administrative problem, due to the increasingly imperative needs imposed on the Roman State by the government of the world. Augustus had tried, by the organization of the Principate, to reconcile them and to solve them so far as their antagonism allowed a solution. For three centuries we shall see these two problems dominating the history of the Empire and gradually determining a constitutional development which only ends with the transformation of the Principate into a " Dominate ", a monarchy.

The Roman, with his practical, observant nature, deaf to the suggestions of theory and little inclined to learn from the past in the case of other peoples (" *Les exemples vivants sont d'un autre pouvoir* " he would have said, with Corneille's hero), preferred to look about him, in the reality of every day, for the solution of the many and complex problems raised by the administration of the world. In the general progress from Principate to " Dominate ", two such examples played a decisive part—Egypt in the Early Empire, and the Persian monarchy of the Sassanids from the third to the fifth century —and modern discoveries throw a light upon both influences which grows brighter every day. At present we need only consider Egypt. The Sassanids will come in when we study the Late Empire.

Egypt, being a Hellenistic monarchy incorporated in the Roman State as a province comparatively late, and being the personal property of the Princeps, a Crown country as we should call it to-day, had a place apart among the possessions of Rome,[1] There the old Roman tradition,

[1] On the special position of Egypt in the Roman State, see especially **CXXXIX**, 5–7, and works cited in the Supplementary Bibliography under Book Four, Chapter II.

embodied by the Senate, had no force. As the direct successor of the Pharaohs and Ptolemies, continuing their system of government, the Emperor acted as an absolute monarch. As such, he was represented in the country by a man of his own, the Prefect of Egypt, who was simply a viceroy, served by an enormous and elaborately graded administrative staff bequeathed to him by a past of thousands of years. The Idiologos, the official in charge of the Roman *Fiscus* in Egypt, was a concrete example of these survivals. So, even in the first century, Egypt offered, not theories and possibilities, but a working realization of the monarchic principle which Cæsar had followed, and to which Rome was doomed, by the exigencies of her position, to come in the end. In the course of the first three centuries after Christ, the Empire took over many of its special institutions, political and administrative. From Egypt came the type of theocratic monarchy which Caligula tried to introduce in Rome from 37 to 41 ; from Egypt came the conception of a great Imperial bureaucracy, the inheritance of the Pharaonic and Lagid monarchies, which was inaugurated as early as the reign of Augustus and systematically developed under his successors ; from Egypt special officials were introduced into the West, such as the Prefect of the Watch and, it seems, the Idiologos, in the Roman form of the Procurator Rei Privatæ, created by Septimius Severus ; from Egypt, too, came the system of district administration which Gallienus extended to all the other provinces at the time of the crisis of the third century ; from Egypt, lastly, came the principle of separating the civil and military powers, which was traditional in the Hellenistic kingdoms but usually unknown to the Mediterranean city-system, and was one of the most characteristic and fruitful innovations of the Late Empire.

The first symptoms of the military danger, which had been warded off for a time by the personal prestige of Augustus and the profound loyalty which bound the army to the Julian house, manifested themselves on the accession of Tiberius (A.D. 14) in the mutiny of the armies of Pannonia and of Germany. Tacitus,[1] at the beginning of his *Annals*, has drawn a vivid and instructive picture of this first military

---

[1] i, 16–45.

movement, which was to be followed by so many others in the coming centuries. The causes, or one should rather say the pretexts, were of a purely professional nature.

> In Pannonia, through their representative, the centurion Clemens, the troops demanded " release after sixteen years, rewards at the end of their service, pay of a *denarius* a day, and that veterans should no longer be kept under the *vexillum* ".[1] In Germany, they all cried with one voice, " that the time had come for the veterans to obtain speedier release, for the young soldiers to get larger pay, for the hardships of all to be relieved, and for the cruelty of the centurions to be punished." [2]

But they did not confine themselves to these first demands. The legions in Pannonia rose against their general and mishandled their officers ; those in Germany went to more serious lengths, not stopping at usurpation and offering the Empire to Germanicus, who refused it at the risk of his life. By the efforts of Drusus, the son of Tiberius, in Pannonia and of Germanicus on the Rhine, all was presently restored to order, but the situation had been alarming, and Tiberius, never good at forgetting, was to remember it all his life.

The military danger, which permanently threatened the authority of the Emperor and the stability of the system and continued to grow without interruption, appeared in two parallel and complementary forms under the Early Empire—the Prætorian Guard in Rome and the provincial armies abroad.

Under the military system of Augustus, the Prætorian Cohorts, nine in number, were stationed partly in Rome and partly in various Italian towns. Their importance was afterwards increased by two successive changes : their strength was increased until there were ten cohorts, under Trajan, and, still more serious, the whole corps was concentrated in Rome itself, in the Prætorian Camp on the Viminal. This latter innovation was the work of the Prefect Sejanus, who sought thereby to strengthen his influence and to have a means of action when he needed it. From then onwards, the political part played by the Prætorian Guard increased from day to day. On the death of Caligula (A.D. 41), it promptly put down the Senate's tentative endeavour to restore the Republic. A soldier discovered Claudius hiding in a far corner of the Palace. He was led off to the Prætorian

---

[1] *Ibid.*, i, 26.   [2] *Ibid.*, i, 31.

camp, he was proclaimed Emperor, and the Senate had, willy-nilly, to bow humbly to the caprice of a soldiery which had made the Empire and did not mean to let go of it.

Later, in 69, the Prætorians gave the Empire to Otho, who had managed to win their favour, and, adding acts to words, killed Galba in the open Forum. The energy of the Flavians, with the attempt at a hereditary system which marks their dynasty, and the long and prosperous rule of the Antonines kept down the Prætorian danger, although they did not remove it for ever. Then the bad times came, and the Prætorian, who had been watching for his chance in the wings, stepped once more upon the stage. The revival of the drama did not lose by having been deferred so long.

It is the year 193 after Christ. The Empire is in the hands of Pertinax, a man of intelligence and strong will. He resolves, as is his duty, to restore in the army a discipline which was destroyed in the long orgy of the reign of Commodus. The Prætorians protest. Pertinax pays no attention. Then they proceed to direct action. One day, in battle order, they come out of their camp, invade the Palace, and cut down the Emperor. Then follows the unique spectacle, unpredecented in the annals of Rome, of the Imperial power being put up to auction and awarded according to the proper rules. Having got possession of the Empire, and being practical men, the Prætorians decide that the best thing to do with it is to sell it. Two men bid against one another—Pertinax's father-in-law, Sulpicianus, and one Didius Julianus, a descendant of the jurisconsult Salvius Julianus, one of the richest men in Rome at the time. The latter secures the lot at the price of 6,250 drachmas a man, and the Senate, under pressure from the Prætorian Cohorts, is compelled to recognize him.

When Septimius Severus triumphed, he dismissed the Prætorian Guard and altered its recruiting. The government gained nothing in stability by this, and the unwholesome influence which the Prætorians had had on the conduct of affairs for two centuries was manifested again on the first favourable occasion. The hostility between civilian and soldier, which had hitherto been exceptional, tended to become permanent. Under Severus Alexander (222–35), the Prætorians and townspeople fought for three days.

Driven from the streets, the Prætorians set the houses on
fire, and a little later they took their revenge by killing
Ulpian, the Prefect of the Prætorium, at the side of the
Emperor himself, who was powerless to save him. At the
end of the reign of Maximin, in 238, the struggle was resumed
more mercilessly than ever. The people, having killed a
number of Prætorians scattered about the town, laid siege
to their camp. In the face of their obstinate and successful
resistance, they cut the water-conduits, to force them to
surrender, but the Prætorians made an unexpected *sortie*
and continued the fight through the streets of the city,
part of which was burned down, whereupon the opponents
joined forces and amicably proceeded to loot the rest. The
excesses of the military provoked another civil reaction
which raised the two Senatorial Emperors, Pupienus Maximus
and Balbinus, to the throne. Some weeks later, the
Prætorians seized them in their own palace, dragged them off
with outrages, and on the way, to make safe, put them to
death. One more crime, a double crime, was recorded in the
annals of the Prætorian Guard. They were a permanent
menace to the Imperial power and to the civil population
of Rome, and they did not cease to do harm until they
disappeared altogether. Constantine had the honour of
ridding the Roman world of their presence.

After the Prætorians in Rome, let us consider the armies
in the provinces. Here the evil will appear more slowly,
as the formation of the armies is gradually completed and
they become local units through the change in their recruiting
and command.

The three great provincial armies which play the chief
part in the political history of the Empire—the armies of
the Rhine, the Danube, and the East—dated from the reign
of Augustus, and therefore from the time when the standing
army was created. At first they contained eight, seven,
and three legions respectively. Both by its numbers and its
quality, the army of the Rhine held the first place among
the armies of the Empire. Later, the situation changed
in both respects. In the third century, just before the
military anarchy, the army of the Rhine had only four
legions, whereas those of the Danube and the East had twelve
and ten respectively. In addition to this great increase of

the strength of the armies of the Danube and the East during the first two centuries, the recruiting changed. In the first century, the Italian element was still numerous in the legion, and for the provincial contingents recruiting was usually largely territorial. The original army of the Danube was in this respect composed of two distinct divisions —the western wing, the legions of Pannonia, and the eastern wing, those of Mœsia. Both were recruited from Italy, and, in addition, the former got its men from Spain and Gaul and the latter from Macedonia and the Asiatic provinces. The army of the East was mainly recruited in the East, whether in Asia or in Europe—Syria, Palestine, Asia Minor, and Thrace. By the end of the first century after Christ, the Italian element was beginning to disappear from the legions, and in the time of Hadrian recruiting was purely local. Henceforth, the army of the Rhine was raised solely in the Rhenish provinces, that of the Danube in the Danubian provinces, and that of the East in the Eastern provinces, and in each case the mass of enrolments came from centres attached to the camps of the legions themselves. The provincial armies now had unity of recruiting, a second element of power and influence.

Lastly, the command developed in the same way. In the first two centuries the Emperors, concerned for the political situation, endeavoured to maintain the Roman character of the army. They reserved the higher commands for Italians or members of the especially Romanized aristocracy and middle class of the West, and, moreover, they practised a system of promotion by transfers from one army to another. Everything changed with the armies of the third century. The officers were soldiers of fortune, who, like their men, belonged to the district in which they were garrisoned and were promoted locally. The evolution was then complete. In respect of numbers, origin, and command, the great armies on the frontiers were now wholly independent ; they had become local armies in the full sense of the term.

The effects of such a state of things on internal politics very soon manifested themselves, and the part played by the provincial armies rapidly increased. The movement began in the reign of Claudius, in A.D. 42, when the Legate of Dalmatia, Furius Camillus Scribonianus, raised a revolt

which was, however, soon brought to an end by the speedy
defection of the troops. This prelude was followed by a
very different affair, the crisis of 68–70, the exceptional
importance of which is noted by Tacitus in a passage full
of significance [1] :—

> " The end of Nero . . . aroused various sentiments, not only in
> Rome among the Senate and people and city troops, but among all
> the legions and generals ; for the secret of the Empire had been
> disclosed, that a man could be made Emperor elsewhere than in
> Rome."

From this time onwards, of the three great provincial
armies, those of the Rhine and the East were evidently
the most homogeneous and solid. It was they, therefore,
which took the chief part in the crisis which ended with the
accession of the Flavians. The army of the Danube, on the
other hand, which lacked unity, being torn between the two
opposite tendencies due to the variety of its recruiting,
merely followed them. The armies of the Rhine and the East
in turn gave the Empire to their leaders, who, of course,
were simply their own champions, the former producing
Vitellius and the latter Vespasian. The army of the Danube
had no candidate of its own ; it first recognized Otho and
then went over to Vespasian, and it was one of its generals,
Antonius Primus, who won the decisive victory for the
latter.

During the second century, the respective importance of
the provincial armies changed altogether. The army of the
Rhine, being reduced in numbers, lost its former military
and political preponderance, while those of the East and,
still more, of the Danube rose to the front rank. The crisis
of 193, the second of the great upheavals which would now
shake the Empire periodically, clearly reflects the new
situation. The military reaction aroused in the provinces
by the action of the Prætorians in killing Pertinax started
from the armies of the Danube and the East, which raised
Septimius Severus and Pescennius Niger respectively to
the Empire. It was the turn of the army of the Rhine to
remain passive. When the moment came, it supported the
successful nominee of the legions of the Danube.

Hitherto the military danger, though always latent, had
become acute only at long intervals and exceptionally.

[1] *Hist.*, i, 4.

Moreover, a man had always appeared—Vespasian in 69, Septimius Severus in 193—who was able to restore the old order and re-establish peace. But now the trouble became permanent, and for nearly a century. First, there was the stubborn feud between the two great provincial armies, those of the East and of the Danube, which triumphed in turn, the former for a time with Elagabalus (218–22) and later with Philip (244–9) and the latter with Decius (249–51) and, permanently, with the Illyrian Emperors ; the great men of the Danube, Claudius II (268–70), Aurelian (270–5), and Probus (276–82), all glorious sons of Illyricum, constituted themselves its mandataries in the direction of the State. In the second half of the third century, in the hands of the Illyrians, the Imperial power became the most absolute and tyrannical military dictatorship ; it was the price paid for the salvation of the whole Roman world. At intervals there was a plague of pretenders, which rose to its height in the period known as that of the Thirty Tyrants. The Emperors, the creatures and toys of their troops, did no more than pass over the scene, which was soon rid of them by a timely assassination. The Senate, the only body left in the universal disorder which could confer legal authority, bowed to the strongest and confined its policy to recognizing one Emperor after another. In the end the enormous evil created by military anarchy disgusted the soldiers themselves, and on the removal of Aurelian the world witnessed the paradoxical spectacle of a return to civil government, demanded by the army itself and effected through the voluntary self-effacement of its own representatives.

The administrative problem was quite different, both in data and in possible solutions. The Republic, for want of a sufficient administrative personnel, which, with its oligarchical character, it could not have, had been compelled to keep the machinery on which the huge task of governing the world depended down to a minimum. This point of view, which was that of an oligarchy, limited in numbers and deliberately exclusive, could not be accepted by the great far-seeing monarchy which came with the Empire. Personal government, by its very nature and programme, had to deal with urgent necessities and fill up ancient deficiencies. In Rome and Italy this was done, in the reign of Augustus, by the creation of new services—great prefectures (of the Prætorium, City, Watch, Corn-supply), executive commissions (water, public works), Italian roads, finance, and Imperial post. In the provinces, Imperial and Senatorial, a complete, co-ordinated administration was set up, such as the Republic had never known. As the Roman Peace, one of the lasting benefits of the Empire, accomplished its work, existing services had to be developed, such as the post, and new ones had to be created, such as those connected with provisions. In the central administration, the State had to create the whole of the necessary organ of transmission; Claudius's freedmen and Hadrian supplied the offices which were lacking. Being short of money and faced with increasing expenses, it had to improve the financial system and, in order to augment the return of taxes, to replace the old method of farming them out by the more modern method of direct collection; this reform was applied to the direct provincial tax at the end of the reign of Tiberius, to the tax of a twentieth on inheritances (*vicesima hereditatium*) under Hadrian, to the customs, probably under Commodus, and to the mines under Septimius Severus at the latest.

A development of the administration on this scale required a large and competent executive personnel. Now, the only governing and administrative personnel which the Republic had bequeathed to the new order was the Senatorial nobility, which did not satisfy the demands of the new situation in either respect. Being limited in its numbers, which had been and would be yet further reduced by proscriptions in the past and executions in the future, made to accept the Imperial system by force, secretly dissatisfied with the real but limited share which the Principate left to it in the control of affairs, and, in addition, being incompetent and pleasure-loving, the Senatorial aristocracy did not offer the Emperor the resources in numbers and capacity now required by the administration of the world. Tiberius and Trajan in turn, in spite of their loyalty to the constitution and their excellent intentions, had painful experience of the fact, and even in the fourth century the historian Aurelius Victor,[1] in a brief but significant passage, observed :—

[1] *De Caes.*, xxxvii, 7.

" Giving themselves up to idleness and, at the same time, fearing
for their wealth . . . they opened the road of dominion over themselves
and their descendants to the military leaders and almost to the
barbarians."

The indispensable organs of administration, which the
Senatorial nobility could not furnish, eventually had, by the
force of things, to be sought elsewhere, particularly in the
Equestrian order. The antagonism between the Senatorial
and Equestrian orders, increasing as the latter rose and the
former decayed more and more hopelessly, further aggravated
the conflict between Emperor and Senate. The centralizing
movement, which, in administration, was the essential
phenomenon of the Early Empire, and necessarily took place
at the expense of the Senate, that embodiment of all survivals
and routines, did the rest. Unable to administer the Empire
with the Senate, the Emperor had to do so without it, and
presently, as was inevitable, against it. Drawn together in
the political domain by the common danger from the armies,
the two powers became opponents in that of administration.
The variations of the policy of the Emperors towards the
Senate during the first three centuries may, in the last
analysis, be summed up in that fundamental antagonism.

The two problems, therefore, political and administrative,
took the form of an irreducible antimony ; the one required
close alliance with the Senate, the other, a fight against its
prerogatives. In this matter of the relations of the Emperor
and Senate, the basis and, as it were, the touchstone of all
the home policy of the Empire, there were two formulas
from which to choose, the Roman formula of Augustus and
the Græco-Oriental formula of Cæsar and Antony. For each
formula there was a corresponding series of Emperors. The
liberal Emperors, who were chiefly concerned with the political
problem, lived on good terms with the Senate, respected
its privileges, and delayed the disappearance of the old concept
of the city as much as they could. Augustus, Tiberius,
Vespasian, Trajan, Antoninus, Marcus Aurelius, and Severus
Alexander were the chief representatives of this type. The
autocratic Emperors were men with a modern spirit, chiefly
alive to the administrative needs of the Empire, who tended
towards absolute monarchy, developed centralization, and
destroyed the vestiges of the past ruthlessly. The great

names among these were those of Claudius, Domitian, Hadrian, and Septimius Severus.

II

LIBERAL EMPERORS AND SENATORIAL RESTORATIONS

By the compromise of 27 B.C., Augustus had carried out the programme of the Principate in concrete and legal form. The Senate held Italy and the Senatorial provinces, the Emperor kept the armies. This programme was maintained, at least in theory, by his successors, the liberal Emperors of the first two centuries. Tiberius, at the celebrated sitting of the Senate at which he consented to accept the burden of the Empire in part, took it up in exactly the same terms, and forty years later Nero, on his accession, renewed the solemn adhesion of the Imperial power to it before the Senate itself.

> "He drew the plan of his coming Principate," Tacitus writes,[1] "especially repudiating the abuses which had recently roused indignation. He would not try all cases, with accusers and accused all shut up within one house, so that the power of a few men had its way ; venality and intrigue would not be admitted into his home ; his household and the Republic would be distinct. The Senate should have its ancient privileges ; Italy and the provinces of the people should take their cases to the courts of the Consuls. Through the Consuls, the Senate should be approached ; he himself would confine himself to the management of the armies, as was his duty."

In the case of Tiberius and in that of Nero, at least in the early part of his reign, there was something more in the Imperial promises than empty phrases. When Augustus died, Tiberius was not a newcomer to power. Having been associated in the Imperial authority by his predecessor, he continued a policy which he had already been pursuing for about ten years, and, as a genuine champion of the formula of the Principate, he endeavoured in practice to make it a reality. He wanted the end, and he also wanted the means— that is, the sincere co-operation of the Senate. Never, as long as the Empire lasted, did an Emperor work with the Senate so honestly and efficiently. He treated it with the utmost consideration, frequently taking part in its sittings and making a point of respecting its liberty of debate. These were not mere formal manifestations. In the desire to give the

[1] *Ann.*, xiii, 4.

Senate a considerable part in the administration of the Roman world, he systematically augmented the powers which the Principate had left to it. He did this in respect of election, legislation, and justice. He abolished the electoral Comitia and transferred their prerogatives to the Senate. He extended the legal force of *Senatus consulta*. Lastly, he made the Senate the supreme court of justice, which dealt with important criminal cases, such as those of crimes against the safety of the State and suits affecting members of the Senatorial order. For various causes—the incurable distrustfulness which was a characteristic of Tiberius on the one side and the ill-will and, perhaps even more, the incapacity of the Senate on the other—the attempt was doomed to speedy failure, and the last part of the reign of Tiberius stands in the history of the Empire as a black period of tyranny. Tiberius had, at least, made an honest effort. He is rightly regarded as the most constitutional of all the line of Emperors.

At first, in reaction against the anti-Senatorial, centralizing policy of Claudius, Nero listened to good advice and solemnly proclaimed his desire to resume the traditional programme of the Principate. He announced this to the Senate, as we have seen, and Tacitus adds [1] : " He did not fail his word, and many measures were taken at the decision of the Senate." Unfortunately, as Nero grew older, his bad instincts soon gained the upper hand, whereupon his earlier policy, which had really been that of his ministers Seneca and Burrhus, to which he had simply given his name, vanished for good.

Tacitus [2] has summed up the programme of the liberal Emperors in a famous phrase : " Nerva Cæsar combined two things once incompatible, Principate and liberty—*res olim dissociabiles, principatum et libertatem.*" That programme, which found practical expression in effective collaboration with the Senate, was applied in succession by Vespasian, Trajan, Antoninus, and Marcus Aurelius, all liberal Emperors and all attached to the political formula of the Principate. Not all did it to the same extent ; Vespasian, whose first relations with the Senate had been rather delicate on account of his humble origin, had somewhat emphasized the monarchical note. But all did it with equal honesty. None

[1] *Ann.*, xiii, 5.   [2] *Agric.*, 3.

of them, however, sacrificed the solid reality of his Imperial rights on the altar of concord.   It is unnecessary to dwell on this series of experiments, which were all similar and repeated in similar conditions.   The essential thing is to observe the result.   Now, in this respect two facts stand out conspicuously.   First, even the Emperors who were most faithful to the principle were compelled, by the requirements of the administration of the world, to make exceptions in applying it.   One example is typical.   Antoninus, to give pledges to the Senate, had abolished the Consulars of Italy, a necessary and useful innovation of Hadrian, and had thus restored the whole administration of the country to the Senate.   Marcus Aurelius, in spite of the trend of his general policy, found himself compelled to revive the institution, and re-established Hadrian's Italian officials under the name of Juridici.   A second, still more important, fact is the ultimate failure of all these attempts, and always for the same reasons as before, the chief being the Senatorial order's incompetence and unfitness for the work.   The liberal policy of Vespasian, of Trajan, and of the last Antonines only ended, with Domitian, Hadrian, and Septimius Severus respectively, in an accentuation of personal rule and a resumption of the centralizing movement.

The chronic evil which had been rudely revealed by the crises of 68–70 and 193 became acute in the third century. Military aggression and civil reaction in turn represent the whole constitutional history of the Empire in that century. The military government of Septimius Severus brought on a first Senatorial reaction which is associated with the reign of Severus Alexander.   The periodic disorders which had followed the death of the founder of the dynasty, the two revolutions by which it had been first overthrown and then restored, the crimes of Caracalla and the orgies of Elagabalus and the very youth and insignificance of the Emperor created an exceptionally favourable atmosphere for another attempt of the kind.   Those highly intelligent women, Julia Mæsa and Julia Mamæa, the Emperor's grandmother and mother, who ruled and inspired the government, saw this, and sought to save the State, which military despotism seemed to be leading to destruction, by a return to the earliest traditions of the Principate.   Civil government

was revived, and the Senate, excluded from affairs in the
previous reigns and injured both in the persons and in the
property of its members, once more became an acting associate
of the Imperial power and the great legislative organ of the
government. A regency council composed of sixteen Senators
took the executive power in charge. The office of Prefect of
the Prætorium, a stronghold of the Equestrian order, became
a Senatorial post, and in Rome itself a municipal council
of fourteen Consulars was attached to the Prefect of the City
for the administration of the capital.

This system of government, which was imposed by the
situation and proved beneficial in practice, had unfortunately
one weak point. The army would not accept it, and presently
there was proof of this. Riots broke out in Rome, and
pretenders arose in the provinces. The inevitable result
occurred in 235 ; Severus Alexander and his mother, who
had been called to the Rhine by an invasion of the Germans,
were murdered by their troops. Three years later, the
Senate engaged in open conflict with Maximin and the
military element represented by that soldier of fortune,
appointed a Senatorial commission which should place the
Mediterranean world in a state of defence, and, on the death
of Gordian in Africa, gave the Empire to two of its most
eminent members, Pupienus Maximus and Balbinus. The
removal of Maximin seemed to establish its victory and
ensure the permanence of the new government. Indeed, the
victory seemed complete. The fact that there were two
Emperors, which, if the government could not be Republican,
was at least a revival of the old tradition of the Consuls,
together with their past record and their political tendencies,
gave the Senate a predominant influence over the conduct
of affairs. Never since the beginning of the Empire, not
even in the happy days of Trajan, the Antonines, and Severus
Alexander, had the Senatorial aristocracy carried out its
programme so completely. It was a house of cards, which
the first breath would overthrow. The soldiers, who had
not forgotten Maximin, their own man and their hero, were
waiting impatiently for the day of vengeance. Three months
after their accession, the two Emperors were assassinated, and
the system which they had represented went down with them.

A last Senatorial reaction, which came as a curious

interlude in the brilliant line of the Illyrian Emperors, especially deserves attention, and for two reasons—because it was a last attempt to save the ancient tradition of the Principate, so far as it could be saved, and because it was only the temporary abstinence or partial assistance of the military power which made this death-bed resurrection of the civil power possible,

For seven years, under Tacitus (275–3) and Probus (276–82), the Senate enjoyed an influence which might have been supposed lost for ever. After the murder of Aurelian, at the request of the army itself and after an interval of about three weeks, the Senate conferred the Empire on one of its most eminent members, the Consular Tacitus. In the Senatorial restoration which resulted from this choice a certain number of the old prerogatives of the Senate were revived, and four especially—the electoral, judicial, administrative, and military privileges, which it had lost, the first after the assassination of Pupienus Maximus and Balbinus in 238, the second at the beginning of the third century, the third under Gallienus and Aurelian, and the fourth under Gallienus. The revival of the electoral right was expressed by the very fact of electing Tacitus, and the three others soon followed.

In respect of justice, Tacitus took a decisive measure : he instituted appeal to the Prefect of the City. The innovation applied to the governors of Senatorial and Imperial provinces and to the Correctors of Italy ; the magistrates of the city of Rome already came under the Prefect of the City in respect of appeals. Before 275, the Prefect of the City was judge of appeal in Rome and within the radius of a 100,000 yards round the capital ; in 275, under Tacitus, this prerogative was extended to the rest of Italy and all the provinces. So, in respect of appeals, the whole Roman world came under his jurisdiction. There was only one limitation to this universal right ; the reform did not include officials who tried cases in virtue of particular and extraordinary delegation by the Emperor (*vice sacra judicantes*). Since they embodied the Emperor's jurisdiction by express delegation, there could not logically be appeal from them to an Imperial agent, even to one as highly placed as the Prefect of the City.

In administration, the Senate traditionally had rights in respect of both kinds of province, Senatorial and Imperial. The restoration of 275 applied to both alike ; the Edict of Gallienus was repealed in respect of both. In the Senatorial provinces there was a complete return to the past ; the Senate recovered both the appointment of governors (Proconsuls) and the administration of these provinces. In the Imperial provinces, the members of the Senatorial order recovered the provincial governorships from which they had been completely excluded by the Edict.

The military privilege of the Senate was restored in its entirety. The repeal of the Edict of Gallienus made the whole army career open to Senators once more. They took their old place, from the bottom of the scale to the top, both as senior officers (Tribunes of legions) and as generals (Legates of legions and Legates governing Imperial provinces). In this respect, therefore, the old state of things was restored.

About the financial privilege the documents tell us nothing. We do not, therefore, know whether Tacitus gave back to the Senatorial treasury its revenues of a general kind. Logically, it seems that he must have done so. The re-establishment of the Senatorial provinces entailed heavy expenses, which the Senatorial treasury, the *Ærarium*, could not meet, now that it had become the mere municipal exchequer of the city of Rome. When the Senate resumed its share in the administration of the provinces, the Emperor ought certainly to have given it the resources needed if it was to cope with its revived obligations suitably. About the privilege of coining money, on the other hand, there can be no doubt. The only copper coins (and they are few) struck in the reign of Tacitus are from the Imperial mint ; the Senatorial signature of S.C. does not appear on any. So this privilege of the Senate was certainly dead since the reform of Aurelian, and even Tacitus, in spite of the extremely Senatorial character of his government, did not revive it.

In sum, with this single exception, the system of government established by Tacitus involved an almost complete restoration of the old administrative privileges of the Senate. The new order of things represented the collapse of the system of Gallienus in the domain of administration, and, if the Senate did not recover its old power in certain

spheres, at least it received considerable compensation in a
sphere in which it had ceased to count since the end of the
second century, namely that of justice.   The institution of
universal appeal to the Prefect of the City, with the corresponding abolition of the powers of the Prefect of the
Prætorium, was a great triumph for the Senatorial nobility
and, if only it lasted, a potent means for action.

Unluckily for the Senatorial aristocracy, the political
and administrative restoration inaugurated by Tacitus was
short-lived. The Emperor was killed after reigning for six
months, and, as was the rule in that cruel time, by his own
troops. At once the whole constitutional edifice set up by
the Senate under favour of exceptional circumstances fell
to pieces.   Ignoring the electoral power restored to the
Senate, Tacitus's brother Florianus took possession of the
Empire without asking its opinion. He broke with his
brother's policy and seems to have returned, at least in
part, for the administration of the provinces, to the arrangements of Gallienus. In any case, he did not keep the power
long. Probus, one of the most brilliant generals of the army
of the Danube, had been proclaimed Emperor by the army
of the East.

A Danubian by birth and a soldier by trade, Probus was
nevertheless a shrewd, clear-headed statesman, and was
well aware of the defects of military government and the
dangers which it could entail for the State. He, too, thought
of restoring a strong civil power, as the obvious and only
thing to counterbalance the omnipotence of the armies.
Of that civil power, it seemed to him, as to so many of his
predecessors, that the essential organ must be the Senate.
No doubt, there could be no question now of going back to
the complete or almost complete restoration of the time of
Tacitus, which fate had condemned without appeal.   Probus
did not intend to abdicate his power into the hands of the
Senate, but he wanted to conclude a fair agreement and
compromise with it.

That agreement, which he regarded as indispensable, he
effected as soon as he came to the throne by a series of
definite concessions. One of these was of a political nature—
the right to ratify Imperial Constitutions by a *Senatus
consultum*. Three others effected the administrative

privileges of the Senate. In its own provinces, it recovered
the right of appointing, either all Proconsul-governors, or
(a more likely hypothesis) a certain number of them. With
regard to the Imperial provinces, we must distinguish between
Consular provinces and Prætorian; in the former, the
Legates appointed by the Emperor might be drawn by him
from the Senate, whereas the governors of the latter, in
accordance with the reform of Gallienus, were still chosen
from the Equestrian order, except that *jus prætorium*, if
required, was conferred by the Senate. A last article of the
compromise of 276 concerns the domain of justice. Probus
abolished appeal to the Prefect of the City as organized
by the system of Tacitus, and replaced it by appeal to the
Senate. The Emperor did not give up his own appellate
jurisdiction in favour of the Senate, but revived the simultaneous appeal to Emperor and Senate which had been a
fundamental principle of the organization of justice in the
first century. We should observe that there was no stipula-
tion—to our knowledge, at least—that the financial and
monetary privileges of the Senate should be restored, and
that its electoral privilege of nominating the Emperor, which
was revived for a moment at the accession of Tacitus, did
not come into question at all.

Between the position given to the Senate by the restoration of 275 and that resulting from the compromise of 276,
there was a very great difference, both in form and in substance. In form : in 275, the privileges of the Senate were
restored as a right and as a legitimate return to the ancient
tradition of the Principate ; in 276, they were regarded
solely as Imperial concessions, the nature and extent of which
were determined by the Emperor alone. In substance : in
275, the Senatorial restoration was almost entire ; in 276,
the concessions made to the Senate, although important,
were only partial. The Edict of Gallienus was put into
force again, both for the government of the Imperial provinces
and for the military commands, save for individual exceptions
which were intended to mitigate its severity. The policy
of compromise which marks the reign of Probus did not
survive that Emperor. His successor, Carus, elected by a
military reaction, abandoned it. Carus's son, Carinus, went
still further, and his relations with the Senate were either

doubtful or frankly bad. The Senate had played its last card with Tacitus and Probus. Diocletian finally put an end to its great traditional rôle. The liberal Emperor was gone, and for ever.

III

AUTOCRATIC EMPERORS AND CONFLICTS WITH THE SENATE

Under the Republic, the Senate, had had two main sets of attributions—political and administrative. It was in these two spheres that the representatives of personal power found the old council in their way and accordingly had to fight it. During the first three centuries, the conflict, in accordance with the general situation, presented two aspects, one political and one administrative.

The political conflict itself varied, if not in spirit, at least in method. Only exceptionally did it take the form of open war. The forces at the disposal of the rival powers were two obviously unequal for such tactics to offer the Senate any chance of success, at least in normal circumstances. Indeed, it only embarked on the adventure twice, and on both occasions it had no Emperor to oppose it. In A.D. 41, Caligula had fallen beneath the sword of the Tribune Chæreas. He left no heir, and the Senate thought of profiting by this fortunate chance to recover the control of affairs. It devoted a regular debate to the constitutional question—Republic or Principate ? It failed lamentably, and thereafter the actual principle of personal power was never again called into question, not at the death of Nero in 68 nor at that of Domitian in 96. In the face of the necessity of monarchical rule, as a fact which everyone must accept, the Republican party itself disappeared in the course of the first century after Christ, and when Tacitus, on the accession of Nerva, congratulates himself on seeing Principate and liberty united for the first time, it is a programme, no doubt, but it is also a funeral oration.

Two centuries later, in 238, we are at the beginning of the military anarchy. Maximin, the first of the great upstarts of the army and the irreconcilable enemy of the Senate, was away from Rome, detained by the wars on the Rhine and Danube. Old Gordian had just seized the Empire

in Africa.   The Senate hastened to recognize him, and
declared Maximin a public enemy.   It appointed a commission of twenty Senators to organize resistance in Italy
and the provinces, and, after the death of Gordian, it gave
the Empire to the two most distinguished members of that
commission, Pupienus Maximus and Balbinus.   Civil war
broke out.   Maximin, marching on the capital, was murdered
before Aquileia, and the Senate, in its own person and in
that of its two nominees, was left master of the situation.
But it was a short-lived victory, for which the army soon
took full vengeance by murdering the two Emperors.

More frequent and more continuous was the underground
struggle.   The Emperors did not attack the Senate as a body,
but the persons and property of its members, in the form of
executions and confiscations.   Tiberius in the later part
of his reign, Caligula, Nero, Domitian, Commodus, and
Septimius Severus excelled in this method.   The Senate
retaliated with conspiracies ;   such were, even in the reign
of Augustus, when the aristocracy as a whole supported the
new regime, the conspiracies of Fannius Cæpio, L. Licinius
Varro, Murena (22 B.C.), and M. Egnatius Rufus (19 B.C.) ;
that of Cn. Cornelius Lentulus Gætulicus, the Legate of
Upper Germany, and M. Lepidus under Caligula (A.D. 39) ;
the great conspiracy of Piso (65), and the *Conjuratio Viniciana*
under Nero ;   that of Quadratus and Lucilla (183) under
Commodus ; and many more.   The war was waged mercilessly
on both sides.   After the defeat of Albinus, Septimius
Severus sent a whole number of Senators to their death (197).
Proscription and plot, plot and proscription, followed one
another in a fatal chain of causes and consequences, from
which the Empire never shook itself free.

By the side of the political conflict went the administrative
conflict, which, as the problems of government increased, took
the form on the Emperor's side of a steady advance towards
centralization.   Claudius and Domitian in the first century,
Hadrian and Septimius Severus in the second, and Gallienus
and Aurelian in the third represent the principal stages.

With the name of Claudius, or rather with those of the
freedmen Narcissus, Pallas, Callistus, and Polybius, who
reigned under his name, a number of very important and
fruitful innovations in the administrative domain are

connected. First of all, organs of transmission were created—
the secretariat, indispensable to a central power, offices
of Correspondence (*ab epistulis*), Petitions (*a libellis*), Inquiries
(*a cognitionibus*), and Preliminary Examinations (*a studiis*),
the directing staff and organization of which were supplied
by the freedmen of the Emperor's household—a significant
evidence of the progress made by the monarchical idea in
the Roman world. Secondly, the Knights made a further
advance at the expense of the Senatorial order, particularly
in respect of provincial administration. Two of the newly
created provinces, Thrace and Judea, were given Equestrian
governors with the title of Proprætor. The centralizing
movement, interrupted for a moment under the successors
of Claudius (Nero at his accession separated the Emperor's
household and the administration of the State completely),
began again under Domitian, a declared enemy of the
Senate in the matter of administration and everything else.
Following Otho's example, he introduced Knights into the
offices by the side of the freedmen, thus opening a new
sphere of activity and influence to the order.

From Nerva to Marcus Aurelius, the Antonines were on
the whole, as we have seen, a line of conservative Emperors,
the fundamental article of whose home policy was the maintenance of good relations with the Senate. But there was
one exception, and a striking one—Hadrian. The experiment
of frank co-operation with the Senate, the ruling idea of
Trajan's reign, had failed, once again, and for the usual
reasons, chief among which was the hopeless incompetence
of the Senate. Hadrian, having seen the Senatorial
aristocracy at work, and knowing what to expect of it, felt
himself obliged to turn elsewhere. Like Claudius and Domitian
before him, but with even more determination and energy,
he went to the Knights for the fellow-workers whom he
needed, and gave that order its final administrative status,
thus taking the Empire a decisive stage further on the road
from Principate to Hellenistic monarchy. Since Otho and
Domitian, the Knights had been at the head of the services
of the secretariat, side by side with the freedmen. Hadrian
gave them the lion's share to themselves. The customary
freedmen were replaced by Knights at the heads of the
offices of Correspondence, Inquiries, and Petitions, and also

of the department of Finance (*a rationibus*), and this change of personnel finally transformed what had been private organs of the Emperor's household into true public departments. When the Imperial post was reorganized, the new heads, the Prefects of Vehicles (*præfecti vehiculorum*) were likewise drawn from the Equestrian order.

This was not all. The Imperial Council, the rival of the Senate in the legislative domain, was reorganized, and Hadrian increased its importance by introducing into it, as regular salaried officials, the first jurisconcults of the day. Lastly, in Italy he dealt the Senate an equally hard blow by the creation of permanent officials, the Consulars, a step towards the inevitable assimilation of Italy to the provinces. All these co-ordinated and convergent measures, the organization of the Equestrian career, the transformation of the offices, the recasting of the Imperial Council, the creation of the Consulars of Italy, constituted a further advance from Principate towards bureaucratic monarchy and administrative centralization.

The less overt war of Emperor and Senate in the sphere of administration went on with increasing bitterness at the end of the second century and through the third. The great names in this connection are those of Septimius Severus, Caracalla, Gallienus, and Aurelian.

Septimius Severus, implacably digging the grave of the Principate, the open enemy of the Senate in every domain of its activity, attacked (from the administrative point of view) both its judicial and its military privilege. In respect of justice, the Senate still had its competency as a criminal court of first instance in respect of Italy for grave cases, and a special jurisdiction, likewise in criminal cases, over its own members. Septimius Severus took the first of these prerogatives from it and gave it to the two great law-officers of the Emperor in Italy, the Prefect of the City for Rome and its environs within the radius of 100,000 yards, and the Prefect of the Prætorium for the rest of the country. He left it its criminal jurisdiction over its own members in theory, but only in theory. In 193, it is true, the Emperor caused a *Senatus consultum* to be passed by which he was formally forbidden to put a Senator to death without a previous discussion by the Senate. In practice, he did not hesitate to infringe this provision, and after his victory over Albinus he caused twenty-nine Senators to be executed without trial. In practice, under Septimius Severus, not one of the former judicial privileges of the Senate was left.

In the military domain Septimius Severus made similar innovations. On the general staff, he replaced the Senatorial *Comites* by Knights. He allowed the existing legions to be commanded by men of the Senatorial order, as his predecessors had done, but introduced the new principle that that privilege should not apply to any legions created in the future. So the three legions which he himself formed, the Parthian legions—I and III Parthica in Mesopotamia and II Parthica at Albanum near Rome—were given senior officers and generals taken exclusively from the Equestrian order. The same was the case with the commander-in-chief of the army of Mesopotamia, who was not a Senatorial Legate, but an Equestrian Prefect similar to the Prefect of Egypt. Of the thirty-three legions then composing the Roman army, twenty-nine received all their generals from the Senatorial order (the legions of Britain, the Rhine, the Danube, the Euphrates, Arabia, Africa, and Spain), and four (those of Italy, Mesopotamia, and Egypt) from the Equestrian. The generals themselves had often really followed the Equestrian career, and had only been admitted to the Senatorial class by *adlectio*. Under Caracalla, of all the legionary Legates collected to take part in the expedition against the Parthians, only one belonged to the Senatorial order by birth.

With Septimius Severus, the constitutional rôle of the Senate came to an end, and at the same time the system of the Principate, resuscitated for a moment under the Antonines, was seen to have received its death-blow. The military element, with the Imperial power at its disposal, the highest grades of the army invaded by it, and even the civil administration reduced to a mere emanation of it since the Severi, now had, in the form of a new Equestrian order, an absolute monopoly of the government. A few years later, in the crisis of the third century, the fact would be fully revealed.

Caracalla, the son and successor of Septimius Severus, followed his father's anti-Senatorial policy in the domain of administration as of other things. He more particularly attacked the administrative privilege of the Senate in Italy, which had already received a severe blow in the preceding century from the institution of the Hadrian's Consulars and the Juridici of Marcus Aurelius. The creation of the Correctors (*correctores*), still an extraordinary function, was a step further towards the abolition of that privilege.

With Gallienus, the anti-Senatorial policy of the Emperors reached its height, although one should not, as is generally done, seek its sole cause, or even its principal cause, in a systematic hatred of the old council. The blame must, above all, be laid on the terrible crisis through which the Empire was then passing and on the exigencies of national defence. Gallienus struck both at its administrative rights in the provinces and at its military privilege, which, indeed, were closely connected in the circumstances. The military question passed to the forefront—*primum vivere*—and the whole Empire was either invaded or directly threatened. In the government by dictatorship which was the necessary consequence of a situation of the kind, the army had to take over all the responsibilities and therefore all the organs and resources of government. The Edict of Gallienus, which was issued when the confusion was at its height, in 261, made this *de facto* necessity an official law. Senators were formally forbidden to perform military duties or to appear in the army at all.

This general principle led in practice to important consequences both of a military and of an administrative kind. First of all, the career of an officer was absolutely closed to members of the Senatorial order ; no more senior officers (Tribunes of legions) or generals (Legates of legions) were taken from that class. With the Senatorial officers of the highest rank—the Legates governing Imperial provinces, who in addition to their military competence acted as civil administrator of their district—we come to the domain of administration. As a result of the Edict of Gallienus, this category of governors entirely ceased to be taken from the Senatorial order. Lastly, as a logical consequence, the measure affected even the Proconsuls governing Senatorial provinces. These latter were purely civil officials, without any military competence, and for this reason one would have expected them to be unaffected by the Edict. But it was

not so, and one can understand the reason. In the frightful
crisis through which the Empire was passing, the Senatorial
provinces had had their share of invasion and of the
correlative evil of usurpation. Therefore the army, contrary
to tradition, now had a part to play there, and the conduct
of affairs could not be entrusted to the Senatorial governors,
who were pure civilians. Apart from the fact that there could
be no question of giving the Senators in the Senatorial
provinces the very powers which were then being taken
from them in the Imperial provinces, their political training
and, one must add, their notorious incapacity put them
out of court. Here, once more, the general situation required
that the power should be concentrated in the hands of
governors who were capable of dealing with it, and such
men the Senatorial class was on the whole quite unable to
furnish. In the presence of the new state of things, therefore,
the Senators governing Senatorial provinces had to suffer
like the rest.

After destroying, Gallienus had to rebuild. He did so
to the profit of the new Equestrian order, which, having
been recruited since the time of Septimius Severus in the
army itself, would give him the safe, experienced men who
were needed if the country was to be saved. Egypt supplied
the model for this administrative and military reform, as
it did for so many others, and its system of administration,
which Gallienus extended to the whole Roman Empire,
gave the Emperor the instrument needed for its regeneration. From top to bottom of the military and administrative scale, the Knights took possession of the posts
relinquished by the Senatorial class, as Tribunes of legions,
Legates of legions, Legates governing Imperial provinces,
and Proconsuls governing Senatorial provinces. In all
this, Gallienus was not inventing an entirely new system
of provincial administration. This particular type had been
working in Egypt since the Principate of Augustus and in
Mesopotamia since Septimius Severus, and both from the
military and from the administrative point of view it had
proved thoroughly efficient. Gallienus only had to make the
system general and to introduce it into the provinces governed
by Legates.

The blow thus struck at the privilege of the Senate in the

provinces was extremely hard. While enforcing the substance, Gallienus endeavoured at least to mitigate the form, and this he did by two methods. First, the Equestrian governor of the new type was not called a Prefect (*præfectus*), as in Egypt and Mesopotamia, but a *Præses*. By this general title Gallienus disguised the Equestrian character of the office, and, since it might in practice be equally well applied to a Senatorial governor, it did not preclude a return to the traditional method of recruiting in the future. Secondly, the new governors were appointed (at the beginning, at least, to smooth over the transition), not as permanent officials, but, officially, as substitutes and stop-gaps (*agens vices præsidis*).[1] Nor was this system of the substitute an innovation ; it was based on a very old tradition of the Roman Empire. We find it employed in the first and second centuries after Christ, but it was under Septimius Severus and especially in the second quarter of the third century that it became general. The career of Timesitheos, the father-in-law and Prefect of the Prætorium of Gordian III, offers a very significant example. So this administrative tradition offered Gallienus a practical means for replacing the Senatorial governors, whom he was turning out of the Imperial provinces, in a suitably tactful manner. He did not fail to apply a procedure which was so convenient in every respect. What was more, he extended it to the new Equestrian commanders-in-chief of the legions. Officially, they held their office as substitutes of the traditional Legate (*agens vices legati*), just as the Equestrian governor of a province was the substitute of the *Præses* (*agens vices præsidis*). But these disguises of form must not blind us to the reality. Under Gallienus, the Senate lost the whole of its two privileges, administrative (in respect of the provinces) and military. Moreover, its financial privilege went at the same time. Gallienus took the revenue of the Senatorial provinces from the treasury of the Senate (*ærarium*), leaving it only one general source of income, the profits of the striking of copper coinage. It did not keep this long.

[1] On this question, see Homo, " L'Empereur Gallien et la crise de l'Empire romain au IIIe siècle," in **XLVII**, cxiii (1913), 258 ; *id.*, " Les Privilèges administratifs du Sénat romain sous l'Empire et leur disparition graduelle au cours du IIIe siècle," *ibid.*, cxxxviii (1921), 12–15 ; cf. A. Rosenberg, " Ein Dokument zur Reichsreform des Kaisers Gallienus," in **XXXVI**, lv (1920), 319–21.

Aurelian, finally, completed the destruction of the privileges of the Senate, in respect of administration and coinage. In Italy the office of Corrector, which had hitherto been of an exceptional character, was transformed. He gave it a regional character by creating Correctors for certain districts in Italy, such as Lucania and Venetia, and he made it a permanent office, thus preparing for the complete assimilation to the provincial governors effected by Diocletian. Lastly, he abolished the last financial privilege of the Senate, that of coinage. In 271, when the workers of the Mint created a riot, he took away the Senate's monopoly of coining copper, and henceforward the whole department of coinage, gold, silver, and copper, was concentrated in the Emperor's hands. So the evolution which had gone on for centuries ended in the disappearance of the traditional privileges of the Senate and the completion of Imperial centralization.

IV

The Development of the Emperor's Power in the Early Empire

Amid the constitutional ebb and flow, offensives of the Emperor interrupted by Senatorial restorations, the evolution which was turning the Principate into a " Dominate " went steadily forward. It was an evolution in form much rather than in substance. In fact, even in the earliest days of the system, the Emperor was master, because he held the army, and he remained master so long as he kept its confidence. What changed was chiefly the details of method. The transition from Principate to " Dominate " in the first three centuries of our era was not so much the rise of a new idea as the falling of a mask and the emergence of a reality.

The first two Emperors of the Julio-Claudian line, the true founders of the system, Augustus and Tiberius, had set themselves to apply the constitutional system of principate with a loyalty which was sincere because it was interested. This is even truer of Tiberius than of Augustus. He had refused to take the *prænomen* of Imperator which Augustus, like Cæsar before him, had regarded as one of the attributes constituting the Imperial power. Everything changed with

Caligula, whose reign represents a first attempt in the history of the Empire at really absolute monarchy. It may, no doubt, have been megalomania, a diseased manifestation of a weak, ill-balanced mind, but that diagnosis is not enough to explain the case. As an heir to the monarchical formula which his great-grandfather Antony, inheriting it from Cæsar, had for a moment put into effect in the East,[1] and his grandmother Antonia, the Triumvir's daughter, had faithfully handed down to himself, Caligula wanted to introduce in Rome the absolute, theocratic monarchy of the Eastern type, in which the sovereign was at once a master and a god, like the Hellenistic Seleucids and Ptolemies.[2] After half a century of principate, there was a return to the monarchical system of Cæsar. But two defects condemned the attempt to failure. It was still premature, for the arguments of political opportunism which had caused Augustus to adopt the system of principate still held good in their entirety ; and the extravagant guise in which the reform was presented could hardly recommend it to the favour of contemporaries. Time had to be allowed to accomplish its usual work. Caligula's successors, through the first three centuries of the Empire—Claudius, Nero at the end of his reign, Domitian, Hadrian, Septimius Severus, Gallienus, and Aurelian most of all—one after another applied themselves to the task, and succeeded.

The practice regarding titles and surnames, the technical description of the Emperor, which was still loose under the Julio-Claudian dynasty, became definitely established and stereotyped under the Flavians and their successors, a concrete manifestation of the continual progress made by the monarchical idea in the first century. Tiberius had refused the *prænomen* of Imperator as a permanent name, although he kept it for his own exclusive use, as a title commemorating a victory. Caligula, Claudius, and Nero (this last only at the beginning of his reign, in his constitutional period), followed his example. Under Galba, Otho, and Vitellius the practice was not regular. With Vespasian, this *prænomen* again came into regular use, as in the time of Augustus, and—a

[1] H. Jeanmaire, " La Politique religieuse d'Antoine et de Cléopâtre," in **XLIV**, 1924 (1), 241–61.
[2] *Ibid.*, 257–9.

characteristic feature—it did not now drive out the bearer's individual *prænomen*. The title of Father of the Country (*Pater Patriæ*), borne by Cæsar and Augustus, had a similar history. Tiberius always refused it. Nero, Hadrian, and Marcus Aurelius did not accept it until fairly late, and only when they considered that they had earned it. The short-lived Emperors did not receive it at all. Pertinax was given the title on his accession, and thenceforward it was part of the official investiture.

So it was with the title of Proconsul. Augustus, by the constitutional act of 23 B.C., received the Proconsular *imperium* over the whole Roman world, including Rome and Italy. But, in view of the fiction by which the Senate and annual magistrates still governed Italy as in the past, the use of such a title would have appeared offensive and contradictory. Augustus and his successors in the first century were content to have the reality without proclaiming the name. We must come down to Trajan to find " Proconsul " among the official titles of the Emperor, and there are still two fundamental reservations ; the Emperor assumes it in respect of the provinces only, and only on inscriptions engraved while he is absent from Italy. Septimius Severus, the great leveller and implacable enemy of the traditional prerogatives of the Senate, introduced the practice of holding it in Italy and even in Rome. So too, the pretence of extension of the Proconsular *imperium,* to which Augustus remained faithful till his death (without, however, deceiving anybody), did not survive its author. It disappeared in the reign of Tiberius. Did this mean an increase of effective power for the Emperor ? Not at all ; a constitutional fiction was falling away, bit by bit.

Augustus exercised the powers of Censor several times, but without bearing the title either in its traditional form or in the new and extended form of the *cura legum morumque,* which he refused three times, in 19, 18, and 11 B.C. But among a form-loving people like the Romans the absence of a legal qualification presented serious disadvantages, and twice, under Claudius in 47–8 and under Vespasian in 73–4, the old magistracy of the Censorship, now exercised by the Emperor, made a reappearance. Domitian finally settled the question in his own favour by taking the title of Perpetual

Censor (censor perpetuus) (85), and, if his successors gave up
the official appellation, at least they were careful to keep the
prerogatives, which were thenceforward permanently included
among the other attributions of the Emperor.

Lastly, the Lex de Imperio, as known to us from the
epigraphic fragment regarding the investiture of Vespasian,[1]
in respect of the right to convoke the Senate and to make
recommendations for the magistracies, formally conferred
new prerogatives on the founder of the Flavian dynasty.

Domitian, always to the fore in the march towards
despotism, was the first to venture to assume the title of
Dominus. The innovation raised an outcry, especially,
as might be expected, in aristocratic circles, but soon, in
spite of the Senatorial reaction under the Antonines, the
appellation became usual. Even Pliny the Younger, in
his official correspondence with Trajan, has no scruples
about calling him by that title regularly—striking proof
of the advance of the monarchical idea. With Septimius
Severus the practice finally became official.

At the end of the third century, the Emperors tried to
give the government the stability which it was steadily
losing by strengthening their despotism. Under the influence
of the Oriental monarchies, and more particularly that of the
Sassanids, the idea had arisen that absolute kingship alone
could save the Empire and avert the ever-menacing return
of military anarchy. Aurelian, in spite of his personal
simplicity, was the first of all the Emperors to appear in
public wearing the diadem and a sumptuous costume covered
with gold and precious stones, and his ceremonial was
completed and systematized by Diocletian and Constantine,
the two great organizers of the monarchy of the Late Empire.

The religious character of the Principate, which was
originally expressed by the title of Augustus, presents an
evolution of the same kind. In virtue of the Imperial
cult, the Emperor is the object of practices and honours
which multiply as we descend through the centuries—
provincial and municipal worships, taking of oaths in the
name of the Emperor, worship of his Genius, fire borne
in front of him, his statue consecrated and endowed with
right of sanctuary like those of the gods, representation

---

[1] C.I.L., vi, 930 ; above, pp. 230–1.

with the radiate crown on his head. Domitian, at least unofficially, caused himself to be given the title of God, *Deus*. From Septimius Severus onwards, everything connected with the Emperor, things and men and the capital itself (*Urbs Sacra*), assumed a sacred character (*sacer*). Finally, Aurelian, after the military anarchy, looked to the religious idea for moral consecration of his power and a means to prevent a renewal of the crisis. His religious reform had made the worship of the Sun a State religion, whereby the Sun became the supreme god of the Empire, *Sol dominus Imperii Romani*. Linking his own cause directly with that of Solar monotheism and making full use of that patronage for the benefit of the Imperial authority, he proclaimed himself the representative and emanation of the Sun-god. He was a god on earth, *Deus*, master by right of birth, *Dominus natus*. These are the titles given him by the official monuments, especially the coins. The new religion not only made for the moral unification of the Roman world. By reinforcing the tottering power of the Emperor, by giving it the solemn consecration of the religious idea, Aurelian legalized depotism and, throwing away all pretences, established absolute monarchy as a permanency.

The problem of the succession, too, was much more one of form than of substance. No doubt, open recognition of the hereditary principle, given the mentality and public law of Rome, was an absolute impossibility ; but it is none the less true that, in practice, when there was no other obstacle, fathers were succeeded by their sons, even in the Early Empire—Vespasian by Titus, Marcus Aurelius by Commodus, Septimius Severus by Caracalla and Geta— and even, where there was no direct descendant, men were succeeded by their brothers, as Titus was by Domitian. But it might happen, and indeed it often did happen during the first two centuries, that the reigning Emperor had no son of his own living, as was the case with Augustus, Galba, Trajan, Hadrian, and Antoninus. To meet this deficiency, which was a danger to the stability of the system, Augustus created a method and left a precedent—the principle of adoption. At first, the adopted son was taken from the Imperial family ; Augustus adopted his step-son Tiberius, Claudius his step-son Nero. In a second period the system

K

was extended in the form of adoption of the most suitable
man, and so might include foreigners. What was an
exceptional act with Galba, who started the method, became
a regular, official law of succession with the Antonines.
Tacitus, in a speech which he makes Galba utter at the time
of the adoption of Piso,[1] sets forth in full the system which
he had seen at work with his own eyes and had known in
its best days :—

> " Even if I were a private citizen, and adopted you by a curiate
> law before the Pontifices in the customary way, it would be a glory
> for me to take into my house a descendant of Pompey and Crassus
> and a distinction for you to augment your nobility with the fame of
> the Sulpicii and Lutatii. But as it is, I, who have been called to the
> Empire by the will of gods and men, have been impelled by your
> eminent character and patriotism to offer the Principate, over which
> our ancestors fought with arms and which I myself have won in war,
> to you who have not fought for it at all. So the Divine Augustus
> summoned his sister's son Marcellus, his son-in-law Agrippa, his
> grandsons, and lastly his stepson Tiberius to his side at the summit
> of power. Yet Augustus sought a successor in his own house ; I
> seek one in the Republic, not because I have no kinsmen or comrades
> in arms, but because I did not take the Empire from ambition, and
> let it be proof of my judgment that I have chosen you not only before
> my own relations but before yours.
>
> " You have a brother, as well-born as yourself and older than you,
> who would have deserved this fortune, if you had not been better.
> You are at an age in which the passions of youth are past ; in your
> past life there is nothing which calls for forgiveness. Hitherto you
> have had only ill-fortune ; good fortune puts the soul to a sharper
> test, for misery is merely borne, while prosperity corrupts. Loyalty,
> frankness, friendship, the highest goods of a man's soul, you will
> doubtless maintain with your usual constancy, but others will weaken
> them by their compliance ; they will be assailed by adulation,
> blandishments, and that worst poison of true feeling, self-interest.
> Even if you and I to-day are talking together in all sincerity, others
> will be more interested in our fortune than in ourselves, for to give
> a prince good advice is a hard task, whereas it is easy to approve of
> any prince without real feeling.
>
> " If it had been possible for the immense body of the Empire to stand
> and balance without a guide, I was worthy to give it a start ; but
> things have come to a point where as an old man I can give the Roman
> people nothing better than a good successor, nor you as a young
> one anything better than a good prince. Under Tiberius, and
> Caligula, and Claudius, we were like the patrimony of one family ;
> the method of election which begins with us shall take the place of
> liberty, and now that the Julio-Claudian house is ended adoption will
> find the best man. For to be born of princes is a matter of chance,
> leaving no room for further appraisement, but in making an adoption
> you use your whole judgment, and if you wish to choose a man you
> are guided by common opinion. Keep Nero before your eyes, swollen

[1] *Hist.*, i, 15–16.

with his long ancestry of Cæsars ; not Vindex with his unarmed
province, nor I with my one legion, but his own monstrous cruelty
and luxury threw him down from the shoulders of the people ; there
was as yet no instance of a Princeps condemned by his people.

" We, who have been raised up by war and public esteem, shall be
unpopular however excellent we may be. But do not be alarmed if
two legions are still restless after that convulsion of the whole world.
I myself did not accede to an untroubled Empire, and when this
adoption is made known I shall cease to be regarded as an old man,
the only thing now objected to me. Nero will always be regretted by
the bad ; it is for me and you to see that he is not regretted by the
good. This is not the time for long warnings, and the task of advice
is done if I have chosen you rightly. The most useful and shortest
way of choosing between good and evil is to think what you wanted
or did not want under another prince ; for we have not here, as in
monarchical countries, an established house of masters and everyone
else a slave ; you will have to command men who can endure neither
complete slavery nor complete freedom."

It is a fine theory, and for once it was not belied by
practice ; to adoption of this wider kind men like Trajan,
Hadrian, Antoninus, and Marcus Aurelius would afterwards
owe their Empire and their contemporaries for nearly a
hundred years would owe such a prosperity as the world
never recovered after that happy time.

The dynasty of the Flavians made a strong effort to
establish the hereditary principle in the succession. One
of the chief arguments which had persuaded Vespasian
to accept the Empire was that he had two sons to succeed
him, and one day he said openly in the Senate, pointing to
Titus, " He will be my successor, or no one." But with
his usual foresight and acute political sense, the Emperor
followed up words with acts. He appointed his son Prefect
of the Prætorium, thus making him the great military chief
of the Empire, associated him with himself in the essential
prerogatives of the Imperial power, Tribunician power,
Proconsular *imperium*, and title of Imperator, and granted
him that basic privilege of sovereignty, the right to issue
coins bearing his image. In practice, although in theory
there was no change in the traditional system of succession
and the hereditary principle was still categorically excluded,
as in the past, Vespasian's two sons, first Titus and then
Domitian, succeeded their father without difficulty.

With the Antonines, circumstances made it necessary to
return to the second form of adoption. But experience
soon revealed its defects, and the Emperors of the second

century considered it advisable to make two improvements.
In Augustus's system, the heir presumptive had no specific,
particular official title. When Vespasian appointed his
son Titus his successor, he shared the *prænomen* of Imperator
with him and gave him the right of issuing coins with his
image, like the sovereign himself, as we have seen. Hadrian
took a decisive step. When, in 136, he chose L. Ceionius
Commodus as his heir, he adopted him and gave him the
surname of *Cæsar*, an official appellation which thus acquired
a definite constitutional meaning and was henceforward
normally applied to the heir presumptive. A second step,
taken twenty-five years later, was complete association in
the Imperial dignity. In 161 Marcus Aurelius associated
his adoptive brother Lucius Verus with himself on an equal
footing, the only Imperial prerogative which he did not share
being the office of Pontifex Maximus, which continued to be
the exclusive apanage of the elder Emperor. Somewhat
later, in 176, the same Marcus Aurelius took another colleague,
his son Commodus, and on the same terms. Following his
example, Septimius Severus conferred the title of Augustus
on his sons Caracalla and Geta in succession. During the
last three years of his reign, from 209 onwards, there were
three Emperors of equal rank, still excepting the Pontificate.
In 238, that last reservation disappeared ; the Emperors
Pupienus Maximus and Balbinus both took the title of
Pontifex Maximus with the other Imperial privileges. The
device of association in the Empire offered two great
advantages. In the present it made the administration
of the Empire easier by dividing the burden, and it made
the transmission of the power more certain in the future.
Pretenders would have to deal, not with a successor designate,
but with an Emperor in the full sense of the word, already
in possession of the whole power. The immense advantage
of the new system was proved in practice, for the throne was
never left altogether vacant. Any such complications as
might arise from the intervention of the Senate, or, still more,
of the army, were *ipso facto* warded off.

Unfortunately, in spite of all these precautions to ensure
the succession, one danger was still possible. The Emperor
might die unexpectedly before he had taken a colleague or
even designated a successor ; this happened, for example,

to Nero, Domitian, and Commodus. The deaths of Nero and Commodus, in 68 and 192, were the signal for the two most terrible crises regarding the succession which the Empire saw, and the murder of Domitian very nearly created a like upheaval. In theory, a constitutional solution was provided by a very simple device : the right of election simply reverted to the Senate, as the legal keeper of the sovereignty of the Roman people. But there was a whole world between the fiction and the reality. The army, as the author and mainstay of the regime, claimed to have a say in the matter ; it intervened to vindicate its rights, and the various troops of the Empire, Prætorians in Rome and legions in the provinces, did not hesitate to dispute the election by force of arms. Whether the new Emperor was designated by his predecessor or chosen by the armies, the Senate had equally little freedom of action ; the only difference was that in the former case order was generally preserved, whereas in the latter the result was often civil war and a breach in the unity of the Empire, as happened in 68 and 192.

In the third century, on account of circumstances which made the public safety and national defence all that mattered, the army definitely took possession of the government. The problem of the succession was affected accordingly. Appointment by the army became the rule ; the troops made and unmade Emperors. There was really no civil constitution. The Senate, which should have had the first and last word in the matter, confined itself to rushing to the aid of victory and legalizing the position of the fortunate nominee of the armies. As for the Imperial Council, which the Severi had tried to set up in the place of the Senate as the pivot of the central power, its bankruptcy in this respect was even more complete. The outward façade of civil government, which the Emperors of the two first centuries had patiently built up, by different methods, but with equal perseverance, collapsed without hope of restoration. Henceforward, the problem of the succession was for the Roman State a matter of life or death. It was for the supreme reformer of the Empire, Diocletian, to solve it.

CHAPTER III

THE CONSTITUTIONAL DEVELOPMENT COMPLETE. THE ABSOLUTE MONARCHY OF THE LATE EMPIRE

BIBLIOGRAPHY : *Ancient Authors* : Ammianus Marcellinus, *History* (A.D. 353–78) ; Aurelius Victor, *De Cæsaribus*, 39–42 (to the death of Constantius II) ; *Epitome*, 39–48 (to the death of Theodosius) ; Eutropius, ix, 19 to x, 18 ; Orosius, vii, 25–43 ; Zosimos, *History*, ii–vi ; Zonaras, xii, 31 to xiii ; *Latin Panegyrics* (i–ii. Claudius Mamertinus on Maximian, Maximian's Birthday ; iii. Eumenius *Pro restaurandis scholis* ; iv. anon. on Constantius I ; v. anon. on Maximian and Constantine ; vi–viii. anon. on Constantine ; ix. Nazarius on Constantine ; x. Claudius Mamertinus on Julian ; xi. Pacatus Drepanius on Theodosius) ; Lactantius, *De Mortibus persecutorum* ; Symmachus, *Letters, Official Reports* ; Julian, *Works* ; Vegetius, *Epitome of Military Matters*.

Administrative Documents : *Laterculus* of Verona (about 297) ; *Notitia Dignitatum* (beginning of fifth century) ; list of Roman Provinces after Polemius Silvius's *Calendar* (about 385) ; *Notitia Galliarum*.

Legal Documents : Imperial Constitutions in the Code of Theodosius (from Constantine to Theodosius), with the supplement of *Novellae* (from Theodosius to Anthemius), and in that of Justinian.

Inscriptions : *C.I.L.*, ii ff., *passim*, especially vol. vi, 1116–98, 31381–419 ; cf. *I.L.S.*, 612–819, 8929–53. Senatorial Album of Thamugadi in *C.I.L.*, viii, 2403 and suppl., 17903 ; *I.L.S.*, 6122.

Coins : H. Cohen, **IV**, vi–viii.

*Modern Works : **CXXXI**, especially i and ii, with the two supplements ; **XXI**, 380–424 ; **I**, 188–202, 236–51 ; **IX**, iii, 159–273 ; **X**, iii, 231–41, 298–306 (E. Kornemann), 461–3 (K. J. Neumann) ; **XXVI**, 599–631 ; **LXIII** ; **XXXI**, 555–647 ; **XVIII**, i, 297–634 ; **XXX**, ii, 3–437 ; **CIV** ; **LXII** ; **LII** ; **CIII** ; **LXXXVI** ; **LXXIX** ; **CXXXII** ; **XC**, Eng. pp., 139–44 ; A. Christensen, " L'Empire des Sassanides : le peuple, l'Etat, la cour," in **XL**, 7th ser., sec. Lettres, i, No. 1 (1907), 3–120.

I

CAUSES AND INFLUENCES : THE ROMAN MONARCHY AND THE SASSANIAN KINGSHIP

THREE essential ideas dominate the political history of the Late Empire—those of absolute monarchy, partition of power, and bureaucracy. None of these ideas was a novelty. Their origins went back to the past of the Early Empire, but it was the circumstances of the end of the third century

*See also Supplementary Bibliography with Prefatory Note (p. 405)

and the fourth which caused them to develop fully. The omnipotence of the army in administrative as well as military matters which ensued from the crisis of the third century, its constant and detrimental interference in public affairs, made all government impossible and jeopardized the very existence of the Roman State. The Emperor, like other men, and even more than others, was in its hands, and the two civil powers in which in turn he sought support against it, the Senate and the Imperial Council, failed him one after the other, blown away like straws before the whirlwind. He must look elsewhere if he was to survive at all. The introduction of Oriental despotism, the partition of the Empire for administrative purposes, and the systematic development of the bureaucracy supplied the Emperors of the end of the third century and of the fourth with the solution needed.

The political and administrative organization of the Roman State in the late Empire was not, any more than in the Early Empire, the result of a purely internal development. The decisive part previously played by Egypt was now taken by a new and altogether foreign influence, the Sassanian kingship.

" After the defeat of the Persians," Lactantius writes,[1] " whose rite and custom it is to deliver themselves in bondage to their kings, who use the people as their personal servants, that criminal (Galerius) wished to introduce a similar practice on Roman soil. From the day of his victory, he extolled it without shame."

The information is valuable, but it would be a mistake to confine it to the narrow and almost episodic limits given to it by the Christian polemic. In reality, the influence of the Sassanian State on the transformation of the Imperial government of Rome began with the Illyrian Emperors and went on until the last days of the Western Empire.

There can be no doubt of the fact, and it is easy to perceive the reasons. About 225 the Parthian Empire had utterly decayed and succumbed to hopeless anarchy in the political, military, and religious domains. Therefore the Sassanian kingship which took its place brought with it a programme of systematic reaction and complete regeneration. Now, after the military anarchy, the Roman State was faced,

[1] *De Mortibus persec.*, xxi, 2–3.

half a century later, with a similar problem. The success of
the Sassanids in their work of revival, the happy results
obtained by their experiment, could not but encourage the
Roman Emperors to follow their example and adopt their
methods. In contrast to the governmental system of the
Parthians, the Sassanids had owed their success to three
great reforms—the strengthening of the power of the King,
the introduction of a centralized bureaucracy, and the
establishment of solid religious unity. The Sassanian King
was an all-powerful monarch, with the prerogatives and
outward signs of absolute power. He lived in the heart
of a palace, clad in gorgeous garments, subject to the strict
laws of etiquette and in general inaccessible to ordinary
mortals. The great feudal lords, who had arrived at a semi-
independence under the Parthians, were severely curbed by
the iron hand of the new dynasty, and henceforward had to
obey, like the other classes of the people.

The execution of the royal will was ensured throughout
the State by a rigid, elaborately graded system of centralization. At the top stood the ministers controlling departments—the Wazurg-Framadhar, or prime minister, the
usual counsellor of the King, to whom he was second in the
State ; the Eran-Spahbedh, or minister of war ; the Wastrio-
sansalar, or minister of finance and director-general of
taxation ; the Eran-Dabirbedh, or secretary-general of the
Empire ; and the two great religious officials, the Mobedhan-
Mobedh, the minister of religion and high-priest of Mazdaism,
and the Herbedhan-Herbedh, who may have had the especial
charge of ecclesiastical jurisdiction. Underneath these there
were the secretaries of State—the numerous and influential
Dabiran, under the Eran-Dabirbedh, or Dabiran-Mihist, who
dealt with diplomatic and administrative correspondence ;
the great officials of the Court, the Keeper of the Seals,
the Director of Intelligence, the Chief of the Guards, the
Administrator of Pious Works, chamberlains, keepers of
the Royal Annals, etc. ; the offices of the secretariat, or
Divans, for correspondence, finance, criminal justice, distribution of honours and offices, and doubtless, too, military
matters, Royal domains, post, coinage ; lastly, the administrators of districts, the Padhghospans or Viceroys, each in
control of a quarter of the kingdom (North, South, East,

West) and the provincial governors (Marzbans, Ostandars), all closely supervised by the central government. Finally, the Sassanid Kings established, in favour of the Zoroastrian priesthood and as a reaction against the incorrigible Hellenism of their Parthian predecessors, a powerful State Church, with its high dignitaries—Mobedhan-Mobedh, Herbedhan-Herbedh—and its enormous staff of Magi (*moghan*), to be a solid support for the Royal house and a living symbol of national unity.

By the middle of the third century after Christ, the whole of this reorganization had received the sanction of success, and thereby the Sassanian kingship had acquired, together with the re-establishment of order at home, a considerable power of expansion. Faced with a situation which was on the whole the same, and ready to learn from an experiment which had been carried out before their very eyes, the Illyrian Emperors of the third and fourth centuries sought inspiration for the revival of the Roman State in Sassanian methods of government and administration. Of course—and it must be expressly remarked—that influence was neither complete nor exclusive. As a result of various influences—imitation of Ptolemaic Egypt, identity of needs at home and abroad suggesting similar solutions—the movement to absolute, centralized monarchy had shown itself irresistible even in the Early Empire. But at least, in the long evolution which ended with the governmental system of the Late Empire, the example of the Sassanian State had an undeniable and important share. In this matter, Aurelian, Diocletian, and Constantine are the great names, and absolute monarchy, centralization, and Solar monotheism are the principal achievements.

II

THE EMPEROR AND THE CENTRAL POWER

The Emperor and the Palace.—In fact and in law, the Principate of Augustus gave place to a complete " Dominate " ; the constitutional programme of Cæsar, born of the actual needs of the Roman world, found complete and permanent realization, three centuries late. In the fourth century the Imperial power was a pure monarchy, in which the State was wholly embodied in the person of the Emperor, as living law and absolute master. That reality found concrete expression in his very title. Since the time of Septimius Severus he had been officially called the Master, *Dominus*, beside whom there was only room for subjects (*subjecti*), sometimes even slaves (*servi*, δοῦλοι). Like an Eastern potentate, he was gorgeously arrayed in diadem and garments of silk adorned with gold and pearls. He lived surrounded by a large and varied household staff, among whom eunuchs, after the Eastern usage, soon came to hold a place of honour. Etiquette and ceremonial were laid down in detail. Hidden in the depths of his palace, like an idol in its shrine, the sovereign did not deign to appear before ordinary men except on rare and carefully organized occasions. He could only be approached with complicated rites of prostration and worship.

There was yet more. The ancients had never imagined a political organization without a corresponding religious idea, and the people who lived in the Roman world in the fourth century after Christ were no exception to that age-old rule. The Late Empire, even more than the governments which had gone before, gave satisfaction to that deep-seated aspiration of consciences and souls. The Emperor was not only the master. Invested with a divine character, he was a scion and a father of gods (*diis genitus et deorum pater*); his acts were described as divine ; everything connected with his person or with those of his family or emanating from his activity was sacred (*sacer*). To disobey him was to transgress religious law and commit sacrilege. In the course of the third and fourth centuries the deification of the Emperor went through two distinct stages. First, there was the pagan stage, that of the Oriental type of Solar monotheism adopted by Aurelian, in which the Sun was the supreme god of the Empire (*Sol dominus Imperii Romani*) and the Emperor was his corporeal emanation (*Deus et Dominus natus*). In the Christian stage the theory changed and the practice survived ; the Emperor kept his former religious qualifications, such as the epithet " Sacred ", and he and his images continued to be worshipped. Only one part of the ceremonial disappeared as being incompatible with Christian doctrine, namely the offer of sacrifice to the

Imperial godhead, but what the Emperor lost thereby he recovered in full in another form, in the tremendous power given him by the Christian religion in its triumph. The recognition of Christianity as the State religion brought to the support of political and administrative centralization a new factor, religious centralization. As the representative of God on earth, and His living image, the Emperor was as it were, a present, corporeal god (*tanquam præsens et corporalis deus*), in the significant phrase of Vegetius,[1] and obedience was owed to him as to God Himself.

The traditional unity of the Empire entailed serious disadvantages, which the crisis of the third century had fully revealed. The thrust of the barbarians on the frontiers, continually growing more violent and widespread, had made the task which national defence laid upon the Emperors very much harder and more engrossing. Claudius II, Aurelian, and Probus, grappling with difficulties which arose in several places at once and grew more and more serious, spent their reigns in rushing from one frontier to another to repel the invader. In spite of their iron determination and tireless activity, in spite of the superhuman efforts which they demanded and, through their example, obtained from their troops, they could not be everywhere at once. They were often compelled to leave matters to their generals, and then a new danger arose, that of usurpation. To avert invasions and usurpations, the twofold curse which the crisis of the third century brought to a head, there was only one remedy—partition of the power. The Illyrian Emperors had put an end to military anarchy and restored the Imperial authority. The crisis seemed to have been overcome, and Diocletian meant to prevent a repetition. He was a clear-minded, methodical man, and he brought with him a whole co-ordinated programme of reforms. The keystone of the system was to be the permanent division of the Imperial dignity among several holders, first in the form of a dyarchy, and later of a tetrarchy.

The idea of partition had, under the pressure of necessity, gradually emerged during the Early Empire, and from the very beginning of personal rule. Augustus had taken colleagues in a subordinate position in the persons of Agrippa

---

[1] *Epit. rei. mil.*, ii, 5.

and Tiberius successively. Claudius, at the end of his reign, had done the same with Nero. After that, the procedure gradually became more definite and was extended. Vespasian took his son Titus as a colleague and, by an important innovation, shared the Imperial prerogatives with him, except only the title of Augustus and the office of Pontifex Maximus. In 161, Marcus Aurelius associated his adoptive brother Verus with himself on similar terms, but went further in giving him the title of Augustus. In 238, Pupienus Maximus and Balbinus, the two Senatorial Emperors, shared the power on absolutely equal terms, including the Pontificate. So far, there had only been a sharing of competence, without any territorial division. In 256, Valerian, having associated his son Gallienus with himself as a colleague, gave him the West as his special sphere of action and kept the East for himself. A few more years, and we see the Roman State split into three distinct Empires—the Empire of Gallienus (Italy, Africa, the Balkan Peninsula, and the Danubian regions) in the middle, the Empire of Postumus (Britain, Gaul, and Spain) in the West, and the Palmyrene Empire of Zenobia and Wahballath (Asia Minor, Syria, and Egypt) in the East. So the notion of partition was on the march. To that notion, which he found in the past, Diocletian for the first time gave full and systematic realization.

Being a cautious man, and well able to profit by experience, Diocletian proceeded in two stages. In 286, only one year after the death of his rival Carinus, he took, as a colleague equal in power to himself, the Pannonian Maximian, who had already distinguished himself as a soldier and a leader. With him he divided the administration of the Empire territorially, giving him the West and himself keeping the East. For seven years the Empire was governed by this dyarchy. The results of the arrangement, both in foreign and in home policy, were so satisfactory that Diocletian resolved to extend it yet further by appointing two more colleagues. So the dyarchy became a tetrarchy. But (and here we see his anxiety to settle the question of the succession at the same time) the new Emperors did not enter the combination on an equal footing with the other two. By the side of and under the two Augusti, they were the two Cæsars, subordinate, assistant Emperors to whom the succession was promised. For these posts, Diocletian, who was a judge of men, once again chose admirably. Constantius Chlorus was a capable general and also (what did no harm) a good statesman ; Galerius was an uneducated man, but a brave soldier and a staunch patriot. Diocletian established a nice balance by attaching Constantius Chlorus to his colleague Maximian and taking Galerius as his own associate. Each of the Cæsars, like the Augusti, received a determined area. After this final partition, the districts were apportioned as follows : Maximian got Italy, Sicily, Africa, and Spain ; Constantius Chlorus, Gaul and Britain ; Diocletian, Thrace, Asia, and Egypt ; and Galerius, Illyricum and Achaia. Each of the four Emperors had his special residence in his own sector, within reach of the frontier which he had to defend—Maximian at Milan, Constantius Chlorus at Treves, Diocletian at Nicomedeia, and Galerius at Sirmium.

But we must not mistake Diocletian's intentions. By establishing the tetrarchy, he did not for a moment mean to divide up the unity of the Empire, but merely to establish special spheres of competence, territorial in form, for the four holders.

This collective system of government, the tetrarchy, offered great advantages, but it presented one great danger, if not in the present, at least in the near or remote future—that of an open or concealed breach of the unity of the Empire. To avert this danger, which could not escape him, Diocletian took two essential precautions. First, he maintained unity of administration ; every official document had to be signed by all four Emperors, so becoming fully valid for the whole extent of the Empire. Secondly, he established a strict order of rank within the tetrarchy by various methods. He created artificial family ties ; the two Augusti were brothers, and the two Cæsars were their respective adopted sons. The Cæsars were subordinate to the Augusti in law (one of the legal bases of the system), and among the Augusti Maximian was subordinate to his colleague Diocletian, the older man (*Augustus Senior*) and the founder and head of the new government. Family alliances were concluded by marriages uniting the Cæsars closely to the Augusti ; Galerius married Diocletian's daughter Valeria, and Constantius Chlorus married Maximian's step-daughter Theodora. Lastly, when, on the abdication of the first two Augusti, Diocletian and Maximian, in 305, the tetrarchy was reconstituted with Constantius Chlorus and Galerius as Augusti and Maximin Daïa and Severus as Cæsars, the honorary title of *Augusti Seniores* was conferred on the two original Augusti.[1]

Thus the political programme of Diocletian, divided administration within a united Empire, seemed, through the system of the tetrarchy, to have found a full and satisfactory realization.

The tetrarchy collapsed in the civil wars which followed the abdication of Diocletian, but the guiding idea, that a partition was necessary in practice, had now become familiar to the Emperors and their subjects alike, and it survived him in both politics and administration. Constantine, who restored the unity of the Empire, himself returned to the system of collective government. By his will of 335, he divided the Empire among five successors—his three surviving sons, Constantine II, Constantius II, and Constans, and his nephews Delmatius and Hannibalianus. This was an excessive partition, which the heirs first, and then events, proceeded to simplify. By 337 only three partners were left, the three sons of Constantine, and three years later the death of Constantine II left only two, Constantius II in the East and Constans in the West. In 350 the death of Constans restored unity for a time, but Constantius was compelled by the pressure of circumstances to associate with himself, as Cæsars, first Gallus in the East (351–4) and, when Gallus was killed, Julian in the West (355–60). From 364 to 375 there were two Emperors, Valentinian I and Valens ; from 375 to 383, three, first Valens, Gratian, and Valentinian II, and then Gratian, Valentinian II, and Theodosius ; finally, on the death of Theodosius, the number became two permanently—Arcadius in the East and Honorius in the West—just because it corresponded to the great racial and linguistic division of the Roman world.

By the side of the Emperor was the Imperial Palace, the total of services attached to the person of the sovereign, comprising several chief elements. As head of the State, the Emperor kept round him, first of all, a staff for his protection and the maintenance of his dignity, his military

[1] *C.I.L.*, vi, 1130 (= Suppl., 31242).

household. From the beginning of the third century, that service was performed by the Protectors (*protectores*), who were later divided (probably before Diocletian's reign) into two distinct bodies, the Protectors properly so called, a mounted troop, and the Domestic Protectors (*domestici*), composed, at least partially, of a contingent of infantry. Under Constantine there appears, by the side of the Protectors commanded by the two Counts of Domestici, a new guard, the Palace Troops (*scholæ palatinæ*), commanded by the Master of Offices.

As the central motor of the administration, himself the first official in the State, the Emperor had his staff of officials and departments which, all together, constituted his civil household. These were divided into three sections—the secretariat, comprising all the organs of transmission; ceremonial, directed by the Master of Offices, who was assisted by the Master of Ceremonies (*magister admissionum*) and a large staff (*admissionales, invitatores, cancellarii*); and the Secret Service, the nucleus of which was formed by the corps of agents (*agentes in rebus*), organized in a *schola*.

Lastly, as absolute master and god on earth, the Emperor maintained an enormous domestic and private staff, divided into several specialized departments—the Emperor's Bed-chamber under the *Primicerius Sacri Cubiculi*, the Palace in general under the Majordomo (*castrensis sacri palatii*), the Wardrobe under the *Comes Sacræ Vestis*, the Imperial Residences under the *Comes Domorum*, and the department of Ushers (*decuriones* and *silentiarii*). A high dignitary, the Grand Chamberlain (*præpositus sacri cubiculi*), had all these services under his general direction.

Organs of Deliberation.—The rivalry of the great organs of deliberation, the Senate and the Imperial Council, ended in the third century with the complete and permanent victory of the latter. Henceforward the whole administration was concentrated in the hands of the Emperor. At the beginning of the military anarchy, the Senate was no more than the shadow of its old self, and in spite of short-lived displays of energy, as in 238 under Pupienus Maximus and Balbinus and in 275–6 under Tacitus, its decline went on steadily all through the remainder of the third century, and appeared in two forms.

First, the Senate gradually lost its last State prerogatives. Of its ancient power, it had saved a few scant privileges, particularly in the administrative, financial, and military domains. These last remnants disappeared for the most part in the storms of the third century. Its administrative privilege received its death-blow, in Italy from the creation of the district Correctors under Aurelian and Diocletian, and in the provinces from the abolition of the Senatorial provinces by Gallienus and his replacement of the old Imperial governors of Senatorial rank by Equestrian officials. Its financial privilege suffered the fate of the Senatorial provinces, and its monetary privilege fell beneath the blows of Aurelian. Lastly, its military privilege came to an end when Gallienus systematically excluded Senators from the higher commands in the army, in favour of the Equestrian order.

Secondly, Rome was finally abandoned as the capital of the Empire and the Emperor's residence. Treves, Milan, Sirmium, and Nicomedeia were raised to the rank of capitals in the reign of Diocletian, and Constantinople in that of Constantine. Thereby the Senate of Rome lost its last practical control over affairs, and sank to the obscure and inglorious rank of a town-council. Drawn down in the shipwreck of the Principate and reduced in the Late Empire to a mere corps of officials which the Emperors filled at their pleasure by the elastic procedure of *adlectio*, it found that its great political rôle was over.

What, then, was left to the Senate in the fourth and fifth centuries ? Its effective competence was confined to two domains only, the Senatorial and the municipal. It played a part in affairs affecting the Senatorial order, in respect of election, justice, and finance. The Senate made appointments to a certain number of magistracies of Senatorial rank (Suffect Consulship, Prætorship, Quæstorship), and partly recruited itself by co-optation, provided, of course, that Imperial ratification was forthcoming. Officials of Senatorial rank accused of serious crimes, such as high treason and lese-majesty (for example, Gildo under Honorius and Arvandus, the Prefect of the Prætorium of Gaul, in 469), were frequently handed over to the Senate for trial, the Emperor always reserving the right to deal with the case himself. Lastly, it dealt with all financial matters affecting the Senate, for example, the *aurum oblaticium*, which Senators had to pay at the beginning of each reign. With regard to the city, the Senate was a real municipal council of Rome. It has a treasury, offices, a municipal gazette (*acta Senatus*). Its competence extended to all municipal matters—civil status, supplies, public works, the University of Rome—but its deliberations were held under the presidency of a high Imperial official, the Prefect of the City, and it was subject to his permanent control ; in case of conflict, in this domain as in all others, the last word lay with the Emperor.

Of the general competence of the Senate, as a deliberative organ of the State, very little remained—the right of requesting the intervention of the Emperor on any matter, of making petitions or recommendations to him, and of collaborating, when required, in the drafting of Imperial Constitutions (edicts, letters, pragmatic sanctions), and, above all, the right of registration. The Senate of the Late Empire, transformed into a corps of officials, had become a kind of registration-office for especially important documents emanating from the Imperial initiative. They were communicated in the form of an Imperial speech read to the Senate by a representative of the Emperor, the Master of Offices, *Primicerius* of Notaries, or Prefect of the City ; it was in this form that the Theodosian Code was laid before the Senate for deliberation in 443 and a Senatorial commission was charged with the task of editing the text.

By the side of the great deliberative organ of the past, now dead, there was the organ of the present, the Imperial Council, the permanent assistant of the Emperor in the work of general administration. It was reorganized by Diocletian and Constantine, with the title of Consistory— Imperial Consistory (*consistorium principis*), or, what meant the same thing, Sacred Consistory (*consistorium sacrum*). Its composition and powers were laid down by new regulations. The Councillors were divided into two sections, Ordinary and Extraordinary. The former, the permanent members of the Council, were themselves subdivided into two classes, a higher class of active high officials like the Quæstor of the Palace, the Master of Offices, and the two financial Counts of the Sacred Largesses and Private Estates, and a lower class, the Counts of the Consistory (*comites consistoriani*), who were chiefly recruited among former heads of offices of the Imperial secretariat.   The Extraordinary Councillors included *Consistoriani vacantes* and, when necessary, heads of departments, such as the Prefect of the Prætorium or the Masters of Troops, summoned to discuss matters within their competence.   The Emperor usually presided over meetings of the Consistory in person. A large office staff of secretaries (*notarii*), under the direction of the chief secretary of State (*Primicerius Notariorum*), and various employees drafted the minutes of sittings.

The attributions of the Imperial Council in the Late Empire were of two kinds.   In administration, it deliberated on big questions of a general nature ; the Emperor held solemn audiences and important laws were publicly promulgated in its presence.   In the matter of justice, it assisted the Emperor in his jurisdiction, both in matters in the first instance which he transferred to his court and in appeals.

Organs of Transmission.—The Imperial secretariat, with its great offices of Correspondence (*ab epistulis*), Petitions (*a libellis*), Inquiries (*a cognitionibus*), Preliminary Examinations (*a studiis*), and "Memory" (*a memoria*), was a creation of the Early Empire.   The rulers of the Late Empire, while maintaining it as a whole, made certain big changes in it. Two of the old offices, those of Preliminary Examinations and Inquiries, disappeared, the second being absorbed by Petitions ;   a new office, that of Dispositions (*dispositiones*), was created ;   and the Office of Memory acquired quite a new importance in the departmental scale.

As a result of all these reforms, the secretariat, now under the general direction of the Master of Offices, comprised four bureaux.   Three of these were organs both of preparation and of transmission.   The Office of Correspondence (*scrinium epistularum*) received the representatives of cities and prepared and dispatched replies to the requests of magistrates or litigants.   The Office of Petitions (*scrinium libellorum*) examined law-suits which came before the Emperor, communicated the sentences to all concerned, and sent replies to the petitions of individuals.   The Office of Dispositions (*scrinium dispositionum*) was an Imperial record-office, in which the decrees, laws, and ordinances of the Emperors regarding individuals and cities were preserved. The fourth office, that of Memory (*scrinium memoriæ*), on the other hand, had become the principal office of transmission ; by it the replies of the Emperor, military commissions, official letters, reports, and other Imperial documents were sent to their destination.

The chiefs of the offices of the secretariat were high dignitaries. The highest in rank, the chief of the office of Memory (*magister sacræ memoriæ*), drew a salary of 300,000 sesterces, and, with the exception of the chief of the office of Dispositions (*magister dispositionum*), who was only a Clarissimus, they all belonged to the class of Spectabiles. Each was assisted by a first and a second deputy-chief (a *proximus* and a *melloproximus*) and a large staff of all ranks.

Organs of Execution.—Magistrates and officials, the two-fold executive organ of the Late Empire, which we shall consider presently, still existed side by side, but their relative importance was not what it had been. There were still magistrates in Rome, but, for one thing, their number was reduced ; the Ædileship had disappeared in the middle of the third century, and the Tribuneship was now a mere honorary title, probably conferred by the Emperor. The others, Consulship, Prætorship, Quæstorship, survived, but, having lost their traditional powers to the Imperial officials, they had hardly any effective attributions left. The Ordinary Consuls, the highest in dignity, were appointed by the Emperor ; the Suffect Consuls, who were very numerous, were appointed by the Senate in a body, often several years in advance. The Consulship had only one real prerogative, that of presiding in the Senate. The Prætorship, which in practice became more and more the first magistracy of the career, was reduced to secondary functions, the charge of guardianships and suits regarding the freedom of persons. Lastly, the only justification for the existence of the Quæstors was the heavy burden of giving games, which they shared with the Consuls and Prætors. The abandonment of Rome as the capital dealt the final blow to the old Republican magistrates ; they gradually descended to the rank of municipal magistrates, while their fortunate rivals, the officials of the Emperor, permanently took their place as the executive organs of the State.

As supreme head of the executive, the Emperor exercised his authority through high officials, ministers, as we should say to-day, similar to those of modern autocratic countries. Some, the Prefect of the Prætorium (minister of the interior) and the Counts of the Treasuries (ministers of finance and Crown property), were survivals from the Early Empire ; others, the Master of Offices (minister of the Imperial household), Quæstor of the Palace (minister of justice), and Masters of Troops (war ministers), were creations of the new regime.

The office of Prefect of the Prætorium underwent two limitations under the Late Empire. Its territorial scope was affected when Diocletian doubled and Constantine quadrupled the number of holders. It also lost in competence. At the time of the tetrarchy, the Prefects of the Prætorium still had the whole of their military and civil functions. Constantine, as a measure of caution, took the former from them and made them into purely civil officials, and so they remained until the fall of the Roman Empire. Yet, in spite of these two diminutions of his authority, the Prefect of the Prætorium, as minister of the interior, continued to be a very important personage in the fourth and fifth centuries, the highest in rank in the administrative scale. He was a Clarissimus in the third century, and was raised to the rank of Illustrious in the reign of Valentinian. A large staff of various officials (*consiliarius, adjutor, commentariensis, ab actis, numerarii, subadjuvæ*) and correspondence-clerks (*regendarius, exceptores, singularii*), all under the supreme direction of a departmental chief (*princeps*), assisted him in his task and carried out his orders.

Financial administration was divided under the Late Empire into two sections—the public treasury, which was descended from the old Imperial *Fiscus* (*ærarium sacrum*), and the privy purse, the former *Res Privata*, whose name it kept. These two departments came under two directors-general—the public treasury under the Count of the Sacred Largesses (*comes sacrarum largitionum*), who was a true finance minister, and the privy purse under the Count of the Private Estates (*comes rerum privatarum*), the minister of Crown property.

Unlike the Prefect of the Prætorium and directors-general

of finance, the other great officials of the central administration, the Master of Offices, Quæstor of the Palace, and Masters of Troops, first appeared under the Late Empire.

The Master of Offices (*magister officiorum*), the minister of the Emperor's household, controlled all the services of the civil household ; in addition, he had the command of half of the military household, the Palatine troops, the general direction of the Imperial secretariat, and the supervision of posts (*cursus publicus*) and arsenals, two attributions taken from the Prefect to the Prætorium at the end of the fourth century. Within the limits of his competence he possessed a jurisdiction over the officials and employees of the Emperor's Palace, and also over the subordinates of the Grand Chamberlain. In the exercise of his functions he employed a large staff of assistants in addition to that of the offices of the secretariat—an *adjutor, subadjuvæ adjutoris, subadjuvæ* of the various arsenals, *curiosi*, and interpreters for all languages.

The Quæstor of the Imperial Palace (*quæstor sacri palatii*), the minister of justice, was, like the Master of Offices, an Illustrious. His chief duty was to prepare, direct, and co-ordinate the work of the Imperial Council. Before a sitting, he saw to the business of preparation and editing in the offices ; in the Council, at which he might have to preside in place of the Emperor, he was the Emperor's natural representative and mouth-piece, and directed the debate ; when decisions had been taken he caused them to be drawn up in their permanent form by the secretariat, presented them to the Emperor for signature, countersigned them, and sent them to their destination.

From the time of Constantine, who finally completed the separation of the civil and military powers in the higher offices, the army came under the Masters of Troops (*magistri militum*), who were professional officers, usually recruited among former Dukes. They had the rank of Counts (*comites*), and in the course of the fourth century they were given the rank of Illustrious. At first they were two in number, but they were increased later ; in addition to the Masters of Troops residing at Court (*præsentales*), or war ministers, district Masters of Troops were created in the East, Thrace, Illyricum, and Gaul. The two Masters of Troops residing at Court together commanded the army of the Empire, or else, as was the case in the East, they specialized, one commanding the cavalry (*Magister Equitum*), and the other the infantry (*Magister Peditum*). Sometimes, however, circumstances caused the office to be concentrated in the hands of a single man (for example Stilicho, Aëtius, Ricimer), who then took the title of *Magister Utriusque Militiæ*. The Masters of Troops had a large staff under two chiefs (*principes*), comprising two *numerarii*, a *commentariensis*, *primoscrinii*, *scriniarii*, *exceptores*, and *apparitores*. These soldiers, lastly, were at the same time judges ; the military chiefs of districts, Dukes and Counts, and the troops directly under their orders were under their jurisdiction, saving the right of appeal to the Emperor.

III

THE SUCCESSION IN THE LATE EMPIRE

All the ground gained by the hereditary idea in the first two centuries had been lost in the third. In that time of intense crisis, Emperors normally ended by a violent death, and their heirs, when they had any, perished with them. This lack of a regular succession, with the uncertainties which it entailed and the ambitions which it inspired, was one of the great curses of the third century. Diocletian set himself to settle the problem, and believed that in the establishment of the tetrarchy he had discovered, in addition to many other advantages, a complete and final solution of a question which had been a chief concern of Emperors since the beginning of the Empire.

A system of succession, especially in the case of an inheritance like the Roman Empire, can only be tested by practice. Diocletian had the unhappiness to see his experiment fail in his own lifetime. The device of the tetrarchy, for all its ingenuity and the wealth of precautions with which its author hedged it round, bore within it a fatal defect. Maxentius, the son of Maximian, and Constantine, the son of Constantius Chlorus, were not the men to sacrifice their hereditary right to a wholly artificial system of succession. Seventeen years of civil wars and confusion, in which the melancholy days of the third century seemed to have returned,

were the price which the Roman world had to pay for a
dream and a mistake.

On the 1st May, 305, Diocletian resigned his powers,
together with his colleague Maximian. The motives of his
decision are plain enough. The partition of power which
had been in force for twenty years, eight years in the form
of a dyarchy and twelve in that of a tetrarchy had produced
all the effects which the author of the system expected of it,
save only one, the settlement of the succession. Consistent
with himself and with the spirit of his whole reform,
Diocletian wanted, on this point as on the rest, to judge his
work in the light of practice and to see it in operation with
his own eyes. This he could only do by voluntary abdication,
an act of which his methodical mind had long foreseen the
possibility and perhaps even determined the date. The
handing over of the power, which, one must allow, took
place on this one occasion in exceptionally favourable
circumstances and, one may well believe, had previously
been arranged in all its details by the far-seeing Emperor,
was effected without serious difficulty. The two Cæsars,
Constantius Chlorus and Galerius, were promoted to the
rank of Augusti, but kept the territorial areas which they
had previously governed, except that Spain and Mauretania
Tingitana were attached to the portion of Constantius.
Then the tetrarchy was made up by the nomination of two
new Cæsars, Severus in the West and Maximin Daïa in the
East, to be their assistants in the present and their successors
in the future. Diocletian and Maximian received the title
of honorary Augusti (*Seniores Augusti*), the former in his
magnificent palace at Salona and the latter in a comfortable
retreat in Lucania. Yet the arrangement had not satisfied
everybody. Maxentius and Constantine posed as martyrs,
but for the time, at least, they could do nothing but wait
for better days.

The better days soon came. The second tetrarchy
maintained itself for a year without serious incident. But
in 306 Constantius Chlorus, one of the Augusti, died, and at
once the problem of the succession was revived, to last for
seventeen years, during which things grew worse and worse.
Legally, the vacant position of Augustus should have gone
to one of the Cæsars, and, logically, to the Cæsar of the West,

Severus. Galerius, the sole survivor of the two Augusti and therefore head of the government, proceeded to appoint him. Then, in the name of that hereditary principle which Diocletian, by the establishment of the tetrarchical system, had tried to eliminate altogether, Constantine appeared upon the scene. He caused his troops to proclaim him and to give him the title of Augustus straight away, without going through the preliminary stage of Cæsarship. Galerius, who had become the soul of the second tetrarchy, as Diocletian had been of the first, could not sanction this double attack on the tetrarchical system without destroying Diocletian's work at one blow. Constantine's action was serious both in itself and as a precedent. However, as a measure of prudence, in order not to drive Constantine too far, Galerius showed a conciliatory attitude and recognized him as Cæsar. This uneven compromise restored the tetrarchy and once again made a kind of settlement of the old and troublesome question of the succession. But Constantine rejected it and kept the title of Augustus. Encouraged by his example, the son of Maximian, Maxentius, likewise had himself proclaimed Augustus, and his father, who had abdicated very unwillingly in the previous year, resumed his former dignity.

As a result of all these usurpations, there were now six Emperors—five Augusti (Severus, Constantine, Maximian, Maxentius in the West, and Galerius in the East), only two of whom, Severus and Galerius, represented the principle of legitimacy, and only one Cæsar, Maximin Daïa, in the East. Diocletian's system of succession, that masterpiece of detail and method, ended in sheer anarchy. Galerius made a last effort to save it. Severus received orders—it was doubtless only a first step—to overthrow Maximian and Maxentius, but failed and was killed in the attempt. Galerius, on his own authority, set Licinius in his place as Augustus of the West. Maximin Daïa, who was officially entitled to the post by his rank of Cæsar, considered that he had been sacrificed, and on his own authority took the title of Augustus himself. The Roman world now had six Augusti, all equal in dignity, and no Cæsar. Galerius's attempt had only made confusion worse confounded. Of the tetrarchical system, as far as the number and relative rank of the co-regents were concerned, nothing at all remained.

Once again in the annals of the Empire, the problem of the succession became a question of strength, to be settled by the gradual elimination of the competitors. In 310, Maximian killed himself; in 311, Galerius died; in 312, Maxentius, defeated at the Milvian Bridge, was drowned in the Tiber; in 313, defeated by Licinius, Maximin committed suicide at Tarsus; lastly, in 324 Licinius was dispossessed by Constantine and perished. The unity of the Empire was restored, with Constantine at its head. When the system of Diocletian failed, irretrievably condemned by the facts, the problem of the succession remained the same in form and as serious as ever.

This problem Constantine settled, or rather tried to settle, in a manner which, if not identical, was at least similar. He revived Diocletian's principle of partition, which the situation of the Roman world made necessary, but, by a radical modification, the need for which he had learned from experience, he made it a partition strictly within his family, thus returning to the hereditary principle usually observed in fact, if not in theory, by the dynasties of the Early Empire. After the execution of Crispus in 326, he had three sons left, Constantine II, Constantius II, and Constans. He divided the administration of the Empire among them, and, since he had also to provide for two nephews, Delmatius and Hannibalianus, he gave them their portion in this general sharing out of the Roman world. Constantine II received Britain, Gaul, and Spain: Constantius, the Asiatic East (except Eastern Asia Minor) and Egypt; and Constans, Italy, Illyricum, and Africa. Of the nephews, one, Delmatius, was to have Eastern Europe—Macedonia, Thrace, and Achaia—and the other, Hannibalianus, Eastern Asia Minor with the title of King of Kings. By this settlement, Constantine returned to Diocletian's system of collective government, but with two fundamental differences. In the old tetrarchy, based on selection, there was no question of heirship, and, moreover, the two classes of holder were not equal, the Cæsars being strictly subordinate to the Augusti. There was nothing like this in Constantine's arrangement; it was a division among the family, representing a return to the offensive on the part of the hereditary principle, and, although in general the two nephews found themselves in a subordinate position with regard to the three sons, the latter, the three principal Emperors, were on a footing of absolute equality. These brothers, who owed their power to the privilege of birth, became far more independent in their respective areas and far less united than Diocletian and Maximian had been during the twenty years of their reign.

The system of succession devised by Constantine fared no better than the tetrarchy. Hardly was the Emperor dead, when his sons came to an agreement to cut out their cousins, whom they regarded as intruders. A military rising instigated by them ended with the murder of Delmatius and Hanni-balianus, not to mention numerous collaterals of less importance. Then, as was to be expected, strife broke out among the sons of Constantine themselves. Three years later, Constantine II commenced hostilities against Constans and invaded his territory, but the attempt was a failure and Constantine was slain. At least, the evil went no further. The survivors, Constantius II and Constans, had the sense to come to an agreement, and for ten years, until the death of Constans in 350, the question of the succession appeared to be settled for good.

Taken all together, the reforms of Diocletian and Con-stantine—the reduction of the power of the Prefect of the Prætorium, the dividing up of the provinces, the severance of the civil and military powers—by making usurpation more difficult and risky, also helped to facilitate hereditary transmission. And, indeed, from then onwards we see sons normally succeeding their fathers, and in 367 Valentinian I, in virtue of that principle, gave his eight-year-old son Gratian the title of Augustus immediately, without first making him a Cæsar. Long dynasties were established—those of Con-stantine, Valentinian, Theodosius. One should note, too, that these dynasties came to an end prematurely in the absence of natural or appointed heirs.

But does this mean that henceforward the system of Imperial succession was definitely established on the hereditary principle ? As in the case of the Early Empire, we must distinguish between theory and practice. In theory, the Imperial power was not, and never would be, hereditary ; even in Constantinople, down to the last days of the Byzantine

Empire, the elective principle was maintained unchanged. But of the fact there is no doubt ; a quasi-hereditary system established itself, whereby the power passed regularly from the Emperor to the heir or heirs designate. Moreover, succession to the Empire was not secured by birth alone ; the traditional processes of designation and association continued in force as in the past, as was the case for Gratian and for the sons of Theodosius, who were nominated Augusti and colleagues of their father, Arcadius in 383 and Honorius ten years later. The innovation, therefore, was not in the methods but in the results. Failing a theory of hereditary succession, which was never admitted by Roman law, a practical hereditary succession established itself in the course of the Late Empire and thenceforward operated with sufficient, if not absolute, regularity. So, after four centuries, the great defect in the constitution created by Augustus was repaired, and the Roman monarchy, the last form of the political and social life of expiring antiquity, assumed its final aspect.

BOOK FOUR

IMPERIAL BUREAUCRACY. ADMINISTRATION AND GREAT PUBLIC SERVICES

CHAPTER I

THE EMPEROR'S ASSISTANTS.   MAGISTRATES AND OFFICIALS

BIBLIOGRAPHY.—*Ancient Authors* : See pp. 201, 238, 274.
Administrative and Legal Documents : See p. 274.
Inscriptions : *C.I.L.*, ii ff., *passim*, especially vol. vi.—(*a*) Senatorial career : Early Empire ; *C.I.L.*, vi, 1331–1583, 31631–826 (*I.L.S.*, 885–1210, 8961–81) ; Late Empire : *ibid.*, 1651–1796, 31879–2083 (*I.L.S.*, 1211–1312, 8982–94) ; (*b*) Equestrian career : *C.I.L.*, vi, 1584–1650, 31827–78 (*I.L.S.*, 1313–1472, 8995–9023) ;   (*c*) Lower careers : civil, *C.I.L.*, vi, 1802, 8398–10228 ; suppl., 32265–317, 33711–936 (*I.L.S.*, 1473–1876, 9024–51) ; military, *ibid.*, 2375–3670, 32515–3061 (*I.L.S.*, 2012–815, 9204–27). Cf. **III**, 91–156.
*Modern Works : **LXXXV**, especially 343–494 ; **VI**, i, 93–120 ; **XIX**, v, 329–404 ; viii–ix ; **CI**, 10–93 ; **CXXXVII** ; **XCVIII** ; **XCIV** ; **LXI**, x (Prefects of the Prætorium) ; G. Tomassetti, " Note sui Prefetti di Roma," in **CXII**, iii, 41–66 (Prefects of the City) ; **CII** (watch) ; O. Horschfeld, " Die Getreideverwaltung in der römischen Kaiserzeit," in **XLIII**, xxix (1870), 1–96 ; L. Cantarelli, " La Serie dei Curatores Tiberis," in **XXXV**, 1889, 185–205 ; " La Serie dei Curatori italici delle vie durante l'Impero," *ibid.*, 1891, 81–131 ; " L'Origine della Cura Tiberis e supplementi alla serie dei Vicarii Urbis Romanæ," *ibid.*, 1894, 39–51 ; " La Serie dei Curatores operum publicorum," *ibid.*, 203–24 ; " Le Distribuzioni di grano a Roma e la serie dei Præfecti frumenti dandi," *ibid.*, 1895, 217–34 ; " Supplementi alla serie dei Curatores Tiberis," *ibid.*, 1900, 134–6 ; " Supplementi alla serie dei Curatores ædium sacrarum et operum publicorum," *ibid.*, 136–9 ; " La Serie dei Curatores aquarum," *ibid.*, 1901, 180–214 ; E. Stein, " Untersuchungen zur spätrömischen Verwaltungsgeschichte," in **XLIX**, lxxiv (1925), 298 ff. ; **LXVIa**, Eng. pp. 119–29 (Italy), 130–412 (the provinces).
For the public services, see also the special bibliography on p. 319.

I

ORGANS OF DELIBERATION : COMITIA, SENATE, IMPERIAL COUNCIL

THE evolution of Cæsarism, in the first five centuries of its existence, is expressed in essence by two symmetrical and connected features—the movement towards absolute monarchy and the development of bureaucracy. We have described the former. Now we have to retrace in its main lines the growth of the Imperial administration.

*See also Supplementary Bibliography with Prefatory Note (p. 405)

As a hybrid compromise between the traditions of the past and the needs of the present, the Imperial regime collected round the person of the sovereign, and in his service, two parallel series of organs, one a survival from Republican times (the Comitia, magistracies, and Senate) and the other mainly a creation of personal government (the Imperial Council and officials of all classes). Moreover, the origins of bureaucracy lay far back. Even in the Republic, the lower posts—those of drafting and correspondence clerks, cashiers, accountants, watchmen, heralds, lictors, beadles, janitors, etc.—when not filled by freedmen or slaves, were in the hands of permanent salaried officials, appointed by the State. In the last century before Christ, as military power advanced and exceptional commands were created, officialdom began to spread and to take hold of the higher employments. In virtue of the *Leges Gabinia* (67), *Manilia* (66), *Vatinia* (59), *Messia* (57), *Trebonia*, and *Pompeia Licinia* (55), and of the pact by which the Second Triumvirate was created (43), the great military leaders—Pompey, Cæsar, Crassus, Octavian, Antony, Lepidus—appointed their own Legates, who thus became their personal representatives and were forerunners of the Legates *pro Prætore* of the Empire.

Nor was that all. In Rome itself, the seat of the government of the City, the movement to bureaucracy continued, from Cæsar's Dictatorship onwards, in a similar form. For the year 45, Cæsar replaced most of the regular magistrates—Prætors, Ædiles, Quæstors—by a series of extraordinary magistrates, who were not appointed by election according to the sacrosanct rule, but chosen direct by himself, and among them, by the side of six vice-Prætors and Ædiles, there appear two Prefects of the City, an innovation from which one of the most typical administrative creations of the Imperial bureaucracy would one day spring—the Prefect of the City. That bureaucracy, which was to be found in rudimentary form in the remote past of the City, the Emperor erected into a system. Henceforward the traditional organs of the City and the newly created officials stood face to face.

With the act of 27 B.C., the former resumed their normal functions, but with the very important difference that they were now under the supervision and guardianship of the head of the State ; the latter came entirely under the

Princeps, and the organs of Republican origin could not interfere with them in any way. Whether it was a matter of deliberative or of executive power, there were two sets of institutions, established side by side and, inevitably, mutual rivals.

Under the Republic, the highest place among the deliberative organs was held by the Comitia, the incarnation of the Roman people and the legal source of all public authority. Augustus took good care not to touch that venerable institution, and was content to take away their judicial powers, which in practice were the least important, leaving them the whole of their legislative and electoral competence. In his reign, the Comitia continued to vote laws, such as the famous *Leges Juliæ* and the *Lex Papia Poppæa*, and to elect the traditional magistrates. But in this domain as in the rest, the fiction very soon collapsed beneath the inexorable pressure of realities. At the beginning of the reign of Tiberius, the electoral powers of the Comitia were transferred to the Senate, and, except for a brief reaction due to a whim of Caligula, the transfer was permanent. Their legislative powers were not abolished legally. Laws were still voted by the Comitia after the time of Augustus, such as the *Lex Julia Norbana* in the early part of the first century after Christ and the law of the Imperial investiture at the accession of Vespasian. But the exercise of the right became more and more infrequent, and finally ceased altogether. In practice, the work of legislation was thenceforward done in the form of *Senatus consulta*, and, still more, of Imperial Constitutions (edicts, decrees, rescripts), which after the second century alone remained in use. So the Comitia, the organs of a political world which no longer existed, played only a brief part in the Imperial system.

The Senate, the chief sufferer by the revolution which had substituted personal rule for Republican government, had emerged from the crisis discredited and very much reduced. One of its essential attributions, the conduct of foreign affairs by diplomacy and war, had been permanently taken out of its hands by the Emperor. In the domain of home politics, at least, by the desire of the Emperor himself, it continued to be closely associated with the work of government. It kept, at least in part, its traditional rôle in the

L

matter of legislation and administration, and on two points it even received new attributions—its judicial competence was increased, and, from the accession of Tiberius, it took over the electoral powers of the Comitia.

As an organ of deliberation, the Senate voted *Senatus consulta*, which were equal in force to laws and Imperial Constitutions. The Emperor might take its advice on matters of home and foreign policy, but he was not bound to follow it, and always reserved the right of final decision. Some have called it an effective dyarchy ; others, a mere constitutional fiction. Both views are wrong. There can be no doubt of the importance of the legislative and administrative powers left to the Senate or conferred on it, but in practice (and it was the chief defect of the system) the Emperor, who was master and knew it, had a thousand ways, constitutional or otherwise, of nullifying them. In practice, from Augustus onwards, the Senate was, in respect of political and administrative competence, wholly in the hands of the Emperor.

With regard to the recruiting of the Senate, the situation was different. On three occasions, in 28, 18, and 11 B.C. (in addition to the partial purgations of 13 B.C. and A.D. 4), Augustus had, in virtue of temporary official powers (the Consulship in 13 and extraordinary functions on the other occasions), undertaken the *lectio Senatus* and the establishment of the Senatorial Album ; he had, by successive eliminations, reduced its numbers to six hundred. For the admission of new Senators, on the other hand, he had adhered to the constitutional rules established by Sulla and confirmed by himself, under which the Senate was filled automatically by the election of the annual Quæstors. No doubt, the Emperor could interfere in the election of Quæstors by using his right of recommendation, and in that of Military Tribunes (the preliminary stage) by his right of direct appointment ; but in practice the exercise of these two prerogatives very soon proved delicate and, above all, insufficient. Another way must be found. The system of *adlectio* (the extraordinary *adlectio* attached to the exercise of the Censorship since Claudius and the ordinary *adlectio* since Domitian, who expressly took the title of Perpetual Censor) remedied this defect of the original Principate and gave the Imperial prerogative the legal form which it had previously lacked. Released from all rules and from all conditions regarding the *cursus*, the Emperor could now introduce into the Senate, and straight into whatever Senatorial category he pleased, those whom he for any reason considered worthy of the honour. The recruiting and the order of dignity of the Senate were completely at the mercy of his discretion.

The truth was that Senate was an organ of the past, no longer answering to the political tendencies and administrative needs of a new world, in which monarchical government alone was seen to be possible and fruitful. Augustus, Tiberius, Vespasian, Trajan, Antoninus, Marcus Aurelius, tried in vain to save appearances and to give the illusion of effective collaboration. It was useless. The history of the Senate under the Early Empire is that of a long decline, during which the political and administrative privileges of the ancient council fall one after another, condemned without appeal by the experience of centuries. Its legislative power, assailed by the competition of the Emperor, grew daily weaker. In the time of Augustus, it was necessary to create a Senatorial commission as permanent representatives of the Senate with the Emperor. It was composed of twenty members, renewable by lot every six months, who should endeavour to effect the constitutional co-operation of the two powers in a more satisfactory form. During the first two centuries, the legislative privilege of the Senate steadily weakened; from the time of the Severi, the Imperial Constitution became the normal, and almost exclusive, instrument of legislative activity. The electoral privilege of the Senate was more and more reduced by the gradual extension of the Emperor's right of presentation of candidates (*commendatio*). That Imperial prerogative, which was at first confined to the lower magistracies, and only to some of the vacancies, was extended in practice to the Consulship under Nero, and became general under Vespasian; thenceforward the elections were a pure formality and, from the beginning of the third century, it was admitted in law that the appointment of all magistrates lay with the Emperor. Lastly, in the same period, the Senate ceased to be the supreme court of justice. Appeal to the Senate had already been effaced in the first century by appeal to the Emperor, represented in practice by the Prefect of the Prætorium, and the Senate's jurisdiction as a criminal court of first instance disappeared under Septimius Severus in favour of the Prefects of the Prætorium and City. Henceforward the Senate had the right of jurisdiction over its own members only, a very small and often illusory privilege.

As the great deliberative organ of the Republic declined, the new deliberative organ of the Empire rose, the Imperial Council (*Consilium Principis*). Being the supreme head of the State, in spite of deliberate pretences and official ambiguities, the Emperor naturally felt it necessary to have by him a consultative body whose opinion he might take or consider. Under Augustus, this Council was still recruited and composed in a very loose manner. The Emperor summoned to it whomever he wished—members of his family (Tiberius, Drusus, Germanicus), ministers (Agrippa, Mæcenas), high officials, friends, Senators, or Knights. The business with which the Council dealt varied in character— foreign policy, questions of war, administration, and justice— and its composition depended on the business to be done and the special qualifications which it seemed in the Emperor's opinion to require.

The Imperial Council became permanent under Tiberius, and was completely reorganized by Hadrian. Hadrian's reform bore on two essential points. First, recruiting : while reserving his own liberty of choice, he introduced a permanent, stable element into the Council, namely, the jurisconsults, whose presence was indispensable to the exercise of the legislative and judicial prerogatives of the Emperor. These permanent councillors, drawn from the Senatorial and Equestrian orders without distinction, were appointed by the Emperor, on presentation by the Senate. Secondly, councillors henceforward received a regular salary, from 100,000 to 200,000 sesterces for permanent councillors and 60,000 for extraordinary councillors.

In the second part of the second century, the Prefect of the Prætorium took a preponderant place in the Council ; as lawful vice-president, he directed its labours when the Emperor was absent and communicated its opinions. From the Severi onwards, the Imperial Council, now rid of the competition of the Senate, became the centre of government and the chief moving force of the Imperial administration.

II

ORGANS OF EXECUTION : MAGISTRATES AND OFFICIALS

In the Republican period, the organs of execution had been the magistracies, extraordinary, like the Dictatorship, and ordinary, one of these latter being five-yearly (the Censorship) and the rest annual (Consulship, Prætorship, Curule and Plebeian Ædileships, Tribuneship, Quæstorship). Two of these magistracies disappeared at the very beginning of the Empire. There was no longer any need for the Dictatorship when the Principate was established, and the Censorship, after a vain attempt to drag it from its grave in 22 B.C., was only held by the Emperors exceptionally. All the others survived, but received two blows which vitiated their working and would one day menace their existence. The Emperor assumed or, when he wished, made members of his family assume, the highest magistracy of all, the Consulship, and, what was even more decisive, the magistracies, which had been the sole organs of execution under the Republic, were now faced with the competition of the Imperial organs. So their history in the three first centuries of the Empire, like that of the Senate, is the story of slow decline and gradual dispossession.

The Consulship, while keeping its prestige, lost in respect of the duration of its powers and of their reality. The annual principle, one of the foundations of the constitutional life of the Republic, was abolished by the creation of Suffect Consuls. Exceptionally under Augustus and regularly from Tiberius onwards, there were supplementary colleges of Consuls. They held office, at first for six months, then for four, then for two ; in the reign of Commodus we hear of a year in which twenty-five Consuls held office in turn. Moreover, the powers of the magistracy were cut down. Gradually shorn of its high civil and judicial functions by the competition of the Imperial agents of centralization, (Prefects and executive commissions) and decentralization (Consulars and Juridici of Italy), it was reduced in the end to purely honorary privileges, such as presidency in the Senate, or burdensome duties such as that of giving games.

The history of the other magistracies was the same. The Prætor lost his two principal attributions, civil jurisdiction in Italy and the presidency on criminal juries, and was reduced to a purely urban sphere. The Curule and Plebeian Ædiles, gradually dispossessed in favour of the Prefect of the City, disappeared in the first years of the military anarchy. The Tribune, who owed his existence to civil strife and was intended for an age of freedom, had no place in the Imperial system ; in the third century his office had no effective powers and was empty of reality. Lastly, the Quæstor did not escape the common lot. The logical consequence was that these magistracies, which no longer gratified the pride of the holder as they had once done, nor, under the new conditions of provincial administration, offered him the certainty of enriching himself afterwards, but were a source of expense without any compensation, became more and more discredited. On the eve of the military anarchy, they were only an empty show, a survival without reality. Their great administrative rôle was ended, and for ever.

Legally, and by express mandate of the people, the Emperor was the master of the whole Roman State. He exercised his powers either in person or through representatives, whom he took in imitation of the Hellenistic monarchies, and particularly of Ptolemaic Egypt, a country where the almost total absence of any municipal system made a very highly developed bureaucracy a necessity. These Imperial officials were divided into two classes—those of the central administration, whose competence, reflecting the master's, extended all over the Empire, and the district and local officials of all kinds.

Among the officials of the central administration, the highest place was held by the Prefect of the Prætorium. His powers were strictly military in origin. The Emperor was the commander-in-chief of all the military forces of the Empire on land and sea, but he could not exercise the whole of that power himself. In the provinces, his representatives were the governors, the commanders-in-chief of the provincial armies. In Rome and Italy, the official residence of the Emperor and permanent seat of his *prætorium,* this duty was given to a Prefect, the Prefect of the Prætorium. He had the chief command of all troops in Rome and Italy, except the Urban Cohorts, which were under the Prefect of the City. He was, therefore, a high military officer, the highest in all the Empire. These original powers, bound up with the very nature of the office, soon became even more important, and from Tiberius onwards the Prefect of the Prætorium was the second man in the State, the first after the Emperor. In war, he accompanied him, and acted as chief of the army under him ; in peace time, he sat on the Imperial Council and took the chair when the Emperor was absent or detained. Therefore lawsuits which the sovereign chose to try and appeals brought to his court came in practice to the Prefect of the Prætorium, and he became the chief judge and jurisconsult of the Roman world. In fact, he was a vice-emperor ; it was " an almost royal office ", as Macrinus said in his accession-message to the Senate, having had experience of it.

But the official powers of the Prefect of the Prætorium are not enough to explain the extraordinary rise of this office ; we must also take realities into account. He lived in Rome at the side of the Emperor, and the nature of his command and the number of men under his orders necessarily made him powerful and dangerous. From weakness or from prudence, the Emperor was obliged to reckon with him. Under Vespasian, Clemens was the brother-in-law of Titus, and under Septimius Severus Plautianus was the father-in-law of Caracalla. Under Tiberius, Sejanus aspired to the supreme power ; at the beginning of the third century, Macrinus won it. The Emperors were not blind to this permanent danger, and to meet it they subjected the office to the principle of the college, a measure of prudence which, if it did not altogether restrain ambitious Prefects, at least somewhat hampered their manœuvres.

One of the essential elements of the authority of the Prefect of the Prætorium was that, like the Emperor's own, his competence extended over the whole Empire. He was a prime minister, and at the same time minister of the interior, justice, war, and the navy, with the fundamental characteristic that, originally at least, he was a minister without colleagues. Others were to appear even in the Early Empire, as the great centralized services came into being. First, there was the minister of Finance (a rationibus). The title is found for the first time in the reign of Tiberius ;

under Claudius the office, already very important, was held by the celebrated freedman Pallas and under Domitian by another freedman, Claudius Etruscus, who was likewise a very great personage. At this time the office, as the condition of the holders shows, was still one of the posts of the household. An important reform was made under Hadrian, when the director of Imperial Finance received the title of Procurator; henceforward he was a Knight, holding one of the highest degrees of the Equestrian career, in respect both of rank and of salary. Thus the Imperial *Fiscus* was transformed from a service of the household into a department of State, a true ministry. Later in the second century, the title of Procurator was superseded by that of *Rationalis*, and in the third century the Emperors attached to the office the highest honour of the Equestrian career, the rank of Perfectissimus.

Two other heads of departments ranked next among the immediate assistants of the ruler. First, there was the director of the Patrimony, later of the *Res Privata*, who took charge of the Emperor's private property. Having been a freedman at the beginning of the Empire, he became a Knight under Claudius and received the title of Procurator. When Septimius Severus reorganized the service, he became still more important; he was one of the highest dignitaries of the Equestrian order and drew an annual salary of 300,000 sesterces. Secondly, the director of Vehicles (*a vehiculis,* a freedman, down to Trajan; Prefect of Vehicles, *præfectus vehiculorum,* of the Equestrian order, from Hadrian onwards) acted as postmaster general. Other ministers, as we have seen, would appear in the Late Empire.

III

Organs of Transmission: the Offices

Complicated as was the administrative machine set up by Augustus, it lacked one essential part—organs of transmission—and the size of the Empire and the centralizing tendencies of the new order made this defect still more noticeable. The creation of these organs, which, one may say, had only existed in the most rudimentary form in the

Republic, was to be the achievement of the Empire, bearing its stamp and revealing its essential methods. An organization of that kind could not be improvised all at once ; it was effected in two stages, represented by Claudius and Hadrian respectively.

The Emperor, an aristocrat who had come to the supreme power, first took his ideas from the traditions of his caste. In the Republic, wealthy Romans had employed a certain number of secretaries, freedmen or slaves, who acted as organs of transmission in the management of their business and patrimony. Cæsar was no exception ; when he became master of the State, he used his private staff for the affairs of the State. Trogus Pompeius, the celebrated historian, was the chief of his correspondence-office. Augustus did the same ; the slave Januarius and the freedman Ti. Julius Agathopus held similar posts in his reign, and two other freedmen, Polybius and Hilarion, helped in the drafting of his will. So the origins of one office, that of Correspondence (*ab epistulis*), went back to the very beginnings of the Empire. A second secretarial office, *A Libellis*, run by a freedman, appears under Tiberius. But under the first Emperors the service was still of a rudimentary kind ; the systematic organization of the Imperial secretariat was the work of Claudius. The freedmen who ruled in his name, men with a modern outlook and representative of the new administrative tendencies, took the initiative and were capable enough to carry through the reform successfully.

The Imperial secretariat, when it left the hands of Claudius, comprised four great offices—*Ab Epistulis, A Libellis,* and two others which appear for the first time in the history of the Imperial administration, *A Cognitionibus* and *A Studiis. Ab Epistulis*, the correspondence-office, received and dispatched all the administrative correspondence of the Emperor—grants of privileges by letter, official correspondence with foreign kings and peoples and provincial officials, commissions appointing officers to the higher ranks. It was divided into two sections, one Greek and one Latin, corresponding to the two languages between which the Empire was officially divided. *A Libellis*, the petition-office, prepared replies to requests addressed to the Emperor ; these replies usually took the form of brief annotations signed by the Emperor. *A Cognitionibus*, the inquiry-office, had the especial duty of working up lawsuits which the Emperor caused to come before his court. Lastly, *A Studiis*, the office of preliminary examinations, was the natural auxiliary of the Emperor in the domains of administration and justice, and gave him the material which he needed for the performance of his duties.

Each office had its own chief, who was designated by the name of his office (*Ab Epistulis, A Libellis, A Cognitionibus, A Studiis*), with assistants (*adjutores, proximi*) and many employees (*scriniarii, custodes*). In spite of its new importance, the secretariat as organized by Claudius was still regarded as a domestic organ and not as a department of the State. It was therefore staffed entirely from the Emperor's household, and free men were never admitted. The higher posts, such as those of heads of offices, were reserved for freedmen, while the lower employees were slaves.

The second stage was passed in the reign of Hadrian, when the secretariat was transformed from a household service into a State department. The fact is explained by the great advance made by the monarchical idea during the first century. A few timid steps had been taken towards the new system by Otho, Vitellius, and Domitian ; Hadrian made it general and permanent. At the head of the four great offices, the freedmen were replaced by Knights. The historian Suetonius was director of the office *Ab Epistulis* under Hadrian, and the jurisconsults Papinian and Ulpian were in charge of *A Libellis* under Septimius Severus and Caracalla respectively. Hadrian, furthermore, completed the organization of the secretariat by the creation of a fifth office, *A Memoria*, whose business it was to aid the Emperor's "memory" by collecting all necessary data for him. Its chief was called the *A Memoria* and was assisted by subordinates (*proximi, adlecti*) all of whom, by an exception which is explained by the late creation of the service, were freedmen and slaves.

The development of the Imperial secretariat went on uninterruptedly along with the centralizing movement, all through the following period. The importance of the different offices increased steadily as their organization was extended. Their chiefs were promoted to the rank of Procurators, and

Septimius Severus still further enhanced their dignity by giving them the title of Perfectissimus. Severus Alexander, giving Hadrian's measure general application, opened the office *A Memoria* to members of the Equestrian order and put the famous jurisconsult Paulus at the head of it. But it was only in the Late Empire that the Imperial organs of transmission attained their full development and assumed their final form.

IV

DISTRICT OFFICIALS : ROME, ITALY, THE PROVINCES

I. ROME AND ITALY.   (*a*) *Survivals of the past : the Senate and magistracies.*—Under the Republic, in virtue of the very concept of the city, the town of Rome had had neither the privileges nor the organization of a self-governing burgh ; it was the City itself, in which general and local administration, State departments and municipal departments were identified and merged in one another.   The administration of the town and the direction of local services were, therefore, in the hands of the great organs of the City, the organs of deliberation being the Comitia and Senate and the organs of execution being the magistracies.   In the Imperial epoch, the Comitia did not survive long, and on the accession of Tiberius they ceased to take effective part in the administration of the town.   The two other organs, the Senate and magistracies, were maintained, but under new conditions and with powers which were more and more restricted by the increasing centralization of everything in the hands of the Emperor.

The Senate had supreme control of public property in the town ; it directed and supervised the magistrates in the exercise of their annual functions ; the Senatorial budget, in respect both of expenditure (public works, roads, food-supply, education) and of revenues (customs, water, various taxes), was in great part a local budget.   The gradual loss of its State privileges confined the Senate more and more to the domain of urban administration.   The evolution, which began in the reign of Augustus and went on through the first two centuries, gained speed under the military anarchy, to culminate under Diocletian and Constantine ; the abandonment of Rome as the capital marked the last stage of the dispossession of the Senate. In the third century, in spite of certain prerogatives, chiefly honorary, the Senate was little more than the town-council of Rome, and even in that limited sphere it ceased to be master. Even in Rome it found the Emperor's authority competing with it, and it came up against the invasive activity of his agents there as elsewhere.

The magistrates, in the early organization of the Imperial system, kept the whole of their urban attributions ; only the Censorship was abolished, leaving vacant its traditional function in matters of civil status, survey, finance, and public works. The Consuls still controlled administration in general, presided in the Senate and Comitia, had the right to initiate measures in those assemblies, and, in theory at least, had supreme executive power with the charge of the safety of the State. The Prætors kept their political and judicial function (presiding at the law-courts). The Tribunes had their old privileges. The Curule and Plebeian Ædiles were maintained at the head of the great urban services which they ran in Republican times—the cleaning and upkeep of roads, the inspection and upkeep of public buildings, the water-service (supply, upkeep, and distribution), the fire-brigade (*familia publica*), police (for the city, for public establishments like taverns and baths, and for morals and religious cults), the food-supply (*annona*), and the organization and policing of the public games, the Roman Games and Megalesia being given by the Curule Ædiles and the Plebeian Games by the Plebeian. The two Quæstors of the *Ærarium* still had the care of the treasury, while the Quæstor of Water worked in collaboration with the Ædiles. Lastly, three colleges of the Vigintivirate continued to take a direct part in the affairs of the town : the *Tresviri Capitales* in police and criminal matters (inspection of prisons, execution of the death-penalty) and the *Quatuorviri Viis in Urbe Purgandis* and *Duumviri Viis extra Urbem propiusve Urbem Romam passus mille Purgandis* in the roads-service of the town and immediate environs respectively, all being under the general direction of the Ædiles.

But, while the magistrates of Rome kept the whole of their

urban functions, they did not exercise them alone, and that was the great innovation of the Empire in that domain. They were now faced with the competition of the Emperor and his servants, particularly the Prefects of the City, Corn-supply, and Watch and the executive commissions, and their administrative history during the first three centuries is one of uninterrupted decline. At the outbreak of the military anarchy, the Consuls and Prætors had nothing left but the competence to try civil suits in Rome and within the 100,000 yards ; the Tribuneship and Quæstorship were purely honorary offices ; and the two Ædileships and the Vigintivirate, drained of their real powers, would disappear, as useless and superfluous organs, before the middle of the third century.

In fact, even at the beginning of the Empire, the old urban administration, with its inadequate organs and its obsolete machinery, was doomed. Its inheritance remained ; the Emperor's officials would take it up.

(b) *New organs : officials and executive commissions.*—The Imperial town-officials, instituted at least in part by Augustus on the model of similar officials in Alexandria, were divided into two main categories—Prefects and executive commissions.

There were three Prefects for the town—the Prefect of the City, the Prefect of the Corn-supply, and the Prefect of the Watch. The Prefect of the City was created under Augustus (25 B.C.) as an extraordinary official, and became permanent when Tiberius left the capital for good (A.D. 26). He was, first and foremost, the chief constable of Imperial Rome ; the maintenance of order, the supervision of associations, the control of traffic, the organization of games, and, in general, everything affecting the public safety was within his competence. As an entirely civil official, he wore the toga and had no forces beyond the police required for his duties, the three Urban Cohorts, numbering 30,000 men. He was not only an administrative official ; in his own sphere of action, he was a judge in civil and criminal cases, and he decided in the last resort on the important cases, including capital cases, referred to him by the Prefects of the Corn-supply and Watch.

These powers, which were connected with the very nature of his function, the Prefect of the City had had since his

office was created. In the course of the first two centuries
of the Empire, they were increased in the domains both of
administration and of justice. In administration he gradually
took over the powers of the traditional urban magistrates,
in particular those of the Ædiles, and became the official
head of the administration of the capital, the other organs
of which were in the end subordinated to him. In justice
there was a similar and parallel development. His original
jurisdiction was presently extended at the expense of the
old Republican organs (Consuls, Prætors, criminal courts).
A reaction in favour of these latter under the Flavians
retarded this irresistible movement, without stopping it.
At the end of the first century, the criminal jurisdiction of
the Prefect of the City covered Rome itself and the whole
of Italy ; when he lost Italy to the Prefect of the Prætorium,
he remained the great criminal judge of Rome and its environs
within the radius of 100,000 yards, where civil jurisdiction
was still in the hands of the Consuls and Prætors.

The Prefect of the Corn-supply (*annona*), another creation
of Augustus, had entire control of the feeding of the capital
(provisioning in corn, oil, meat, and other foodstuffs, the
supervision of the market, the control of sale-prices), except
for the free distributions, which were done by special officials
(*Præfecti Frumenti Dandi*). He had a civil and criminal
jurisdiction within the limits of his competence, with
the reservation that the more important cases, capital cases
in particular, were referred to the Prefect of the City, and
he had special rights of policing all the corporations (bakers,
boatmen, dockers) connected in any way with the food-supply.

The Prefect of the Watch, lastly, who was created by
Augustus in A.D. 6, was in charge of the night-police and
fires. For this purpose he had seven cohorts of watchmen
(*vigiles*), with 1,200 men in each, divided among the fourteen
districts of the city, with one barracks to every two districts
and one guard-house per district. Like the two other
Prefects, he had judicial powers in civil and criminal cases
coming within his competence, but for criminal cases he was
in the same position as his colleague of the Food-supply,
having to refer especially grave cases, including capital
cases, to the Prefect of the City.

With the Prefects, we must consider the executive commissions, the second great element in the Imperial administration of the city of Rome. Two, the Water Commission and that of Public Buildings, were created by Augustus. The Water Commission (*cura aquarum*), which was instituted in 11 B.C. and consisted of three members, a Consular as president, who was really the head of the department, and two Prætorians as assistants, was in charge of everything connected with the water-supply of Rome. The Commission of Public Buildings (*cura ædium sacrarum et operum locorumque publicorum*), consisting of two members of Prætorian rank, saw to the upkeep of public monuments. A third commission, created by Tiberius in A.D. 15, was that of the Bed and Banks of the Tiber (*cura alvei et riparum Tiberis*), and had to keep the channel of the river in good condition and take such steps as were possible against the permanent danger of floods. It contained five members of Consular rank, one of whom was president ; at first they were chosen by lot, but later they were appointed direct by the Emperor, like the members of the other similar commissions. Trajan added the maintenance of the drains to its duties, and its name was expanded accordingly (. . . *et cloacarum urbis*). All these commissions, like the Prefects, in accordance with the general principles of Roman public law, had in addition to their administrative competence judicial powers within their own sphere.

In Italy, outside the capital and its environs, there were the same administrative organs and the same duality of powers : on the one side, the Senate and the old magistrates, Consuls, Prætors, and Quæstors, who had had charge of the whole peninsula in Republican times ; on the other, the new organs created by Augustus—Prefect of the Prætorium, Prefect of the City, Prefect of the Corn-supply, Prefect of the Watch, and, of the executive commissions of the city, the Water Commission, whose powers extended to the whole system of aqueducts and therefore to a large area outside the town. To these administrative departments, which were common to the city and a considerable part of the peninsula, one should add the service of Italian Roads, which was created by Augustus in 20 B.C. and entrusted to Curators (one to a road) of Senatorial or Equestrian rank, according to the importance of the route.

II. The Provinces. (a) *Senatorial provinces.*—The settlement of the 13th January, 27 B.C., by which the provinces were distributed between the Senate and the Emperor, allotted ten to the former—Bætica, Sardinia, Sicily, Illyricum, Macedonia, Achaia, Asia, Bithynia, Crete-and-Cyrenaïca, and Africa. These were on the whole pacified, except Africa, where the legion III Augusta was in garrison, and Illyricum, which was held by a few military contingents, frontier-posts rather than a real army. Nor did this anomaly last long; in 11 B.C. Illyricum was transferred to the Emperor, and in A.D. 37 Caligula took the command of the legion in Africa from the governor of the province and gave it to a lieutenant of his own.

The governors of Senatorial provinces were drawn from the Senate and were of various ranks. Those of Asia and Africa were Consulars and those of the eight other provinces Prætorians. The former were entitled to twelve lictors and the latter to only six, but, apart from this difference, their title, mode of appointment, and powers were exactly the same. All Senatorial governors, whatever their rank, alike bore the title of Proconsul. They were appointed by the Senate, lots being drawn. The drawing was done within each of the two categories (Consulars and Prætorians) in conformity with the *Lex Pompeia de Provinciis* of 52 B.C., which required an interval of five years between the holding of a magistracy and admission to the pro-magistracy; therefore the two lists continued only Consulars and Prætorians who had laid down their office at least five years before. They were usually appointed for one year, but their office might be extended. In respect of powers, the Senatorial Governor, except, for a time, those of Illyricum and Africa, was a purely civil official, wearing the toga and not having the " right of the sword "; of the universal competence of the Republican governors, he had kept only the civil and judicial powers. He was assisted in his administration by one or more Legates and a Quæstor who specialized in finance, the former being chosen by the Senate and the latter by lot.

In 27 B.C., the Emperor had given over the administration of the so-called Senatorial provinces to the Senate, but not without reservation. The universal character of his Proconsular *imperium*, as based on the constitutional act of 23, allowed him to interfere even in the provincial domain of the Senate, legally in virtue of the *imperium majus*, and this power, though not obvious at first sight, manifested itself in various forms in practice. He could intervene officially or unofficially, according to the circumstances, in the recruiting of Senatorial governors, and had the right, if he chose, to appoint candidates without the formality of drawing lots (*extra sortem*). In justice, appeal could always be made from the decrees of the governor to the Emperor. In finance, the Quæstor was no longer, as in Republican times, the sole director of the finances of the Province ; he was in charge of only the taxes and the funds which went into the Senatorial treasury (*ærarium*), while those destined for the Emperor's treasury (*fiscus*) were under the exclusive control of a special Imperial official, the Procurator, who was independent of the governor. Lastly, the arrangement of the provinces of 27 was not a permanent settlement. The Emperor could always transfer a province from one category to the other, especially if foreign or civil wars broke out which required direct action by the army, and therefore by the Imperial authority. Thus, Illyricum in 11 B.C., Sardinia in A.D. 6, again under Vespasian, and for good under Commodus, Bithynia in 135, and Macedonia and Achaia from A.D. 15 to 44, were made temporarily or permanently into Imperial provinces. As a rule, but not always, the Emperor gave a province in exchange ; Narbonensis and Cyprus, which were Imperial provinces under the settlement of 27, were returned to the Senate in 22, and the same was done with Pamphylia and Lycia, combined in a single province, under Hadrian in 135.

Moreover, the general equilibrium established in 27 between the Senatorial and Imperial provinces soon broke down in the Emperor's favour. From Augustus to Trajan, in spite of various transfers, the share of the Senate was increased by only one province, while the number of Imperial provinces grew very much greater. In 27 B.C., there were ten Senatorial provinces and seven Imperial provinces (including Egypt), plus the vast area of Gallia Comata ; in A.D. 117, there were eleven Senatorial provinces and thirty-three Imperial. These figures leave no doubt that the balance between the two powers was breaking down more and more.

(b) *Imperial provinces.*—In virtue of the partition of 27,
Augustus kept the Imperial provinces to himself, that is,
he had direct administration of Gallia Comata (the equivalent
of the future provinces of Belgica, Lugdunensis, Aquitania,
and the two Germanies), and also of Narbonensis, Tarraconensis, Lusitania, Cilicia, Cyprus, Syria, and Egypt,
which were the less Romanized provinces, those in which
the presence of Roman troops was generally indispensable.
These provinces the Emperor governed in virtue of his
higher *imperium*, Consular *imperium* from 27 to 23 B.C., and
Proconsular *imperium* from 23 onwards. He was represented by personal delegates, the Imperial governors (*legati
pro prœtore*). Of these Imperial provinces,the more important
(Hither Spain or Tarraconensis and Syria) were of Consular
rank and were governed by former Consuls ; others (Narbonensis, Lusitania, Cilicia, and Cyprus) were Prætorian and
governed by former Prætors. Gallia Comata at this time still
constituted an extraordinary command, and Egypt had a
special type of administration, with an Equestrian Prefect
as governor.

These Imperial governors, whatever their category, had
one thing in common with those of the Senatorial provinces,
namely their origin. Like them, they were drawn from the
Senate, from the Consular or Prætorian class as the case
might be. But in all other respects their status was radically
different. Being appointed by the Emperor, they were
responsible to him and might be recalled at his pleasure.
He kept them in their office as long as he chose, generally
for five years. As his representatives, they embodied, by
delegation, his full *imperium*, civil, military, and judicial.
In dispensing justice, they were assisted by one or more
Legates (*juridici*) who acted as their substitutes when
required. In financial matters they were assisted by an
Imperial Procurator, chosen by the Emperor from the
Equestrian order. The Imperial governor was in charge of
the civil administration of his province (general government
of the country, finance, public works, post), and at the same
time was commander-in-chief of all troops garrisoned there,
both legions and auxiliary corps. He tried civil and criminal
cases, and was invested with the power of life and death (*jus
gladii*), save that appeal might always be made to the Emperor.

The province governed by a Legate represented the original and usual type of Imperial province, but soon, even in the reign of Augustus, another class appeared. These were newly created and less important provinces, the Maritime Alps, Rætia, and Noricum, the organization of which was copied from that of Egypt, except that the government was conducted by Prefects of lower rank, who were superseded in the reign of Claudius by Equestrian Procurators (*procuratores jure gladii*). The mode of nomination and powers of this second class of provincial governors were similar to those of the Legates, but they had no legions under their orders, only corps of auxiliaries.

V

THE GREAT PUBLIC SERVICES

BIBLIOGRAPHY.—*Ancient Authors* : For public services in general, see the bibliographies on pp. 201, 238, 274 above.—For the water-supply the fundamental authority is Frontinus, *De Aquæductibus Urbis Romæ*, of which there are an edition with a full commentary by R. Lanciani, **C**, in *Atti dell' Accademia dei Lincei*, ser. 3a, vol. iv, Rome, 1880, and a critical edition by F. Krohn, Leipzig, 1922.

Inscriptions : Urban public services : *C.I.L.*, vi, 8398–10228 ; suppl., 33711–936.—Water : Inscriptions on lead pipes in Lanciani, **C**, "Silloge epigrafica aquaria," pp. 211–308, and *C.I.L.*, xv, 7235–913.

Modern Works : Public services in general : **LXXXV**, 1–342 ; **XIX**, v, 344–56 ; bibliography, p. 299 above.—Water in Rome : **C** ; **LXXXV**, 273–84 ; H. Thédenat, art. " Cura Aquarum," in **V**, i (2), 1615–17 ; Ett. di Ruggiero, art. " Aqua," in **XXVIII**, i, 544–56 ; L. Cantarelli, " La Serie dei Curatores aquarum," in **XXXV**, 1901, 180–214 ; D. Vaglieri, " Nuove Scoperte al Foro romano," *ibid.*, 1900, 71–3 ; **LXXXIV**.

Apart from bureaucracy in general, the Empire saw, if not the first blossoming, at least the expansion and growth to full maturity of great public services of a special kind—police, food-supply, fires, water, public buildings, and Tiber and drains. There were Prefects of the City for police, of the Corn-supply for food, and of the Watch for fires, and executive commissions (*curatelæ*) for water, public buildings, and the Tiber and drains. One of these services, by a happy chance, is particularly well known to us. In constitution, organization, and general development, the water-department in Rome offers us a definite example, the best known of all, thanks to the treatise of Frontinus, of that supremely original creation of the Romans, the great public services. These services were rudimentary under the Republic, since the oligarchy had neither the men nor the material means needed for their development ; under the Empire they gradually took on their complete and permanent form. But here again the political and administrative policies which dominate and, by their antagonism, condition the whole history of personal government are found confronted. The latter led, as early as Augustus, to the creation of specialist departments, strictly graded ; the former took the form of the control given to Senators of Consular or Prætorian rank. But in this particular domain we find the general evolution of the Roman administration complete in all its three aspects. The Equestrian order gradually superseded the Senatorial (an expert Procurator was created under Claudius, and thenceforward rose at the expense of the Senatorial head of the department) ; the public service became a strictly graded department under a great Imperial dignitary (in Rome, the Prefect of the City) ; and the staff gradually fell into the grip of the system of bureaucracy and rigid discipline which, under the Late Empire, became one of the fundamental principles of the whole Roman administration. The water-service, therefore, gives us a concrete picture, with all its virtues and vices, of what the Imperial administration became in the five centuries of its existence.

CHAPTER II

THE ADMINISTRATIVE UNIFICATION OF THE ROMAN WORLD

BIBLIOGRAPHY.—*Ancient Authors* : See pp. 201, 238, 274, above.

Administrative and Legal Documents : See p. 274 above.

Inscriptions : *Lex Julia Municipalis*, in *C.I.L.*, i, 2nd ed., 2, 593 ; *I.L.S.*, 6085 ; Municipal Laws of Salpensa (*ibid.*, ii, 1963 = *I.L.S.*, 6088) and of Malaga (*ibid.*, ii, 1964 = *I.L.S.*, 6089) ; Senatorial Album of Canusium (*ibid.*, ix, 338 = *I.L.S.*, 6121).

*Modern Works : **I**, 211–16 ; **X**, iii, 281–95 (E. Kornemann) ; **XCII** ; **LXXXI** ; **LXVI**a, Eng. pp. 119–29 (Italy), 130–412 (provinces). Egypt : **CXXXIII** ; **CXXXIX**, 6–16 ; **XCI**, and the administrative regulation regarding the Idiologos, recently discovered in a Berlin papyrus, T. Reinach, " Un Code fiscal de l'Egypte romaine : le gnomon de l'idiologue," in **XLVIII**, xliii (1919), 583–636 ; xliv (1920), 5–134 ; **CXXXI**, especially ii, 3–336, and suppl., 461–570 ; L. Homo, " Les Privilèges administratifs du Sénat sous l'Empire et leur disparition graduelle au cours du IIIe siècle," in **XLVII**, 1921 (cxxxvii), 161–203 ; (cxxxviii), 1–52.

I

ROME

AT the time when the Republican regime was abolished, the Roman State was without administrative unity. Three different elements entered into its composition—Rome and Italy (the domain of the city), protectorates, and provinces. The establishment of the Empire, far from automatically reducing this variety, increased it. The Principate, a body foreign to the traditional constitution, brought a new complication into the administration of Rome and Italy ; the provinces were divided into two distinct categories, Senatorial and Imperial ; and there entered into the Roman organization a country of a special type, Egypt, where the Emperor, as successor of the Ptolemies, had the authority of an absolute monarch. In the end unity emerged from this diversity, but it took three centuries to happen.

When the Empire was established, the town of Rome had long overflowed its traditional bounds. In the earliest days

*See also Supplementary Bibliography with Prefatory Note (p. 405)

of the Republic, the Aventine, the Velabrum, and the out-lying parts of the Quirinal, Viminal, Esquiline, and Cælian had become covered with houses. The Hill of Gardens (the present Pincian) had become a quarter of villas and parks, and the district across the Tiber, which had long preserved a purely rural character, had been transformed, through the proximity of the port, into one of the most populous quarters of the town. Lastly, large suburbs had grown up outside the so-called Wall of Servius Tullius, along the great roads which radiated from the city to the various parts of Italy—the Flaminian Way to the north, the Salarian, Nomentane, and Tiburtine to the north-east, the Prænestine and Labicane to the east, the Latin, Appian, and Ostian to the south, and the Aurelian to the west.

But, while the limits of the agglomeration had extended greatly through the centuries, the old administrative com-partments of the city properly so-called, the Urbs, which a tradition, perhaps too flattering, ascribed to King Servius Tullius, remained the same. The four traditional districts, Suburane, Esquiline, Palatine, and Colline, still covered only the centre of the city, while the Campus Martius, the Pincian, the plain across the Tiber, the Janiculum, and the suburbs remained outside. This abnormal, anachronistic state of things, which answered neither to the realities nor to the administrative necessities of the new age, could not continue. The creation of Imperial Rome was the work of Augustus.

Augustus not only enlarged the official city; he rearranged it. The Campus Martius and Pincian on the north, the Quirinal, Esquiline, and Cælian on the east, the principal suburbs, particularly those on the Flaminian, Appian, and Ostian Ways, and the plain to the west across the Tiber were annexed to the city. The Emperor then gave the enlarged capital a new organization, and divided it, on a strictly geographical principle, into fourteen districts (*regiones*). The old quarters of Republican Rome formed five districts in the centre (III, IV, VIII, X, XI), the newly annexed parts constituted four (V, VII, IX, XIV), and five were mixed (I, II, VI, XII, XIII). At first these new districts were known by their numbers. Later, in the fourth century, they were given topographical names in addition : I, Porta

Capena ;   II, Cælemontium ;   III, Isis and Serapis ;
IV, Temple of Peace ;   V, Esquiliæ ;   VI, Alta Semita ;
VII, Via Latina ;   VIII, Forum Romanum ;   IX, Circus
Flaminius ; X, Palatium ; XI, Circus Maximus ; XII, Piscina
Publica ;   XIII, Aventine ;   XIV, Transtiberim—but these
late denominations were probably of popular origin, and it
is not certain that they were ever official.   The district was
subdivided into wards (*vici*) whose number varied in different
districts and periods ;   there were 265 under Vespasian, 307
in the fourth century, and 424 just before the barbarian
invasions.

The administration of the city was brought into line with
the new organization in districts.   The district was a purely
topographical division, and neither governed itself nor
elected political representatives.   At its head one of the
urban magistrates of the year was placed, a Prætor, Ædile,
or Tribune, who was chosen by lot.   Severus Alexander,
true to his general policy of Senatorial restoration, raised
the dignity of this office by entrusting it to Consulars, and
gave the Senate a large share in the administration of the
city.   These magistrates in charge of districts had under
their orders one or two Curators to a district in the second
century, and two in the fourth, who were drawn from the
freedman class.

The ward or *vicus* was the centre of a local cult, a revival
of the old worship of the Lares of the Crossways (*Lares
compitales*), who, under the influence of the worship of the
Emperor, were given the name of Imperial Lares (*Lares
Augusti*).   Henceforward there was a shrine of the Lares
in each ward. at the principal street-crossing.   This local
worship was served by the magistrates of the ward (*vicomagistri*), four in number, who were chosen from the men
of middle status of the ward.   In the fourth century after
Christ, by an innovation the author of which is unknown,
the number of *vicomagistri* was made independent of that
of the *vici* and fixed at forty-eight for each district.

Both out of prudence and in pursuance of a local policy
bound up with its whole system, the Empire always made
a point, at least in appearance, of safeguarding Republican
traditions in respect of the administration of the capital.
Comitia, Senate, and magistracies kept their old powers.

But, in Rome as elsewhere, in spite of precautions of form, they were faced with the competition of the new Imperial magistrates, the Prefects of the City, Corn-supply, and Watch, and great executive commissions, the *curatelæ* of Public Buildings, Water, and Tiber. The evolution was completed at the beginning of the third century. From the Severi onwards, the old Roman city, shorn of its traditional character, was the *Urbs Sacra*, the City of the Emperor.

II

ITALY

Italy, since the *Leges Julia* and *Plautia Papiria* (90–89 B.C.), had been an integral part of the City like Rome itself. In spite of its size, its territory was not cut up into administrative districts, and the State was not represented there by permanent local officials ; these were two great points of difference from the traditional government of the provinces. As a collection of *municipia* with a citizen population (*conventus Italiæ*), it was one of the proudest boasts of Italy to be governed direct from Rome by the great organs of the City—Comitia, Senate, and magistracies. The Comitia passed laws for the whole State and appointed magistrates. The Senate, as guardian of Italy, had supreme control of the affairs of the peninsula, political, administrative, judicial, and financial. The magistrates (Consuls, Prætors, Quæstors) had charge of administration in general, while some of them, such as the Quæstor of Ostia, who looked after the food-supply, and the other Italian Quæstors, had special employments in various parts of the country.

The establishment of personal government and the very principle of monarchy necessarily created a great upheaval in the administration of Italy, the effects of which did not make themselves felt at once. In virtue of the constitutional act of 23, Augustus received the Proconsular *imperium* for Italian soil as well as for the rest of the Empire. Although prudence bade him disguise the effects, the opposition between survivals of the past and creations of the present, between the Senate and magistracies on one side and the

Emperor and his servants on the other, was as real in Italy as in Rome, a conflict of old traditions and present needs, an unequal struggle, in which the old powers were condemned to defeat and disappearance.

The Senate, under the Principate, retained its administrative privilege in Italy ; general administration and the control of local affairs continued, at least in theory, to be within its competence. The Emperors of the Julio-Claudian line even added to these powers a jurisdiction, appellate and of first instance, in Italian cases. But both prerogatives were attacked in the first century and disappeared in the second under the repeated assaults of the Imperial power and its agents. By the time of the military anarchy, the Italian privileges of the Senate, finally destroyed by the Severi, were no more than a memory.

The magistracies had the same fate. The Consuls, who had been the administrators and supreme judges of Italy under the Republic, were attacked in both capacities, their powers being transferred to the two great representatives of the Emperor, the Prefect of the City in Rome and within the 100,000 yards and the Prefect of the Prætorium in the rest of Italy. The Prætors lost their criminal jurisdiction to the same officials and in similar circumstances ; in civil cases their traditional jurisdiction was given to the Consulars and Juridici created by Hadrian and Marcus Aurelius, but at least they succeeded in keeping their competence in Rome and within the 100,000 yards. The creation of new Prætorships, such as that of Guardianships and that of Bequests on Trust, was a very small return for their humiliation. Finally, the last specifically Italian Quæstorships were abolished under Claudius in 44, and the college in charge of roads in the immediate environs of Rome (*Duumviri Viis extra Urbem Purgandis*) disappeared in the reign of Augustus, their duties being taken over by the Curators of the Roads of Italy.

The gradual absorption of Italian administration by the Emperor was effected by means of two kinds of officials, agents of centralization and agents of decentralization, the former being concentrated in Rome and the latter established in various districts in the country.

(a) *Italian agents of centralization.*—These were divided

into two classes, Prefects and executive commissions. Of the Prefects the most important was the Prefect of the Prætorium. He was the great military chief of Italy at the beginning of the Empire, and he subsequently became the supreme judge of the country. All the troops in Italy were under his command. These were, apart from the garrison of Rome, the constabulary (*stationarii*) posted about the country to preserve order and put down brigandage, the fleets of Misenum and Ravenna and, from Septimius Severus onwards, the legion II Parthica, which was encamped in the neighbourhood of the capital at the foot of the Alban Mount.

As vice-president of the Imperial Council, the Prefect of the Prætorium was the chief judge of Italian suits brought before that court by order of the Emperor or on appeal. In the second century, his competence in this respect was augmented by a very important power, that of criminal jurisdiction. In the preceding century, that jurisdiction had belonged to the Prefect of the City, who had gradually extended it from the town itself to the whole of Italy. But the Prefect of the City had neither the troops nor the police-force needed to exercise his authority over an area of that size, whereas the Prefect of the Prætorium, as commander-in-chief of the army in Italy, was in a much better position in this respect and inevitably came in the end to take the place of his colleague. But the Prefect of the City was not wholly deprived of his powers ; at the end of the second century, under Septimius Severus, the matter was settled by a division of competence between the rival Prefects. The Prefect of the City kept his criminal jurisdiction within the 100,000 yards, that is, in the district where he had the means to enforce it in practice.

The Prefect of the Prætorium was the chief instrument by which the Emperor exercised his *imperium* in Italy at the expense of the old organs of the Republic, but he was not the only one. The three town Prefects, those of the City, Corn-supply, and Watch, also played a part in this gradual encroachment. The authority of the Prefect of the City extended outside the town proper over the wider environs of Rome, to a distance of 100,000 yards, that is, over a considerable part of Central Italy. In that area, he had an *imperium* similar to that of the governor of a Senatorial province, the military power being given, as in the rest of Italy, to the Prefect of the Prætorium. His attributions were purely civil (administration of his district, command of the police) and judicial (criminal and civil). In this last respect, again, one should note that he came into competition with the Republican organs, the Senate, the Roman magistrates, and, in a less degree, the magistrates of the Italian *municipia*.

The Prefect of the Corn-supply, being in charge of the provisioning of the capital, had under his supervision the great ports by which goods came into Italy—Ostia, Portus Trajani, and Puteoli. There he had a large staff of all kinds to carry out his orders and enforce his decisions. The authority of the Prefect of the Watch extended to Ostia, where a detachment of the watch, furnished by the cohorts of the capital and relieved at intervals, acted as a fire-brigade, just as in Rome.

The executive commissions created by Augustus were, on principle, confined to the city. But there was an exception in the Water Commission, whose powers, as we have seen, covered the whole system of Roman aqueducts and necessarily extended over a great part of the environs of the city.

Lastly, there appear under the Empire two Imperial services which were more especially Italian. The Italian Roads Department (*cura viarum*) as we have seen, was created by Augustus in 20 B.C. The department of Provisions, instituted under Trajan, was ensured by the Curators of Roads for their respective districts, and these officials were called Prefects of Provisions (*præfecti alimentorum*) in addition to their previous title. In exceptional cases, from Marcus Aurelius to Macrinus, directors-general (*præfecti alimentorum*) of Consular rank centralized the supply of food to the whole of Italy in Rome.

(*b*) *Italian agents of decentralization.*—The territorial indivisibility of Italy and the direct subordination of the Italian burghs to the central government without any intermediate machinery were among the most ancient administrative privileges of the country. In the Late Empire, we shall find this exceptional situation gone and Italy divided into provinces like the other regions of the Roman State. That great transformation, due both to political causes and to administrative necessities, was not effected all at once, but in a series of stages covering more than three centuries.

A first step was an act of Augustus dividing Italy into eleven districts (*regiones*)—I, Latium and Campania ; II, Apulia and Calabria ; III, Lucania and Bruttium ; IV, Samnium ; V, Picenum; VI, Umbria; VII, Etruria; VIII, Æmilia (the country of the Boii, Ravenna, Ariminum) ; IX, Liguria ; X, Venetia and Istria ; XI, Western Transpadane Gaul. But it was still a very mild innovation. The new districts were not called by the name of provinces, and lacked that essential character-istic of a province, the presence of a governor representing the central power. Yet, in spite of all these prudent reserva-tions, a start had been made towards the administrative splitting-up of Italy, and nothing would stop it.

Struck by the chaos reigning permanently in the adminis-tration of Italy, particularly in the domain of justice, and by its ill effect on the successful conduct of affairs, Hadrian resolved upon a drastic step. Shortly after 120, he divided the peninsula into four judicial districts, to be intermediate between the organs of justice in Rome and the local authorities, and at the head of each he placed a Consular, a high official of Senatorial rank. The institution was keenly combated by the Senate, whose interests and prejudices were alike affected, and did not survive its author. Antoninus, in a spirit of conciliation, consented to abolish it. But it was not for long. Marcus Aurelius was compelled by administrative necessities to restore it, this time permanently, but he changed the title of the heads of districts from Consulars to Juridici and their rank from Consular to Prætorian.

For the administration of justice, Italy was now divided into four districts : Transpadane Gaul, which always kept the same boundaries, and three others which varied, but were generally the following : Etruria-and-Liguria, Umbria, and Southern Italy (Apulia, Calabria, Lucania, Bruttium), Central Italy being attached to óne or other of the adjoining districts. Rome and its environs remained outside this organization. The Italian Juridici had administrative and judicial powers. In administration, they had the general supervision of their district, dealt with provisions and the privileges of the colleges (*sodalicia*), and had a share in the appointment of the Advocates of the *Fiscus* ; in this respect, they were regarded as the natural intermediaries between the Italian burghs and the central power. In justice, the main part of their duties, while they did not possess criminal jurisdiction, which was reserved for the Prefect of the Prætorium, they had all civil jurisdiction (guardianships, bequests on trust, formal acts of adoption, manumission, etc.) and administrative jurisdiction (a share in the nomination of Decurions, the recruiting and supervision of municipal officials).

The beginning of the third century was marked by a third step in the same direction—the institution of the Italian Correctors. Under Caracalla, between 214 and 217, a Corrector, C. Octavius Suetrius Sabinus, was given the task of " correcting " or reforming the condition of Italy (*electus ad corrigendum statum Italiæ*). A second Corrector of the same kind, Pomponius Bassus, likewise a very high personage of the Senatorial order, held office about fifty years later, at the end of the reign of Gallienus or at the beginning of that of Claudius II. The powers of these new officials were on the whole similar to those of the governors of Imperial provinces. They had the *imperium* in the full sense of the word, with civil, military, and judicial attributions, but the effects of the innovation were toned down, at least in form, and its application was facilitated, by the fact that the Correctorship was an exceptional post, and there was only one for the whole of Italy. Both reservations were abolished, at least in part, in the reign of Aurelian (270–5). Aurelian made the office permanent, and, while preserving the general title of Correctors of Italy for all of them, he gave them certain districts to govern, in particular the first (Campania), third (Lucania), and tenth (Venetia). Diocletian had only to make this reform general, so taking another step towards the final abolition of the administrative privilege of Italy. The Juridici disappeared at the same time, and the Correctors took their place as permanent governors of the various Italian districts.

Another fact of the same kind, tending to the same result, was the interference of the central power in the municipal life of the Italian burghs ; it was discreet in the first century after Christ, but grew more marked in the second. The fact is certain, but the interpretation of it is open to discussion. Was it intentional encroachment on the self-government of the burghs ? Or a favour requested by the burghs themselves and granted by the Emperor ? Both theories contain a portion of truth, but both are exaggerated. The Emperor's intentions towards the Italian towns were not always evil, but the fact remains that the encroachment of the central power on the municipal life of Italy increased from the end of the first century after Christ. At that time, the burghs found themselves in a difficult and in some cases serious financial position. Carried away by the general prosperity which developed under the Roman Peace, they had spent money recklessly, chiefly on public works,. and had not always conceived their grandiose programmes in a duly methodical and prudent spirit. Moreover, having no civil personality, they could not be the object of legal donations, which might have restored the shaken balance of their budgets. To improve their financial position, Nerva decided that they might in the future be made legatees, and this permission was afterwards confirmed by Hadrian in more regular form. It presently became fashionable for individuals to make such bequests, to the great profit of the Italian burghs, whose revenues were considerably augmented from this source.

The Emperors gave proof of equal generosity, but, as might be expected, the burghs did not get these pecuniary advantages for nothing. They had to relinquish their financial autonomy and accept the control of the Imperial power in the person of a new official, the *Curator Reipublicæ* or *Curator Civitatis*. The Curator was appointed by the Emperor from the Senatorial or Equestrian order, according to the case. His functions were in essence financial—the supervision of municipal finance, the keeping of the landed or movable capital of the town—but, as usual, he also had a jurisdiction within the limits of his competence. The whole municipal budget, expenditure and revenue, came under the Curator. This interference was a delicate and often ungrateful task, and the Emperors tried to make it as tolerable as possible by hedging it round with a number of guarantees. Thus, the Curator was always an Italian, never a provincial, and, although he never belonged by birth to the town whose administration he had to control, at least the central power was careful to select him from a neighbouring or not too distant town. Lastly, the Emperor made a point of checking unnecessary or misplaced zeal. We must not, however, be blind to the despotic nature of the institution. In practice, the control of the Curator became more and more complete. In the fourth century, he had driven the local magistracies into the shade and had become the real head of the town.

By the accession of Diocletian, the process which had gradually stripped Italy of her privileges was complete in respect of politics; under Diocletian and Constantine, it reached its term in respect of administration, finance, and military matters.

Even before 292, Diocletian took up the administrative reform of Aurelian and completed it in so far as it was incomplete. Italy was divided into eight districts, Transpadane Gaul, Venetia and Istria, Æmilia and Liguria, Flaminia and Picenum, Etruria and Umbria, Campania and Samnium, Lucania and Bruttium, Apulia and Calabria, each of which was given a permanent Corrector. Moreover, the title of the office was simplified and even the pretence of indivisibility was abandoned. From 298, at the latest, a Corrector was no longer called Corrector of Italy for such-and-such a district, but simply Corrector of the particular district. Thenceforward he was, in name as in fact, a real governor of a province, and his district was a province like those of the rest of the Empire.

In the fifth century, there were eleven district administrators of Italy, seven being called Consulars, two *Præsides*, and only two, those of Lucania and Apulia, Correctors.

This was not all. Hitherto the Roman world had been divided, from the territorial and administrative point of view, into two quite distinct parts—Italy on the one hand and all the provinces on the other. Diocletian, in his general reorganization of the Empire, established two new administrative units—Dioceses and Prefectures of the Prætorium. Henceforward, every piece of the Empire was territorially part of a province, every province (except Asia and Africa, the governors of which came under the Emperor direct), part of a Diocese, and every Diocese part of a Prefecture. With this territorial scale went an administrative scale;

the province had a governor, the Diocese a Vicar, the Prefecture of the Prætorium a Prefect. Italy was treated like
the rest of the Empire; together with Rætia and the
islands of the Western Mediterranean (Sicily, Sardinia, and
Corsica), it formed the Diocese of Italy (*diœcesis Italiciana*),
and the three Dioceses of Italy, Africa, and Pannonia constituted the Prefecture of the Prætorium of Italy. Italy was
just one among the neighbouring provinces; like them, it
had its three officials, governors, Vicar, and Prefect of the
Prætorium, and in this respect as in others its administrative
privilege was a distant memory.

The abolition of the financial privilege of Italy was likewise
the work of Diocletian, and of two of his successors, Galerius
and Constantine. This important reform was dictated by two
chief considerations, one general and one purely opportunistic.
On the one hand, it was a part of the general policy of
Diocletian, who, in this matter as in others, aimed at completing the administrative unification which had been going
on since the beginning of the Empire. Moreover, when
Diocletian divided the Roman world into spheres of competence, Italy was permanently incorporated in one of those
areas. It was evidently impossible that, inside that organization, Italy alone should be exempt from the land-tax and
leave the adjoining provinces to bear the whole burden.
As the historian Aurelius Victor justly observes, the partition
of the Empire was what brought upon Italy " the great
evil of tribute ".[1]

In Diocletian's reign, a little before 292, a survey of
Italy was taken, and henceforward the country had to pay
the land-tax like the rest of the Empire. Galerius, on
becoming an Augustus with Constantius Chlorus in 305,
enforced the application of the reform systematically and
with the energy with which he did everything, and even
went further, making Italy liable not only to the land-tax
but to the capitation-tax paid by non-landowners in the
provinces, so that Italians not owning land henceforward
had to pay like the rest. The people of certain great cities
in the Empire were exempted from taxation by a law of
Diocletian; Galerius repealed it. The usurpation of
Maxentius in Italy delayed the execution of Galerius's

---

[1] Aurelius Victor, *De Caes.*, xxxix, 31.

decrees, but only for a short time. Maxentius himself, hard-driven by financial difficulties, had to re-establish the capitation-tax, which fell on the whole population, urban and rural. Lastly, when Constantine defeated Maxentius at the Milvian Bridge in 312, he resumed and finally completed the financial legislation of his predecessors in respect of the land-tax and capitation-tax, but prudently introduced two alleviations. Reviving a measure of Diocletian which Galerius had repealed, he exempted the townspeople of Rome from capitation-tax, and he seems to have abolished the old tax of Augustus on inheritances, a perfectly fair measure, since Italy now paid land-tax like the provinces, and this substitute tax was no longer justified. But this relief did not alter the facts. Italy paid taxes on the same terms and in the same form as the Provinces. It had finally lost its traditional immunity in financial matters.

The only military privilege left to Italy after the reign of Septimius Severus was the fact that the capital had special troops, the Prætorian and Urban Cohorts. Even these were special in name only, since they were now recruited just like the others, and this last shred of the ancient fiction disappeared when Constantine abolished the two corps altogether. So Italy, in military matters as in all others, was reduced to the rights common to the Roman world. By the beginning of the fourth century, its assimilation to the provinces was complete; the evolution of three centuries was at an end.

Only Rome enjoyed favoured treatment. It is true that under Diocletian it ceased to be the Emperor's residence and the centre of government, and the creation of Constantinople by Constantine, the expression of the military needs to which the Empire was now subject, and the con-secration of the predominance acquired since the third century by the Illyrian element, put an end to its privilege as the capital of the world. But at least, in the midst of the unified Empire, it preserved its old administration with its two sets of traditional organs. It kept its Senate, now nothing, or very little, more than a town council, its magistrates, and its Imperial officials. At the beginning of the fourth century, the town and its environs were detached from the Diocese of Italy and made into a special diocese.

M

It was a vain show, a last tribute paid to the stupendous past of the city and to the incomparable glory which still attached to its name. Nor did this arrangement long remain a peculiar privilege of Rome, for the new capital of Constantinople was before long placed on a footing of absolute equality with it in respect of administration.

III

THE PROVINCES

At the beginning of the Empire, the territory outside Italy subject to Roman rule comprised three distinct elements —protectorates, provinces, and Egypt.

The protectorates were vassal States, usually kingdoms, which kept the whole of their native institutions. Rome had the sovereign direction of their foreign policy and also, as far as she chose, of their internal affairs. This arrangement is found chiefly in the East, both in Europe (Thrace) and in Asia (Cappadocia, Galatia, Paphlagonia, Polemoniac Pontus, Abilene, Commagene, Chalcis, Judea, and the States of Damascus and the Nabatæan Arabs). In the West it is only found exceptionally (Mauretania in Africa, the kingdom of Cottius in the Alps). Moreover, it was by definition only a transitional system, and did not last long. The protectorates were gradually absorbed into the provincial system; the process began in the reign of Augustus and went on, quickly in the West and more slowly in the East, to terminate in the first years of the second century. In the West, Mauretania, a vassal kingdom under Kings Juba II and Ptolemy, was annexed at the beginning of the reign of Claudius and made into two provinces, Mauretania Cæsariensis (Western Algeria) and Mauretania Tingitana (Northern Morocco). The same fate befell the Cottian Alps under Nero. Before the middle of the first century, therefore, the protectorate system had ceased to exist in the West.

In the East, Galatia became a Roman province under Augustus, on the death of the last King, Amyntas (25 B.C.); Paphlagonia, rather later, about 5 B.C.; Judea, in A.D. 6; Cappadocia, under Tiberius, in A.D. 18; Thrace and the

Lycian Confederation, under Claudius, in 45 and 43 respectively; and Pontus, under Nero, in 63. The Syrian principalities (Abilene, Commagene, Chalcis) were annexed to the Province of Syria by the Emperors from Claudius to Domitian, and the Nabatæan State, conquered by Trajan, was made into a province under the name of Arabia in 105–6. Only a few protectorates were then left, outside the true territory of the Empire—the kingdom of the Cimmerian Bosphorus in Europe and, save for a short period of annexation (114–17), that of Greater Armenia in Asia.

By the side of the protectorates there were the provinces. The system of provincial administration established by Augustus did not remain unchanged all through the Early Empire. It underwent two important series of modifications —the gradual increase of the number of Imperial provinces and, among these provinces, the promotion of some from one category to another.

The increase of the number of Imperial provinces was due to three main causes—conquest, the transformation of protectorates into provinces, and the dividing up of existing provinces. On principle, all those recently conquered became Imperial provinces. These were, in order of date : under Augustus, Rætia and Noricum (15 B.C.), the Maritime Alps (14 B.C.), Mœsia (A.D. 6), and Pannonia (A.D. 10); under Claudius, Britain (A.D. 43); under Trajan, Arabia (105–6), Dacia (107), Armenia for a time (114–17), Assyria (115–17), and Mesopotamia, first in 115–17 and finally under Septimius Severus. The same treatment was applied to the protected countries which were made into provinces—under Augustus, Galatia (25 B.C.); under Tiberius, Cappadocia (A.D. 18); under Claudius, Mauretania Cæsariensis and Tingitana (41–2), Lycia-and-Pamphylia (42), and Thrace (46); under Nero, the Cottian Alps.

The dividing-up of provinces was in the interest both of the central power, to which over-powerful governors might be a danger, and of the provincials, who were better governed in consequence. Under Augustus, between 16 and 13 B.C., Gallia Comata was divided into three provinces, Belgica, Lugdunensis, and Aquitania, and this measure was completed in A.D. 17 by the abolition of the single governor-general. At the end of the first century or beginning of the second,

Epeiros, detached from Achaia, was made a separate province. Under Domitian, two new Gallic provinces, Upper Germany and Lower Germany, were permanently organized, and Mœsia was divided into Upper and Lower Mœsia. Under Trajan, the same thing was done to Pannonia, and about the same time the Pennine Alps were detached from Rætia. Under Septimius Severus, in 197, Britain was divided into Upper and Lower Britain, and, in 198, Syria into Syria Cœle and Syria Phœnice. In the same reign, Numidia was detached from Africa ; so too, provisionally under Caracalla, about 216, and finally from Diocletian onwards, Asturia-and-Gallæcia was separated from Tarraconensis. By these three processes the number of Imperial provinces was more than trebled by the time of Trajan's death, and, although we lack exact figures for the following period, we can at least conclude from the statistics of the Late Empire that at the end of the second century and beginning of the third provinces were divided up very extensively.

Nor was this all. As the Imperial provinces of the lower class, the Procuratorial provinces, became populated and Romanized, they rose one or more steps in the administrative scale. Rætia and Noricum were made Prætorian provinces under Marcus Aurelius, Thrace became Prætorian under Trajan, and Cappadocia became Consular under Vespasian. But this was not a general rule ; certain provinces, such as the Pennine, Cottian, and Maritime Alps, Epeiros, and Mauretania Cæsariensis and Tingitana, being of less importance, always remained in their original condition.

Lastly, by the side of the protectorates and true provinces, we must give a special place to Egypt. It was officially a province, but the Senatorial element was strictly excluded from it, and it was the personal property of the Emperor, wholly dependent on his administration and provided with special institutions, some of which, such as the Idiologos, the official in charge of the revenues, were survivals from the Ptolemaic kingdom. The Emperor was represented by a viceroy, the Prefect of Egypt, who belonged to the highest ranks of the Equestrian scale and commanded a large army, several legions strong.

The administrative unification of the Roman world, the great internal achievement of the Empire, for which Egypt, the typical Hellenistic monarchy absorbed into the Roman State, served as a model, may be summed up in three chief facts—the disappearance of the protectorates, the gradual abolition of the privileges of Italy, and the assimilation of the provinces one to another. We have spoken of the first ; let us pass on to the two others.

Italy had inherited from the Republican period a whole series of important privileges which gave her, as against the domain of the State outside Italy—protectorates and provinces—a peculiar and definitely favoured position. In justice, it was part of the City ; it was the only region in the Empire where a free man was a citizen by birth and, unless officially degraded, could not be anything else. In respect of administration, Italy was a collection of autonomous *municipia*, governed direct by the organs of the City without any intermediate machinery. In respect of finance, Italy, unlike the provinces, paid no land-tax. In military matters, lastly, Italy was the domain of the civil *imperium*, and under the constitution provincial armies could not enter it. This favoured position of Italy Augustus had been careful to maintain. After the creation of the Principate, as before, the peninsula was the centre of all political and administrative organization.

But in this domain as in others the national needs which were drawing the Roman State along the road to unification and centralization soon began to exert their growing influence.

Even in the early Empire, these various privileges were assailed by the Imperial power and began to collapse one after another. The judicial privilege gradually decreased in importance as the number of citizens in the provinces grew larger, and disappeared the day when the Edict of Caracalla conferred the citizenship on all the inhabitants of the Empire. The administrative privilege was damaged by the intervention of the Emperors in the administration of the Italian burghs from the time of the first Antonines onwards, by the control obtained by the Imperial power over the general government of Italy, which was complete under the Severi, and by the creation of district officials and the division of Italy into provincial areas, reforms which had been started in the first two centuries by Augustus and Hadrian and assumed their final shape after the military anarchy, under Aurelian and Diocletian. The financial privilege, in spite of disturbing symptoms like the extension of Italian rights to certain parts of the provinces, was maintained intact until the decisive measures of Diocletian, Galerius, and Constantine.

Lastly, the military privilege received a severe blow at the very beginning of the Empire. The Emperor had established his general headquarters, his *prætorium*, in Italy, and he maintained there, to protect his person, a permanent guard, the main nucleus of which was formed by the Prætorian and Urban Cohorts. But, true to his policy of circumspection and prudence, Augustus had at least been careful to observe two precautions : the Prætorian and Urban Cohorts were entirely recruited among the Italians, and the legions, the provincial army, were rigorously kept out of the country. Both reservations soon disappeared. Even in the first century, the shortage of men had made it necessary to open the garrison of Rome to provincials from Spain, Noricum, and Macedonia, and Septimius Severus systematically excluded Italians from the guard, giving their places to legionaries from the provinces, and especially to trustworthy Illyrians. During the first two centuries, the Italian garrisons had been reinforced by other provincial elements, *equites singulares* and *frumentarii.* ' Septimius Severus took the decisive step, and a legion, II Parthica, was for the first time permanently established on Italian soil. From that moment, the military privilege of Italy, or rather the fiction which was all that was left of it, was gone. Constantine, by abolishing the Prætorian Cohorts, put the finishing touch to an evolution which had been going on for three centuries.

The unification of the provinces was, lastly, the result of two concordant tendencies, the unification of the provinces with Italy, and their unification with one another. The extension of the citizenship, which gradually bridged the legal gulf separating Italy from the provinces, was one of the most potent and efficacious instruments for the unification of the world. The citizenship was already widely spread in the provinces, when, in 212, Caracalla issued his

Edict,[1] the *Constitutio Antoniniana*, which at a stroke conferred the much-desired privilege on all free inhabitants of the Empire who did not possess it already, except the large class of *dediticii*. The measure was the crowning act of a very old policy rather than a legal revolution, but, by officially consecrating the unification of Italy and the provinces, it was a turning-point in the history of Italy and of the world.

The administrative unification of the two great classes of provinces, Senatorial and Imperial, followed a parallel course. By the settlement of 27 B.C., the Emperor not only was absolute and sole master in his own provinces, but could interfere in those of the Senate, both in practice and by right. In particular, he could, if necessary, take over the administration of any Senatorial province, and there are many instances of this in the history of the Early Empire—Illyricum in 11 B.C., Sardinia in A.D. 6, Macedonia from 15 to 44, Bithynia shortly after 160, and Bætica about 172. In such cases, the Emperor usually gave the Senate something to compensate it for the deprivation. In 22 B.C., even before he took away Illyricum, Augustus gave the Senate Cyprus and Narbonensis ; in A.D. 67, when Nero solemnly proclaimed the independence of Achaia, he restored Sardinia to the Senate ; about 172, Marcus Aurelius again gave Sardinia to the Senate in exchange for Bætica. But, apart from the fact that these exchanges were not always to the advantage of the Senate, the Emperor could take a province back from it without any compensation. Thus, Trajan took Bithynia from the Senate for a time and governed it direct through his Legates.

In the course of the first two centuries of the Empire, the intervention of the Imperial power in the administration of the Senatorial provinces steadily increased. Two things are especially characteristic in this respect—the appropriation by the Emperor of appointments of Senatorial governors and the abolition of the special financial organization of the

---

[1] Ulpian, cited in the *Digest*, i, 5, 17 ; Dion Cass., lxxvii, 9. The text is given in Greek in an abridged form in *Greichische Papyri zu Giessen* (see ref. on p. 377, below), No. 40, pp. 29 ff., 164 ff., and in **CXI**, i, 1, 55 ff. ; ii, 1, 288 ff. ; ii, 2, No. 377. There is an allusion to the *Constitutio Antoniniana* in the inscription on the triumphal arch at Volubilis in Mauretania Tingitana, *I.L.A.*, 608 ; cf. A. Piganiol, " Note sur l'inscription de l'arc de triomphe de Volubilis," in **XLIV**, 1924 (1), 114–16.

Senatorial provinces. Constitutionally and normally, the Emperor had no say in the appointment of Senatorial governors, which was done by the Senate alone, by drawing lots. In the end, however, he obtained the legal right to nominate these governors, an important innovation which was brought about in two stages, first collective appointment and then individual appointment. The first step was taken in the reign of Severus Alexander; the Emperor himself drew up the two lists of candidates for the Senatorial provinces, Consulars and Prætorians, the number of names being equal to that of the provinces, and the candidates in each class merely had to draw lots among themselves for the governorships. The second and final stage ended in direct appointment by the Emperor, as in the case of the Imperial provinces. This reform was very probably the work of Gallienus. In virtue of the edict of 261, that Emperor had debarred Senators from the government of Imperial provinces. The measure which transferred the appointment of the governors of Senatorial provinces to the Emperor was conceived in the same spirit and was logically connected with the other. It was justified not so much by a systematic policy of opposition to the Senate as by the urgent needs of national defence resulting from the terrible crisis in which the Roman Empire was then floundering.

By definition, the Senatorial provinces were unarmed provinces (*inermes*), and, unlike those of the Imperial provinces, their governors had only civil powers. They were, moreover, internal provinces, far from the frontiers, and consequently the army had nothing to do there. Now, in the reign of Gallienus, when the crisis of the third century was at its worst, the breakwater of the frontiers was broken in by the barbarians and the whole Empire was invaded. Consequently, all or almost all the Senatorial provinces became the zone of the armies. In the course of the first two centuries, when, for any reason, such as invasion from outside or internal disorders, troops had to be sent to a Senatorial province, the Emperor had transformed it temporarily into an Imperial province and then taken the necessary action. This had been done, for example, to Illyricum in 11 B.C. and to Bætica about A.D. 172. Gallienus was only doing the same thing, with the important difference that, since all the Senatorial provinces had to be protected at the same time, he did it to them all. At the same time as he took the government of the Imperial provinces away from the men of the Senate, he treated the Senatorial provinces in a similar way, claiming the direct, personal appointment of the governors for himself. With the Senatorial restoration under Tacitus, which repealed the measures of Gallienus, and the conciliatory policy of Probus, the old Senatorial provinces reappeared. But this revival did not last long. Diocletian made an end of it. From the last years of the third century onwards, all governors of provinces, of those which had been Senatorial and those which had been Imperial alike, were uniformly and without exception appointed by the Emperor.

At the very time when the Senate was losing all share in the appointment of Senatorial governors, it also lost the financial privileges, the collection of the direct tax in particular, which had been reserved for it in this domain by the partition of 27 B.C. Although we do not know it for certain, it is logical to suppose that Gallienus was responsible for this deprivation as for the other. It is probable that, in this matter as in so many others, Diocletian did no more than confirm a previous reform and systematize a change which had already been accomplished.

As for Egypt, the introduction of the system of Curiæ under Septimius Severus, about 202, and the general extension of the municipal system in the first years of the third century prepared the way for the complete assimilation of the country to the rest of the Roman world.

The levelling-up of the administration was completed in the Late Empire by four series of measures.

(i) *Assimilation of Provinces.*—Egypt lost its previous administrative unity and was divided into three districts, Jovian Egypt, Herculian Egypt, and the Thebaïd. Simultaneously and symmetrically, Italy and Egypt, administratively the antipodes of the Early Empire, were both turned into provinces. The administrative unity of the Roman State was now complete.

(ii) *Breaking up of Provinces.*—The breaking-up of provinces, which had been commenced during the first three centuries, went on in the Late Empire. In 297, there were ninety-six provinces, including those of Italy ; in 369, there were a hundred and four ; in 385, a hundred and thirteen ; at the beginning of the fifth century, a hundred and twenty. This process was due to reasons of a political kind, the desire to weaken the power of the governors, and of an administrative kind, the desire to ensure good government.

(iii) *Separation of the Civil and Military Powers.*—The traditional *imperium* meant the possession of the whole executive power, civil and military, by one man, and when Augustus established personal government he maintained this old conception of the ancient city-system intact. Diocletian, applying a principle taken, like so many others, from the administrative system of the Hellenistic monarchies, separated the civil power from the military in the provinces (a first step towards Constantine's application of the same principle to the central administration). The military power was taken from the governors and given to the heads of military districts, called Dukes (*duces*). The governors, now called by the generic name of Rectors (*rectores*) and divided into four classes (Proconsuls, Consulars, Correctors, and Præsides) according to the importance of the province, possessed, save in a very few cases, only civil powers, administrative, financial, and judicial.

(iv) *Creation of Intermediate Organs.*—Under the Early Empire, there was no intermediate organ between the central power and the province. This defect entailed many disadvantages, two of which were particularly grave ; the central administration was overwhelmed by business, especially the appeals which came pouring in from every quarter of the Roman world, and the local administration, being far from supervision, often took things too easily. Moreover, the great size of the Empire, the diversity of races which it contained, and the number of economic interests conflicting within it naturally led, as regards administration, to the formation of district organizations. The crisis of the third century and the temporary collapse of the Imperial unity which ensued not only revealed in acute form the fundamental opposition of the Greek and Latin worlds, but, in the absence of a central power, led to the creation of local Empires—the Gallo-Roman Empire in the West and the Empire of Macrianus, followed by the Palmyrene

State, in the East. These were transitory appearances, no doubt, but they were significant symptoms, by which a wary statesman like Diocletian would not fail to profit. Moreover, as early as the middle of the third century Emperors had not hesitated, under the pressure of political and administrative necessities, to take a step in that direction deliberately. In 256, Valerian and Gallienus had divided the territory of the Empire, the former taking the East and the latter the West. These needs and these precedents gave rise, in the Late Empire, to two series of intermediate organs. The Prefectures were large districts varying in number at first and permanently fixed at four in the course of the fourth century ; the Dioceses were subdivisions of the Prefectures and collections of provinces, numbering twelve under Diocletian and fourteen at the beginning of the fifth century. The former were governed each by a Prefect of the Prætorium, who was a purely civil official after the reform of Constantine, and the latter by a Vicar, who was purely civil from the beginning and always.

Lastly, there were special officials, coming directly under the central power—Count-inspectors (*comites*), *Notarii* or secretaries of the Consistory, *Agentes in Rebus*—who provided the permanent control of local administration which was needed.

CHAPTER III

THE ADMINISTRATIVE PERSONNEL

BIBLIOGRAPHY.—*Ancient Authors* : See above, pp. 201, 238, 274.
Administrative and Legal Documents : See above, p. 274.
Inscriptions : *C.I.L.*, ii ff., *passim*, especially vol. vi (cf. *I.L.S.*) ;
for details of various careers, see above, p. 299.
Modern Works : **LXXXV,** especially 343–486 ; **III,** 157–250
(the Emperor), 91–111 (Senatorial career under the Early Empire),
112–29 (Equestrian career, do.), 129–34 (administrative careers after
Diocletian), 134–56 (lower careers in general) ; **CXXXI,** ii, 3–336,
and suppl., 461–570 ; A. von Domaszewski, " Die Rangordnung
des römischen Heeres," in **XXXIV,** cxvii (1908), 1–278 (army
grades) ; **LXXIX,** 107–98 (do. in the late Empire) ; **I,** 236–51 ;
VII, i, 100–20, 190–5 ; **XCIV** ; **XCVIII** ; **CI** ; **CXXXIII** ; O.
Hirschfeld, " Die Rangtitel der römischen Kaiserzeit," in **LI,** 1901
(i), 579–610 ; C. Lécrivain, art. " Officiales, Officium," in **V,** iv (1),
155–9 ; and the articles by L. Cantarelli quoted above, p. 299.

I

THE EARLY EMPIRE : CAREERS AND SALARIES

THE bureaucracy which was one of the most characteristic
creations of the Empire was also one of the most complicated. This was due to deep-seated reasons, bound up with
the very conception of the Empire. Augustus, who neither
could nor would dispense with the services of the Senatorial
aristocracy, could not and would not entrust it with the sole
administration of the Empire. From the beginning,
therefore, the administrative personnel of the Empire was
not homogeneous in origin, social position, or prospects of
preferment. Two series of careers were open to officials
of the different categories—the higher careers, Senatorial
and Equestrian, and the lower, civil and military.

The Senatorial career [1] was the highest and, in theory
at least, the most honourable. It was the administrative
form in which the old nobility, willingly or otherwise, entered
the service of personal government. It was a legacy of
the Republican past, but, while Augustus and his successors

[1] **III,** 91–111.

*See also Supplementary Bibliography with Prefatory Note (p. 405)

maintained its fundamental principle, the mixed character in which, by the ancient tradition of the Republic, military and civil powers were combined, they made it subject to new regulations. It required two fundamental qualifications, Senatorial birth and the minimum property of 1,000,000 sesterces demanded by the Senatorial census. This career supplied the Senate, part of the Imperial Council, the magistracies, and a certain number of high offices in Rome, Italy, and the provinces.

There were six chief stages. Two of these were preparatory ; a man had to hold a post on the Vigintivirate, as *Decemvir Stlitibus Judicandis* (jurisdiction regarding the status of citizens), *Triumvir Auro, Argento, Ære Flando Feriundo* (the coinage of copper money in the name of the Senate), *Triumvir Capitalis* (judicial and police work, involving the execution of death-sentences), or *Quatuorvir Viis in Urbe Purgandis* (management of the streets of the city), and he had to do a year's military service as Tribune *laticlavius* (after the Vigintivirate from the Flavians onwards, often before it in earlier times). Then came the four Senatorial magistracies properly so-called, the Quæstorship, for which the minimum age was twenty-five, the Tribuneship of the Plebs or Plebeian Ædileship, two magistracies which under the Empire represented the same step in the scale and, as their title shows, were only held by Plebeians, the Prætorship, at the minimum age of thirty, and lastly, at the minimum age of thirty-three, the Consulship, Ordinary or Suffect.

Apart from this succession of magistracies, men of the Senatorial order might fill a certain number of posts in Rome, Italy, and the provinces. These posts were divided into three categories, Quæstorian, Prætorian, and Consular, each being legally held after the corresponding magistracy. Moreover, in each series there was an exact order of rank, according to the nature of the duties and the importance of the province in which they were performed. The chief of these Senatorial offices were as follows. The Quæstorian offices were those of Legates of the governors of Senatorial provinces. The Prætorian posts were those of Legates of legions and Legates governing Prætorian Imperial or Prætorian Senatorial provinces. The Consular posts were

those of Prefect of the City, members of certain executive
commissions in Rome, governors of Consular Senatorial
provinces, and Legates governing Consular Imperial provinces.
Lastly, a member of the Senatorial order might hold a
priesthood, as Pontifex, Augur, Fetialis, Flamen, Arvalis,
Lupercus, *Quindecimvir Sacris Faciundis*, Salius, *Septemvir
Epulonum*, or *Sodalis Augustalis*.

The Senatorial career was mixed and, in virtue of the
traditional principle of the combination of powers, comprised
civil, military, and judicial functions. These legal arrangements were maintained as a whole until the crisis of the
third century. Only one noteworthy change should be
mentioned : after Caracalla, the Military Tribuneship ceased
to be obligatory before the Quæstorship. One last point :
this Senatorial nobility bore a generic title, that of
Clarissimi, which had an official meaning from Hadrian
onwards.

The Equestrian career,[1] unlike the Senatorial, was a creation
of Augustus, and was the great administrative invention of
the Empire. It was re-fashioned by Claudius, the author
of the system of the *tres militiæ*, and by Hadrian, who completed its constitution by giving a place in it to the office
staff and great officials of the Court and permanently
establishing its status. Admission to this career was henceforward subject to two conditions—possession of the minimum
property required for the Equestrian order in the past
(400,000 sesterces) and, a new restriction, the right to a
" public horse ", that is, inscription in an active or honorary
capacity on the list of Knights *equo publico*, which was drawn
up under the Emperor's supervision and included those who
were Knights by birth and those who had been raised to the
order by special favour. The Equestrian career supplied men
for part of the Imperial Council and for a certain number
of executive offices. It was mixed in character, like the
Senatorial career and in virtue of the same principle.

A preliminary condition was military service in one or
more Equestrian posts (as Prefect or Tribune of an auxiliary
cohort, Tribune *angusticlavius* of a legion or of a cohort of the
Roman garrison, Prefect of a wing of cavalry), usually in
that ascending order, which was permanently established

[1] III, 112–29.

by Hadrian's regulations.   The average age of Military Tribunes of the Equestrian order was twenty-five years.

Between the ages of twenty-seven and thirty, that is, rather later than in the Senatorial career, a man started upon the Equestrian career properly so called, in which there were two big stages.   First, there were the junior Procuratorships, chiefly financial, the higher posts of Procurators governing provinces, whose duties were both civil and military, and, at the top of the scale, those of Procurator *a Rationibus* (minister of finance), chiefs of offices of the secretariat, Sub-prefects of the Corn-supply, Watch, and Navy, and Equestrian members of the Imperial Council. Secondly, there were the Prefectships, some purely civil (the Corn-supply), the greater number military (one of the Italian fleets) or mixed (Egypt, the Watch, the Prætorium, the last office being the top of the Equestrian tree, the " field-marshal's baton " of the Knight).   To this list one must add some priesthoods of a lower class (Haruspices, Luperci). All through, the Equestrian career was of a mixed civil and military character.

Certain important changes were subsequently made in the Equestrian career, chiefly because administration became a larger and more complicated task.   In the reign of Hadrian, a turning-point in the genesis of the Roman bureaucratic system, a severe blow was dealt to the old principle of combination of powers, and, although it did not disappear altogether, at least we find a purely civil Equestrian career emerging, in which the preliminary military service is replaced by administrative offices (the new post of Advocate of the *Fiscus* and other subordinate employments).   In the time of Septimius Severus, the post of centurion was attached to the Equestrian military service, as a preliminary stage, if not as an essential part.   The result of this important innovation was that the whole Equestrian career, civil functions no less than high commands, was open, in the form of a new Equestrian career, to soldiers risen from the ranks.   The invasion of that career by the army and the resulting militarization of the civil service were a fundamental characteristic of the bureaucracy of the Empire from the third century onwards. Lastly, under Hadrian and permanently under the last Antonines, the administrative order of rank within the

Equestrian career was accompanied by a scale of honorary appellations which were true titles of nobility—*Viri Egregii* (*primipili*, Prefects of Wings, junior Procurators), *Viri Perfectissimi* (first-class Procurators, Prefects of the Corn-supply and Watch, *A Cognitionibus*), *Viri Eminentissimi* (Prefects of the Prætorium and, from Septimius Severus onwards, of Mesopotamia and Egypt)—all of which titles, unlike that of Clarissimus, reserved for the Senatorial and hereditary nobility, kept a strictly personal character.

The Prefecture of the Prætorian was the summit of the Equestrian career, but a Knight might rise still higher and enter the Senatorial career. This he did by the process of *adlectio*, by which he was promoted either to the rank of ex-Tribune (*adlectio inter Tribunicios*) or to that of ex-Prætor (*adlectio inter Prætorios*), which in the end became the rule. This favour gave him the right of holding offices reserved for the corresponding class of the Senatorial order. The Emperor made use of this convenient procedure to admit capable Knights to the Senatorial career, so turning the Equestrian order into a kind of nursery for the Senate.

Magistrates and officials were equally the Emperor's assistants. Their careers had one characteristic in common; in accordance with the Republican tradition, at least down to the second century, it was both military and civil. But their respective status entailed certain differences in their position, two of which were fundamental. (1) Mode of appointment. The magistrates were the representatives of the Roman people, and the traditional principles of annual office and election were maintained in their case. The officials, whether of the Senatorial or of the Equestrian order, were delegates of the Emperor, who appointed them without any time-limit and recalled them at his pleasure. (2) Salary. To represent the Roman people was an honour; therefore, in conformity with the Republican tradition, the magistrates still exercised their functions for nothing. The officials of all ranks, on the other hand, received a fixed salary in proportion to the importance of their duties. The practice was commenced by Augustus, who founded the system, and completely organized by Hadrian, who has a place of honour in the history of the Imperial bureaucracy. The following are some figures. The highest provincial office, the Senatorial governorship of Africa, and doubtless also that of Asia, carried a salary of 1,000,000 sesterces. We have no exact information for the other Senatorial posts, but their salaries must have ranged between the above figure and that of 300,000 sesterces, the highest pay received by officials of the Equestrian order.

The Equestrian salaries comprised four rates :—

(a) *Sexagenarii*,[1] receiving 60,000 sesterces, the lowest salary. In Rome, all higher employees of the central administration—the clerk in charge of Greek Correspondence (*ab epistulis Græcis*), the assessor (*consiliarius*) of the Prefects of the Prætorium and City, the Procurator *ab Actis Urbis*, directors of public libraries, the assistant of the Prefect of the Corn-supply (*adjutor præfecti annonæ*), the Vice-director of Inheritances (*promagister hereditatium*), the Procurator of the Great Gladiatorial School (*procurator ludi magni*), the Sub-curator of Sacred Buildings and Public Works (*subcurator ædium sacrarum et operum locorumque publicorum*), the assistant of the Tiber Conservancy (*adjutor alvei Tiberis*), the Procurator of Pavements (*procurator silicum*), that of Urban Districts (*procurator regionum sacræ Urbis*), that of the Minicia (*procurator ad Miniciam*), and that of the Property of Condemned Persons (*procurator ad bona damnatorum*).

In Italy, the official in charge of the Corn-supply (*ad annonam*) at Ostia, the Procurators of the *Ratio Privata* (*per Tusciam et Umbriam, per Salariam Tiburtinam*, etc.), Curators and Sub-curators of Roads (*curator et subcurator viarum*), Procurators of Provisions (*procuratores alimentorum*), and the Sub-prefects of the Italian fleets.

In the provinces the junior Procurators, chiefly financial —the Epistrategi of Egypt, the *Ad Diocesim* of Alexandria, the Procurator of the Corn-supply in Narbonensis (*procurator annonæ provinciæ Narbonensis*), the Procurators of the *Ratio Privata* in Bithynia and Mauretania Cæsariensis (*procuratores rationis privatæ per Bithyniam, per Mauretaniam Cæsariensem*), Census-officials (*censitores*), the Procurators of the Troop of Gladiators (*procuratores familiæ gladiatorum*), Patrimony (*procuratores patrimonii*), and Twentieth on Inheritances (*procuratores vicesimæ hereditatium*), the Prefects of Vehicles (*præfecti vehiculorum*), the Prefects of the provincial fleets of Alexandria, Mœsia, Pannonia, and Syria

[1] A. v. Domaszewski, in **XXXIV**, cxvii (1908), 160–9 ; **LXXXV**, 440–1.

(*Alexandrina, Mœsiaca, Pannonica, Syriaca*), and the Advocates of the Fiscus (*advocati fisci*).

(*b*) *Centenarii*,[1] receiving 100,000 sesterces. In Rome, the clerk in charge of Latin Correspondence (*ab epistulis Latinis*), the Procurators of the Mint (*procurator monetæ*), Morning Gladiatorial School (*procurator ludi matutini*), Water (*procurator aquarum*), and Public Works (*procurator operum publicorum*), the *A Commentariis* of the Prefect of the Prætorium, the Advocate of the Fiscus, and the Sub-prefects of the Corn-supply and Watch.

In Italy, the Procurator of the *Ratio Privata* for the District of Ariminum (*procurator rationis privatæ regionis Ariminensium*) and the Prefect of Vehicles *per Flaminiam*.

In the provinces, the financial Procurators of Prætorian Imperial provinces (Upper and Lower Dacia, Galatia, Cilicia, Arabia, etc.), the Procurators governing (*procuratores præsides*) the Alpine provinces (Graian, Cottian, and Maritime Alps), the Procurators of Prætorian Senatorial provinces (Sicily, Macedonia, Crete, etc.), those of Neapolis and Pelusium in Egypt (*procurator Neapoleos, procurator Pelusii*), of indirect taxation in the provinces, such as the *vectigal* in Illyricum and the *quadragesima Galliarum*, of the Imperial mines (silver in Pannonia, iron in Dalmatia—*argentariæ Pannoniæ, ferrariæ Delmatiæ*), and of the Imperial domains in Africa (of the District of Hadrumetum and of the *tractus* of Carthage and Theveste—*regio Hadrumetica, tractus Carthaginiensis, tractus Thevestinus*), and Prefects of the provincial fleets of Britain, Germany, and the Euphrates (*Britannica, Germanica, Parthica*).

(*c*) *Ducenarii*,[2] receiving 200,000 sesterces. In Rome, the Procurators at the head of departments—Inheritances (*procurator hereditatium*), the Patrimony (*procurator patrimonii*), the Twentieth on Inheritances (*procurator vicesimæ hereditatium*)—the Postmaster General (*præfectus vehiculorum*), the *Magister Rei Privatæ*, and the *Magister a Studiis*.

In Italy, the Prefects of the Prætorian fleets of Misenum and Ravenna.

In the provinces, the Procurators of Consular Imperial provinces (Spain, Cappadocia, Syria, etc.), those of Prætorian

---

[1] A. v. Domaszewski, art. cit., 153–60 ; **LXXXV**, 439–40.
[2] Domaszewski, art. cit., 141–53; **LXXXV**, 438–9.

Imperial provinces comprising more than one province (Lugdunensis and Aquitania, Belgica and the two Germanies, Asturia and Gallæcia in Spain), the financial Procurators of Consular Senatorial provinces (Asia, Africa), the Procurators governing (*procuratores præsides*) Imperial provinces which had once been kingdoms (Thrace, Osrhoëne, the Mauretanias) and also Rætia and Noricum, the Procurators of indirect taxation in the provinces (*vectigal Illyrici, IV Publica Africæ*), and high officials of Egypt like the *Idiologos* and *Juridicus*.

(d) *Trecenarii*,[1] receiving 300,000 sesterces. In Rome, the great chiefs of the central administration—Prefect of the Prætorium, heads of offices of the secretariat, director of Finance (*a rationibus*), and director of the Private Estates (*rationis privatæ*)—and of the urban administration—Prefects of the Corn-supply and Watch. In the provinces, the two highest Prefect-governors, those of Egypt and Mesopotamia.

The lower careers,[2] like the higher, fell into two main classes, but here the difference was not one of rank, but of character, one being civil and the other military.

(1) *Lower civil career*.[3] This career comprised all the lower-grade officials (*officiales*) of the public services—cashiers (*tabularii*), records-clerks (*commentarienses, librarii*), dispatch-clerks (*scribæ*), assistants of all kinds (*adjuvæ*), various employees and workmen of the Mint (*exactores, signatores*), paving department (*pavimentarii*), water (*aquarii*), and baths (*thermarii*), watchmen (*custodes, villici*), ushers (*apparitores*), lictors (*lictores*), heralds (*præcones*), and janitors (*æditui*), who were often freeemen or slaves. To this large and complex category we must attach the services of the Court and Imperial household, most of whose personnel did not belong to the public services.

(2) *Lower military career*.[4] Whereas the posts of senior and general officers were so many stages in the Senatorial and Equestrian careers, those of junior and non-commissioned officers constituted a lower military career, independent and self-contained. The bottom rung was the ranks (*miles gregarius*), and the top was normally the post of centurion

---

[1] Domaszewski, art. cit., 183.
[2] **III**, 134–56.
[3] *C.I.L.*, vi, *passim*, esp. 1802, 31827–78 (*I.L.S.*, 1473–1876, 9024–51).
[4] *C.I.L.*, iv, *passim*, esp. 2375–3670, 32515–3061 (*I.L.S.*, 2012–774, 2815–914, 9061–202, 9218–27).

in the infantry and of decurion in the cavalry. There were two main grades in this career—non-commissioned officers and junior officers.

The private soldier, after serving for a time which varied in length, might, by his capacity or services, become a non-commissioned officer (*principalis*), and, as such, be given one of two appointments. In the fighting troops, he would become centurion's assistant (*optio*) in the infantry, decurion's assistant (*duplicarius, sesquiplicarius*) in the cavalry, *tesserarius*, who took the commander's orders, ensign (*aquilifer, signifer, imaginifer*), instructor (*doctor, campidoctor, exercitator*), or orderly N.C.O. to generals or senior officers (*cornicularius, singularis, secutor tribuni, adjutor tribuni*). Or he might be given office work, as accountant (*librarius, notarius, codicillarius*) or cashier (*tabularius, capsarius*), or in the commissariat (*horrearius, pecuarius, lanius*), armoury (*armorum custos*), or hospital (*optio valetudinarii*).

The second stage was that of junior officer—centurion in the infantry (legions or auxiliary corps) and decurion in the cavalry. Of the centurions, those commanding maniples were of higher rank than the rest, and the first centurion of the whole legion, the *primipilus*, was a man trusted by the senior officers, whom he replaced in case of need, and therefore had a special position among the juniors.

On principle, in conformity with the general organization of Roman society, the lower careers, civil and military, were closed and self-contained. In practice, although only as an exception, the higher careers were not altogether inaccessible, and the Emperors did not hesitate on occasion to promote deserving men from the lower careers to higher posts. Civil officials, after going through the lower civil career, might rise in the administrative scale and enter the Equestrian career, either by holding certain intermediate offices or by obtaining enrolment on the Equestrian lists by an Imperial decree. Mixed careers of this kind were not infrequent in the Empire.

We find the practice more frequently in the case of the lower military career, from which, in the face of the growing needs of the army and national defence, the Emperors had to take men in greater and greater numbers as time went on. First, the post of Prefect of the Camp (*præfectus castrorum*), who looked after the guarding and upkeep of the legionary camps, was reserved by the Imperial power for centurions. From Domitian, it was an absolute rule that there was never more than one legion in a camp, and that legion was usually the same. In consequence, the Prefect of the Camp tended to become an executive officer, a senior officer of the legion in question, and his position in the military scale rose accordingly. Moreover, for motives both of military efficiency and of personal security, the Emperor entrusted men who had been *primipili* with the duties of senior officers in the troops of the garrison of Rome, as Tribunes of the Urban and Prætorian Cohorts and those of the Watch. Lastly, junior officers might rise still higher by receiving the " public horse " admitting them to the Equestrian career, and in exceptional cases they might even be raised by *adlectio* to the Senatorial career, and so to the regular functions to which these two higher careers gave access. This tendency continued during the second century and became more marked under the Severi. Hadrian placed the new bodies of infantry called *numeri* under the command of former centurions, whom he raised to the rank of *præpositi*. Extraordinary commands of detachments (*vexillationes*) or armies of operations were created outside the regular organization, and given to especially deserving junior officers, as chiefs of *vexillationes* or even of armies (*duces*). Lastly, Septimius Severus made the post of centurion a preliminary stage to the Equestrian career, a radical measure which prepared the way for the invasion of the high commands by men from the ranks, one of the fundamental characteristics of the army and civil service in the third century.

As the higher grades of the army came to be filled more and more by professional soldiers (*viri militares*), those who had formerly held these posts, Senators and Knights, gradually found themselves excluded. The classes from which the Senatorial and Equestrian careers were normally fed lost the military tradition. Therefore a great number of the officials who went through those careers tried, as far as possible, to avoid the strictly military duties, such as the Tribuneship, which constituted the first stage. A few young men of the Senatorial order who liked army life rejoined the service at the end of their legal Tribuneship (Trajan served in this grade ten years, and Hadrian three), but most of them regarded the obligation of a year's service as a burden from which they were glad to be released when the time came. Moreover, some even managed to obtain exemption from this one year's service, and their number increased during the first two centuries. The number of exemptions, which was on the average 35 per cent under Augustus and Tiberius, fell to 10 per cent under Trajan, who did not treat military service as a joke, varied between 28 per cent and 31 per cent from Hadrian to Commodus, and rose to 57 per cent under Septimius Severus and 61 per cent under Caracalla. Even the men who duly served their Tribuneship were officers of no great brilliance, from whom the high command could expect little in the military line.

The gradual invasion of the higher grades by professional soldiers and the desertion of the lower grades by candidates for the Senatorial and Equestrian careers led, as a logical consequence, to the introduction of a new principle, practically unknown to Roman antiquity, the divorce of the civil and military careers. In exceptional cases from Maximin onwards and regularly after the great crisis of the time of Valerian and Gallienus, the career which led to the Imperial throne was purely military. Maximin, Claudius II, Aurelian, Probus, all the pretenders (Postumus, Victorinus, Aureolus, Proculus, Bonosus), and the Emperors of the tetrarchy (Diocletian, Maximian, Constantius, Galerius, Licinius, Maximin Daïa) were professional soldiers from the ranks, who as such had gone through all the stages of the lower military career, as *principalis* and centurion, as *præpositus* and *dux*. Gallienus, by the famous edict which barred Senators from admission to the high commands and from an army career of any kind, made the Senatorial career a purely civil one, but he did not press the application of his principle to the very end. At the head of the provinces, legions, and auxiliary corps he replaced the Senators by men of the Equestrian order, who held all the civil, military, and judicial powers constituting the traditional *imperium*. The last stage in the separation of the civil and military careers, as in so many other things, was passed by Diocletian and Constantine.

The Bureaucracy of the Late Empire : The Legal Status of Officials

Absolute in principle, the monarchy of the Late Empire took the practical form of an administrative monarchy. It merged the various careers of the Early Empire in a single Imperial civil service. The personnel was numerous, and, at least in the higher ranks, constituted a new and strictly graded nobility. The service had been developed during the Early Empire, particularly in the decisive reigns of Claudius, Hadrian, and Septimius Severus, and it was completed by the Emperors of the fourth and fifth centuries. Diocletian and Constantine share the chief honours of the final organization.

In respect of the administrative personnel in particular, the Late Empire achieved three things—the final constitution of the bureaucracy, the systematic separation of the civil and military careers, and the establishment of the status of officials.

1. *Final constitution of the Imperial bureaucracy.*—The first chapter of the *Notitia Dignitatum* [1] gives us officially the general organization of the bureaucracy. The officials of the central administration included the Prefect of the Prætorium, the Masters of Troops *in præsenti*, the *Præpositus* of the Sacred Bedchamber, the Master of Offices, the Quæstor of the Palace, the Counts of the Sacred Largesses and Private Estates, the Counts of the Domestici, the *Primicerius* of the Sacred Bedchamber, the *Primicerius* of Notaries, the *Castrensis* of the Sacred Palace, and heads of offices of the secretariat. In the administration of the districts there were the Prefects of the City in Rome and Constantinople, Vicars, Proconsuls, Counts, civil and military, Dukes, Consulars, Correctors, and Præsides. Each branch contained a vast number of elaborately graded departments.

There were two orders of rank in the civil service of the Late Empire, one of classes and one of titles, which were strictly co-ordinated. At the top were the great civil and military officials, the heads of the Imperial administration. Some were ministers—the Prefect of the Prætorium, the

[1] *Not. Dign.* : East, i, 2–128 ; West, i, 2–121.

Counts of the Treasuries, the Master of Offices, the Masters of Troops, the Quæstor of the Palace. Others were the great officials of districts—Vicars, governors of provinces of all classes, the Prefects of the two capitals, Dukes, Counts, and financial agents. Underneath these came the great mass of lower posts, the offices. Every high official of the central or local administration had his staff (*officium*) of employees, known by the generic name of *officiales*, who were distributed in offices (*scrinia*) which varied in number according to the importance of the service. Heads of departments were called variously—*primiscrinius, primicerius, princeps*—and had sub-directors or assistant directors under them (*proximus, secundicerius, melloproximus, cornicularius, adjutor*). All these people had their special duties, as drafting and dispatch clerks (*notarii, exceptores*), assistants (*adjutores*), ushers (*nomenclatores*), or couriers (*singularii*).

The power of this bureaucracy lay in its numbers, its organization, and its privileges of all kinds. Certain exact figures, given by an official document, the Theodosian Code, are particularly suggestive. A governor of a province had 100 employees ; a Vicar, 300 ; the Proconsul of Africa, 400 ; the Count of the East, 600 ; the Count of the Sacred Largesses of the West, 546 regular employees and 300 supernumeraries ; that of the East, 224 regular employees and 600 supernumeraries ; the Prefect of the Prætorium of the East, over 1,000 dispatch clerks.

2. *Separation of the civil and military careers.*—In spite of a temporary reaction under Tacitus and Probus, the Edict of Gallienus excluding men of the Senatorial career from the army had remained in force under his successors. Diocletian went further. He extended the same principle to the Equestrian order of former times, at least in respect of governors of provinces. Of the great Imperial officials, only the Prefects of the Prætorium still held all civil and military powers as in the past. Lastly, Constantine took away their military functions and gave them to the Masters of Troops, thus completing the reform and making it permanent.

After the reforms of Diocletian and Constantine, the military career in the Late Empire [1] was distinguished

------

[1] *C.I.L., passim* (*I.L.S.*, 2775–815, 9204–17) ; **LXXIX**, 107–98.

from that in the Early Empire by two fundamental characteristics—independence, since it had no connexion whatever with the civil career, and unity, since it was open to men from the ranks, without bar or restriction, from the bottom of the scale to the top. The least private soldier might rise to the intermediate rank of non-commissioned officer and junior officer (as in the past) and so (under the new order) to a general command, as Prefect of a legion, *dux*, or Master of Troops. In respect of the higher military career, the great innovation of the Late Empire lay in the new conception of the post of Duke and the creation of Masters of Troops (*magistri militum*), the former being due to Diocletian and the latter to Constantine.

Even before 289, Diocletian had taken away all the military powers of the governors of provinces, and given them to general officers, the Dukes. These new *duces*, though called by the same name as those of the Early Empire, were a different institution. They were no longer commanders of armies of operations, but the heads of territorial districts which were permanently established and varied in extent. The Dukes were all professional officers, and therefore originally came from the ranks. Those most distinguished received the title of " Duke and Count " (*dux et comes*), in practice abbreviated to " Count ".

Lastly, when Constantine reduced the Prefects of the Prætorium to their civil functions, he gave their military powers to purely military officers, likewise professional soldiers, the Masters of Troops. At the beginning of the fifth century, there were eight—four at Court (*præsentales* or *in præsenti*, two in each Empire) and four over large districts (three in the Eastern Empire, in the districts of the East, Illyricum, and Thrace, and one in the Western Empire, in Gaul). In the Late Empire this was the highest stage in the military career. As a general rule, it was the Dukes who were called, by special promotion, to hold the office.

3. *Establishment of the status of officials.*—In addition to the strict order of rank established by regulation among the various posts, the Imperial officials (*officiales*) were organized on a thoroughly military system, a creation and legacy of the terrible days of the third century when the army alone mattered in the State. In the offices of the

central and provincial administrations, service and retirement were called by the same names as in the army—*militia, honesta missio.* Civil officials wore the belt (*cingulum*), as if they were soldiers. The various grades were frequently designated by military titles—*cohortales, primipilares, principes, equites, circitores, biarchi.* Men who had retired from the civil service and army were alike called " veterans " (*veterani*).

Lastly, the Imperial officials had an exact administrative status, which, in return for definite professional duties, entitled them to a variety of privileges.

(*a*) *Appointment.*—Employees were appointed by a decree of the Emperor (*probatoria*) [1] on the recommendation of the head of the department. In practice, they were recruited in their own caste, by the application of two processes—hereditary succession, a special application to the administrative personnel of the hereditary principle which became general in all classes of society in the Late Empire, and the sale of offices, usually to the auxiliaries (*adjutores*), who found this device the quickest means of obtaining a regular official position. Both practices constituted a limitation to the rights of the central power. When the Emperor had issued his decree of appointment, the applicant's name was entered on a list, the official warrant of his position in the service.[2] The *officiales* thus appointed learned their work or improved their knowledge of it, as the case might be, in special schools (*scholæ*) attached to the offices. These were divided into two main categories according to the standard of knowledge required from the employees on leaving them. The *ministeria litterata* gave a general literary education (e.g. the *scholæ scrinianiorum* for the post of *scriniarius*, and the *scholæ exceptorum* for that of *exceptor*), while the *ministeria illitterata* supplied the lower office personnel (ushers, messengers, etc.).

---

[1] Law of Theodosius and Valentinian III to Hierius, Prefect of the Prætorium (22nd June, 426), *Cod. Theod.*, viii, 7, 21 : " *Nemo aliter ad tuæ sublimitatis admittatur officium, nisi eum emissa ex sacris scriniis probatoria consecrarit.*"

[2] Law of Arcadius, Honorius, and Theodosius II (17th March, 407), *Cod. Theod.*, viii, 4, 20 : " *Quicumque ad chartas vel tabulas vel quodcumque aliud ministerium cohortalis optaverit, non ante accedere permittatur, nisi ejus nomen matriculis receptum primitus fuerit, pœna proposita his qui contra statuta cælestia crediderint suscipiendos aliquos aut quodlibet eis officium injungendum.*"

(*b*) *Promotion.*—The status of officials was strictly defined, and promotion was by seniority. Constantine laid down the principle definitely in a Constitution of the 8th March, 315 [1] : " The order of promotion must be observed in such a way that the highest rank in the *officium* shall go to him whose Imperial warrant of appointment is older—*Promotionis ordo constituendus est, ut primus in officio sit, qui prior fuerit in consequendo beneficio principali.*" This rule did not, of course, put an end to *suffragium*, which we should call favouritism and all the abuses of recommendation, and those concerned were already complaining of it.

(*c*) *Financial privileges.*—A regular salary, exemption from certain taxes and services (*munera personalia et sordida*) and retirement (*honesta missio*) after fifteen, twenty, or twenty-five years of service, according to the importance of the post (twenty-five years for employees of the governor, twenty and fifteen for those of high officials, the central administration, the Prefects of the Prætorium and City, Vicars, etc.).

(*d*) *Judicial privileges.*—Government employees were not subject to the regular courts. The head of their department was their natural judge in civil and criminal cases, and they had no appeal from his sentence.

(*e*) *Honours.*—With the scale of functions there went a scale of titles, some attached to the function itself and some conferred, as the crown of a man's career, when he retired.

From the point of view of recruiting, officials under the Early Empire had been divided into three great careers, Senatorial, Equestrian, and lower. The administrative reorganization of Diocletian maintained these three divisions on the whole—the Senatorial order, or Clarissimi ; the Equestrian order, or Perfectissimi (the ranks of Egregius at the bottom of the Equestrian scale and Eminentissimus at the top were abolished) ; lower functions. The title of Clarissimus was borne by the highest officials of the State, civil (Prefects of the Prætorium and City, Master of Offices, Quæstor of the Palace, the highest provincial governors, Proconsuls, Consulars, some of the *Præsides* of Italy, and even several *Præsides* of Egypt) and military (Masters of Troops, Counts of the Domestici). The Perfectissimi were

[1] *Cod. Theod.*, viii, 7, 1.

the other great officials of the central administration, namely, the two directors of the Treasuries, the employees of the offices of the secretariat and financial services, Tribunes and Notaries of the Consistory, decurions and *silentiarii* ; those of the capitals, namely, the Prefects of the Corn-supply and Watch in Rome and Constantinople and the *Magister Census*, the chief assistant of the Prefect of the City ; those of the provinces, namely, all governors who were not Clarissimi (certain Correctors and all *Præsides*) and financial officials (*Rationales*, Procurators, *Præpositi*, and employees of the *Fiscus*) ; and of the army, namely, Dukes and Counts, Prefects of legions, Tribunes of cohorts, *Primipilus*-centurions, Domestici, Protectors, and agents. The lower career, lastly, was in general that of the subordinate office personnel. Moreover, many employees of this class rose to the rank of Perfectissimus, either at the end of their career or, more frequently, on the day of their retirement.

In the fourth century, two important changes, correlative one with the other, were made in this scale of honours. First of all, the Perfectissimi gradually disappeared, as they became Clarissimi. This was the case with the two Counts of the Treasuries, the Prefects of the Corn-supply and Watch, the Counts, the Correctors and Præsides governing provinces, and, in the army, the Dukes. In the first years of the fifth century, this upward movement came to an end. Secondly, the Clarissimi were divided into different grades. Two new titles were created, that of Illustrious about 350 and that of Spectabilis, intermediate between the two others, about twenty years later, under Valentinian I. The title of Clarissimus survived, but it took on a narrower sense, designating the lowest grade of the career. In consequence of these innovations, there was a general reclassification of the Imperial officials, the results of which we have in the *Notitia Dignitatum*. The grade of Illustrious, the highest of all, was given to the Prefects of the Prætorium, the Prefects of the City in Rome and Constantinople, the Master of Offices, the Quæstor of the Palace, the Grand Chamberlain, the two Counts of the Treasuries, the Counts of the Domestici, and the Masters of Troops. That of Spectabilis was given to Consulars and Correctors, Tribunes, Notaries, Advocates of the *Fiscus*, Dukes, and others.

Lastly, this new scale of titles entailed a corresponding series of official attributes. The Illustrious had the lion's share, as was his due—*auctoritas, celsitudo, culmen, eminentia, magnificentia, magnitudo, præstantia.* The Spectabilis did not do so badly, with *excellentia, prudentia, sollertia, sublimitas, summitas.*   The plain Clarissimus had to be content with the milder gratification offered by *experientia, gravitas,* and *sinceritas.*

CONCLUSION

FROM primitive horde to Mediterranean Empire, through the intermediate forms of City and Italian State, Rome made a constitutional journey covering fifteen centuries. The origins of the city by the Tiber lay deep down in the tribal system ; her final development was a realization, for the first time, of the constitutional type of the great state, the heritage and tradition of which would be taken up by modern peoples after the long interlude of the barbarian invasions. In this service as a kind of link lay the novelty of her rôle and the fundamental originality of her achievement.

In the tenth century B.C., perhaps earlier, when the settlers from Alba came and set up their homes on the top of the Palatine, the city-system was still unknown in Italy, and still more so to the primitive peoples of Lower Latium. Ligurians and Latins, the two racial elements and germ-cells of the future Roman people, led the life of the horde, with all its blemishes and shortcomings, but it was a horde already marked with the stamp of constitutional development. These inveterate nomads began to settle down in refuge-villages, *oppida*, and the exact moment when this general phenomenon happened in the story of the beginnings of Rome is marked by the establishment of the old Latin colony on the Germal.

Three centuries went by. With the Etruscans in Central Italy, with the Greeks in the South, a new concept appeared, the introduction of which was one of the greatest political revolutions known by our Western world, the concept of the City. Before that more highly developed constitutional form, the horde receded, as the primitive does in contact with civilization. In the middle of the seventh century, the kings of the Etruscan line, being masters of the soil of Rome, effected a synœcism of the villages and made Rome a city for the first time in its history, with the fundamental political organs—King, Assembly of the People,

Senate—implied by that constitutional form at that first stage of its existence. The Revolution of 509 B.C., a national reaction accompanied by a political change, led to a second stage of the ancient city, government by an aristocracy, in the orthodox forms of aristocracy of birth first, the Patrician Republic of the fifth century, and aristocracy of wealth, the Patricio-Plebeian Republic of the fourth and third centuries, after it.

From the middle of the fourth century onwards, the great facts of external history, the conquest first of Latium, then of Italy, and lastly of the Mediterranean, resulted in the old Roman City changing into a vast territorial state and new constitutional forms developing in consequence. First, in the second century B.C., behind the safety-curtain of the traditional constitution, there grew up a powerful oligarchy which, from its Senatorial citadel, imposed its political supremacy on the other organs and finally obtained the practical direction of all public affairs. Next the idea of monarchy advanced, military power gradually came to the fore, and personal government was established in the Roman State, taking the concrete form first of the Principate and then of the " Dominate ".

In general, then, Rome knew all the forms of government common to the whole of classical antiquity. She tried kingship, aristocracy, and oligarchy. But her constitutional development presents two original features : democracy is missing and military dictatorship is added. Democracy never gained a footing in Rome, and this most important fact is explained by several reasons. One was the Roman temperament. The Roman was a conservative, fiercely attached to tradition, who mistrusted radical novelties and professed only the mildest enthusiasm for seductive programmes and visionary formulas. Circumstances, too, played a part. That the Roman constitution was on the way to democracy in the third century and down to the eve of the second Punic War, is amply proved by the *Leges Hortensiæ* of 287 and the reform of the Comitia Centuriata at the middle of the century on the one hand and by the great political influence of such a man as Flaminius on the other. But Roman democracy was killed in its infancy by the ruin of the agrarian class, the very backbone of the

democratic party. The Greek democracies, Athens most of
all, thanks to an intense economic development which had
transformed the life of the lower classes, rested on a vigorous
element, full of life, and so had a solid constitutional basis.
In Rome there was nothing of this kind. As early as the
second century, the town proletariate, coming to the front as
the rural class gradually disappeared, stood for nothing but
lack of programme, debasement, and servility. The democratic movement was taken up first by the big capitalists
and then by the ambitious soldiers, and sold itself body and
soul to the army and money, the two powers of the day.
It could destroy, but it never succeeded in doing anything
constructive on its own account. Rome had democratic
disturbances enough, but she never had democracy.

In compensation, the Roman State found its final political
form in the military dictatorship which was its chief constitutional originality. This was a system to which neither
the great cities of the Greek world nor the Semites of the
East had ever come definitely. Some, like Sparta, had
preferred the maintenance of their traditional constitution
to the safety of their Empire ; others, like Athens and
Carthage, had lost their power when they were on the very
point of entering upon that last phase and supreme
transformation.

Such are the main features of the great constitutional
lesson which Rome has bequeathed to the world, and which
modern aristocracies, whether they have called themselves
Tsardom, Napoleonic Empire, or Catholic hierarchy, have
tried to put into practice, with the necessary modifications.
But in constitutional matters, more perhaps than in any
other, it is not enough to state the facts. Two very important
questions remain, that of causes and that of results.

Among all peoples and in all countries, the connexion
between foreign politics and internal constitutional development, the actions and reactions of each of these primary
elements of any national history on the other, are clearly
facts of an experimental nature, requiring no demonstration.
But the contribution of each in that process which is called
the life of a people varies. In Rome, foreign policy very

N

soon assumed a predominant influence, which became greater
as time went on. The Roman was a soldier and an
administrator, by nature and, as it were, by vocation, and
had little bent for the theoretical constructions, the play
of the creative imagination, which in the Greeks, for instance,
had taken the form of an incomparable virtuosity. He
bent himself, patiently and tirelessly, to the growing needs
of his Empire, and it may be said without paradox that
with him constitutional development was not a spontaneous
creation but a gradual, constant adaptation. One scene
follows another on the stage ; the real drama is acted in
the wings. The facts are there to give us striking proof
of this.

Let us go over the great stages—the village on the Germal,
the Etruscan kingship of the Tarquins, the Patrician city,
the Patricio-Plebeian rule, the Principate, the " Dominate "
—which represent the constitutional development of Rome.
That the old Latin settlement on the Germal, that cradle
of Roman national life, a Latin outpost on the Etruscan
border, and the united city of the Tarquins which was a direct
result of the Etruscan conquest, were immediately connected
with the great military events which mark the history of
Central Italy at intervals from the tenth century to the
sixth, is too obvious to need emphasizing. The Plebs,
that people of conquered subjects, traders, craftsmen,
which would soon hold a place of honour in the constitutional
development of Rome, was almost entirely a product of the
conquest. The Patriciate, too, after the Revolution of
509, owed to the part which it had played at the head of
the national movement the privileged position on which
it founded its monopoly of the government for half a century.
When the Plebs succeeded in forcing the gates of the city
in the course of the fifth and fourth centuries, it was above
all to the stern exigencies of the situation abroad, which
were too much for the Patriciate, that it owed its final
victory. The war against Veii, by revealing the numerical
insufficiency of the Roman cavalry, led to an important
innovation, that of compulsory cavalry service for the First
Class of the census, to which the Equestrian order was to
owe its later political and administrative influence. At the
end of the fourth century, again, it was for like motives of

foreign policy, namely the formation of the great Italian coalitions, that Appius Claudius introduced a new element into the establishment of the census, movable wealth, thus giving the last touch needed to the Centuriate organization. But in return for these new services in men and money the Plebs demanded a *quid pro quo* in the form of greater and greater political concessions. The pressure from without was ably exploited by the Plebs, whose great legislative actions of the fifth and fourth centuries—the Convention of the Sacred Mount, the Laws of the XII Tables, the *Leges Valeriæ Horatiæ*, the creation of the Military Tribuneship with Consular Power, and the Licinian Laws—were a direct result of that pressure ; and from it civil and political equality was born, a new and fruitful constitutional principle, of which the old Patriciate, the representative of a vanishing past, had to pay the cost.

This was not all. An expanding state and an increasing population need more and better organs. The successive appearance, during the fifth and fourth centuries, of the Roman magistracies composing the *cursus honorum*— Quæstorship, Censorship, Prætorship, Curule Ædileship— the most characteristic expressions of the Roman constitutional spirit, was doubtless a direct result of internal struggles, that is, of the conflict of the two orders ; but it also (perhaps one should say, chiefly) answered to administrative needs arising from the conquest. Therefore, in this definite point once again, a large share of the credit must be given to external politics.

After the Punic Wars, the decay of the traditional constitution became more apparent every day, and the admirable balance of the third century was soon only a memory. The Equestrian order rose up as a rival to the Senatorial order, while the middle class, whose foundation was the small landowner, disappeared. So much for the facts. Of the causes there can be no doubt—the formation of capitalism on a large scale and the policy of expansion, both concrete manifestations of the same phenomenon, the conquest. The Punic Wars, by their long duration, by the increasing extension of the theatres of operations, and by the measures of national defence which they required of the State, gave the Senate a veritable dictatorship, the origin of the oligarchical government which was finally constituted in the first half of the second century B.C. To it the conquest of the world offered not only immense profits but the most effective justification of its authority.

With the problem of conquest went that of organization. The oligarchy had neither the men nor the methods required, if the State was to survive at all, for the accomplishment of such a new and vast programme. It would neither throw over the constitutional framework of the ancient city nor renounce the rule of the Mediterranean, and indeed the existing facts did not allow it the choice. It got out of its difficulties, as is usual in such cases, by a series of opportunistic measures which were nothing more than shifts, the best example of which is the extension of the term of magistracies. But, as usual, these devices soon proved inadequate. All ambiguities were blown away and all prejudices hustled aside by one brutal fact. Rome, as everybody came in the end to see, had not the diplomatic and military instruments or the political and administrative machinery wanted for the domination and systematic organization of the Mediterranean world. An empire of such huge dimensions cannot be governed by such anomalies as local Comitia, annual magistrates, and the rudiments of a civil service. Two reforms, the agrarian and the Italian, were intended to give Rome the men whom the citizen body had lost by the ruin of the middle class, but the former had been killed by the tenacious opposition of the ruling oligarchy and the latter remained inoperative through a deliberately defective application. The obsolete machinery of the City was breaking down under a strain for which it was not made. The administration and exploitation of the world called, every day more loudly, for the concentration of powers. The oligarchy was a first step in this direction, but the system did not go far enough and was soon discredited. Something more was needed, and things developed relentlessly. The idea of monarchy, which had its origin in realities, took shape and gained in strength. It appeared in civil form in Caius Gracchus, as a temporary power in Sulla, and presently in permanent form in Principate and " Dominate " successively. At the head of the State there must henceforward be a brain and a will. Both were provided by the military power, which for over a century had been growing up within the oligarchy, in spite of it and against it, the only active, living element amid the general decomposition. The long drama of a constitution which could not live and yet clung to life desperately ended in the gloom of the Civil Wars and the awful bloodshed of the Proscriptions. The City went down beneath the repeated blows of the Empire. The day of personal rule was come.

In the course of a constitutional development covering three centuries, the Principate, the first, cautious manifestation of personal government, was transformed into a monarchy pure and simple, the " Dominate ". There were many causes for the fact, and among them, as we have seen, internal politics had had a large place ; but the crisis of the third century was the decisive factor, and the immediate explanation of that crisis lay abroad. At a time when the repeated attacks of the barbarians were endangering the existence of the Empire, and the demands of national defence over-shadowed all other interests, however legitimate, the Emperor resigned the power to the great military leaders. The army came to the forefront and the last privileges of the Senate, the anachronistic vestiges of a past now dead, crumbled away. In absolute monarchy, as Diocletian and Constantine left it, the new situation found its systematic, permanent consecration.

So then, once again and always, down to the last hours of the Western Empire, the external problem remains the initial motive and essential factor in the history of the Roman constitution. *Tu regere imperio populos, Romane, memento*—the line is not merely a maxim of foreign policy. The whole constitutional development of Rome bears its stamp and expresses its spirit.

In the series of political forms which have in turn gone to make the constitutional past of this ancient Europe of ours, Rome occupies an exact point and marks a definite phase— the transition from the system of the city to that of the state. She grew up in the framework of the city ; it was as a state that she expanded and disappeared. Of the ancient city, Rome had the four characteristic *differentiæ*—a small territory, direct exercise of sovereignty, combination of powers, and absence of bureaucracy.

The territory of the Roman City properly so called, namely, the annexed land, was confined for nearly three centuries to the immediate environs of the town, and when it was extended, by a succession of conquests, to the rest of Italy the city-system received its death sentence.

The people possessed sovereignty in its three forms, voting laws, electing magistrates, and judging important suits, and it exercised that sovereignty direct, meeting in its Comitia and only at the very seat of the City, in Rome.

The separation of powers was unknown to the Roman City. The *imperium*, the highest and most perfect expression of executive authority, as held by the Dictators, Consuls, and Prætors, comprised all military, civil, and judicial powers. Some magistracies, namely the Censorship, Ædileship, and Quæstorship, were purely civil, but their holders also had, like magistrates with the *imperium*, judicial authority within their sphere of action.

As a last characteristic inherent in the ancient city, the executive power, which was monopolized by the magistrates elected by the people, had room for few or no officials. The only representatives of this class were the subordinate staff— lictors, ushers, dispatch-clerks, messengers—and much of the work was done by slaves.

In every point the modern state which we see working round us, with its large territory, delegated sovereignty, separated powers, and bureaucracy, is the opposite of the ancient city. And it was Rome which brought these political and administrative factors into the common possession of mankind, in the course of a development eight centuries long.

Out of the humble Italian city she made an immense state, comprising Britain, Gaul, Mesopotamia, and the Mediterranean frontage of three continents.

Although the principle of popular sovereignty remained intact, direct government gave place to the system of delegated sovereignty, and as the magistracies gradually decayed, the power fell chiefly, and in the end solely, into the hands of the Emperor.

Under the pressure of needs and circumstances, the old dogma of combination of powers disappeared in favour of the new principle of their separation. District administrators—governors of provinces from Diocletian onwards and Prefects of the Prætorium from Constantine— lost their military attributions and, with a few exceptions, kept only their civil competence. Henceforward the military power was held by generals who were officers by profession— Masters of Troops, Counts, Dukes.

Lastly, all through the administrative scale, the magistrates gave way to the officials. The bureaucracy inaugurated in the last period of the Republic and extended during the Principate reached its height in the Late Empire. The State now had great ministers—the Prefect of the Prætorium for home affairs, the Count of the Sacred Largesses for finance, the Count of the Private Estates for Crown lands, the Quæstor of the Palace for justice, the Masters of Troops for the army and navy, and the Master of Offices for the Imperial household. It had a Council of State in the Sacred Consistory, a secretariat in the four offices of *Epistulæ*, *Libelli*, *Dispositiones*, and *Memoria*, and, at least in the two capitals, specialized technical services under their own directors—police, fires, food-supply, water, public buildings, and Tiber and drains. It had a numerous and strictly graded administrative nobility, some of whose members have left their titles to modern aristocracies (Count, Duke). In the domain of justice, finally, it generalized and systematized the procedure of appeal, one of the most successful and fruitful measures of the Imperial system.

No doubt, Rome did not create these principles and institutions lock, stock, and barrel, or evolve them from her imagination, for inventiveness was never her strong point. She took them chiefly from the great Eastern monarchies which had met like needs with like solutions, first the Hellenistic kingdoms and Egypt in particular, and then the Persian kingdom of the Sassanids. But Rome was able to adapt what she borrowed, and, whatever her models may have been, she initiated in this respect in a decisive manner.

The type of state which Rome, after all, gave to the constitutional heritage of our Western world therefore represents, in relation to earlier political systems, a certain number of important and lasting achievements. But, like every human creation, the picture has its dark parts ; there are failures, both deficiencies and faults.

Of the deficiencies, the first was the absence of political liberty. Provincial liberties such as really mattered were hardly known under the Republic. Municipal liberties, what with the general disappearance of the Comitia in the first century after Christ, the increasing interference of the Emperor in the administration of the towns, and the creation of officials delegated by the central power, such as the Curators, were reduced to very little even before the Late Empire. There remained the two deliberative organs created by the Roman State itself, the provincial assemblies founded in the Early Empire and the Diocesan assemblies instituted, or rather authorized, at the end of the fourth century. But, although the former were able to do good work in controlling local representatives of the government and reporting the more flagrant abuses on occasion, they never played, or even aspired to playing, a serious part in politics ; and the latter appeared too late, just when the Empire was about to fall a prey to the barbarians, to show what they could do. The Roman Empire never knew representative government, any more than the rest of antiquity. That system might, by the intimate association of the peoples with the government of the commonwealth, have been a mighty element of vitality in all ages, and a very strong guarantee of safety in the hour of supreme peril.

A second deficiency was the lack of administrative services, which are so important in our eyes and have therefore been highly developed by the modern state. First, certain ministerial departments did not exist at all. Foreign affairs were treated direct by the head of the State and his Council. There were no ministries of agriculture, public works, education, or labour. The army and navy were combined in the hands of the Masters of Troops. Trade was divided up into a number of local departments—the East and Egypt, Mœsia, Scythia, Pontus, Illyricum—under Counts of Commerce (*comites commerciorum*), and, instead of having an independent central direction, came under the Count of the Sacred Largesses, that is, the finance minister. There was no diplomatic corps, and there was no specialized legal body. Even when the Roman State was at the height of its development, there was never an independent organization of justice in the form of professional magistrates; this was a logical consequence of the ancient conception which made no distinction between the ideas of State and government, which are to us, at least in theory, quite different. Although the notion of the separation of powers made such progress, it was not carried to its final conclusion in this matter. There were now definitely specialized civil and military officials, but both continued to have judicial powers in addition to their main functions, as in the past. The absence of a public ministry (again a feature common to all antiquity) in which the duty falls on the magistrates and, eventually, on every citizen, is, in our modern eyes and from the strict judicial point of view, another deficiency of the same kind. Rome created this institution only in one special domain, that of finance. Corresponding to the *synegoroi* of Athens, there was under the Empire, from Hadrian onwards, an Advocate of the *Fiscus*, whose business it was to defend the material interests of the treasury. The duties given to the municipal Curiæ in the matter of collecting taxes reduced the financial services to a minimum. Lastly, the department of education in Rome was only concerned with "university" education, and that to a very small extent; the State supported a few chairs of philosophy or rhetoric, particularly in Athens and Rome. Secondary and primary education was regarded as a purely family matter and the State left it alone altogether.

In addition to its deficiencies, the system of the State in the form which it assumed in the Late Empire had its positive faults. Here it will suffice to mention the two chief— excessive despotism and bureaucratic tyranny. In the third century after Christ, the Empire had been transformed into a monarchy of the Eastern type, with the usual cruelties and the palace intrigues in which underlings, women and eunuchs (such as Paul Catena and Eusebius in the reign of Constantius II) presently took far too prominent a part. Secondly, there were the excesses of an omnipotent and practical irresponsible bureaucracy, beneath the sovereign and under his protection; proof of this is furnished by the affair of Tripolitana under Valentinian I, who was certainly not a man who treated government service lightly.

Favouritism, caste-spirit, cabal-spirit, arbitrary action, extortion, greed, cruelty, slackness, slavery to routine, and a hundred other vices—such are the reproaches which contemporary writers—Lactantius, Ammianus Marcellinus, Salvianus—heap on the civil service of their day with a unanimity too complete to be unfounded. If one leaves a large margin for the usual exaggerations, their statements are on the whole in conformity with historical truth. Against that bureaucracy, a veritable state within the State, on which, in the last analysis, the working of the whole machine of government depended, the Emperor, a despot with feet of clay, often ill-secure on his throne, threatened by invaders and pretenders, and paralysed by the lack of an unassailable law of succession, was too often helpless. Diocletian, Constantine, Valentinian I, or Theodosius, men with clear heads and iron wills, might turn upon it, at least occasionally and in flashes ; the rest, being weaker or too young, allowed things to go on, and presented the world with the paradoxical sight, not an exclusive privilege of Rome, of an autocratic monarch held prisoner by his household and reduced to creating special administrative machinery as a protection against the tyrannical encroachment of his own servants.

In the fifth century after Christ, the Roman Empire broke up under the assault of barbarism, at last triumphant, but the great lesson remained, and Constantinople, escaping the catastrophe, still stood to carry on its tradition. Achievements and deficiencies alike, what Rome on the day of her fall bequeathed to mankind was not only her own original work, it was also what she herself had taken up, the constitutional heritage of all antiquity.

BIBLIOGRAPHY

[Certain English and other editions are added in square brackets.
The footnotes do not refer to these editions unless it is so stated.—Trs.]

I. SOURCES
(A) *Literary Sources*

Abbreviations.	Authors.	Works.
	Aulus Gellius . .	*Attic Nights.*
	Appian . . .	*Roman History (Civil Wars)*
	Aristotle . . .	*Politics*, ed. by O. Immisch, Leipzig, 1909
	Aurelius Victor .	*De Cæsaribus*
	Cato the Elder .	*Origins, Speeches (Catonis præter librum de Re Rustica quæ extant*, ed. by H. Jordan, Leipzig, 1860)
	Cæsar . . .	*Commentaries on the Gallic War ; on the Civil War*
Cic. . .	Cicero . . .	*Brutus, Letters (to Atticus, to Quintus, to Family), Speeches (Pro Balbo, De Lege Agraria, Pro Marcello, Pro Murena, Philippics, Pro Plancio, Pro Sestio), De Legibus, De Officiis, De Oratore, De Republica*
	Cornelius Nepos .	*De Illustribus Viris*
Dion. Hal. .	Dionysios of Halicarnassos	*Roman Antiquities*
Dion C. .	Dion Cassius . .	*Roman History* Epitome of Oxyrrhynchos, ed. by E. Kornemann, in *Klio*, Beiheft ii, Leipzig, 1904 ; by Rossbach, Leipzig, 1910
	Eusebios . . .	*Chronicle*, ed. by A. Schöne, Berlin, 1866–75
	Eutropius . .	*Breviarium.*
	Festus . . .	*De Verborum significatione*, ed. by M. Lindsay, Leipzig, 1913
F.H.G. . . .		*Fragmenta Historicorum Græcorum*, ed. by C. Müller, Paris, 1849–53
	Florus . . .	*Epitome*

Abbreviations.	Authors.	Works.
F.P.R. . .		Fragmenta Poetarum Romanorum, ed. by Æm. Bæhrens, Leipzig, 1886
	Frontinus . .	De Aquæductibus Urbis Romæ
	Hieronymos (Jerome)	Chronicle, ed. by A. Schöne, Berlin, 1866–75
H.R.F. . .		Historicorum Romanorum Fragmenta, ed. by H. Peter, Leipzig, 1883
H.R.R. . .		Historicorum Romanorum Reliquiæ, ed. by H. Peter, 2nd ed., Leipzig, 1914
	Horace . . .	Odes
	Josephus . .	Jewish Antiquities (Ant. Jud.)
	Lactantius . .	De Mortibus persecutorum
	Livy . . .	Roman History ; Periochæ
	Nicolaos of Damascus	Life of Augustus, in F.H.G., iii, 427–56, and in L. Dindorf, Historici Græci Minores, Leipzig, 1870–1, i, 93 ff.
O.R.F. . .		Oratorum Romanorum Fragmenta, ed. by H. Meyer, Zurich, 1842
	Orosius . .	Histories against the Pagans
	Pliny the Elder .	Natural History
	Pliny the Younger	Panegyric of Trajan ; Letters
	Plutarch . .	Parallel Lives ; Roman Questions
Polyb. . .	Polybios . .	History
	Procopios . .	Gothic War
Sall. . .	Sallust . .	Jugurthine War
	Solinus . .	Collectanea rerum mirabilium
	Strabo . .	Geography
Suet. . .	Suetonius . .	Twelve Cæsars
	Tacitus . .	Annals ; Histories ; Agricola
	Valerius Maximus .	Factorum ac dictorum memorabilium libri IX
	Varro . . .	De Lingua Latina ; De Re Rustica
	Vegetius . .	Epitome rei militaris (of Military Matters)
	Velleius Paterculus	Roman History
De Viris illustr.		De Viris illustribus
	Zonaras . .	Chronicle
	Zosimos . .	History

(B) *Administrative Sources*

Abbreviations.		Works.
Not. Dign.	.	*Notitia Dignitatum* (with the *Laterculus* of Verona, POLEMIUS SILVIUS's list of provinces, and the *Notitia Galliarum*), ed. by O. SEECK, Berlin, 1876

Notitia de Regionibus Urbis Romæ ; Curiosum Urbis Romæ ; in C. L. URLICHS, *Codex Urbis Romæ topographicus*, Würzburg, 1871, pp. 1–27

(C) *Legal Sources*

Cod. Theod. . Theodosian Code : (*a*) *Theodosiani libri XVI cum constitutionibus sirmondianis et leges novellæ ad Theodosium pertinentes*, ed. by T. MOMMSEN and Paul MEYER (Academia Regia Borussica), Berlin, 1905 ; (*b*) *Codex Theodosianus cum perpetuis commentariis Jacobi Gothofredi*, ed. by RITTER, Leipzig, 1730–50

Cod. Just.; Dig. Code of Justinian and Digest, in *Corpus Juris Civilis*, ed. by T. MOMMSEN, P. KRUEGER, E. SCHŒLL, Berlin, 1872, etc.

(D) *Papyri*

Papyri (griechische) im Museum des Oberhessischen Geschichtsvereins zu Giessen, ed. by E. KORNEMANN and P. MEYER, in association with O. EGER, Leipzig, 1910–12

(E) *Inscriptions*

C.I.G. . . *Corpus Inscriptionum Græcarum*, ed. by A. BOECKH, continued by J. FRANZ, E. CURTIUS, A. KIRCHOFF, H. ROHL, Berlin, 1828–77

C.I.L. . . *Corpus Inscriptionum Latinarum* (Academia Regia Borussica), Berlin, 1863, etc.

Ditt., *Syll.* . DITTENBERGER (W.), *Sylloge inscriptionum Græcarum*, 3rd ed., Leipzig, 1915–23

Ephemeris Epigraphica, Rome and Berlin, 1872, etc.

Consular *Fasti*, in *C.I.L.*, i, 1, 2nd ed., pp. 79–167

Triumphal *Fasti*, *ibid.*, pp. 168–81

I.G. ., . *Inscriptiones Græcæ* (Academia Regia Borussica), Berlin, 1873, etc.

I.G. ad R.R.p. . *Inscriptiones Græcæ ad res Romanas pertinentes*, ed. by R. CAGNAT, G. LAFAYE, J. TOUTAIN (Acad. des Inscr. et belles-lettres), Paris, 1901, etc.

I.L.A. . . *Inscriptions latines d'Afrique*, published by R. CAGNAT, A. MERLIN, L. CHÂTELAIN, Paris, 1923

I.L.S. . . *Inscriptiones Latinæ selectæ*, ed. by H. DESSAU, Berlin, 1892–1916

I.O. . . DITTENBERGER (W.), *Orientis Græci inscriptiones selectæ*, Leipzig, 1903–5

Mon. Anc. . *Res gestæ Divi Augusti* (Will of Augustus, Monument of Ancyra), ed. by T. MOMMSEN, 2nd ed., Berlin, 1883, with a full commentary. See also the editions of W. FAIRLEY, " Monum. Ancyr.,

Works.

the Deeds of Augustus," in *Transactions and Reprints from the Original Sources of European History*, v, 1, Philadelphia, 1898, and H. MALCO-VATI, "Imperatoris Cæsaris Augusti operum fragmenta*," in *Corpus Scriptorum Latinorum Paravianum*, Turin, 1821 ; also, for the many questions raised by the establishment and interpretation of the text, M. BESNIER, " Récents Travaux sur les *Res Gestæ Divi Augusti*," in **CVI**, 118–51, and J. COLIN, in **XXXV**, 1922, 171–3

A certain number of fragments of other copies of the *Res Gestæ* have been found at Apollonia and Pisidian Antioch, the latter recently, also in Galatia. Collation of the texts of Antioch and Ancyra has made it possible to verify the Ancyra text and in some cases (see, e.g., above, p. 208, n. 1, and p. 214) to fill up its lacunæ. On this subject, see especially W. M. RAMSAY, " Monumentum Antiochenum," in *Journal of Roman Studies*, vi (1916), 105 ff. ; E. KORNEMANN, " Neues zum Monumentum Ancyranum," in **XXXVIII**, xv (1924), pp. 214–15 ; A. VON PREMERSTEIN, " Zum Monumentum Antiochenum," in **XLII**, 135–44 ; *id.*, " Zur Aufzeichnung der *Res Gestæ Divi Augusti* in Pisidischer Antiochia," in **XXXVI**, lix (1924), 95–107 ; and, lastly, V. EHRENBERG, " Monumentum Antiochenum," in **XXXVIII**, xix (1925), 189–213

(F) *Coins*

COHEN (H.), *Description historique des médailles frappées sous l'Empire romain*, 2nd ed., Paris, 1880–92

ROHDE (T.), *Die Münzen des Kaisers Aurelianus, seiner Frau Severina, und der Fürsten von Palmyra*, Miskolcz, 1881

II. GENERAL WORKS

BLOCH (G.), *L'Empire romain : évolution et décadence*, Paris, 1922 . . . .   **I**

—— *La République romaine : conflits politiques et sociaux*, Paris, 1913 . . . .   **II**

CAGNAT (R.), *Cours d'épigraphie latine*, 4th ed., Paris, 1914   **III**

COHEN (H.), *Description historique des médai les frappées sous l'Empire romain*, 2nd ed., Paris, 1880–92 . .   **IV**

DAREMBERG (C.) and SAGLIO (E.), *Dictionnaire des antiquités grecques et romaines*, Paris, 1877–1918 . . .   **V**

DESSAU (H.), *Geschichte der römischen Kaiserzeit :* i. *Bis zum ersten Thronwechsel*, Berlin, 1924 ; ii, 1. *Die Kaiser von Tiberius bis Vitellius*, Berlin, 1926 . . .   **VI**

—— KLEBS (E.), and ROHDEN (P. v.), *Prosopographia Imperii Romani saec, I, II, III*, Berlin, 1897–8 . .   **VII**

DOMASZEWSKI (A. v.), *Geschichte der römischen Kaiser,*
Leipzig, 1909 VIII
FERRERO (G.) and BARBAGALLO (C.), *Roma antica,* Florence,
1921 IX
GERCKE (A.) and NORDEN (E.), *Einleitung in die Altertums-
wissenschaft,* iii, 2nd ed., Berlin, 1914 . . . X
GOYAU (G.), *Chronologie de l'Empire romain,* Paris, 1891 . XI
HOMO (L.), *L'Empire romain,* Paris, 1925 . . . XII
—— *L'Italie et les débuts de l'impérialisme romain (Évolu-
tion de l'humanité),* Paris, 1925 [*Primitive Italy,* trans.
by V. Gordon CHILDE (*History of Civilization*), London,
1927] XIII
—— *Lexique de topographie romaine,* Paris, 1900 . . XIV
—— *Rome antique,* Paris, 1921 XV
LANGE (L.), *Histoire intérieure de Rome jusqu'à la bataille
d'Actium,* trans. by A. BERTHELOT and DIDIER, Paris,
1885–8 [extract from his *Römische Alterthümer,* Berlin,
1876, Leipzig, 1879] XVI
MEYER (Eduard), *Geschichte des Altertums,* 1st–3rd eds.,
Stuttgart, 1893–1913 XVII
MISPOULET (J. B.), *Les Institutions juridiques des Romains,*
Paris, 1882–3 XVIII
MOMMSEN (T.), MARQUARDT (J.), and KRUEGER (P.),
[*Handbuch der römischen Alterthümer,* 1st–3rd eds.,
Leipzig, 1871–88] *Manuel des antiquités romaines,*
French trans., Paris, 1887–1907 XIX
MOMMSEN (T.), *Histoire romaine,* trans. by C. A.
ALEXANDRE, Paris, 1863–72 [*The History of Rome,*
trans. by W. P. DICKSON, London, 1872, etc.] . . XX
NIESE (B.), *Grundriss der römischen Geschichte nebst Quellen-
kunde,* in I. v. MÜLLER, *Handbuch der klassischen
Altertumswissenschaft* (re-ed. by W. OTTO), 5th ed.,
Munich, 1923 XXI
PAIS (E.), *Ricerche sulla storia e sul diritto pubblico di
Roma,* Rome, 1913–16 XXII
—— *Storia critica di Roma durante i primi cinque secoli,*
Rome, 1913–20 XXIII
—— *Storia dell' Italia antica,* Rome, 1925 . . . XXIV
PAULY (A. F. v.) and WISSOWA (G.), *Real-Encyclopädie der
classischen Alterthumswissenschaft,* Stuttgart, 1894, etc. XXV
PFLUGK-HARTUNG (J. v.), *Weltgeschichte* (in *Weltgeschichte
des Ullsteinschen Verlags*) : i, *Altertum* (K. J. NEU-
MANN, *Die hellenistischen Staaten und die römische
Republik,* 329 ff. ; R. v. POEHLMANN, *Römische
Kaiserzeit und Untergang der antiken Welt,* 507 ff.),
Berlin, 1909 XXVI
ROSENBERG (A.), *Geschichte der römischen Republik,*
Leipzig, 1921 XXVII
RUGGIERO (E. DI), *Dizionario epigrafico di antichità romana,*
Rome, 1886, etc. XXVIII
SANCTIS (G. DE), *Storia dei Romani,* Turin, 1907–23 XXIX
SCHILLER (H.), *Geschichte der römischen Kaiserzeit,* Gotha,
1883–7 XXX
WILLEMS (P.), *Le Droit public romain,* 7th ed., Louvain,
1910 XXXI

III. PERIODICALS

Abhandlungen der Königlichen Gesellschaft der Wissen-
　schaften zu Göttingen, Philol. Hist. Klasse, Berlin   **XXXII**
Bollettino dell' Associazione Archeologica romana, Rome .   **XXXIII**
Bonner Jahrbücher, Bonn . . . .   **XXXIV**
Bullettino della Commissione Archeologica communale di
　Roma, Rome . . . .   **XXXV**
Hermes, Berlin . . . .   **XXXVI**
Historische Zeitschrift, Munich and Berlin . . .   **XXVII**
Klio, Berlin . . . .   **XXXVIII**
Neue Jahrbücher für das klassische Altertum, Geschichte,
　und deutsche Litteratur, Leipzig . . . . .   **XXXIX**
Mémoires de l'Académie royale des Sciences et des lettres
　de Danemark, Copenhagen . . . . . .   **XL**
Monumenti antichi, pubblicati per cura della R. Accademia
　dei Lincei, Milan . . . .   **XLI**
Philologische Wochenschrift, Leipzig . . . .   **XLII**
Philologus, Göttingen and Leipzig . . . .   **XLIII**
Revue Archéologique, Paris . . . . . .   **XLIV**
Revue des Études anciennes, Bordeaux . . . .   **XLV**
Revue des Études grecques, Paris . . . . .   **XLVI**
Revue Historique, Paris . . . .   **XLVII**
Revue historique de Droit français et étranger, Paris .   **XLVIII**
Rheinisches Museum für Philologie, Frankfort on the Main   **XLIX**
Sitzungsberichte der Heidelberger Akademie der Wissen-
　schaften, Phil. Hist. Klasse, Heidelberg . . .   **L**
Sitzungsberichte der Kgl. Preuss. Akad. der Wissenschaften,
　Phil. Hist. Klasse, Berlin . . . . . .   **LI**

IV. SPECIAL WORKS

ALLARD (P.), *Julien l'Apostat*, Paris, 1900–3 . . .   **LII**
BEAUFORT (L. de), *Dissertation sur l'incertitude des cinq
　premiers siècles de l'histoire romaine*, new ed., Paris,
　1886 . . . .   **LIII**
BELOCH (J.), *Die Bevölkerung der griechisch-römischen Welt*,
　Leipzig, 1886 . . . .   **LIV**
—— *Der italische Bund unter Roms Hegemonie*, Leipzig,
　1880 . . . .   **LV**
BERGE (C. de la), *Essai sur le règne de Trajan*, Paris, 1877   **LVI**
BEURLIER (E.), *Le Culte impérial*, Paris, 1891 . . .   **LVII**
BINDER (J.), *Die Plebs : Studien zur römischen Rechts-
　geschichte*, Leipzig, 1909 . . . .   **LVIII**
BLOCH (G.), *Les Origines du Sénat romain*, Paris, 1883 .   **LIX**
BOISSIER (G.), *La Conspiration de Catilina*, Paris, 1905 .   **LX**
BORGHESI (B.), *Œuvres complètes*, Paris, 1862–97 . .   **LXI**
BROGLIE (A. de), *L'Église et l'État romain au IVe siècle*,
　Paris, 1856, etc. . . . .   **LXII**
BURY (J. B.), *History of the Late Roman Empire*, London,
　1923 . . . .   **LXIII**
CAGNAT (R.), *Étude historique sur les impôts indirects chez les
　Romains jusqu'aux invasions des barbares*, Paris, 1882   **LXIV**
—— *Le Portorium chez les Romains*, Paris, 1880 . .   **LXV**
CEULENEER (A. de), *Essai sur la vie et le règne de Septime
　Sévère*, Brussels, 1880 . . . .   **LXVI**

CHAPOT (V.), *Le Monde romain* (*Évolution de l'humanité*), Paris, 1927 [*The Roman World*, trans. by E. A. PARKER (*History of Civilization*), London, 1928] .   **LXVIa**

CHRIST (W.), *Geschichte der griechischen Litteratur bis auf die Zeit Justinians*, 4th ed., Munich, 1905 . . **LXVII**

DECLAREUIL (J.), *Rome et l'organisation du Droit* (*Évolution de l'humanité*), Paris, 1924 [*Rome the Law-giver*, translated by E. A. PARKER (*History of Civilization*), London, 1927] . . . . . . **LXVIII**

DOMASZEWSKI (A. v.), *Die Rangordnung des römischen Heeres*, repr. from **XXXIV**, No. 117, Bonn, 1908 . **LXIX**

DRUMANN (W.) and GROEBE (P.), *Geschichte Roms in seinem Übergange von der republicanischen zur monarchischen Verfassung*, 2nd ed., Berlin, 1899–1919 . **LXX**

McFAYDEN (D.), *The History of the Title Imperator under the Roman Empire*, Chicago, 1920 . . . **LXXI**

FERRERO (G.), *Grandeur et décadence de Rome*, French trans., Paris, 1904–8 [*The Greatness and Decline of Rome*, trans. by A. E. ZIMMERN and H. J. CHAYTOR, London, 1907–9] . . . . **LXXII**

—— *La Ruine de la civilisation antique*, Paris, 1921 [*The Ruin of the Ancient Civilisation*, trans. by the Hon. Lady WHITEHEAD, N.Y., 1921] . . . **LXXIII**

FUCHS (C.), *Geschichte des Kaisers Septimius Severus*, Vienna, 1886 . . . . **LXXIV**

GARDTHAUSEN (V.), *Augustus und seine Zeit*, Leipzig, 1891–1904 . . . . **LXXV**

GELZER (W.), *Cæsar der Politiker und Staatsmann*, Stuttgart, 1921 . . . . **LXXVI**

—— *Die Nobilität der römischen Republik*, Leipzig and Berlin, 1912 . . . . **LXXVII**

GREGOROVIUS (F. v.), *Der Kaiser Hadrian*, 3rd ed., Stuttgart, 1884 . . . . **LXXVIII**

GROSSE (R.), *Römische Militärgeschichte von Gallienus bis zum Beginn der byzantinischen Themenverfassung*, Berlin, 1920 **LXXIX**

GSELL (Stéphane), *Essai sur le règne de l'empereur Domitien*, Paris, 1894 . . . . **LXXX**

GUIRAUD (P.), *Les Assemblées provinciales dans l'Empire romain*, Paris, 1887 . . . . . **LXXXI**

HASEBROEK (J.), *Untersuchungen zur Geschichte des Kaisers Septimius Severus*, Heidelberg, 1921 . . **LXXXII**

HENDERSON (B. W.), *The Life and Principate of the Emperor Nero*, London, 1903–5 . . . . **LXXXIII**

HERSCHEL (C.), *Frontinus and the Water Supply of Ancient Rome*, Boston, 1899, and London, 1913 . . **LXXXIV**

HIRSCHFELD (O.), *Die kaiserliche Verwaltungsbeamten bis auf Diokletian*, 2nd ed., Berlin, 1905 . . **LXXXV**

HODGKIN (Thomas), *Italy and her Invaders*, Oxford, 1892–9 **LXXXVI**

HOMO (L.), *De Claudio Gothico*, Paris, 1904 . . **LXXXVII**

—— *Essai sur le règne de l'empereur Aurélien*, Paris, 1904 **LXXXVIII**

—— *Problèmes sociaux de jadis et d'à présent*, Paris, 1922 **LXXXIX**

HUART (C.), *La Perse antique et la civilisation iranienne* [*Évolution de l'humanité*), Paris, 1925 [*Ancient Persia*, translated by M. R. DOBIE (*History of Civilization*), London, 1927] . . . . . **XC**

JARDÉ (A.), *Études critiques sur la vie et le règne de Sévère Alexandre*, Paris, 1925 . . . .   XCa

JOUGUET (P.), *La Vie municipale dans l'Égypte ancienne*, Paris, 1911   XCI

JULLIAN (C.), *Les Transformations politiques de l'Italie sous les empereurs romains*, Paris, 1883 . . .   XCII

KAHRSTEDT (U.), *Die Annalistik von Livius, B. XXXI–XL: Vorschläge und Versuche*, Berlin, 1913 . . .   XCIII

KORNEMANN (E.), *Mausoleum und Tatenbericht des Augustus*, Leipzig and Berlin, 1921 . . .   XCIV

KEYES (C. W.), *The Rise of the Equites in the third century of the Roman Empire*, Princeton and Oxford, 1915 .   XCV

KORNEMANN (E.), " Die neue Epitome aus Oxyrynchos," in **XXXVIII**, Beiheft ii, Berlin, 1904   XCVI

KROMAYER (J.), *Die rechtliche Begründung des IIIvirats*, Marburg, 1888   XCVII

LACEY (R. H.), *The Equestrian Officials of Trajan and Hadrian : their careers, with some notes on Hadrian's reforms*, Princeton, 1927   XCVIII

LACOUR GAYET (G.), *Antonin le Pieux et son temps*, Paris, 1888   XCIX

LANCIANI (R.), *I Commentarii di Frontino intorno le acque e gli acquedotti*, repr. from *Atti dell' Accademia dei Lincei*, ser. 3a, vol. iv   C

LÉCRIVAIN (C.), *Le Sénat romain depuis Dioclétien à Rome et à Constantinople*, Paris, 1888   CI

McFAYDEN (D.), see **LXXI** above . . . . .

MAGISTRIS (E. de), *La Militia Vigilum della Roma imperiale*, 2nd ed., Rome, 1898   CII

MARSH (B.), *The Founding of the Roman Empire (Publications of the University of Texas)*, Austin, 1922 . .   CIII

MAURICE (A.), *Constantin le Grand : l'origine de la civilisation chrétienne*, Paris, 1924   CIV

Mélanges Appleton, Lyons, 1903   CV

Mélanges Cagnat, Paris, 1912   CVI

MERLIN (A.), *L'Aventin dans l'antiquité*, Paris, 1906 .   CVII

MESS (V.), *Cæsar (Das Erbe der Alten*, vii), Leipzig, 1913   CVIII

MEYER (Eduard), *Cæsars Monarchie und das Prinzipat des Pompeius*, Stuttgart and Berlin, 1918 . . .   CIX

—— " Kaiser Augustus," in *Kleine Schriften*, Halle a. S., 1910   CX

MITTEIS (L.) and WILCKEN (U.), *Grundzüge und Chrestomathie der Papyruskunde*, Berlin, 1912 . .   CXI

Museo italiano di antichità classica, Florence, 1885–90 .   CXII

NEGRI (G.), *L'Imperatore Giuliano l'Apostata*, 2nd ed., Milan, 1902   CXIII

NEUMANN (K. J.), *Die Grundherrschaft der römischen Republik, die Bauernfreiung, und die Entstehung der servianischen Verfassung* (Acad. address), Strasburg, 1900   CXIV

NISSEN (H.), *Untersuchungen über die Quellen der 4. and 5. Dekade des Livius*, Berlin, 1863   CXV

NITZSCH (K. W.), *Die römische Annalistik von ihren ersten Anfängen bis auf Valerius Antias*, Berlin, 1873 .   CXVI

PAIS (E.), *Ancient Legends of Roman History*, N.Y. and
London, 1906 CXVII
—— *Fasti triumphales populi Romani*, Rome, 1920 . . CXVIII
PETER (C.), *Zur Kritik der Quellen der älteren römischen
Geschichte*, Halle, 1879 CXIX
PIGANIOL (A.), *Essai sur les origines de Rome*, Paris, 1917 CXX
PLATNAUER (M.), *The Life and Reign of the Emperor L.
Septimius Severus*, Oxford, 1918 CXXI
RENAN (E.), *Marc Aurèle et la fin du monde antique*, Paris,
1882 CXXII
ROSENBERG (A.), *Einleitung und Quellenkunde zur römischen
Geschichte*, Berlin, 1921 CXXIII
—— *Der Staat der alten Italiker*, Berlin, 1913 . . CXXIV
SANDS (R. C.), *The Client Princes of the Roman Empire under
the Republic*, Cambridge, 1909 CXXV
SCHILLER (H.), *Geschichte des römischen Kaiserreichs unter
der Regierung des Nero*, Berlin, 1872 . . . CXXV*a*
SCHULTEN (A.), *Numantia: die Ergebnisse der Ausgrabungen*,
1905–12. i. *Die Keltiberer und ihre Kriege mit Rom*,
Munich, 1914 CXXVI
SCHULZ (O.), *Vom Prinzipat zum Dominat : das Wesen des
römischen Kaisertums des III. Jahrhunderts (Studien
zur Geschichte und Kultur des Altertums*, vol. ix),
Paderborn, 1919 CXXVII
—— *Die Rechtstitel und Regierungsprogramme auf römischen
Kaisermünzen*, Paderborn, 1925 CXXVIII
—— *Das Wesen des römischen Kaisertums der ersten zwei
Jahrhunderte (ibid.*, vol. viii), Paderborn, 1916 . . CXXIX
SCHULZE (W.), *Zur Geschichte lateinischer Eigennamen*,
(**XXXII**, N.S., v), Berlin, 1904 CXXX
SEECK (O.), *Geschichte des Untergangs der antiken Welt*,
2nd ed., Stuttgart, 1897–1921 CXXXI
STEIN (E.), *Untersüchungen über das Officium der
Prätorianer-Präfektur seit Diokletian*, Vienna, 1922 . CXXXII
—— *Untersuchüngen zur Geschichte und Verwaltung
Ægyptens unter römische Herrschaft*, Stuttgart, 1915 CXXXIII
TAEUBLER (E.), *Imperium Romanum : Studien zur Ent-
wicklungsgeschichte des römischen Reichs. i. Die
Staatsverträge und Vertragsverhältnisse*, Leipzig and
Berlin, 1913 CXXXIV
—— *Untersuchungen zur Geschichte des Decemvirats und der
Zwölftafeln*, in E. EBERING, *Historische Studien*,
vol. cxlviii, Berlin, 1921 CXXXV
THIELE (W.), *De Severo Alexandro Imperatore*, Berlin, 1909 CXXXVI
VIGNEAUX (P. E.), *Essai sur l'histoire de la Præfectura Urbis
à Rome*, Paris, 1896 CXXXVII
VOGT (J.), *Die alexandrinischen Münzen*, Stuttgart, 1924 . CXXXVIII
—— *Römische Politik in Ægypten (Der Alte Orient*,
Beiheft ii), Leipzig, 1924 CXXXIX
WALTZ (R.), *La Vie politique de Sénèque*, Paris, 1919 . CXL
WILLEMS (P.), *Le Sénat de la République romaine*, 5th ed.,
Louvain, 1883 CXLI

INDEX

NOTE.—Romans are indexed under their cognomen, except those usually known by their gentile name. Men indexed under the same name are given in order of date.

Greek names are transliterated on the usual English system, except that Roman terminations (-*us*, etc.) are avoided for choice.

o

SUPPLEMENTARY BIBLIOGRAPHY

Over thirty years have elapsed since L. Homo's *Les institutions politiques romaines* was first published. The need for an additional bibliography in this unrevised reprint of the English version is therefore absolute. The author's own bibliography, though still, of course, of value, is outdated and, as it stands, misleading, while several of the opinions which are presented as orthodox in the text have since been shown, either by scholarly argument or by the subsequent discovery of new evidence, to be false or improbable. Although, therefore, it is hoped that this supplement will prove sufficiently comprehensive in certain fields to be of some value to the serious scholar, it has been designed primarily as a companion for the convenient use of the reader. It does not cover the period prior to the original publication of the book, and, except in a few cases where writings are listed on highly relevant themes which for one reason or another have only comparatively recently occasioned detailed discussion, its scope has been determined by Homo's own subject-matter. In view of the volume of material to be cited, it has been thought desirable for ease of reference not only to arrange it under Homo's chapter headings, but also, where convenient, to isolate any appreciable number of works on a common subject in a separate subsection.

E. S. STAVELEY.

Bedford College, London.

406

ABBREVIATIONS (SUPPLEMENTARY BIBLIOGRAPHY)

ABAW   *Abhandlungen der Bayerischen Akademie der Wissenschaften, Philos.-Hist. Klasse.*

AC   *L'Antiquité Classique*

AJP   *American Journal of Philology*

APAW   *Abhandlungen der Preussischen Akademie der Wissenschaften*

BAB   *Bulletin de la Classe des Lettres de l'Académie Royale de Belgique*

BCAR   *Bolletino della Commissione Archeologica Comunale in Roma*

BIDR   *Bulletino dell'Istituto di Diritto Romano*

CHJ   *Cambridge Historical Journal*

CP   *Classical Philology*

CQ   *Classical Quarterly*

CR   *Classical Review*

CRAI   *Comptes Rendus de l'Académie des Insçriptions et Belles-Lettres*

JRS   *Journal of Roman Studies*

MAAR   *Memoirs of the American Academy in Rome*

MC   *Il Mondo Classico*

MH   *Museum Helveticum*

NJAB   *Neue Jahrbücher für Antike und deutsche Bildung*

PBSR   *Papers of the British School at Rome*

PP   *La Parola del Passato*

RAL   *Rendiconti della Classe di Scienze Morali, Storiche e Filologiche dell'Accademia dei Lincei*

RBPh   *Revue Belge de Philologie et d'Histoire*

RD   *Revue Historique de Droit Français et Étranger*

REA   *Revue des Études Anciennes*

REL   *Revue des Études Latines*

RFIC   *Rivista di Filologia e d'Istruzione Classica*

RH   *Revue Historique*

RhM   *Rheinisches Museum für Philologie*

RIDA   *Revue Internationale des Droits de l'Antiquité*

RIL   *Rendiconti dell'Istituto Lombardo, Classe di Lettere, Scienze morali e storiche*

RPAA   *Rendiconti della Pontificia Accademia di Archeologia*

RPh   *Revue de Philologie*

RSI   *Rivista Storica Italiana*

SDHI   *Studia et Documenta Historiœ et Iuris*

TAPA   *Transactions of the American Philological Association*

ZRG   *Zeitschrift der Savigny-Stiftung für Rechtsgeschichte*

GENERAL WORKS

ADCOCK (F. E.), *Roman Political Ideas and Practice*, Ann Arbor, 1959
ALTHEIM (F.), *Römische Geschichte :* I. *Die Grundlagen ;* II. *Bis zur Latiner Frieden* 338 *v. Chr.*, Frankfurt, 1951–3
BELOCH (K. J.), *Römische Geschichte bis zum Beginn der Punischen Kriege*, Berlin, 1926
The Cambridge Ancient History : VII. *The Hellenistic Monarchies and the Rise of Rome ;* VIII. *Rome and the Mediterranean ;* IX. *The Roman Republic,* 133 *to* 44 *B.C. ;* X. *The Augustan Empire,* 44 *B.C. to A.D.* 70 *;* XI. *The Imperial Peace, A.D.* 70 *to* 192 *;* XII. *The Imperial Crisis and Recovery, A.D.* 193 *to* 324, Cambridge, 1928–39
CHARLESWORTH (M. P.), *The Roman Empire*, Oxford, 1951
DE MARTINO (F.), *Storia della costituzione romana*, I—III, Naples, 1951–8
GELZER (M.), *Vom römischen Staat*, Leipzig, 1943
Histoire Romaine : I. PAIS (E.), *Des origines à l'achèvement de la conquête* (133 av. J.C.) ; II, i. BLOCH (G.) and CARCOPINO (J.), *Des Gracques à Sulla ;* II, ii. CARCOPINO (J.), *César ;* III. HOMO (L.), *Le Haut-Empire ;* IV, i. BESNIER (M.), *L'empire romain de l'avènement des Sévères au concile de Nicée*, Paris, 1928–37
KORNEMANN (E.), *Das Imperium Romanum. Sein Aufstieg und Niedergang*, Breslau, 1941
LOMBARDI (G.), *Lo sviluppo costituzionale dalle origini alla fine della repubblica*, Rome, 1939
VON LÜBTOW (U.), *Das römische Volk. Sein Staat und sein Recht*, Frankfurt, 1955
The Methuen History of the Roman World : I. SCULLARD (H. H.), *A History of the Roman World from* 753 *to* 146 *B.C.*, 2nd ed., London, 1951 ; II. MARSH (F. B.), *A History of the Roman World from* 146 *to* 30 *B.C.*, 2nd ed., London, 1953 ; III. SALMON, (E. T.), *A History of the Roman World from* 30 *B.C. to A.D.* 138, 3rd ed., London, 1957 ; IV. PARKER (H. M. D.), *A History of the Roman World from A.D.* 138 *to* 337, 2nd ed., London, 1958
MEYER (ERNST), *Römischer Staat und Staatsgedanke*, Zürich, 1948
PARETI (L.), *Storia di Roma e del mondo romano*, I–IV, Rome, 1952–5
ROSTOWTZEFF (M.), *The Social and Economic History of the Roman Empire*, 2nd ed., Oxford, 1956
SIBER (H.), *Römisches Verfassungsrecht in geschichtlicher Entwicklung*, Lahr, 1952.
SOLARI (A.), *L'impero romano :* I. *Unità e universalità di Augusto ;* II. *Conflitto tra Senato e province* (14–69) ; III. *Compromesso costituzionale* (69–193) ; IV. *Impero provinciale. Restaurazione* (193–363), Rome, 1940–7
STEVENSON (G. H.), *Roman Provincial Administration till the age of the Antonines*, Oxford, 1939
Storia di Roma (a cura dell' Istituto di Studi Romani) : I. PARIBENI (R.), *Le origini e il periodo regio. La repubblica fino alla conquista del primato in Italia ;* II. GIANELLI (C.), *Roma nell'età delle guerre puniche ;* III. CORRADI (G.), *La grande conquiste mediterranee ;* V. PARIBENI (R.), *L'età di Cesare e di Augusto ;* VII. CALDERINI (A.), *I Severi. La crisi dell' impero nel terzo secolo ;* VIII. PARIBENI (R.), *Da Diocleziano alla caduta dell' impero d'Occidente*, Bologna, 1938–54
TÄUBLER (E.), " Grundfragen der römischen Verfassungsgeschichte " in *Tyche*, Leipzig, 1926

BOOK I

THE INSTITUTIONS OF THE EARLY CITY

CHAPTER I—The Birth of the Roman State. The Etruscan
Kingship

(A) *The Origins of Rome*

Accame (S.), *Le origini di Roma*, Naples, 1957

van den Bruwaene (M.), *La société romaine :* I. *Les origines et la
formation*, Brussels, 1955

Cardinali (G.), *Le origini di Roma*, Rome, 1949

Ciaceri (E.), *Le origini di Roma. La monarchia e la prima fase dell'
età repubblicana dal secolo VIII alla metà del secolo V a.c.*, Milan,
1937

Devoto (G.), " Le origini trepartiti di Roma," *Athenæum* XXXI
(1953), 335–43

Peremans (W.), " Notes sur les origines de Rome," *Bulletin de
l'Institut historique Belge de Rome* XV (1934), 97–108

Romanelli (P.), " Le origini di Roma. I dati della ricerca archeologica,"
Capitolium XXIV (1949), 49–64

Westrup (C. W.), " Quelques recherches sur le problème des origines de
Rome," *RIDA* III (1949), 551–76

(B) *The Primitive Society and Institutions of Regal Rome*

Alföldi (A.), *Der frührömische Reiteradel und seine Ehrenabzeichen*,
Baden-Baden, 1952

Altheim (F.), " Altrömisches Königtum," *Welt als Geschichte* I (1935),
413–34

Bernardi (A.), " Periodo sabino e periodo etrusco nella monarchia
romana," *RSI* LXVI (1954), 5–20

van den Bruwaene (M.), " Curies et tribus," *AC* XXI (1952), 74–83

Coli (U.), *Regnum*, Rome, 1951

De Francisci (P.), " La formazione della comunità politica romana
primitiva," *Annali Triestini* XXI (1951), 5–36

—— " La comunità sociale e politica romana primitiva," *SDHI* XXII
(1956), 1–86

De Martino (F.), " La gens, lo stato e le classi in Roma antica," *Studi
Arangio-Ruiz* IV (Naples, 1953), 25–49

—— " Note sul regnum," *Iura* IV (1953), 181–92

Ferrero (G.) and Barbagallo (C.), *Das alte Rom*, Stuttgart, 1927

Hoffman (W.), " Die römische Plebs," *NJAB* II (1938), 82–98
and Siber (H.), " Plebs," *RE* XXI, 73–187

Hülsen (C.), " I veri fondatori di Roma," *RPAA* II (1923–4), 83–6

Peremans (W.), " Over de romeinische plebs," *Philologische Studiën*
V (1933–4), 227–32

—— " Note sur les tribes et les curies de la Rome primitive," *AC* V
(1936), 443–7

Taylor (L. R.), " The four urban tribes and the four regions of ancient
Rome," *RPAA* XXVII (1952–4), 225–38

Westrup (C. W.), " Sur la royauté primitive de Rome," *Archives
d'Histoire du Droit oriental* IV (1949), 85–116

—— " Sur les *gentes* et les *curiæ* de la royauté primitive de Rome,"
RIDA, 3rd ser., I (1954), 435–73

(C) *The Servian organization*

Coli (U.), " Tribù e centurie dell'antica repubblica romana," *SDHI* XXI (1955), 181–222

d'Arms (E. F.), " The Classes of the Servian Organization," *AJP* LXIV (1943), 424–6

De Sanctis (G.), " Le origini dell'ordinamento centuriato," *RFIC* LXI (1933), 289–98

Fraccaro (P.), " La storia dell'antichissimo esercito romano e l'età dell'ordinamento centuriato," *Atti del 2° Congresso Nazionale di Studi Romani* (1931) III, 91–9

—— " Ancora sull'età dell'ordinamento centuriato," *Athenæum* XII (1934), 57–71

Friezer (E.), *De Ordening van Servius Tullius*, Diss. Amsterdam, 1957

Gianelli (G.), " Origini e sviluppi dell'ordinamento centuriato," *Atene e Roma* XVI (1935), 229–43

Mattingly (H.), " The Property Qualifications of the Roman Classes," *JRS* XXVII (1937), 99–107

Momigliano (A.), " Studi sugli ordinamenti centuriati," *SDHI* IV (1938), 509–20

Nillson (M. P.), " The Introduction of Hoplite Tactics at Rome : its date and its consequences," *JRS* XVIII (1928), 1–11

Piganiol (A.), " Un document d'histoire sociale romaine : la classification servienne," *Année d'histoire économique et sociale* V (1933), 113–24

Schönbauer (E.), " Die römische Centurien-Verfassung in neuer Quellenschau," *Historia* II (1953), 21–49

Staveley (E. S.), " The Constitution of the Roman Republic 1940–1954: I. The origin and early development of the centuriate organization," *Historia* V (1956), 75–84

Taylor (L. R.), " The Centuriate Assembly before and after the Reform," *AJP* LXXVIII (1957), 337–54

Zancan (L.), " Per la storia dell'ordinamento centuriato," *Atti del reale Istituto Veneto di scienze, lettere e arti* XCIII (1933–4), 869–77

CHAPTER II—The Patrician Republic and the Conflict of the Two Orders

(A) *The Genesis of the Republic : the Nature and Powers of Primitive Magistracy*

Bernardi (A.), " Ancora sulla costituzione della primitiva repubblica romana," *RIL* LXXIX (1945–6), 15–26

—— " Dagli ausiliari del *rex* ai magistrati della *res publica*," *Athenæum* XXX (1952), 3–58

Cohen (D.), " The Origin of the Roman Dictatorship," *Mnemosyne* X (1957), 300–18

De Francisci (P.), " Dal *regnum* alla *respublica*," *SDHI* X (1944), 150–66

—— " Intorno alla natura e alla storia dell' *auspicium imperiumque*," *Studi Albertario* (Milan, 1953) I, 397–432

—— " Intorno all'origine etrusca del concetto di *imperium*," *Studi Etruschi* XXIV (1955–6), 19–43

Frezza (P.), " L'istituzione della collegialità in diritto romano," *Studi Solazzi* (Naples, 1948), 507–42

410

GINTOWT (E.), " Dictator Romanus," *RIDA* II (1949), 385-94

GIOFFREDI (C.), " *Rex, prœtores* e *pontifices* nella evoluzione dal regno al regime consolare," *BCAR* LXXI (1943-5), 129-35

GUARINO (A.), "La formazione della *respublica* romana," *RIDA* I (1948), 95-122

GROH (V.), " La cacciata dei re romani," *Athenæum* VI (1928), 289-324

HANELL (K.), *Das altrömische eponyme Amt*, Lund, 1946

HEINLEIN (S.), " Über die römische Diktatur," *Egyetemes Philologiai Közlöny*, 1943, 63

HEUSS (A.), "Zur Entwicklung des Imperiums der römischen Oberbeamten," *ZRG* LXIV (1944), 57-133

LEIFER (F.), *Studien zum antiken Ämterwesen :* I. *Zur Vorgeschichte des römischen Führeramts*, Leipzig, 1931 (*Klio*, Beiheft X)

McFAYDEN (D.), " A Constitutional Doctrine re-examined " [on the consular right of veto], *Studies in honour of F. W. Shipley* (St. Louis, 1942), 1-15

MANNI (E.), " Appunti sull'origini di alcune magistrature romane," *MC* IX (1939), 260-72

MAZZARINO (S.), *Dalla monarchia allo stato repubblicano*, Catania, 1945

MEYER (ERNST), " Zur Frühgeschichte Roms," *MH* IX (1952), 176-182

NOCERA (P.), " Il fondamento del potere dei magistrati nel diritto pubblico romano," *Annali Perugia* LVII (1946), 142 ff.

PACCHIONI (G.), " Dalla monarchia alla repubblica," *Atti della reale Accademia di Scienze di Torino* LX (1925), 675-97

RUDOLPH (H.), " Das Imperium der römischen Magistrate," *NJAB* III (1939-40), 145-64

STARK (R.), " Ursprung und Wesen der altrömischen Diktatur," *Hermes* LXXV (1940), 206-14

STAVELEY (E. S.), " The Constitution of the Roman Republic 1940-1954 : III. The origin of the consulship ; IV. The origin of the dictatorship ; V. The nature of *imperium*," *Historia* V (1956), 90-112

VOCI (P.), " Per la definizione dell' Imperium," *Studi Albertario* (Milan, 1953) II, 67-102

VOGEL (K. H.), " Imperium und Fasces," *ZRG* LXVII (1950), 62-111

WAGENVOORT (H.), *Roman Dynamism*, Oxford, 1947

WESENBERG (G.), " Prætor maximus," *ZRG* LXV (1947), 319-26

—— " Zur Frage der Kontinuität zwischen königlicher Gewalt und Beamtemgewalt in Rom," *ZRG* LXX (1953), 58-92

(B) Plebeian Institutions

ALTHEIM (F.), *Lex sacrata. Die Anfänge der plebejischen Organisation*, Amsterdam, 1940

DE SANCTIS (G.), " La origine dell'edilità plebea," *RFIC* LX (1932), 433-445

—— " La *lex tribunicia prima*," *Miscell. G. Mercati* V, *Studi e Testi* 125 (1946), 539-44

VON FRITZ (K.), "*Leges sacratæ* and *plebi scita*," *Studies presented to D. M. Robinson* (St. Louis, 1951) II, 893-905

GIOFFREDI (C.), " Il fondamento della *tribunicia potestas* e i procedimenti normativi dell'ordine plebeo," *SDHI* XI (1945), 37-64

GUARINO (A.), " L' *exæquatio* dei *plebiscita* ai *leges*," *Festschrift Schulz* (Weimar, 1951) I, 458-65

Latte (K.), " Zwei Exkurse zum römischen Staatsrecht : II. Das Vorbild der römischen Aedilitat," *Nachrichten von der Gesellschaft der Wissenschaften zu Göttingen, Philol.-Hist. Klasse*, I (1934), 73–7

Momigliano (A.), " Ricerche sulle magistrature romane : III. L'origine del tribunato della plebe ; IV. L'origine della edilità plebea," *BCAR* LIX (1931), 157–77, LX (1932), 217–32

Niccolini (G.), " Le *leges sacratæ*," *Historia* II (1928), 3–18

—— " Origini e primo sviluppo del tribunato della plebe," *Historia* III (1929), 181–207

—— *Il tribunato della plebe*, Milan, 1932

Roos, (A. G.), *Comitia Tributa—Concilium Plebis, Leges—Plebiscita*, Amsterdam, 1940

Sabatucci (D.), " L'edilità romana : magistrato e sacerdozio," *Memorie della Accademia Nazionale dei Lincei—classe di scienze morale storiche e filologiche, ser.* 8, VI (1954), 255–334

Siber (H.), *Die plebejischen Magistraturen bis zur lex Hortensia*, Leipzig, 1938

—— " Plebiscita," *RE* XXI, 54–73

Staveley (E. S.), " Tribal Assemblies before the Lex Hortensia," *Athenæum* XXXIII (1955), 3–31

(C) *Varia*

Adcock (F. E.), " Consular Tribunes and their Successors," *JRS* XLVII (1957), 9–14

Altheim (F.), " Patriziat und Plebs," *Welt als Geschichte* VII (1941), 217–33

Bernardi (A.), " Patrizi e plebei nella costituzione della primitiva repubblica romana," *RIL* LXXIX (1945–6), 3–14

Biscardi (A.), " Auctoritas patrum," *BIDR* XLVIII (1941), 403–521

Boddington (A.), " The Original Nature of the Consular Tribunate," *Historia* VIII (1959), 356–64

Cornelius (F.), *Untersuchungen zur frühen römischen Geschichte*, Munich, 1941

Costanza (V.), " Sul divieto di connubio fra patrizi e plebei," *Atti del 1° Congresso Nazionale di Studi Romani* (1929) II, 171–7

De Francisci (P.), " Per la storia dei *comitia centuriata*," *Studi Arangio-Ruiz* (Naples, 1953) I, 1–32

Dell' Oro (A.), *La formazione dello stato patrizio-plebeo*, Milan, 1950

Faravelli (A. L.), *Origini della censura romana*, Como, 1937

von Fritz (K.), " The Reorganization of the Roman Government in 366 B.C. and the so-called Licinio-Sextian laws," *Historia* I (1950), 3–44

von Gerkan (A.), " Zur Frühgeschichte Roms," *RhM* C (1957), 82–97

Grosso (G.), " Monarchia, *provocatio* e processo popolare," *Studi De Francisci* (Milan, 1954) II, 1–9

Guarino (A.), " La genesi storica dell' *auctoritas patrum*," *Studi Solazzi* (Naples, 1948), 21–31

Latte (K.), " Zwei Exkurse zum römischen Staatsrecht : I. Lex curiata et coniuratio," *Nachrichten von der Gesellschaft der Wissenschaften zu Göttingen, Philol.-Hist. Klasse*, I (1934), 59–73

—— " The Origin of the Roman Quæstorship," *TAPA* LXVII (1936), 24–33

412

von Lübtow (U.), "'Lex curiata," *ZRG* LXIX (1952), 154–71

Siber (H.), "Die ältesten römischen Volksversammlungen," *ZRG* LVII (1937), 233–71

—— "Provocatio," *ZRG* LXII (1942), 376–91

—— "Zur Kollegialität der römischen Zensoren," *Festschrift Schulz* (Weimar, 1951) I, 466–74

Staveley (E. S.), "The Significance of the Consular Tribunate," *JRS* XLIII (1953), 30–6

—— "*Provocatio* during the fifth and fourth centuries B.C.", *Historia* III (1955), 412–28

—— "The Constitution of the Roman Republic 1940–1954 : II. Lex curiata," *Historia* V (1956), 84–90

Tibiletti (G.), "Evoluzione di magistrato e popolo nello stato romano," *Studia Ghisleriana*, Ser. 2, I (1950), 359–77

Literature on the centuriate organization of the early Republic is listed above under I (C). Further discussion of the nature of the Roman *plebs* is to be found among the relevant works cited under I (B).

CHAPTER III—The Republican Constitution Complete

(A) *The Reform of the Centuriate Assembly*

Arangio-Ruiz (V.), "La riforma dell'ordinamento centuriato," *Scritti C. Arno* (Modena, 1938), 1–13

Dell' Oro (A.), "Rogatio e riforma dei comizi centuriati alla luce della Tabula Hebana," *PP* V (1950), 132–50

Fraccaro (P.), "La riforma dell'ordinamento centuriato," *Studi Bonfante* (Milan, 1930) I, 105–22

Gallo (F.), "La riforma dei comizi centuriati," *SDHI* XVIII (1952), 127–57

Meyer (Ernst), "Neuere Erkenntnisse und Forschungen auf dem Gebiete des römischen Staatsrechts," *Welt als Geschichte* XIII (1953), 137–48

Nicholls (J. J.), "The reform of the *comitia centuriata*," *AJP* LXXVII (1956), 225–54

Schönbauer (E.), "Die Centurien-Reform," *Studi Albertario* (Milan, 1953) I, 701–37

Staveley (E. S.), "The Reform of the Comitia Centuriata," *AJP* LXXIV (1953), 1–33

—— "The Constitution of the Roman Republic 1940–1954 : VI. The reform of the *comitia centuriata*," *Historia* V (1956), 112–9

Tibiletti (G.), "Il funzionamento dei comizi centuriati alla luce della tavola Hebana," *Athenæum* XXVII (1949), 210–45

See also the articles by Coli, Momigliano, Schönbauer, and Taylor, cited above under I (C).

(B) *Varia*

Afzelius (A.), "Lex Annalis," *Classica et Medievalia* VIII (1946), 263–78

Astin (A. E.), "The Lex Annalis before Sulla," *Collection Latomus* XXXII (Brussels, 1958)

Bleicken (J.), *Das Volkstribunat der klassischen Republik*, Munich, 1955

Bourne (F. C.), "The Roman Republican Census and Census Statistics," *Classical Weekly* XLV (1952), 129–35

Cavaignac (E.), " Le cens romain aux 3ᵉ et 2ᵉ siècles av. J.-C.", *RPh*
LX (1934), 72–82

Coli (U.), " Sui limiti di durata delle magistrature romane," *Studi
Arangio-Ruiz* (Naples, 1953) IV, 395–418

Fraccaro (P.), " Tribules ed ærarii. Una ricerca di diritto publico
romano," *Athenæum* XI (1933), 150–72

—— " I *decem stipendia* e le *leges annales* repubblicane," *Per il XIV
centenario della codificazione giustinianea. Studi di diritto* (Pavia,
1934), 475–503

Frank (T.), " Roman Census Statistics from 225 to 28 b.c.", *CP* XIX
(1924), 329–41

—— " Roman Census Statistics from 508 to 225 b.c.", *AJP* LI (1930),
313–24

Gabba (E.), "Ancora sulle cifre dei censimenti," *Athenæum* XXX
(1952), 161–73

Garzetti (A.), " Appio Claudio Cieco nella storia politica del suo
tempo," *Athenæum* XXV (1947), 175–224

Jacobs (K.), *Gaius Flaminius*, Leiden, 1937

Klotz (A.), " Zur Geschichte der römischen Zensur," *RhM* LXXXVIII
(1939), 27–36

Nocera (P.), *I potere dei comizi e i suoi limiti*, Milan, 1940

Staveley (E. S.), " The Political Aims of Appius Claudius Cæcus,"
Historia VIII (1959), 410–33

Further literature on the magistracies and *comitia* is listed above
under II.

CHAPTER IV—The Genesis of Oligarchy

Balsdon (J. P. V. D.), " History of the Extortion Court at Rome,
123–70 b.c.", *PBSR* XIV (1938), 98–114

Bernardi (A.), " I ' cives sine suffragio'," *Athenæum* XVI (1938),
239–77

De Regibus (L.), " L'evoluzione costituzionale romana dopo la secondo
guerra punica," *Paideia* II (1947), 129–40

Frank (T.), " The Provincial Activities of the Equestrian Corporation,"
CP XXVIII (1933), 1–11

Haywood, (R. M.), *Studies on Scipio Africanus*, Baltimore, 1933

Hill (H.), *The Roman Middle Class in the Republican period*, Oxford,
1952

Jenny (B.), *Der römische Ritterstand während der Republik*, Diss.
Zürich, 1936

Kienast (D.), *Cato der Zensor*, Heidelberg, 1954

Klingner (F.), " Cato Censorius und die Krisis des römischen Volkes,"
Die Antike X (1934), 239–63

McDonald (A. H.), " Scipio Africanus and Roman Politics in the
Second Century b.c.", *JRS* XXVIII (1938), 153–64

Marmorale (E.), *Cato Maior*, Catania, 1944

Salmon (E. T.), " Roman Colonization from the Second Punic War to
the Gracchi," *JRS* XXVI (1936), 47–67

Scalais (R.), " La politique agraire de Rome depuis les guerres puniques
jusqu'aux Gracques," *Musée Belge* XXIV (1930), 195–241

Schur (W.), *Scipio Africanus und die Begrundung der römischen
Weltherrschaft*, Leipzig, 1927

SCULLARD (H. H.), *Scipio Africanus in the Second Punic War*, Cambridge, 1930

—— *Roman Politics, 220–150 B.C.*, Oxford, 1951

TIBILETTI (G.), " Il possesso dell' *ager publicus* e le norme *de modo agrorum* sino ai Gracchi," *Athenæum* XXVI (1948), 173–236 ; XXVII (1949), 3–42

—— " Ricerche di storia agraria romana," *Athenæum* XXVIII (1950), 183–266

BOOK TWO
FROM OLIGARCHY TO MILITARY RULE

CHAPTER I—THEORIES AND REALITIES

(A) *Polybius and Cicero on the Roman Constitution*

BRION (A.), *La controverse autour de l' idée du princeps chez Cicéron*, Diss. Louvain, 1940

VON FRITZ (K.), *The Theory of the Mixed Constitution. A critical analysis of Polybius' political ideas*, New York, 1954

GRENADE (P.), " Remarques sur la théorie cicéronienne dite du principat," *Mélanges d'Archéologie et d'Histoire de l'École Française de Rome* LVII (1940), 32–63

—— " Autour de *De Republica*," *REL* XXIX (1951), 162–83

HAMMOND (M.), *City State and World State in Greek and Roman Political Theory*, Cambridge (Harv. Univ.), 1951

HOW (W. W.), " Cicero's Ideal in his *De Republica*," *JRS* XX (1930), 24–42.

KORNEMANN (E.), " Zum Staatsrecht des Polybius," *Philologus* LXXXVI (1931), 169–84

LEPORE (E.), *Il princeps ciceroniano e gli ideali politici della tarda repubblica*, Naples, 1954

PÖSCHL (V.), *Römischer Staat und griechisches Staatsdenken bei Cicero. Untersuchungen zu Ciceros Schrift De Republica*, Diss. Heidelberg, 1936

PONTEVILLE (G.), *Cicéron et les formes de gouvernement*, Diss. Louvain, 1945

WALBANK (F. W.), " Polybius and the Roman Constitution," *CQ* XXXVII (1943), 73–89

—— *Commentary on Polybius*, I (Oxford, 1957), 673–697

ZANCAN (L.), " Dottrina delle costituzioni e decadenza politica in Polibio," *RIL* LXIX (1936), 499–512

(B) *Varia*

AFZELIUS (A.), " Zur Definition der römischen Nobilität in der Zeit Ciceros," *Classica et Medievalia* I (1938), 40–94

—— " Zur Definition der römischen Nobilität vor der Zeit Ciceros," *Classica et Medievalia* VII (1945), 150–200

SAGE (E. T.) and WEGNER (A. J.), " Administrative Commissions and the Official Career, 218–167 B.C.", *CP* XXXI (1936), 23–32

SCHUR (W.), " Homo Novus," *Bonner Jahrbücher* CXXXIV (1929), 54–66

VOGT (J.), *Homo Novus*, Stuttgart, 1926

CHAPTER II—The Decline of Oligarchy and the First *Coups d'État*

Accame (S.), " Il primo consolato di Mario," *RFIC* LXIV (1936), 64–9
Badian (E.), *Foreign Clientelœ* (264–70 B.C.)—Part II, Oxford, 1958
Balsdon (J. P. V. D.), " Q. Mucius Scævola and *Ornatio Provinciœ*," *CR* LI (1937), 8–10
Ensslin (W.), " Die Democratie und Rom," *Philologus* LXXXII (1927), 312–28
von Fritz (K.), "Emergency Powers in the last centuries of the Republic," *Annual Review of the American Historical Association* III (1942), 221–37
Gabba (E.), " Le origini dell' esercito professionale in Roma. I proletari e la riforma di Mario," *Athenœum* XXVII (1949), 173–209
—— " Ricerche sull' esercito professionale romana da Mario a Augusto," *Athenœum* XXIX (1951), 171–272
Jashemski (W. F.), *The Origins and History of the Proconsular and the Proprœtorian Imperium to 27 B.C.*, Chicago, 1950
Last (H. M.), Review of F. B. Marsh, *A History of the Roman World from 146 to 30 B.C.*, *AJP* LVIII (1937), 467–74
Levi (M. A.), *La costituzione romana dai Gracchi a Giulio Cesare*, Florence, 1928
Scalais (R.), " L'échec des Gracques et l'avènement de la monarchie militaire," *Études Classiques* II (1933), 9–28
Smith (R. E.), *The Failure of the Roman Republic*, Cambridge, 1955
Valgiglio (E.), " La riforma mariana del sistema di arruolamento," *MC* XIX (1952)
Wiehn (E.), *Die illegalen Heereskommanden in Rom bis auf Cæsar*, Marburg, 1926

CHAPTER III—In Search of a New Formula. The Principate of Pompey and the Monarchy of Cæsar

Adcock (F. E.), " The Legal Term of Cæsar's Governorship in Gaul," *CQ* XXVI (1932), 14–26
Alföldi (A.), " Studien über Cäsars Monarchie," *Bulletin de la société des Lettres de Lund*, 1952–3, 1
Balsdon (J. P. V. D.), " Consular Provinces under the Late Republic," *JRS* XXIX (1939), 57–73 ; 167–183
—— " Roman History, 58–56 b.c. : Three Ciceronian Problems," *JRS* XLVII (1957), 15–20
Bersanetti (G. M.), "La tradizione antica e l'opinione degli storici moderni sul primo triumvirato," *Rivista Indo-Greca-Italica di filologia*, XI (1927), 1–20 ; 185–204 ; XII (1928), 21–42
Borle (J. P.), " Pompée et la dictature, 55–50 av. J.C.", *Études Classiques* XX (1952), 168–80
Buchan (J.), *Julius Cæsar*, London, 1936
Julius Cæsar, 44 B.C.-A.D. 1957, Bimillenary number of *Greece and Rome*, 2nd ser., IV, i (1957)
Cobban (J. M.), *Senate and Provinces, 78–49 B.C.*, Cambridge, 1935
Cuff (P. J.), " The Terminal Date of Cæsar's Gallic Command," *Historia* VII (1958), 445–71

416

EHRENBERG (V.), " *Imperium maius* during the Roman Republic,"
AJP LXXIV (1953), 113–36

ELTON (G. R.), " The Terminal Date of Cæsar's Gallic Proconsulate,"
JRS XXXVI (1946), 18–42

GELZER (M.), " Das erste Konsulat des Pompeius und der Ursprung des
grossen Imperien," *APAW* I, 1943

—— *Pompeius*, Munich, 1949

HEUSS (A.), " Der Untergang der römischen Republik und das Problem
der Revolution," *Historische Zeitschrift* CLXXXII (1956), 1–28

HOLMES (T. RICE), *The Roman Republic and the Founder of the Empire*,
I–III, Oxford, 1923

LEVI (M.), " La *tribunicia potestas* di Giulio Cesare," *Atti del* 1° *Congresso
Nazionale di Studi Romani* (1929) I, 352–7

LOADER (W. R.), " Pompey's command under the Lex Gabinia,"
CR LIV (1940), 134–6

McDONALD (W. F.), " Clodius and the Lex Aelia Fufia," *JRS* XIX
(1929), 164–79

MARSH (F. B.), *The Founding of the Roman Empire*, 2nd ed., Oxford,
1927, rp. Camb., 1959

—— " The Policy of Clodius from 58 to 56 B.C.", *CQ* XXI (1927),
30–5

—— " The Gangster in Roman Politics," *Classical Journal* XXVIII
(1932–3), 168–78

VAN OOTEGHEM (J.), *Pompée le Grand, bâtisseur d'Empire*, Brussels, 1954

PERPILLOU (A.), " La question du droit entre César et le Sénat," *RH*
CLVIII (1928), 272–82

POCOCK (L. G.), " Publius Clodius and the Acts of Cæsar," *CQ* XVIII
(1924), 59–64

—— " A Note on the Policy of Clodius," *CQ* XIX (1925), 182–4

ROSSI (R. F.), " Cesare e l'opposizione tribunicia," *Annali Triestini*
XXIII (1953), 335–44

SALMON (E. T.), " Cæsar and the Consulship for 49 B.C.," *Classical
Journal* XXXIV (1939), 388–95

SANDERS (H.), " The so-called First Triumvirate," *MAAR* X (1932),
55–68

SEALEY (R.), " Habe meam rationem," *Classica et Medievalia* XVIII
(1957), 75–101

STEVENS (C. E.), " The Terminal Date of Cæsar's Command," *AJP*
LIX (1938), 169–208

SYME (R.), " Cæsar, the Senate, and Italy," *PBSR* XIV (1938), 1–31

—— *The Roman Revolution*, Oxford, 1939

TAYLOR (L. R.), *Party Politics in the Age of Cæsar*, Berkeley, 1949

UTTSCHENKO (S. L.), *Der weltanschaulich-politische Kampf in Rom am
Vorabend des Sturzes der Republik*, Berlin, 1956

VOGT (J.), " Zum Herrscherkult bei Julius Cæsar," *Studies presented to
D. M. ROBINSON* (St. Louis, 1951) II, 1138–46

WALTER (G.), *César*, Paris, 1947

WEINSTOCK (S.), " Clodius and the Lex Aelia Fufia," *JRS* XXVII
(1937), 215–22

WIRSZUBSKI (C.), *Libertas as a Political Idea at Rome during the late
Republic and early Principate*, Cambridge, 1950

BOOK THREE

CÆSARISM : PRINCIPATE AND " DOMINATE "

CHAPTER I—Augustus and the Principate

Augustus. Series of articles in *Die Antike* XIII (1937)

Augustus. Studi in occasione del bimillenario Augusteo, Rome, 1938

Probleme der augusteischen Erneuerung—a series of articles, Frankfurt, 1939

Adcock (F. E.), " The Interpretation of *R.G.D.A.* 34.1," *CQ* XLIV (1951), 30–5

Anderson (J. G. C.), " Augustan Edicts from Cyrene," *JRS* XVII (1927), 33–48

Béranger (J.), *Recherches sur l'aspect idéologique du principat,* Basle, 1953

Berlinger (L.), *Beiträge zur inoffiziellen Titulatur der römischen Kaiser,* Breslau, 1935

Birkenfeld (G.), *Augustus,* London, 1935

Buchan (J.), *Augustus,* London, 1937

Chilver (G. E. F.), " Augustus and the Roman Constitution, 1939–1950," *Historia* I (1950), 408–35

De Francisci (P.), " Genesi e struttura del principato Augusteo," *Memorie dell'Accademia d'Italia* VII, 2, 1 (Rome, 1940)

De Sanctis (G.), " Imperator," *Miscellanea Riccobono* (Palermo, 1935), II, 55–61

de Visscher (F.), " La *tribunicia potestas* de César à Auguste," *SDHI* V (1939), 101–22

—— *Les édits d'Auguste découverts à Cyrène,* Louvain, 1940

Di Marzo (S.), " Il principato," *BIDR* XLII (1934), 291–8

Gagé (J.), " De César à Auguste," *RH* CLXXVII (1936), 279–342

Grant (M.), *From Imperium to Auctoritas. A historical study of æs coinage in the Roman Empire,* 49 *B.C.–A.D.* 14, Cambridge, 1946

—— " The Augustan 'Constitution'," *Greece and Rome* XVIII (1949), 97–112

van Groningen (B.-A.), " De Octaviani Cæsaris ante principatum conditum imperio," *Mnemosyne* LIV (1926), 1–9

Hammond (L.), " L'empire romain, sa naissance et sa évolution de 44 av. J.C. à 96 ap. J.C.", *L'Information Historique* XV (1953), 13–16

Hammond (M.), *The Augustan Principate in Theory and Practice during the Julio-Claudian period,* Cambridge (Harv. Univ.), 1933

—— " Imperial Elements in the Formula of the Roman Emperors during the first two and a half centuries of the Empire," *MAAR* XXV (1957), 17–64

Henderson (M. I.), " Potestas regia," *JRS* XLVII (1957), 82–7

Holmes (T. Rice), *The Architect of the Roman Empire,* I–II, Oxford, 1928

Instinsky (H.), " Consensus Universorum," *Hermes* LXXV (1940), 265–78

Jones (A. H. M.), " The Imperium of Augustus," *JRS* XLI (1951), 112–9

—— " Imperial and Senatorial Jurisdiction in the early Principate," *Historia* III (1955), 464–88

418

KOLLE (W.), " Vom Werden des Prinzipats," *Klio* XXXVI (1943), 1–25

KORNEMANN (E.), " Volkstribunat und Kaisertum," *Festschrift Wenger* II (Munich, 1945), 284–316

LAST (H. M.), " Imperium Maius : a note," *JRS* XXXVII (1947), 157–64

—— " On the Tribunician Power of Augustus," *RIL* LXXXIV (1951), 93–110

LEVI (M.), *Ottaviano Capoparte*, Florence, 1943

McFAYDEN (D.) " The Rise of the Princeps' Jurisdiction within the City of Rome," *Washington University Studies*, 1923.

—— " The Newly-discovered Cyrenean Inscriptions and the Alleged *imperium maius proconsulare* of Augustus," *CP* XXIII (1928), 388–93

MAGDELAIN (A.), *Auctoritas Principis*, Paris, 1947

MASCHKIN (N. A.), *Zwischen Republik und Kaiserreich. Ursprung und sozialer Charakter des augusteischen Prinzipats*, Leipzig, 1954

NESSELHAUF (H.), " Von der feldherrlichen Gewalt des römischen Kaisers," *Klio* XXX (1937), 306–22

PIGANIOL (A.), " Les pouvoirs constitutionels et le principat d' Auguste," *Journal des Savants*, 1937, 150–66

VON PREMERSTEIN (A.), " Von Werden und Wesen des augusteischen Prinzipats," *ABAW* XV (1937)

RICCOBONO (S.), " Augusto e il problema della nuova costituzione," *Annali del Seminario Giuridico di Palermo* XV (1936), 363–507

SALMON (E. T.), " The Evolution of Augustus' Principate," *Historia* V (1956), 456–78

SCHMITTHENNER (W. C. G.), *Oktavian und das Testament Cæsars. Untersuchungen zu den politischen Anfängen des späteren Augustus*, Diss. Heidelberg, 1949

SIBER (H.), " Die Entwicklung der Prinzipatsverfassung," *Abhandlungen der Sächsischen Akademie der Wissenschaften* XLII, 3 (1933)

—— " Cäsars Diktatur und das Prinzipat des Augustus," *ZRG* LV (1935), 99–158

—— " Das Führeramt des Augustus," *Abhandlungen der Sächsischen Akademie der Wissenschaften* XLIV, 2 (1940)

—— " Zur Prinzipatsverfassung," *ZRG* LXIV (1944), 233–74

STRACK (P. L.), " Zur *tribunicia potestas* des Augustus," *Klio* XXXII (1939), 358–81

SYME (R.), " Imperator Cæsar : a Study in Nomenclature," *Historia* VII (1958), 172–88

WAGENVOORT (H.), " Princeps," *Philologus* XCI (1936), 206–21 ; 323–45

WEBER (W.), *Princeps. Studien zur Geschichte des Augustus*, Stuttgart, 1936

WICKERT (L.), " Cäsars Monarchie und der Prinzipat des Augustus," *NJAB* IV (1941), 12–23

—— " Princeps und βασιλεύς," *Klio* XXXVI (1943), 1–25

—— " Princeps," *RE* XXII, 1998–2296

CHAPTER II—FROM PRINCIPATE TO " DOMINATE "

(A) *Tiberius and his Julio-Claudian Successors*

BALSDON (J. P. V. D.), *The Emperor Gaius*, Oxford, 1934
CHARLESWORTH (M. P.), " The Tradition about Caligula," *CHJ* IV (1933), 105–19
CIACERI (E.), *Tiberio, successore di Augusto*, Rome, 1934
FRANZERO (C. M.), *The Life and Times of Nero*, New York, 1956
KUNTZ (O.), " Tiberius and the Roman Constitution," *University of Washington Studies in Social Sciences* II, 1 (1924)
LEVI (M.), *Nerone e i suoi tempi*, Milan, 1949
MARAÑON (G.), *Tibère*, Paris, 1941
MARSH, (F. B.), " Tiberius and the Development of the Early Empire," *Classical Journal* XXIV (1928), 14–27
—— *The Reign of Tiberius*, Oxford, 1931
MOMIGLIANO (A.), *Claudius, the Emperor and his Achievement*, Oxford, 1934
PASSERINI (A.), " Per la storia dell'imperatore Tiberio," *Studia Ghisleriana* I (1948), 195–233
PIPPIDI (D. M.), " Tacite et Tibère," *Ephemeris Dacoromana* VIII (1938), 233–97
—— *Autour de Tibère*, Bucharest, 1944
ROGERS (R. S.), " Tiberius' Reversal of an Augustan Policy," *TAPA* LXXII (1940), 532–6
—— *Studies in the Reign of Tiberius*, Baltimore, 1943
SCRAMUZZA (V. M.), *The Emperor Claudius*, Cambridge (Harv. Univ.), 1940
TARVER (J. C.), *Tibère*, Paris, 1934
WALTER (G.), *Nero*, London, 1957
WEIGALL (A.), *Nero : Emperor of Rome*, London, 1930

(B) *The Year of the Four Emperors*

CHILVER (G. E. F.), " The Army in Politics, A.D. 68–70," *JRS* XLVII (1957), 29–35
MANFRE (C.), *La crisi politica dell' anno 68–69 d.C.*, Bologna, 1947
MANNI (E.), " Lotta politica e guerra civile nel 68–69 d.C.", *RFIC* LXXIV (1946), 122–56
ZANCAN (P.), *La crisi del principato nell' anno 69 d.C.*, Padua, 1939

(C) *Vespasian to Hadrian*

BERSANETTI (G. M.), *Vespasiano*, Rome, 1941
D'ORGEVAL (B.), *L'empereur Hadrien. Oeuvre législative et administrative*, Paris, 1950
FORTINA (M.), *L'imperatore Tito*, Turin, 1955
GARZETTI (A.), *Nerva*, Rome, 1950
HENDERSON (B. W.), *The Life and Principate of the Emperor Hadrian*, London, 1923
—— *Five Roman Emperors : Vespasian, Titus, Domitian, Nerva, and Trajan*, Cambridge, 1927
HOMO (L.), *Vespasien, l'empereur de bon sens*, Paris, 1949
LEVI (M.), " I principii dell' impero di Vespasiano," *RFIC* LXVI (1938), 1–12

420

PARIBENI (R.), *Optimus princeps. Saggio sulla storia e sui tempi dell'
imperatore Traiano*, Messina, 1926–7
PERRET (L.), *La titulature impériale d'Hadrien*, Paris, 1929

(D) *The Antonines and Severi*

BARBIERI (G.), " Aspetti della politica di Settimio Severo," *Epigraphica*
IV (1952), 3–48
CARRATA (T. F.), *Il regno di Marco Aurelio*, Turin, 1953
CASTAGNA (R.), *L'imperatore Settimio Severo*, Naples, 1937
DE FRANCISCI (P.), " La politica imperiale di Settimio Severo," *Atti
della Societa italiana per il Progresso di Scienze* XXV, 3 (1937), 19–30
DOVE (C. CLAYTON), *M. Aurelius Antoninus, his Life and Times*,
London, 1930
FARQUHARSON (A. S. L.), *Marcus Aurelius. His Life and World*,
Oxford, 1951
GÖRLITZ (W.), *Marcus Aurelius Kaiser und Philosoph*, Leipzig, 1936
HAMMOND (M.), " Septimius Severus, Roman Bureaucrat," *Harvard
Studies in Classical Philology* LI (1940), 137–73
HAYWARD (F. H.), *Marcus Aurelius, a saviour of men, sixteenth emperor
of Rome*, London, 1935
HOMO (L.), *Le siècle d'or de l'empire romain*, Paris, 1947
HÜTTL (W.), *Antoninus Pius :* I. *Historisch-politische Darstellung ;*
II. *Römische Reichsbeamte und Offiziere unter Antoninus Pius*,
Prague, 1933–6
MACKENZIE (D.), *The Reign of Caracalla*, Diss. Princeton, 1949
MURPHY (G. J.), *The Reign of the Emperor L. Septimius Severus from the
Evidence of the Inscriptions*, Jersey City, 1945
TRAUPMAN (J. C.), *The Life and Reign of Commodus*, Diss. Princeton,
1956.
WEBER (W.), *Roms Herrschertum und Reich im zweiten Jahrhunderte*,
Stuttgart, 1937
VON WILAMOWITZ-MÖLLENDORFF (U.), *Kaiser Marcus*, Berlin, 1931

(E) *The Crisis of the Third Century*

ALTHEIM (F.), *Die Soldatenkaiser*, Frankfurt, 1939
BARBIERI (R.), " La politica amministriva e successoria dell' imperatore
Caro," *RAL*, Ser. 8, II (1947), 523–8
BERSANETTI (G. M.), " Studi su Massimino il Trace : i rapporti fra
Massimino e il Senato," *Rivista Indo-Greca-Italica di filologia*
XVIII (1934), 215–22
—— " La pretesa restaurazione senatoria dell'imperatore Tacito,"
Rivista Indo-Greca-Italica di filologia XIX (1935), 131–6
—— " Valeriano ed Aemiliano," *RFIC* LXXVI (1948), 257–79
CARATELLI (G. P.), " La crisi dell'impero nell'età di Gallieno," *PP* II
(1947), 48–73
DE REGIBUS (L.), " Le riforme militari dell'imperatore Gallieno,"
Historia IX (1935), 446–64
—— *La monarchia militare di Gallieno*, Genoa, 1939
GIGLI (G.), *La crisi dell'impero romano*, Palermo, 1947
HORNSBY (R. A.), *Studies in the Reign of Valerian and Gallienus*, Diss.
Princeton, 1952
JONES, (T. B.), " Three Notes on the Reign of M. Claudius Tacitus,"
CP XXXIV (1939), 366–9

KENNEDY (M. L.), *The Reign of the Emperor Probus*, 276–282 *A.D.*, Diss. Minnesota, 1952

MANNI (E.), *L'impero di Gallieno*, Rome, 1949

MULLENS (H. G.), " The Revolt of the Civilians, A.D. 237–8," *Greece and Rome* XVII (1948), 65–77

VAN SICKLE (C. E.), " Changing Bases of the Roman Imperial Power in the third century," *AC* VIII (1939), 153–70

SOLARI (A.), *La crisi dell'impero romano*, Rome, 1933

TOWNSEND (P. W.), " The Revolution of A.D. 238. The Leaders and their Aims," *Yale Classical Studies* XIV (1955), 49–105

VITUCCI (G.), *L'imperatore Probo*, Rome, 1952

(F) *The Succession*

BÉRANGER (J.), " L'hérédité du principat. Note sur la transmission du pouvoir impérial aux deux premiers siècles," *REL* XVII (1939), 171–187

CARCOPINO (J.), " L'hérédité dynastique chez les Antonins," *REA* LI (1949), 262–321

GAGÉ (J.), " Divus Augustus. L'idée dynastique chez les empereurs julio-claudiens," *Revue Archéologique* XXXIV (1931), 11–41

GEER (R. M.), " Second Thoughts on the Imperial Succession from Nerva to Commodus," *TAPA* LXVIII (1936), 47–54

GRENADE (P.), " La réglement successorial d'Hadrien," *REA* LII (1950), 258–77

HAMMOND (M.), " The Transmission of the Powers of the Roman Empire from the death of Nero in A.D. 68 to that of Alexander Severus in A.D. 235," *MAAR* XXIV (1956), 61–133

TIMPE (D.), *Untersuchungen zur Kontinuität des frühen Prinzipats*, Diss. Freiberg, 1957

VILLERS (P.), " La dévolution du principat dans la famille d'Auguste," *REL* XXVIII (1950), 235–251

(G) *Imperial Cult*

ABÆCHERLI BOYCE (A. L.), " The Institution of the Imperial Cult in the Western Provinces of the Roman Empire," *Studi e Materiali di Storia delle Religioni* XI (1935), 153–86

CHARLESWORTH (M. P.), " Some Observations on Ruler Cult, especially in Rome," *Harvard Theological Review* XXVIII (1935), 5–44

—— " The Refusal of Divine Honours : an Augustan Formula," *PBSR* XV (1939), 1–10

LAMBRECHTS (P.), " La politique apollienne d'Auguste et le culte impérial," *La Nouvelle Clio* V (1953), 65–82

LEVI (M.), " Culto imperiale e genesi della monarchia augustea," *RSI* LV (1938), 1–14

PIPPIDI (D. M.), " Le *numen Augusti*. Observations sur une forme occidentale du culte impérial," *REL* IX (1931), 83–112

—— *Recherches sur le culte impérial*, Paris, 1939

ROSTOVTZEFF (M. I.), " L'empereur Tibère et le culte impérial," *RH* CLXIII (1930), 1–26

SCOTT (K.), *The Imperial Cult under the Flavians*, Stuttgart, 1936

TAYLOR (L. R.), " Tiberius' Refusal of Divine Honours," *TAPA* LX (1929), 87–101

—— *The Divinity of the Roman Emperor*, Middletown, 1931

422

(H) *Legions and Prætorian Cohorts*

DE LAET (S. J.), " Cohorts prétoriennes et préfets de prétoire de haut-Empire," *RBPh* XXIII (1944), 489–506

DURRY (M.), *Les cohorts prétoriennes*, Paris, 1938

FORNI (G.), *Il reclutamento delle legioni da Augusto a Diocleziano*, Milan, 1953

LORENZ (H.), *Untersuchung zum Prätorium. Katalog der Prätorien und Entwicklungsgeschichte ihrer Typen*, Diss. Halle, 1936

PARKER (H. M. D.), *The Roman Legions* (with a bibliography by G. R. WATSON), Cambridge, 1958

PASSERINI (A.), *Le coorti pretorie*, Rome, 1939

TULLIO (R.), " Le coorti pretorie nella recente critica storia," *RSI* LIX (1942), 208–24

For literature on the Prætorian Prefecture see below under BOOK IV, Chapter I (B).

CHAPTER III—THE CONSTITUTIONAL DEVELOPMENT COMPLETE. THE ABSOLUTE MONARCHY OF THE LATE EMPIRE

BAYNES (N. H.), " Three Notes on the Reforms of Diocletian and Constantine," *JRS* XV (1925), 195–208

VAN BERCHEM (D.), *L'armée de Dioclétien et la réforme constantinienne*, Paris, 1952

BOAK (A. E. R.), " Constantine and Rome," *Queen's Quarterly* LVII (1950), 182–96

DE ROBERTIS (F. M.), " Dal potere personale allo competenza dell' ufficio," *SDHI* VIII (1942), 255–307

DÖRRIES (H.), *Konstantin der Grosse*, Stuttgart, 1957

GERLAND (E.), *Konstantin der Grosse in Geschichte und Sage*, Athens, 1937

HÖNN (K.), *Konstantin der Grosse*, Leipzig, 1940

HOLSAPPLE (L. B.), *Constantine the Great*, New York, 1942

KLINDERT (W.), *Die diokletianisch-konstantinische Heeresreform*, Diss. Vienna, 1949

KORNEMANN (E.), *Doppelprinzipat und Reichsteilung im Imperium Romanum*, Leipzig, 1930

PALANQUE (J.), *Constantin*, Brussels, 1936

—— " Collégialité et partage dans l'empire romain aux IVe et Ve siècles," *REA* XLVI (1944), 47–64, 280–98

PASSERINI (A.), " Osservazioni su alcuni punti della storia di Diocleziano e Massiminiano," *Acme* I (1948), 131–94

PIGANIOL (A.), *L'empereur Constantin*, Paris, 1932

SALVATORELLI (L.), *Constantino il Grande*, Rome, 1928

SCHÄFFER (A.), *Kaiser Konstantin, eine Zeitwende*, Leipzig, 1929

SEGRE (G.), " Alcune osservazioni sulla costituzione dell'impero da Diocleziano a Giustiniano," *Atti del Congresso Internazionale di Diritto Romano* (1933), 209–33

SESTON (W.), *Dioclétien et la tétrarchie : I. Guerres et réformes*, Paris, 1946

—— " Du comitatus de Dioclétien aux comitatenses de Constantin," *Historia* IV (1955), 284–96

STERN (H.), " Remarks on the *adoratio* under Diocletian," *Journal of the Warburg Institute* XVII (1954), 184–9

VOGT (J.), *Constantin der Grosse und sein Jahrhundert*, Munich, 1949
ZEILLER (J.), " L'œuvre politique et administrative de Dioclétien,"
Journal des Savants, 1948, 148–55

BOOK FOUR
IMPERIAL BUREAUCRACY. ADMINISTRATION AND GREAT PUBLIC SERVICES

CHAPTER I—THE EMPEROR'S ASSISTANTS. MAGISTRATES AND OFFICIALS

(A) *Senate, Comitia, and Council*

BARBIERI (G.), *L'albo senatorio da Settimio Severo a Carino*, Rome, 1952
BÉRANGER (J.), " La démocratie sous l'empire romain. Les opérations
électorales de la Tabula Hebena et la *destinatio*," *MH* XIV (1957),
216–40
BIRLEY (E.), " Senators in the Emperor's Service," *Proceedings of the
British Academy* XXXIX (1953), 197–214
COLI (U.), " La *destinatio magistratuum* in una nuova iscrizione dell'
epoca di Tiberius," *BIDR* LIII–LIV, 369–91
―――― " Nuove osservazioni e congetture sulla Tabula Hebana," *Jura* III
(1952), 90–131
CROOK (J. A.), *Consilium Principis. Imperial Council and Counsellors
from Augustus to Diocletian*, Cambridge, 1954
DE LAET (S. J.), *De samenstelling van den romeinschen Senaat gedurende
de eerste eeuw van het principaat*, Antwerp, 1941
DELL' ORO (A.), " Comitia ad patres," *Archivio Giuridico* CXLIV (1953),
58–68
DE REGIBUS (L.), " La decadenza del senato romano nel terzo secolo,"
Atti della Accademia Ligure di Scienze e Lettere IX, 2 (1952)
DE VISSCHER (F.), " La destinatio," *PP* V (1950), 118–31
―――― " Tacite et les réformes électorales d'Auguste et de Tibère,"
Studi Arangio-Ruiz (Naples, 1953) II, 419–34
―――― " La Table de Heba et la décadence des comices centuriates," *RD*
XXIX (1951), 1–38
―――― " La Tabula Hebana e les aspects politiques de la réforme électorale
d'Auguste," *BAB* XXXVII (1951), 169–82
HAMMOND (M.), " Composition of the Senate, A.D. 68–235," *JRS*
XLVII (1957), 74–81
JONES (A. H. M.), " The Elections under Augustus," *JRS* XLV (1955),
9–21
LAMBRECHTS (P.), *La composition du Sénat romain de l'accession au
trône d'Hadrien à la mort de Commode* (117–192), Antwerp, 1936
―――― *La composition du Sénat romain de Septime Sévère à Dioclétien*
(193–284), Budapest, 1937
MCALINDON (D.), " Entry to the Senate in the Early Empire," *JRS*
XLVII (1957), 190–5
PIGANIOL (A.), " La procédure électorale de la *destinatio* selon la Table
de Magliano," *CRAI*, 1951, 204–14
SESTON (W.), " La table de bronze de Magliano et la reforme électorale
d'Auguste," *CRAI*, 1950, 105–11
SIBER (H.), " Die Wahlreform des Tiberius," *Festschrift Koschaker*
(Weimar, 1939) I, 171–217

TIBILETTI (G.), " Il funzionamento dei comizi centuriati alla luce della tavola Hebana," *Athenæum* XXVII (1949), 210–45

—— *Principe e magistrati repubblicani. Ricerca di storia Augustea e Tiberiana*, Rome, 1953

ZAKRZEWSKI (G.), " Le Consistoire impérial au Bas-Empire romain," *Eos* XXXI (1928), 405–38

(B) *Magistrates and Officials*

BESNIER (R.), " Les procurateurs provinciaux pendant le règne de Claude," *RBPh* XXVIII (1950), 439–59

DE LAET (S. J.), " La préfecture du prétoire sous le haut-empire et le principe de la collégialité," *RBPh* XXII (1943), 73–95

—— " Cohorts prétoriennes et préfects de prétoire au haut-empire," *RBPh* XXIII (1944), 489–506

—— " Les pouvoirs militaires des préfets du prétoire et leur développement progressif," *RBPh* XXV (1946–7), 509–54

ENSSLIN (W.), " Præfectus, *RE* XXII, 1257–1347

—— " Præfectus prætorio," *RE* XXII, 2381–2502

GROAG (E.), " Zum Konsulat in der Kaiserzeit," *Wiener Studien* XLVII (1929), 143–6

HOROWITZ (P.), " Essai sur le pouvoir des procurateurs gouverneurs," *RBPh* XVII (1938), 53–62 ; 775–92

HOWE (L. L.), *The Prætorian Prefect from Commodus to Diocletian*, Chicago, 1942

LAST (H. M.), " The *Præfectus Aegypti* and his Powers," *Journal of Egyptian Archæology* XL (1954), 8–73

PALANQUE (J.), *Essai sur la préfecture du prétoire sous le Bas-Empire*, Paris, 1933

PETERSEN (H. E.), " Senatorial and Equestrian Governors in the third century A.D.", *JRS* XLV (1955), 47–57

PFLAUM (H. G.), *Les procurateurs équestres*, Paris, 1950

REINMUTH (O. W.), " The Prefect of Egypt from Augustus to Diocletian," *Klio*, Beiheft XXXIV (1935)

SACHERS (E.), " Præfectura, præfectus," *RE* XXII, 2247–53

—— " Præfectus urbi," *RE* XXII, 2502–34

SINNIGEN (W. G.), " The Officium of the Urban Prefecture during the later Roman Empire," *Papers and Monographs of the American Academy at Rome* XVII (1957)

—— " The *Vicarius urbis Romæ* and the Urban Prefecture," *Historia* VIII (1959), 97–112

STEIN (A.), " La dignità senatoria dei prefetti del pretorio," *BCAR* LII (1924), 9–25

—— *Die Präfekten von Aegypten in der römischen Kaiserzeit*, Berne, 1950

VITUCCI (G.), *Ricerche sulla præfectura urbi in età imperiale*, Rome, 1956

WHITE (A. N. SHERWIN-), " Procurator Augusti," *PBSR* XV (1939), 11–26

CHAPTER II—THE ADMINISTRATIVE UNIFICATION OF THE ROMAN WORLD

(A) *Constitutio Antoniniana*

BICKERMANN (E.), *Das Edikt des Kaisers Caracalla in pap. Giessen* 40, Berlin, 1926

DE VISSCHER (F.), " La constitution antonine et la persistance des droits locaux," *Cahiers d'Histoire mondiale* II (1954–5), 788–811

—— " L'expansion du droit de cité romain et la diffusion du droit romain," *BAB* XLI (1955), 29–46

D' ORS (A.), " Estudios sobre la Constitutio Antoniniana : Caracala y la unificacion del imperio," *Emerita* XXIV (1956), 1–26

JONES (A. H. M.), " Another Interpretation of the *constitutio Antoniniana*," *JRS* XXVI (1926), 223–35

SCHÖNBAUER (E.), " Rechtshistorische Urkundenstudien. Die Inschrift von Rhosos und die Constitutio Antoniniana," *Archiv für Papyrusforschung* XIII (1939), 177–209

SEGRE (A.), " La costituzione antoniniana," *RFIC* LIV (1926), 471–87

STRONG (J.), " Die Constitutio Antoniniana," *Philologus* LXXXVIII (1933), 257–95

(B) *Finance*

BOTT (H.), *Die Grundzüge der Diokletianischen Steuerverfassung*, Darmstadt, 1928

DELEAGE (A.), *La capitation du bas-empire*, Mâcon, 1945

GARZETTI (A.), " *Aerarium* e *fiscus* sotto Augusto. Storia di una questione in parte di nome," *Athenæum* XXXI (1953), 298–327

JONES (A. H. M.), " The Aerarium and the Fiscus," *JRS* XL (1950), 22–9

LAST (H. M.), " The Fiscus : a note," *JRS* XLIV (1944), 51–9

PIGANIOL (A.), " La capitation de Dioclétien," *RH* CLXXVI (1935), 1–13

SUTHERLAND (C. H. V.), " *Aerarium* and *fiscus* during the early Empire," *AJP* LXVI (1945), 151–70

(C) *Varia*

BELL (H. I.), " Roman Egypt from Augustus to Diocletian," *Chronique d'Égypte* XIII (1938), 347–63

DE ROBERTIS (F. M.), " La *cura regionum urbis* nel periodo imperiale," *Athenæum* XIII (1935), 171–86

GARZETTI (A.), " Le basi amministrave del prinzipato romano," *Aevum* XXX (1956), 97–114

HOMO (L.), " Auguste et la création des grands services municipaux à Rome," *Mélanges Glotz* (Paris, 1932), I, 439–51

JOHNSON (A. C.), *Egypt and the Roman Empire*, Ann Arbor, 1951

JONES (A. H. M.), " The Cities of the Roman Empire. Political, administrative and judicial institutions," *La ville* I (Brussels, 1954), 135–76

REYNOLDS (P. R. BAILLIE-), *The Vigiles of Imperial Rome*, Oxford, 1926

VAN SICKLE (C.), " Diocletian and the Decline of the Roman Municipalities," *JRS* XXVIII (1938), 91–8

THOMSEN (R.), " The Italic Regions from Augustus to the Lombard invasion," *Classica et Medievalia*, Diss. IV (1947).

CHAPTER III—THE ADMINISTRATIVE PERSONNEL

BIRLEY (E.), " The Equestrian Officers of the Roman Army," *Durham University Journal* XI (1949), 8–19

DE LAET (S. J.), " La composition de l'ordre équestre sous Auguste," *RBPh* XX (1941), 509–31

426

DUFF (A. M.), *Freedmen in the early Roman Empire*, 2nd ed., Cambridge, 1959

HILL (H.), " The ' equites illustres '," *CQ* XXII (1928), 77–83

JONES (A. H. M.), " The Roman Civil Service (clerical and sub-clerical grades)," *JRS* XXXIX (1949), 38–55

LOPUSZAMSKI (G.), " La transformation du corps des officiers supérieurs dans l'armée romaine du 1ᵉʳ au IIIᵉʳ siècle ap. J.-C.", *Mélanges de l'École Française de Rome* LV (1938), 131–83

McALINDON (D.), " Senatorial Advancement in the reign of Claudius," *Latomus* XVI (1957), 252–62

SEGRE (A.), " A Note on the classes of Roman Officials in the age of Diocletian," *TAPA* LXXIV (1943), 102–8

STEIN (A.), *Der römische Ritterstand*, Munich, 1927

Date Due